Tromsø
Jiehkkevàrri
×1833

Harstad
Hinnøya
Narvik

Bodø
1907
Suliskongen

Norwegian Sea

Arctic Circle

1915
×
Oksskolten

Steinkjer

TRONDHEIM
Kristiansund
Molde
Ålesund
Snøhetta
2286
Galdhøpiggen Rondslottet
2469× ×2178
2465× Glittertind
Lillehammer
Gjøvik Hamar
BERGEN
Hønefoss
Drammen OSLO
Kongsberg
Haugesund Tønsberg Moss
Skien Fredrikstad
Stavanger Larvik
North
Sea Arendal
Lindesnes Kristiansand
Skagerrak

- ● Large city
- ● Smaller city
- ✈ Airport
- —— Railway
- —— Main road
- —— County boundary
- —— International boundary

0   100   200 km

© Statens kartverk 1995   STATENS KARTVERK

Making a Historical Culture

Making a Historical Culture
Historiography in Norway

Edited by William H. Hubbard,
Jan Eivind Myhre, Trond Nordby,
and Sølvi Sogner

SCANDINAVIAN UNIVERSITY PRESS
Oslo – Copenhagen – Stockholm – Boston

Scandinavian University Press (Universitetsforlaget AS),
P.O. Box 2959 Tøyen, N-0608 Oslo, Norway
Fax +47 22 57 53 53

Stockholm office
SCUP, Scandinavian University Press
P.O. Box 3255, S-103 65 Stockholm, Sweden
Fax +46 8 20 99 82

Copenhagen office
Scandinavian University Press AS
P.O. Box 54, DK-1002 København K, Denmark
Fax +45 33 32 05 70

Boston office
Scandinavian University Press North America
875 Massachusetts Ave., Ste. 84, Cambridge MA 02139, USA
Fax +1 617 354 68 75

ISBN 82-00-22699-9

Published with a grant from the Research Council of Norway

Design: Astrid Elisabeth Jørgensen
Typeset in 9.6 on 11.7 point by Engers Boktrykkeri A/S, Otta, Norway
Printed on Carat Offset by Engers Boktrykkeri A/S, Otta, Norway

Contents

Introduction

The fifteen contributions to this anthology attempt two things. First, they try to convey an impression of the intimate connection between Norwegian society, culture, and politics, on the one hand, and Norwegian historiography, on the other. Norwegian historical scholarship has primarily been a *national* historiography, thus inspiring the title of this volume: *Making a Historical Culture*. Second, the articles trace the development of professional historical studies in Norway, mapping the themes and problems, and examining the presuppositions, approaches, and methods Norwegian historians have been wrestling with over the decades. The editors hope that the collection thereby presents a clear and comprehensive picture of the current state of Norwegian historiography.

From its beginnings, historical scholarship in Norway has been connected with the building of the Norwegian nation and its state. This applies both to the nature of historians' themes and topics as well as to the role historians and interpretations of history have played in public affairs. The interconnection was particularly evident in the nineteenth and early twentieth centuries. The names of scholars such as Rudolf Keyser, P. A. Munch, Ernst Sars, and Halvdan Koht appear frequently in several articles, not only because they pioneered many historical subdisciplines, but also because they formulated and carried out the main task assumed by Norwegian historians: explaining how Norwegians derived political and cultural identity and, ultimately, sovereignty from deep historical roots, stretching as far back as the Iron Age. These historians were public figures, acting as teachers of the nation, telling politicians and the public *why* cultural and political sovereignty were historically necessary. In the twentieth century, the liberal-democratic nationalism that had dominated the historiographical paradigm earlier received strong competition from Marxism and historical materialism. But the Marxism of Norwegian historians has usually been diluted with the nineteenth-century national-democratic heritage. Knut Kjeldstadli calls these historians "maverick Marxists", the most typical being Halvdan Koht, with his blend of nationalist and class issues. Koht and his colleague Edvard Bull sen. also continued the Norwegian historians' tradition of public service. Both served periods as the country's foreign minister during the inter-war years.

Since 1945 these public roles and state/nation-building paradigms have diminished in influence. The retreat from public politics has been considerable: The few politically active historians today serve in advisory positions or appear as commentators; they are no longer central actors like Koht and Bull were. This withdrawal was partly caused by factors outside historical scholarship – for example, the increased professionalization of politics and the mass media – but also by developments within the profession itself. Historians have also retreated from a concentration on national issues and have directed their attention both towards international–global questions and towards local and regional topics. The major intellectual reason for this shift has probably been historians' widespread adoption of *impartiality* as the supreme value in historical scholarship. To some extent this position was adopted as part of a larger endeavour to make history more "objective" and "scientific", following the model of the social sciences. Even more, however, impartiality was the ethos attached to the building of the discipline of history as an academic profession. Scientifically, professionalization is undoubtedly a positive development; socially, its effect is more ambiguous. Kåre Lunden, for example, connects the ideal of impartiality to what he perceives as the "decline in social relevance" of history writing in Norway over the past five decades.

Lunden's concept of social relevance is closely tied to the question of national identity. But people have several identities; being Norwegian is only one of them. Countering Lunden, one could interpret the rise of social history and related subdisciplines after 1970 as a quest for social relevance. This was to be achieved by giving hitherto invisible groups – women, workers, the Sami – a historical identity and by insisting on new perspectives in the writing of history: history from below, from a local perspective, from the perspective of everyday life, and so on. These "socially relevant" perspectives loom large in the articles on social history, local history, women's history, historical demography, and the history of ethnic minorities. Whether the decline in public visibility of the country's historians can be attributed to a lack of social relevance in their writings is thus debatable. Certainly, as mentioned in several chapters, publicly and privately commissioned works written by professional historians constitute a substantial part of scholarly historical research in Norway, and these works are widely read – or at least widely purchased.

How does one write the history of a country's historical scholarship? Our solution – a collection of articles written by different authors – offers both disadvantages and advantages. One drawback is obvious: Having fifteen authors instead of one inevitably weakens the book's unity and coherence. The risk of thematic overlapping is also increased. In our case this is especially evident for period before 1940. The reason is simple: Most of the historians then were *polyhistorians* working in an age of poorly developed historical subdisciplines. In the treatment of post-1945 historians, overlapping has been avoided to the best of the editors' abilities. Here the problem of duplication has been replaced by the problem of trying to cover all important fields of historical research. Some gaps have, nonetheless, been unavoidable. For example, important aspects of domestic history, such as the growth the labour movement and the development of political parties, could have been presented more fully. The highly diverse field of international history is represented only by the chapter on foreign relations. The latter neglect means that our collection has heightened further the role played by the nation–state in Norwegian historiography. At the same time we have included an article on the history of mentalities, a field that is still poorly defined but whose influence is growing. The main advantage of using many authors is that the fields are presented by specialists in their respective areas; no one author could have mastered the entire Norwegian historiography. The editors hope that the competence and insight of the individual contributors compensate for the inevitable degree of fragmentation and duplication.

The collection is divided into three parts, representing a logical progression from the general concerns of the discipline to specific concerns of individual subdisciplines.

The first part deals with what we have called the *contexts and concepts* of Norwegian historical scholarship. The opening chapter surveys the long-term interrelationship between *history and society* and gives an overview of Norway's history as well as of the social function of historical discourse. This is followed by a discussion of *history as a scientific discipline*, examining the ebb and flow of philosophies of history, epistemological questions, and other central issues in the writing of history. The closing chapter in this section explains the *infrastructure of history* in Norway, that is, the institutions of historical scholarship and education, which differ somewhat from Continental and North American models.[1]

The second part presents surveys of the historiography of the three *major eras* in Norway's past: the Middle Ages to *c.* 1536; the era of subordinated union with Denmark from 1536 to 1814; and the modern era of semi-independence in personal union with Sweden from 1814, followed by full sovereignty in 1905. This admittedly conventional classification is employed because many of the pivotal questions in Norwegian history writing centre on these eras. Since the bulk of modern Norwegian history writing concentrates on the modern era, the chapter on that period focuses on general methodological and philosophical approaches to the study of Norwegian history after 1814.

The third part looks at various subdisciplines. For the most part work in these areas concentrates on the modern era since *c.* 1800. The major exceptions are historical demography and the history of mentalities, which both have a strong presence in research on the seventeenth and eighteenth centuries.

In the Norwegian language, unlike in English, the term historiography (*historiografi*) is unambiguous, meaning only the history of

---

1 One of these differences deserves special mention: The *hovedfag* (main subject) thesis that caps the basic university degree in history (*cand. philol.*) is a considerable piece of independent research and could be considered equivalent to a modest American Ph.D. dissertation, although it is typically translated as Master's thesis. Its closest equivalent is perhaps the M.Phil. research degree once granted by British universities.

historical writing. Writing historiography is, nonetheless, an ambiguous undertaking. What kinds of themes and problems ought to be in the forefront? Apart from those for the first three articles, the subject assignments for this anthology – as expressed in the titles – did not provide the authors instructions on how to define historiography. As a result, authors have used different emphases: 1) historiography as the *development of institutions* and *groups of historians or individual scholars* in the field; 2) historiography as an account of the *debate over what history is about*, including its themes, methods, and aims; 3) historiography as *debate over major historical problems*; and 4) historiography as the *interconnection* between the development of historical studies and the unfolding of history itself.

Finally, some comments about the occasion behind this publication are in order. Norwegian historians, consonant with the concern for national identity, organized early; the Norwegian Historical Association (HIFO) and its journal, *Historisk tidsskrift*, were founded in 1869. The present publication is thus a belated homage to the association's 125th anniversary. Despite the centrality of national concerns, Norway's historians have by no means been out of touch with the international community of historians. Halvdan Koht was elected the first president of the Comité International des Sciences Historiques upon its foundation in Geneva in 1926, and Norwegian historians have regularly taken part in international conferences in the discipline. However, the focus on national history, combined with the habit of writing in a little-known language, has effectively restricted the purview of history writing in Norway.

The tide is now changing. Norwegian historians increasingly undertake research in international history, and more of them now write about Norwegian history in an international language, usually English. The publication of *Making a Historical Culture: Historiography in Norway* thus reflects this growing internationalization of Norwegian historical scholarship. It is the result of internationalization in another way as well, for the anthology was initially proposed by a newcomer to the county and its history, the Canadian historian William H. Hubbard. One of his important functions in the editorial group has been to challenge his Norwegian colleagues when they threatened to become myopic.

Part I
Context and Concepts

1. History and Society[1]
Kåre Lunden

This chapter mainly deals with the period from 1771, the year Gerhard Schøning began to publish *Norges Riiges Historie* (three volumes, 1771–81). A dominating *theme* of Norwegian historiography from Schøning right up to the start of the present century, however, had been the relation between the new and the old Norway, back to the Middle Ages and Viking times. Icelandic–Norse historiography (the saga literature) of the twelfth and thirteenth centuries was a correspondingly dominant *material*. We shall therefore take a brief look at older historiography. As in other countries, Norwegian historiography also received its character through interaction with social and natural surroundings.

Geography and society[2]

As well as the mainland, which is part of Finno-Scandinavia, Norway comprises several detached territories acquired between 1920 and 1931: Svalbard, Jan Mayen, Bouvet Island, Peter I's Island, and a part of the Antarctic continent. The mainland covers 323,917 square kilometres. Mean height above sea level is 480 metres.

Glacial activity in the Quaternary period formed the river and

---

1 Translated by Eamonn Noonan.
2 General works: Helvig 1974; Popperwell 1972. On geography: Ahlmann 1962; Dent 1957; Hohle 1956; Holtedahl 1960; Myklebost 1963; Sømme 1954. On society and politics: Lafferty 1981; Norway's official statistics XII 1978; Ramsøy 1974; Selbygg 1986; Statistical Yearbook (annual); Valen and Katz 1964. On language and culture: Beyer 1979; Haugen 1966; Mortensen and Vogt 1955.

fjord landscape which characterizes the west coast. Langfjella, generally ranging over 1,000 metres above sea level, divides East Norway and West Norway. Part of this massif is Hardangervidda, Europe's largest plateau. An east-going part of Langfjella marks the border to the third region, Trøndelag. The fourth region, Northern Norway, lies mainly above the Arctic Circle.

Of the total land mass, about 74 percent is mountainous and unproductive, 23 percent productive forest, and 3 percent arable land. East Norway alone has more than half of both the forest area and the arable land. The mainland lies on roughly the same latitudes as Alaska, between 58° and 71° North. Southerly winds and the Gulf Stream nevertheless keep the fjords generally free of ice, even in Finnmark above the Arctic Circle. Annual mean temperatures are in Oslo (East Norway) 5.9°C, in Bergen (West Norway) 7.8°C, and in Tromsø (Northern Norway) 2.9°C, all well over the average for such latitudes.

Fir and pine forests cover large parts of the broad valleys of East Norway and Trøndelag. West Norway has very little coniferous forest, but some deciduous forest. Northern Norway, which is mainly mountainous, has some forest, including coniferous forest, especially in the inland valleys.

Up to around one hundred years ago, large beasts of prey – bears, wolves, and lynx – were common in the whole country; now they are found only in small areas. Arctic animals such as reindeer and wolverine are still found over the whole country, though in the south only in the mountains. Moose are common in the coniferous forests, and deer in the western coastal areas.

The population was around 450,000 in the fourteenth century; 883,000 in 1801; 2,240,000 in 1900; and 4,300,000 in 1992. Of these around 30,000 speak the Lapp language. The remainder speak Norwegian, a member of the Northern Germanic group of languages. From around 1500 the written language was Danish, which still greatly marks *riksmål* (or *bokmål*). This is one of the two written languages which have formally stood on equal footing since 1885. The other written language, New Norwegian (*nynorsk*), is based on modern dialects and was codified around 1850.

The labour force has been distributed as follows:

	1875	1946	1970	1990
Primary industries	53%	30%	12%	6%
Industry, mining	18%	32%	38%	23%
Services, trade	29%	38%	52%	69%

Among the primary industries, forestry has been important, with considerable exports from around 1500. Fish was the only large export trade between 1100 and 1500, and has always been one of the main trades, both in consumption and in export. In 1994 agriculture produced about half of domestic food consumption, on the basis of estimated caloric values. The country has been dependent on imports of grain since the Middle Ages.

The pattern of agricultural settlement has always been one of individual farms rather than villages. There has not been serfdom since slavery was ended around 1200. In older times farmers were mainly tenants, but after a development from c. 1600, by far the larger part have been freeholders since the mid-nineteenth century. In addition farmers now own around two-thirds of the productive forestry.

Since the 1890s industry has to a large extent built on hydroelectric power; in this area Norway ranks fourth in the world in terms of resources, and first in per capita terms. Since the 1970s North Sea oil and gas have been the most important export items, corresponding since around 1980 to the combined value of the traditional export goods.

Shipping has been an important sector, especially since the end of the seventeenth century. In 1973 the Norwegian merchant fleet accounted for 10 percent of the world's tonnage.

Per capita income approximately trebled between 1945 and 1970, and by this measure Norway has been among the world's ten richest countries in recent years. The country has had a means-tested state pension system since 1936 and universal social security since 1967. The latter covers old age, illness, and loss of income for other reasons.

Norway is a constitutional hereditary monarchy, with an advanced multi-party system since 1884. The Norwegian Labour Party has been the dominant party since 1927.

The country has had state schools for all since 1739. A Norwegian university was first established in 1811, and the annual number of examination candidates has developed as follows:

1815	1875	1925	1960	1975	1991
16	158	1,559	5,179	16,135	20,919

Of the 1991 figure, 13,104 were women.

Around 5,000 books are published annually in Norway, and the country has around 5,000 public libraries (including school libraries), which lend c. 24,000,000 books a year.

History[3]

"Norway" and "Norwegians" are first clearly described around 890, in the forward to King Alfred's translation of Horace's *Historiarium adversum*. Political consolidation under a monarchy began at around the same time, in the decades around 900, under King Harald Fairhair.

The oldest traces of settlements go back to the period 11,000–8,000 BCE, along the coast where the ice first melted after the last ice age. New immigrants between 3,000 and 2,500 BCE were cultivators, who mainly displaced the earlier hunting peoples.

From the time of the downfall of the Roman Empire in the West (400–600), the graves of chieftains and other sources show that the country must have had local "states" or mini-kingdoms.

In the Viking era (800–1050), the Norsemen conducted raids against, or settled in, Ireland, Scotland, parts of England and France, the Isle of Man, the Hebrides, the Orkneys, the Shetlands, the then generally unpopulated Faroe Islands, and Iceland. They settled in Greenland, and made expeditions to Vineland in North America. Others travelled eastwards, to Russia and Constantinople.

The hundred years after the death of Harald Fairhair around

3 General history: Andersen 1977; Bagge and Mykland 1987; Derry 1957; Derry 1973; Fladby 1986; Furre 1991; Helle 1974; Ingstad 1985; Mykland (ed.) 1976–80; Nerbøvik 1967; Pryser 1985; Steen 1951–62. Economic history: Galenson 1986; Hodne 1975; Hodne 1983; Moe 1977.

930 were marked by military conflicts, partly among his successors, partly between these and other Norwegian chieftains, and
also between all these together and the Danish kings. Danish kings
occasionally had supremacy over the whole country, as in the
years up to the death of Canute the Great in 1035. More often they
had hegemony over Vika, the south-eastern part of the country. In
this era it was only for short periods, as under Olav I (994–1000)
and St. Olav II (1015–28), that a united royalty could operate relatively efficiently, at least over the entire coastal area. Under these
two kings the country was Christianized, and a Norwegian church
was organized. Despite conflicts between king and church from the
end of the twelfth century, after the church itself had become rich
and powerful, co-operation between church and king must be considered as a bulwark of the political and administrative consolidation of Norway from 1035.

Approximately one hundred years of "civil wars" followed the
relatively peaceful period 1035–1130. The main feature was conflict between and among the secular and the religious aristocracy
about state and church resources. These grew strongly before and
during this period, in the form of state and church taxes and tolls.
Contributory to the internal conflicts was that after *c.* 1130 there
was a definite end to the ability of the Norwegian rulers' ability to
profit from raids abroad, which had been a feature of the chieftain
system earlier in the Viking period, and to a lesser extent subsequently. A strongly increasing population also made for internal
conflicts, also among the main clans.

Up to 1260 kingship was fairly commonly divided between several kings at a time, and the succession custom gave equal rights to
all the king's sons. Through the civil wars a sole kingship developed, codified in 1260.

The latter part of the reign of Håkon IV Håkonsson (1217–63)
and his successors up to Håkon V Magnusson (1299–1319) is
"Norway's golden age", marked by a high degree of internal peace,
relatively strong international position, the institutional development of the kingdom and the church, and otherwise by a cultural
flourishing, especially in literature and building. The social basis
was a secular and religious aristocracy of landowners, who also
collected public revenues.

Territorially the Norwegian kingdom – *Noregsveldet*, the Norwegian realm – reached its greatest extent under Håkon Håkonsson. The mainland then comprised, in addition to the present lands, Båhuslen, Jemtland, and Herjedalen. The Isle of Man, the Hebrides, the Orkneys, the Shetlands, the Faroes, Iceland, and the Norwegian settlements on Greenland (which had indefinite borders) also belonged to the kingdom.

King Håkon V had no sons, and thus in 1319 a personal union with Sweden was established, which lasted to 1355. After a separate Norwegian kingdom under Håkon VI (1355–80) followed a personal union with Denmark between 1380 and 1389, extended in the latter year to union with Sweden: the Calmar union. Norway remained in union with Denmark until 1814, while Sweden seceded in 1521.

The legal basis for the Danish–Norwegian union was set down in the union treaty of 1450. This placed the two kingdoms on equal footing within an eternal union. After an uprising by the most important Norwegian potentate, the Archbishop of Nidaros (the archbishopric was established in 1152 or 1153), King Christian III promised the Danish nobility in 1536 that Norway would not subsequently be or be called a separate kingdom, but a province of the Danish kingdom. A separate Norwegian royal council did not exist after 1536.

Norway's legal–constitutional status between 1536 and 1814, and especially between 1536 and 1660, is a matter of dispute. Legally, the most correct view seems to be that Norway should be seen as a separate kingdom in terms of international law, and as a separate nation in the natural law sense, in the whole period.[4] Thus a separate constitutional act was issued for Norway, and a separate royal election was held for Norway, when absolutism was introduced in Denmark–Norway in 1661. Factually, politically, and administratively, Denmark–Norway with its centre in Copenhagen was nevertheless in the main a Danish-dominated entity. State and local officials were in large part Danish. Only occasionally and for some of its internal matters did Norway have a distinct government, in the form of a governor or a government collegium in Christiania.

4 Castberg 1961:15; 1964:73ff.

The social basis for the establishment of the union in the Late Middle Ages, and for the fact that Norway thereafter assumed a subordinate position, was complex. Firstly, through marriage ties a common Nordic and gradually a (mainly Danish) Danish–Norwegian nobility was formed. Secondly, as long as the economy was mainly based on agriculture, Denmark was inevitably several times more powerful than Norway. It was also important that the Norwegian population was perhaps more than halved by the Black Death of 1349–50 and succeeding plagues.

Norwegian resources in fisheries, forestry, and water mills (water power), as well as expanding interaction with the growing West European economy, nevertheless brought strong growth and a much more differentiated Norwegian economic basis from the 1500s. This also formed the basis for a much increased population. After Denmark had ceded the provinces east of Øresund to Sweden following the wars of 1643–60, the two kingdoms of Denmark and Norway were much more balanced than before in population and in resources. A Norwegian merchant class, involved in lumber, mining, and the fisheries trade, had become relatively strong by the late eighteenth century. This bourgeoisie was aware that Norway did not always have the same economic and political interests as Denmark. The government in Copenhagen carried on a policy for a unitary state, especially from the 1730s. This concentrated in Copenhagen not only the central administration, but also institutes of higher education, banks, trade monopolies, and manufacturing. Norwegian discontent with the effects of the unitary-state policy was expressed, especially in a period of press freedom from 1771 to 1773.[5] Especially unfortunate for Norway was the fact that Denmark–Norway from 1807 came into war with England and Sweden on Napoleon's side. The continental blockade stopped Norwegian exports and hindered corn imports, which were vital at this stage. Central Norwegian political figures, led by Count Wedel Jarlsberg, felt that the union with Denmark was unfortunate, and that a self-governing Norway in union with Sweden was a better alternative.

After Napoleon's defeat King Frederik VI ceded Norway to the

5 Lunden 1992:116ff.

king of Sweden through the Peace of Kiel in 1814. The Norwegians rebelled against this, led by the heir to the Danish throne, Christian Frederik. A Norwegian national assembly at Eidsvoll elected Christian Frederik as a separate king of Norway on 17 May 1814. It also gave the country a constitution based on irrevocable popular sovereignty and the division of powers. The popular representation, the Storting, was elected on the basis of a broad franchise, including farmers.

After a short war with Sweden, the Convention of Moss of 14 August 1814 established Norway as an independent monarchy in personal union with Sweden.[6] The constitution of 17 May was retained, with the alterations entailed by the personal union. The conduct of foreign affairs lay with the king. This union lasted until 1905.

With the Peace of Kiel, the Faroes, Iceland, and Greenland were ceded from the Norwegian kingdom and retained under the Danish crown. The Orkneys and the Shetlands were mortgaged by King Christian I to the king of Scotland in 1468 and 1469, and never released. The Norwegian provinces of Jemtland, Herjedal, and Båhuslen were ceded to Sweden after defeats in war in 1645 and 1658.

After the crisis for the export trade which followed the Napoleonic Wars and England's tariff policy, the Norwegian economy was marked by the expansion of agriculture in the early nineteenth century and the modernization of this sector from around 1850. Fish exports increased around sixfold between 1815 and 1880, and timber exports grew strongly from the 1840s. The strongest expansion was in shipping, especially between 1850 and 1880. By the turn of the century, the country had the world's third-largest merchant marine, after Great Britain and the USA.

A certain industrialization began around the middle of the century. The first railway was built in 1854, and commerce and crafts liberalized from 1842. Measured by per capita GNP, Norway around 1870 was not backward in relation to most European countries, and was for example ahead of Sweden. Politically, the 1814 constitution, and thereby Norwegian independence, was defended against royal attempts at revision in the 1820s.

6 Castberg 1961:23; 1964:104–12.

The leading political class up to 1884 was the civil servants. From the 1830s, however, farmers made greater use of the position granted them by the constitution. From the end of the 1840s, the rule of civil servants met opposition also from the Storting representatives of the expanding bourgeoisie. A left-wing coalition mainly of farmers and bourgeoisie was formalized as the Venstre (Left) party in 1883. This put an end to the "rule of officials" with a judgement of the court of impeachment which deposed the government in 1884. Parliamentarianism was thereafter practised. The conservatives organized their party, Høyre (Right), in 1884.

Venstre, together with the Norwegian Labour Party, which was founded in 1887, introduced universal suffrage for men in 1898, and for women in 1913.

In conflict with the left-wing elements, the officials supported the king from the 1840s. Conflict between farmers and officials, left and right, therefore came to assume the form of a struggle about the strength of royal power, and hence about the strength of the union. The left-wing coalition, which especially from the 1840s was able to base itself on a blossoming cultural nationalism, exalted Norwegian independence, and tried to keep royal power and the strength of the union at a minimum. There were bitter constitutional disputes, especially between 1872 and 1884, after a period in the 1850s and 1860s when a Nordic pan-nationalism ("Scandinavianism") appeared.

After 1884 the constitutional and union dispute concerned the conduct of foreign policy. The Norwegian demand was initially for a separate Norwegian foreign minister, but later for a separate and Norwegian-ruled consular service. When the king refused to concede this in 1905, against the advice of the Norwegian government, following a Storting resolution on such a consular service, the government resigned. The king was not able to find an alternative Norwegian government. On 7 June 1905 the Storting declared the union with Sweden dissolved, "as a consequence of the fact that the king has ceased to function as Norwegian king". The dissolution of the union was acknowledged by Sweden by the Agreement of Karlstad in September 1905.

The subject of the conflicts with Sweden – or with the common king – which destroyed the union might in retrospect not seem to be especially important. But the principle at stake was Norway's sovereignty. The union conflict also had the power to disrupt internal politics, mainly because the union and the royal authority were used to defend the old upper class against the expanding farmers and bourgeoisie.

The main lines in economic and social development between 1875 and 1920 were the reorientation of agriculture towards market production and mechanization, the motorization of the fisheries fleet from around 1900, industrial exploitation of wood for pulp and cellulose, the quadrupling of industrial employment, the expansion of hydroelectric power from around 1905, the transition from sail to steam power in the merchant fleet from the 1880s, and the trebling of goods imports.

From the 1860s the reorientation of agriculture and these other conditions led to emigration, notably to the USA and Canada. This was at times greater than from any other country except Ireland.

A politically dominant conflict between 1905 and 1914 concerned concession laws regarding the national control of natural resources, especially water power. The language question also caused political conflict, in the context of the new orthography in 1907 and 1917, which also rendered *riksmål* more Norwegian.

During the First World War, Norway was formally neutral, but was forced by the western powers to cease the export of strategically important goods such as metal and fish to Germany. Around half the merchant fleet was sunk by Germany. The wartime boom brought growing economic and social inequalities.

The inter-war period was marked by sharp economic crises, but also by growth. Industry production grew by 75 percent between 1913 and 1938. Total merchant tonnage nearly trebled from 1918 to 1939, and Norway's fleet was then the world's most modern, leading for instance in tankers.

The trend in unemployment was sharply upwards, from nearly full employment during the world war to 20 percent unemployment among the organized work-force in 1927 and 33 percent in 1933. In the Great Depression, which hit Norway from 1930, both the export trade and agriculture had huge problems. Despite temporary falls in per capita GNP, this grew by around 60 percent from 1918 to 1939.

Politically the period up to 1935 was especially turbulent, in the context of unemployment; the problems of the farmers; the radicalization of the labour movement after 1917; and a right-wing reaction with some quasi-fascist organizations from the 1920s and an entirely fascist party, the National Coalition, led by Vidkun Quisling from 1933. The farmers, who had earlier mainly supported Venstre, in 1920 formed their own party, the Farmers' Party. The Christian People's Party, founded in 1933, was a political defence of traditional values, religion, and abstinence from alcohol. Together with the Communist Party, formed as a splinter from the Labour Party in 1923, all of this was an expression of political and social polarization during the economic crises.

A socialist revolution did not, however, occur, and the fascist party remained without representation in the Storting. The Labour Party came to power in 1935, through a compromise with the Farmers' Party. An agreement between the Trade Union Congress (Landsorganisasjon) and the Employers' Federation in 1935 set down rules for the solution of industrial conflicts.

The Labour Party pursued a moderate reform policy, with the development of a welfare system and with measures against unemployment, which was still around 20 percent in 1939. The Labour Party government was a minority one, replacing earlier non-socialist minority governments.

Norway entered the Second World War with the German invasion of 9 April 1940. On the same day the government elected to fight, and after new talks on 11 April, it rejected German pressure for a government led by Vidkun Quisling.

From 7 June 1940 the king and the government took refuge in London for the duration of the war, with Norway under German occupation. Actual political power was exercised by the Reich's Commissioner Josef Terboven. But Vidkun Quisling, who from 9–14 April 1940 had placed himself at the head of a self-proclaimed "national government", was appointed "Minister President". His party, the National Coalition, had 43,000 members at its height in 1943. The other political parties were forbidden after 25 September 1940. From this time on a "reorganization" was carried out, with an implemented or attempted Nazification of local government, the school system, and the associations. This was met with civil resistance; sports, theatre, and cinema strikes; protests by teachers and bishops; and more. Resistance was organized by a Co-ordination Committee from the winter of 1941–2, and this was met by the arrest of 1,100 teachers, as well as other German acts of terror. Military resistance was organized from 1942.

The merchant fleet made a significant contribution on the Allied side, and half of it was lost. Finnmark and northern Troms were laid waste during the German retreat in 1944–5.

The post-war period from 1945 to 1965 was dominated by the Labour Party, which held power for the entire period with a brief interruption in 1963. It held an absolute majority in the Storting up to 1961. Reconstruction proceeded under regulated economic planning, and the social reform policies of the 1930s were resumed. There was full employment up to the early 1980s. Annual growth in GNP from 1946 to 1974 was around 4–5 percent, and at times higher. In 1945 there was one car per sixty-four inhabitants, and in 1983 one car per three inhabitants.

The post-war period, especially up to the 1970s, was the period of most rapid change in known history. The changes may be summed up as a transition from semi-urbanization to full urbanization (a quarter of farms ceased to exist from 1949 to 1969), from industry to services (see table, p. 17), equalization between classes and regions in lifestyle, and ever-greater participation of women in the work-force and politics. For a time in the early 1990s, the three largest parties all had female leaders, and the fourth-largest had a woman as parliamentary leader. Since November 1990 the prime minister has been a woman, Gro Harlem Brundtland, who first attained that office in 1981.

Norway has become much more integrated with the outside world, economically and institutionally. Exports comprised 17 percent of GNP in 1950, and 31 percent in 1982. The country became a member of the OECD in 1949, and of EFTA in 1960. It concluded a free trade agreement with the EC (EU) in 1973, replaced in 1994 by membership in the European Economic Area. Norway has been a member of NATO since 1949, thus abandoning the neutrality which had been its policy since 1905.

From the 1970s a new phase began, with an economic slump, growing unemployment, and less political stability. There were

70,000 unemployed persons in 1983, rising to around 6 percent of the labour force in 1994. The extension of the welfare state measures culminated in the 1970s, with a certain contraction subsequently. Since 1965 the country has had five non-socialist governments, all but one being coalitions, and six Labour Party minority governments.

The sharpest political conflicts in recent decades have concerned political integration with Western Europe. In 1972 the government signed a membership agreement with the EEC (EU), but in a referendum the people voted no. The government signed a new membership agreement in 1994, but on 28 November of the same year the people again said no. On both occasions it was only in the more densely populated areas of the south-east that there was a yes majority, apart from a few cities.

Particularly strong resistance to EU membership in Norway reflects a relatively strong belief that it is possible, despite internationalization, to use a relatively free-standing nation–state as an instrument of the nation's interests. The resistance probably also reflects an especially strong mistrust in the periphery of the geographical and political centre. A background to the resistance is also the perception of the unhappy experience with the earlier, long-lasting unions with Denmark and Sweden. The strong Norwegian opposition to EU membership thus reflects deeply rooted features of the Norwegian country and Norwegian history. The same features mark its historiography; they may to a certain extent be created, or at least strengthened, by historical writings.

Historiography and society

Under the first state formation and the unions, c. 1170–1770

Norse literature of the twelfth and thirteenth centuries -mainly Icelandic, partly Norwegian – comprises twenty-three distinct known sagas about the Norwegian kings.[7] The best known is *Heimskringla* by Snorre Sturlason (1178/9–1241). The three oldest compendia,

---

7 Schier 1970:9ff.

and perhaps others, have Norwegian authors, although most of the mainly anonymous writers must have been Icelandic.[8] The Icelandic aristocracy in this period, before Iceland became part of the Norwegian kingdom in 1262–4, were often the Norwegian king's men in the feudal sense, and participated to some extent in Norwegian political and military conflicts.[9] This was the case with Snorre. An awareness of a Norwegian political and ethnic identity finds expression in the sagas about the Norwegian kings, at times in a strongly chauvinistic form.[10] The struggles between the Danish and Norwegian kings and other chieftains presumably lie behind this.

All subsequent Norwegian historiography about the Middle Ages, as well as the general modern awareness of the Norwegian nation's past, is based mainly on the Norse sagas of that period.

The fourteenth and fifteenth centuries were a virtual literary vacuum for Norway. A renaissance in historical work came after around 1550, notably in the form of collections, translations, and versions of the Norse saga literature.[11] The work of the Bergen circle, whose central figures are Mats Størssøn (c. 1500–69), Laurits Hanssøn (d. 1558), Absalon Pederssøn (1528–75), and Peder Claussøn Friis (1545–1614), had an important background in the struggle with the German Hanseatic League, whose main Norwegian base was in Bergen.[12] With their work a Norwegian national awareness was renewed, which is also clearly expressed in the kings' sagas of the Middle Ages.[13] In Friis's work are found main themes similar to those which became prominent during the "first national breakthrough" in the 1770s.[14] These included hostility between the Norwegians and the Danes and the assertion of a specifically Norwegian heroism, developed through bear hunting and similar activities in the harsh Norwegian wilderness. His version of Snorre Sturlason's king's saga of around 1240, *Heimskringla*, was very well known, and from around 1760 also among the farmers.

8 Ibid.
9 Sigurdsson 1993.
10 Koht 1977 (1920):3ff.; Lunden 1994a.
11 Bull 1958:1–88 on sixteenth-century historians.
12 Ibid.:29ff.
13 Ibid.:52; Lunden 1994a.
14 Winsnes 1924:263; Lunden 1992:75ff.

It is said to have been one of the most important preconditions for Norwegian politics and literature in the period 1770–1814.[15]

The same romanticization of the Norse past is found in the anonymous Hamar Chronicles of around 1550, and to a lesser extent in the historical work of the Oslo humanists such as Halvard Gunnarssøn.

In the seventeenth century a number of historical–topographical works were produced, by Arent Berntsen (1610–80), the Danish-born Jens Lauritssøn Wolf (c. 1583–1660), Edvard Edvardsen (1630–95), and others.[16] A certain Norwegian patriotism was expressed in several of these, but not to the same intensity as in the earlier Bergen circle.

Tormod Torfæus (1636–1719), an Icelander who lived in Norway for many years, wrote (in Latin) *Historia rerum Norvegicarum* (1711), which for a hundred years was the most important single overview of Norwegian history.[17] Arni Magnusson (1663–1730), like Torfæus an Icelander who spent some time in Norway, made an extensive collection of mainly Icelandic but also Norwegian and Danish medieval manuscripts, which has been important for all subsequent work on the period.[18]

The Norwegian-born dramatist Ludvig Holberg (1648–1754), professor in Copenhagen from 1717, is regarded as the most prominent historian in Denmark–Norway in the eighteenth century.[19] Holberg wrote in Danish "for the general populace of both kingdoms". As a spokesman of popular enlightenment, he sought to forge links between Denmark–Norway and the rest of Europe, especially in *Introduktion til de fornemste Europæiske Rigers Historie* (1728). His history writings expressed consciousness of a particularly Norwegian identity, having equal chapters "On Norway" and "On Denmark". In *Danmark og Norges Beskrivelse* (1729), he portrayed a Norwegian national character, unlike the Danish. In this way Holberg anticipated viewpoints found in Schøning and the historians of the 1840s.

15 Bull 1958:54, 62.
16 Ibid.:89ff. on seventeenth-century historians.
17 Ibid.:151–5; Dahl 1990:13.
18 Ibid.:153ff.; Dahl 1990:14.
19 Ibid.:252 ff.; Dahl 1990:14f.

The historical and literary work of Holberg in itself and the viewpoints expressed therein reflected the fact that Norway had now become a more important part of the unified state. It also strengthened the basis for Norwegian national consciousness and patriotism.

The main precondition for Norwegian historiography from Mats Størssønn to Holberg was the continuity of an objectively existing and subjectively experienced Norwegian nationality through the period of union. Its main function was, in turn, to strengthen this.

The re-establishment of an independent state, 1771–1830[20]

Despite the earlier, important work, Gerhard Schøning is often reckoned to have laid the foundations for a specifically Norwegian historiography in modern times, notably with his *Norges Riiges Historie* (1771–81) on the period up to 996 CE.

Even as a student in the 1730s, Schøning was called "the fatherland's man". His historical writings were full of national pride, and contained some chauvinism; however, this was often simply extracted from the kings' sagas of the High Middle Ages, more than has generally been appreciated. Schøning wanted to show, especially in *De Norske og en deel andre Nordiske Folks Oprindelse* (1769), that the Norwegians were a distinct people from the beginning. In his unfinished history of Norway, he intended to demonstrate that Norway had been a distinct kingdom though its entire history. He also believed, in line with an opinion widespread in Europe at the time, that the general idea of liberty had spread with the Germanic tribes from the north. For Schøning Norway was its very breeding ground.

As a Norwegian intellectual, Schøning was a typical representative for his time of what A. D. Smith calls a "sociological minority", in reaction to the policy of centralization and homogenization of a pluri-national dynastic state.[21] The Danish–Norwegian Olden-

20 Dahl 1990:15–42; Bull 1958:400ff. on historians in this period.
21 Smith 1971:230ff.; Lunden 1992:25ff., 51–74.

bourg dynastic state had from 1720 to the 1740s concentrated foreign trade and manufacturing in the capital, Copenhagen. It expanded the unified state's banking system there between 1736 and 1791, and gave Danish exporters a monopoly over grain exports to large parts of Norway between 1735 and 1788.[22]

Norwegian dissatisfaction with the policies of the unified state, and the Norwegian demand for a university, a bank, and partly for a distinctly Norwegian arm of government in Christiania (Oslo), was expressed particularly in a short period of press freedom from 1771 to 1773.[23]

Schøning's historical writings were partly a cultural expression of the Norwegian reaction against the unitary-state policy, and illustrate a great "awakening" of national consciousness which nevertheless is also clearly documented earlier. But his writings also strengthened what one might call the "national wave", and formed a foundation for the powerfully patriotic literature of many poets and others in the last decades of the eighteenth and the first decades of the nineteenth century. Hans Arentz (1731–93), Even Hammer (1732–1800), Johan Nordal Brun (1745–1816), Claus Frimann (1746–1829), Edvard Storm (1749–94), and Christen Pram (1756–1821) were to an extent direct students of Schøning, or built on his writings.[24]

The patriotism of the general European enlightenment in the late eighteenth century included a demand to promote the general good through the work of enlightenment, the study of nature, and initiatives for the strengthening of commercial activities. The task included the production of topographical writings, which also had historical content.[25] The Royal Norwegian Scientific Society in Trondheim, of which Schøning was a co-founder, took up this work from 1767. Among the important topographical–historical works were Hans Strøm's *Physisk og oeconomisk Beskrivelse over Fogderiet Søndmør* (1762–4) and H. F. Hjorthøy's corresponding work on Gudbrandsdal.

22 Lunden 1992:46–50.
23 Ibid.:116–49; Bull 1958:255.
24 Lunden 1992:80–102; Winsnes 1924.
25 Sandnes 1970:18ff.

All of these works, which strengthened Norwegian self-awareness, together with the new idea of popular sovereignty, were necessary preconditions for the Norwegians' 1814 rebellion against
the cession of Norway by the Peace of Kiel, and for their adoption
of a constitution and the establishment of an independent Norwegian state.

The demand for a Norwegian university was conceded in 1811.
This improved the conditions for Norwegian historical research. In
the first period it was, however, "amateurs" outside the university
who did the most important work. These were also – and typically
– people who were directly involved in or especially preoccupied
with the establishment of the state in 1814. One such person was
the prefect and later supreme court judge Christian Magnus Falsen
(1782–1830), one of the most important political leaders of
1814. He held that the constitution of 1814 to a great extent re-
established Norwegian popular liberty from the Early Middle Ages.
He sought to underpin this view in *Norges Odelsret med Hensyn paa
Rigets Constitution* (1815) and with a general presentation of Norwegian history in the saga period.[26] Falsen's view of the historical
connection with the Middle Ages at least had consequences for the
names given to the two chambers of the Storting: Odelsting and
Lagting. But the wide franchise gained by farmers in the 1814
constitution was also based on ideas about the position of farmers
in the old Norwegian state.

The great importance which the generation of 1814 accorded
history and historiography found expression in the relatively
numerous circle of prominent officials who themselves engaged in
historical research. The circle included the district governor and later chief justice Jens Christian Berg (1775–1852), Captain Gerhard
Munthe (1795–1876), and economics professor Gregers Fougner
Lundh (1786–1836). In addition to writing history, these made an
important contribution by editing sources (*Samlinger til det norske
Folks Sprog og Historie* I–IV, 1833–9) and periodicals (*Budstikken. Et
Ugeblad av statistisk-økonomisk og historisk Indhold*, from 1817, and
others), and by their organizational work (Association for the Norwegian People's Language and History, from 1831).

26 Dahl 1990:22.

This generation's most significant historian was the poet and national archivist Henrik Wergeland (1808–45), especially with *Norges Konstitutions Historie* (1841–3). Wergeland was the son of one of the leaders of 1814, and was himself a great patriot in word and deed. Although he was hardly an outstanding empirical researcher, he can be considered one of the foremost thinkers in Norwegian historiography. Wergeland looked for chronologically extensive connections and socially profound causes in history. He developed the main lines in theories which later became more known through Ernst Sars. Wergeland explained the fact that the freedom of the Norwegian farmers could persist through the union with Denmark by reference to the virtual extinction of the Norwegian nobility in the Late Middle Ages. He sharply stressed that an independent Norwegian state did not follow automatically from the cession of Norway from Denmark to Sweden in 1814. An active *Norwegian* contribution was still required. Wergeland found the necessary preconditions for such a contribution in the growth of Norwegian national consciousness over a long time before 1814, and additionally in the continuity in social structure back to the saga era. This was especially the case for the conditions of the farmers.[27]

It is clear that the historical work of this generation was deeply integrated with the main features of contemporary history. Older historiography, as Wergeland suggested, was a precondition for the uprising of 1814, and for the form the constitution took. More recent works extended and maintained the Norwegian self-image, which among other things was a precondition for the maintenance of independence against the royal attempts at revision in the 1820s.

Although I have here stressed the connection between historiography and contemporary Norwegian – and Nordic – political history, more specifically intellectual impulses from Europe as a whole were also a decisive factor throughout. The work of Arni Magnusson in the early eighteenth century was strongly influenced by professional impulses from French and German writers such as Mabillon and Leibnitz.[28] Schøning and the topographical

27 Koht 1965:189ff.; Dahl 1990:39ff.
28 Dahl 1990:18.

writers of the late eighteenth century were influenced by the phys-
iocrats and by the patriotism of the enlightenment. Falsen, Wergeland, and the others of the generation of 1814 elaborated the constitution and wrote history under direct and indirect influence
from Rousseau's teachings of irrevocable popular sovereignty,
Montesquieu's overall view of history, and gradually from the bud-
ding romanticism of Herder and others.[29]

There is throughout an interaction between social and political
life, which gave motivation and deep relevance to historical work,
and intellectual impulses. The latter decisively influenced not only
the forms taken by historical works but also the problems that historiography identified and addressed.

Further nation-building and agrarian emancipation, 1830–1860[30]

It is usually stated that a new generation of historians appeared
from the 1830s. In contrast to the generation of 1814, one can
now speak of professional academic historians, rather than of
"amateurs". The foremost were the professors Rudolf Keyser
(1803–64) and Peter Andreas Munch (1810–63). These historians show notable parallels in central viewpoints, and have been
called the "Norwegian historical school". Connections with the
previous generation are, however, strong. It was one of their leading predecessors, G. F. Lund, who formulated in 1832 what has
been considered their common programme. The task was to show
that the Norwegian people were "one of Europe's oldest, most historically renowned peoples, not just a puny offshoot of the fermentations of the current times".[31] This was a nation-building programme typical of the times, and it was especially topical in the
newly restored Norwegian nation–state.

Though continuity from earlier ideas is strong, and the close
relation to current political tasks was clear, the historiography of
the Norwegian historical school is in a particular manner deter-

---

29 Bull 1958:411; Paasche 1959:21, 24, 28ff., 74ff.; Koht 1929; Koht
   1977:75ff.
30 Dahl 1990:43–85; Worm-Müller 1920:19–22 on this period.
31 Dahl 1990:44.

mined by its links to the "national romanticism" of the 1840s. National romanticism was a movement and an ideology which was especially preoccupied with "folk individuality". The basic idea was that an independent nation must seek its right to exist in the fact that the "people" or "tribe" which constituted the nation could demonstrate its separate individuality far back in history, from the "beginning".[32] Historians were accordingly mainly interested in the oldest history. They developed special theories about the first settlers of the country, and about the relationship between the Norwegian and the Nordic elements of saga literature. The Norwegian historians claimed, in contrast to their Nordic colleagues, that Norway from the first was "the actual main seed of the Nordic tribe". It was the Norwegians who had authors' rights to most of the most important Norse literature of the Middle Ages. This was despite the fact that most of these were found in Icelandic script, and that most of their authors were Icelandic, insofar as their identity was known.

Similarities in purpose and in key viewpoints between the Norwegian historical school and its predecessors are so marked that the differences were essentially clearest in the technical, professional sense. The new writers were professional, with a general, international education in the discipline. New and stricter principles in source criticism were taken from the German historians Niebuhr and Ranke. P. A. Munch and others also laid more secure foundations for theories with links to other disciplines, especially philology and archaeology.

This generation conducted groundbreaking work in the editing of sources (*Norges gamle Love* I–II in the 1840s and *Diplomatarium Norvegicum* in 1847). Especially important historical works were Keyser's "Nordmændenes Herkomst og Folkeslegtskab" (1839), *Den norske Kirkes Historie under Katolisismen* I–II (1856–8), and Munch's monumental *Det norske Folks Historie* I–V (1851–63) on the period up to 1397.

Keyser was the most systematic thinker of this generation. His theories about medieval history can be seen as a historical explanation of contemporary society, in which the relatively egalitarian

32 Ibid.

character of Norwegian society had recently found expression in the "farmers' Stortings" of 1833 and 1836, and in the 1837 law on municipal councils, which provided for democracy in local government. Keyser presented Norwegian medieval society as relatively egalitarian, especially through the farmers' right to the *freehold* ownership of land (*odel*). For comparison he presented Denmark and Sweden in the Middle Ages as marked by feudalism (*lensvesen*), with a much more prominent stratification.

According to both Keyser and Munch, the causes of Norway's "decline" in the Late Middle Ages did not lie in any fundamental economic and social weakness.[33] The reasons lay in political–institutional conditions, and particularly in the fact that royal power was too strong. This had fatal consequences in relation to the unions. This viewpoint was clearly based on the perception that even in the historians' own times, Norway had the ability to stand on its own feet, provided the correct political solutions were found.

Other members of the Norwegian historical school were Christian C. A. Lange (1810–61), C. R. Unger (1817–97), and Frederik Peter Brandt (1825–91). These carried on the work of Keyser and Munch along the same general lines, especially with the editing of sources and with specialist studies such as Brandt's *Forelæsninger over den norske Retshistorie* I–II (1880–3).[34]

The Norwegian historical school's historiography was to be just one element of a more extensive phenomenon which is often called "the national breakthrough" in Norway. It is more accurate to call it, as did A. H. Winsnes, the *second* and strongest national breakthrough, since the first occurred in the 1770s.[35] (Even here Winsnes overlooks an even earlier case, which according to Halvdan Koht followed the struggle with the Danes around the year 1000.)[36] However, just as Schøning's historical writings were fundamental for the poetry and the other manifestations of national sentiment in the 1770s, the writings of the Norwegian historical school laid a basis particularly for (and forged a link to) the work of national cultural revival of this period. Central elements are Peter

33 Ibid.:69.
34 Ibid.:75ff.
35 See note 14 above.
36 Koht 1977 (1920).

Christian Asbjørnsen and Jørgen Moe's collection of Norwegian folk tales (1841), Moe's *Samling af Sange, Folkeviser og Stev i norske Almuedialekter* (1840), Magnus Brostrup Landstad's *Norske Folkeviser* (1848, 1852–3), Ludvig M. Lindeman's *Norske Fjeldmelodier* (1841), and Ivar Aasen's grammar and dictionary of vernacular Norwegian (1848, 1849). Other examples are the national romantic poetry of Johan Sebastian Welhaven (1838–59) and the farmers' tales and historical dramas of Bjørnstjerne Bjørnson and Henrik Ibsen from 1856. There was also national romantic painting by J. C. Dahl (1788–1837), Adolph Tidemand (1814–76), and others, as well as a corresponding music by Ole Bull (1810–80) and Halfdan Kjerulf (1815–68).[37]

All were concerned with clarifying that which was specifically Norwegian by means of the study of popular culture or peasant culture. Even if this was a fairly general feature of the nationalist movement of the time, the national breakthrough in Norway entailed that farmers and peasant culture gained a more prominent position than was otherwise usual in high cultural life as a whole, and in the self-image of the nation. This was because an earlier Norwegian high culture, linked to a separate Norwegian court with an associated corps of officials, had mainly disappeared since the High Middle Ages. That which was distinctively Norwegian was thus regarded as having to do with farmers, and national romanticism in Norway was an agrarian romanticism.

All this cultural work, with historiography as a central component, formed a general foundation for the political alliance between the farmers and the Venstre bourgeois movement in the following period, and with the development of democracy. This was linked to the assertion of Norwegian independence in the union.

Towards parliamentarianism and the dissolution of the union, 1860–1905[38]

A biological and to some extent an intellectual change of generation occurred in the 1860s. The new leading figures were the con-

---

37 Paasche 1959:465ff.
38 Dahl 1990:86–228; Koht 1920:1–18; Worm-Müller 1920:23–47; Bull 1920:52–129 on this period's historiography.

servatives Michael Birkeland (1830–96) and Ludvig Daae
(1834–1910), the radical Ernst Sars (1835–1917), and the jurist
and economist T. H. Aschehoug (1822–1909), a conservative.

The general interweaving of historiography and political struggle was unusually pronounced in this period. It has been said that
the main question was, "Should the future of Norway be Norwegian or Scandinavian? Should the Norwegians strive to build their
own independent national society, or should they enter in a wider
entity?"[39] But the political conflict which seemed to concern the
national question was closely linked to one which concerned the
class problem.

Yet the connection between historiography and politics, here as
elsewhere, is only *one* element in the weave. The historians of the
1860s, divided by political faction, had one fundamentally professional characteristic: they believed in the evolutionary perspective,
in the context of a professed belief in progress. This common feature can also be set in the context of both long- and short-term
economic development. The period from 1850 to 1875 was one of
continuous prosperity.[40] This was especially true of urban activities, which were especially profitable during the Crimean War
(1853), the American Civil War (1861–5), and the Franco-Prus-
sian War (1870–1). In a more or less clear connection with the
long-term development of technology and the economy, evolutionism and belief in progress among Norwegian historians also
had a more purely intellectual origin in the writings of Darwin and
Spencer. The influence came directly, and also indirectly through
the writings of Guizot, Michelet, Tocqueville, and others.[41]

Common to the opposing factions of historians was that they
wished to elaborate the continuities in the *whole* of Norwegian history, and not just to stress the beginnings and the oldest times. In
practice this entailed a wholly new emphasis on the "Danish
period" (1536–1814).

The main dividing lines on the national question between the
two historical factions were clearly articulated in a joint publication by Birkeland and Sars in 1867 (*To Foredrag om Skandinavisme*

39 Koht 1920:1.
40 Try 1979:111.
41 Dahl 1990:159.

og Norskhed, Christiania, 1867).[42] Birkeland asked who were the current Norwegians' real forefathers. He found them in the Danish period; the last traces of the old Norway disappeared in 1537. *True* historical continuity was thus linked to the Danish period. This view stressed at the same time the historical connection between Norway and the other Nordic countries, especially Denmark. The historical acceptance of the union with Denmark in the past assumed an implicit or explicit acceptance of the current union with Sweden, perhaps in a strengthened form. Another conservative historian, Aschehoug, here personified the ties between historiography and politics. He was the Norwegian head of the Swedish–Norwegian Committee on the Union from 1865 to 1867 and wanted a closer union. At the same time he wrote *Statsforfatningen i Norge og Danmark indtil 1814* (1866) and attributed Norwegian weakness in the Danish period to *natural conditions* in Norway, which produced poverty.

This point had wide-ranging implications, in history and in the contemporary situation. First of all, it entailed refuting earlier tendencies to accuse Denmark of causing Norwegian weakness in the period of union. Secondly, Aschehoug's view also exonerated the Norwegian nobility from responsibility for "Norway's decline", a responsibility which Munch for example wished to attribute to them.[43] Moreover, Norway's naturally determined poverty cast doubt on the appropriateness and the validity of the view that the nation could stand alone in the present and in the future. Aschehoug's historical explanation in general reduced the importance of politics and of social institutions in explaining the course of the country's history.

This was the context of a proposal put forward by the Committee on the Union under Aschehoug's leadership in 1867. The proposal entailed codifying a practice which confirmed a certain Norwegian subservience to Sweden, especially in that Sweden's foreign minister would conduct the foreign policy of both countries. The proposal was also linked to "Scandinavianism", a pan-national movement on a Scandinavian basis, established in the

1830s and especially popular among students. From the 1850s the movement gained support in broader circles and among officials. A union of the three Scandinavian kingdoms was discussed. The Danish–Prussian war of 1864 was, however, a decisive reverse, in that the Scandinavian slogans proved to have little to do with reality. But a strain of "little Scandinavianism" in favour of close co-operation between Norway and Sweden persisted. The Committee on the Union's 1867 proposal was the response to this.

Norwegian political opposition to closer union with Sweden, and against either version of the Scandinavian programme, found its great historical proponent in Ernst Sars, co-author of the 1867 publication with Birkeland. Sars must be considered the main heir to the great tradition in Norwegian historiography, from the Norwegian historical school back to Schøning and beyond. From 1856 Sars elaborated what remains the most wide-ranging synthesis of Norwegian history, especially with his *Udsigt over den norske historie* I–IV (1873–91).[44] A main political goal was to show that the conservative historians, together with the supporters of the union and the Scandinavianists, were historically and politically wrong. The Norwegian policy which had a historical basis, and which therefore in Sars's view had to succeed, was that which aimed at a fully independent Norway, not at a union.

Sars was not content just to study the oldest times in order to demonstrate this, as the Norwegian historical school had mainly done, or to study only the Danish period, to which the conservatives largely confined themselves. Sars drew lines through the whole story. An especially strong Norwegian clan and local nobility in the oldest times prevented the development of a strong central aristocracy. This lack was the main reason for Norway's being superseded by a neighbouring country from the Late Middle Ages. But this had advantages in the long run. Under the union with Denmark, Norwegian farmers were to a large extent left to themselves. Thus they were able to salvage the peasant freedom of the saga period, and to forge the link between this period and the new Norway from 1814. The latter was also to be understood in the sense that the social characteristics which the farmers had pre-

44 Koht 1977:24–39; Dahl 1990:156ff.

served through the Danish period, together with the new bourgeois class, constituted the underlying conditions for the Norwegian uprising against the Peace of Kiel in 1814.

Sars's view of history entailed a rehabilitation of political and
institutional conditions as main causes in history, in relation to the
ideas of Aschehoug and the other conservatives. Politics, not economics, would also be decisive in the future. More specifically
Sars's stress on farmers in history well suited the left-wing alliance
of farmers and radical officials of his times.

Sars was an especially important historian, all the more so
because in the 1870s the traditional officials' regime tried to
defend itself by taking refuge in a relatively strong united monarchy. Social radicalism and Norwegian radical union politics were
here in a notable way two sides of the same coin. Sars's historical
work was the main legitimization of Venstre's policies, which first
led to parliamentarianism in 1884, and then to the dissolution of
the union in 1905.

Some of this period's historical writings had less direct connections to the political conflict. Gustav Storm (1845–1903) put forward results which greatly weakened the argument of Keyser and
Munch that the Icelandic sagas drew on oral traditions in Norway.
He conducted a series of investigations of older history on the basis
of a more rigorous application of the principle of source criticism.
He was especially influenced by J. G. Droysen.[45]

Oluf Rygh (1833–99) gathered the material and edited the first
parts of the major work *Norske Gaardnavne* I–IXX (1899–1936).
This is a register of all farm names in Norway, based among other
things on a near-complete registration and use of medieval
sources, and a selection of more recent sources. At the time there
was no comparable work for any other country, and very few have
since appeared. A necessary precondition for such work was the
Norwegian pattern of individual farm settlement, as distinct from
village settlement. Norwegian topography was also a precondition,
in that each settlement had a distinct name, or a name of a certain
type. On a deeper level, the fact that Rygh, a professor of history in
succession to Munch, took up a work of this kind can show conti-

45 Dahl 1990:196ff.

nuity from Keyser, Munch, Sars, and others. All of these looked for the essential in Norwegian history and Norwegian nationality among the farmers, and in the results of their work. To this extent Rygh's work also belonged to the same main picture as that which encompassed Venstre's political alliance with the farmers.

More distinctly, Rygh's work was a component of and a precondition for the especially strong local history movement which blossomed in Norway in the twentieth century.[46]

The uniting of "the national idea" and Marxism, 1905–1939[47]

Industrialization from the mid-nineteenth century continued at an increased tempo after 1905. This found expression in the fact that this period's two leading historians, Halvdan Koht (1873–1965) and Edvard Bull sen. (1881–1932), both considered themselves Marxists. They had a correspondingly keen interest in the working class and the class issue generally. Nevertheless, historical writing was still more traditional in choice of subject than one might have expected, in view of the transformation in social conditions.

Halvdan Koht was enormously productive, and his writing was particularly wide-ranging both thematically and chronologically. He combined a boundless energy for detailed research with a striking capacity to discern larger connections and long lines. The latter found expression in various works rather than in a collected great synthesis, as in the case of Sars. Koht's achievement was to form his own overall view of Norwegian history, a view which combined the earlier main theme, the national, with a class perspective which he genuinely considered Marxist. (Nevertheless he saw himself as "a heretic in Marxism as in all other things".) Koht must be considered the giant of Norwegian historiography.

Koht accorded historical writing the function of answering questions which were generally relevant in the present. To this extent, historical writing which was interesting could never be

46 Johnsen 1920:277–306; Reinton 1970:33–54.
47 Dahl 1990:229–268 on this period's historiography.

politically neutral: "This is what has always kept historical research alive – that the fire of social conflict burns in its veins."[48] He had grand ideas about the role historical research could play. In 1884, as in the conflict about the union, he suggested that it was "as much Sars who succeeded, as Sverdrup [the leading Venstre politician]".[49]

A consequence of Koht's general programme was that "we cannot be satisfied with dry professional science.... If there is no spirit to bind everything together ... such science becomes useless."[50] This is a manifesto for historical synthesis as that which is actually important, and in Koht this is explicitly in the service of the class struggle: "when the social classes are shown the roots of their own struggles in the past, it strengthens their self-consciousness, and above all people learn to think along the lines of class struggle."[51] It is surely no accident that this especially sharp formulation of Koht's was made in 1920, during the radicalization which followed the Russian Revolution.

Although Koht wanted particularly to advance the class struggle among the workers, one of his main works was *Norsk bondereising* (The Norwegian farmers' emancipation, 1926). This was somewhat typical of Koht, and on a deeper level of much left-wing Norwegian historiography. Koht energetically carried forward the work of earlier historiography, which particularly sought to render the Norwegian nation–state legitimate: "all great historiography in this country has impressed upon us that we are a *nation*" (on Schøning, Munch, and Sars).[52]

Koht summed up his views of Norwegian history in a formula: the nation grew as various classes successively stepped up as active political protagonists, conscious of *both* class and nation. A narrow stratum of Norwegian aristocracy came into conflict with the Danes around the year 1000, and through this struggle came to consider themselves as Norwegian. This stratum then carried the Norwegian state. After the denationalization of the aristocracy in

48 Koht 1920:18.
49 Ibid.:5.
50 Koht 1977 (1921):46.
51 Koht 1920:18.
52 Koht 1977 (1921):51.

the Late Middle Ages, the growth of new occupations from the six-teenth century created the bourgeois basis for a Norwegian nation, and this was the social precondition for the state uprising of 1814.

In the nineteenth century the nation was again extended, in that farmers became aware that they constituted a consolidated and *Norwegian* class, in their efforts to establish their interests against the officials, and partly against the bourgeois, notably in the Storting. Finally, in the twentieth century the workers had the same experience. They made a contribution corresponding to that of the farmers hitherto, and also through country-wide organiza-tions and in political work inside and outside the Storting.

Koht was active in both local and national politics, and served as foreign minister from 1935 to 1941, in the first lasting Labour Party government. Koht's synthetic presentation of Norway's past and present, in which each class appeared in turn to make the active nation larger and richer, was easily assimilated into a view of society which accorded the Labour Party a moderate reformist role, on the basis of the existing society.

The same symbiosis between historiography and politics is embodied by Edvard Bull sen., who was foreign minister of the first, short-lived Labour government in 1928.[53] Bull was less pre-occupied with national and agrarian history than Koht. But Bull too worked extensively with older history. It is typical of the rural focus in Norwegian historical research that even Bull set up an extensive, comparative cultural history project in 1928 which concerned the agrarian society.

Similarly to Koht and other Norwegian historians of the period, Bull was influenced by researchers oriented towards cultural and social history, such as Karl Lamprecht, Werner Sombart, and Marc Bloch.[54] This brought a lessening of emphasis on political history. Bull conducted studies on older institutional history (*Leding*, 1920), and was a pioneer in the local history research which was then flourishing (*Kristianias historie* I–II, 1922–7).

The social history manifesto, coupled with the maintenance of the earlier interest in agrarian history, was expressed in important works by Oscar Albert Johnsen (1876–1954) and Sigvald Hasund

53 Bull 1933.
54 Dahl 1990:229, 232ff.

(1868–1959). Like Koht and Bull, Hasund was a cabinet minister, from 1928 to 1931.

Arne Bergsgård (1886–1954) was especially preoccupied by the national issue. Like Sars and Koht, he stressed that the Danish cession of Norway to Sweden in 1814 could not in itself have produced an independent Norwegian state, without an active Norwegian contribution on a broader historical basis. Bergsgård also represented a social historical viewpoint. On a deeper level of abstraction, this viewpoint harmonized with the participation of steadily broader groups in the active life of society, through political, professional, and cultural organizations.

Even if the political function of historiography was strongly emphasized and regarded favourably in this period, there was no slackening of technical–professional demands on research work. On the contrary, leading figures such as Koht and Bull were also pioneers of a new and stronger source criticism which dated from around 1913, under the direct influence of the Swedish historian Lauritz Weibull.[55]

In the course of the 1930s, a number of historians emerged who were later to assume primary importance. These were in their first works students of Edvard Bull sen., a particularly talented teacher, and were often referred to as "Marxist influenced". It gradually transpired that the younger historians were to travel in different directions than had Bull and Koht. They therefore belong to the next era.

Growth, differentiation – and lesser social relevance? 1945–1994[56]

In this period the most influential Norwegian historiography – and the bulk of historical work – acquired a radically different stamp from the leading historical research of any previous period. Among those who exercised the greatest influence was Jens Arup Seip (1905–92),[57] who wrote major and consequential works both

55 Ibid.:236.
56 Dahl 1990:269–326; Myhre 1994:320–37; Sejersted 1993:305–28 on this period's historiography.
57 Fure 1983:117–56; Lunden 1985:220–68.

on the Middle Ages and on modern Norwegian history. Another was Ottar Dahl (b. 1924), who is mainly a theorist and a methodologist.[58] The principle difference from earlier generations was a changed view of the relation between historiography and society, including politics. The new conception was articulated by both Seip and Dahl in the form of methodological and theoretical perspectives. Referring directly to Norwegian historiography in the second half of the nineteenth century, Dahl in 1959 wrote: "the linking of historical research to current political conflict can at times be remarkable, but it is largely superficial. Ultimately pure quest for knowledge and understanding is a stronger motif in research than a polemic interest determined by topicality."[59]

This sounded like a statement of facts, but also included a programme for Dahl, and for much of the historical writing of the period. Clearly, one could discern direct polemic against Koht's motto about what constitutes "living" historiography. The polemic is explicit in Seip, when he describes politically partisan historical works of the type produced by Sars as "political pamphlets".[60] Seip observed in 1958 that the historian in the exemplary case did not need to attempt anything other "than to find out how things are", and that this "is in accordance with the main tendency in current historical research".[61] Here he is referring to an empiricist tendency, as part of a more general neo-positivism or logical empiricism, which was transmitted to Norwegian historians in the post-war period especially by the philosopher Arne Næss.

Evidently, empiricist historiography of this kind lacks a "standard of significance"[62] corresponding to that found among the earlier leading historians. The latter regarded it as *professionally* important to demonstrate the nation's existence through time, or in the special case of Koht, to show the successive integration of classes into the nation. The empirical research programme (mani-

58 Fure 1993:37–66.
59 Dahl 1990:195.
60 Seip 1963:83.
61 Seip 1963:149.
62 Lunden 1994:18, after Carr 1961.

festo) to this extent paved the way for a fragmentation of activities, with no other structuring or professional identity-giving principle than that entailed in "pure quest for knowledge".

It is also easy to see that Norwegian historiography in the post-war period, in connection with a quantitatively much larger activity, has had the kind of fragmented character that one could fore-see on the basis of the empiricist programme. The result was in 1994 characterized as follows, with a mildly polemic intention:

Historians have been "out in fishing boats, down the mines, in the graveyards, on the factory floor, at the nurseries, in the prisons, into the subconscious, at the looms, at the employment agencies, under the covers, in the prayer houses, barns, and backyards", in short everywhere, in addition to the earlier activity in the main political and economic fields.[63] This summation is given in the context of a demand for more unified programmes of activity, and with a view to social relevance.

The numerous thematic areas covered in this period can, however, be considered more positively. Traditional classifications allow us to summarize a few main features as follows: Jens Arup Seip, with prominent students such as Alf Kaartvedt (b. 1921), Rolf Danielsen (b. 1922), Knut Helle (b. 1930), and others, conducted political and political–institutional history. Research into older agrarian and local history was conducted by Andreas Holmsen (1906–89), with his students Halvard Bjørkvik (b. 1924), Jørn Sandnes (b. 1926), Kåre Lunden (b. 1930), and others. General economic history, with a new emphasis on urban-based businesses, has been taken up, after Johan Schreiner (1903–67), notably by Francis Sejersted (b. 1936) and his many students. General social history, of demographic and other varieties, has been researched by Ingrid Semmingsen (b. 1910), Sølvi Sogner (b. 1932), Ståle Dyrvik (b. 1943), and others.

The history of the 1940–5 occupation is a huge research area in itself, examined by Magne Skodvin (b. 1915) and many followers. The increasing political and economic integration of Norway into the outside world has had fewer historiographical consequences than one might have expected. But there has been an

63 Nielsen 1994:28.

expansion, represented by John Sanness (1913–84), Edvard Bull
jun. (1914–86), Jarle Simensen (b. 1937), and others.

The history of the working class continues to receive less investigation than one might expect, but here too Edvard Bull jun. was a
pioneer, and he has had followers.

Norwegian local history research is still growing substantially,
and in the post-war period it has often been conducted by professional historians. The Norwegian Institute of Local History, under
the direction of Rolf Fladby (b. 1918) for many years, has been
important in this regard. There are around 200 local history associations, and at any given time around 100 of a total of 448
municipalities have a new or revised work on local history in
progress.[64] The relative weight of this work is a lasting testimony
to the special significance of the periphery, and especially the rural
areas, in Norway. This has found expression in, among other
things, the no vote in the EU referenda of 1972 and 1994.

The greatest expansion in the last twenty years has been in the
area of women's history. A bibliography of works in this area from
1970 to 1990 has around 450 entries.[65] This expansion corresponds closely to the rise of women in business and politics.
Women's history research has arguably assumed a political function similar to that accorded by Halvdan Koht to class history (or
history in general) in the inter-war period.

Norwegian historiography since 1945 in general must be said
to answer well to Dahl and Seip's empiricist programme, with
research based on "pure quest for knowledge". Nevertheless, in
recent times this programme has been called into question. The
question partly concerns its professional fruitfulness, and more
radically the extent to which it is possible to divorce historical
research from socially decisive forces.[66]

As far as this latter point is concerned, it is easy to show marked
similarities in the development of society, on the one hand, and
historiography on the other, in the period after 1945. Thus
"growth and differentiation" can apply equally to either area. One

64 *Heimen* 1991:28 and 1992:35; Fladby 1970:55ff; Fladby and Winge 1981.
65 Fløystad 1990:403ff., 598ff.
66 Lunden 1985; Fure 1983 and 1993.

can here mention the 4–5 percent annual growth in GNP from 1945 to 1974, with consequent strong differentiation in activities (see table, p. 17), and the entry of women into working life.

If one wishes to propose a mirror theory for the relationship between historiography and society, one could point to the fact that growth and differentiation have occurred both in historiography and in society. It is at least to that extent superficial to say that historiography is determined by "pure quest for knowledge" also in the era of empiricism. Quantitative growth is evident in that the number of university professors of history was 3 in 1911, and 33 in 1994. The expansion came mainly after the Second World War, and especially from around 1960. There were 80 registered, professional researchers in 1961, and 169 in 1972; in 1994 the Norwegian Historical Association had around 500 members.[67]

The economic precondition for this growth in the number of historians, as well as the corresponding growth in other disciplines, is, of course, the growth in the social economy. But one may also ask how such an extensive historical research activity can be justified. It seems that an empiricist research programme, with no other criteria of relevance or structuring principle than "pure quest for knowledge", could serve as a justification for unlimited research. The research programme of Seip and Dahl can in this light appear as a research ideology which is itself not divorced from social or economic interests. It corresponds directly to "the interests of the professional association" among the strongly expanding historians' guild. The programme may be functional, for the *profession*, in that it does not prescribe qualifications other than source criticism, applied to larger or smaller subjects. Demand for clearer relevance in relation to combined professional or social goals would be more theoretically demanding, and could thus exclude a large number of candidate researchers.

Yet a combined historical researcher contribution which was mainly characterized by dispersed, uncoordinated presentations may also be functional for dominating political interests in society. Historical writing along the lines of "pure quest for knowledge" will tend to be *uncritical*; it does not address the question of the

67 Norges allmennvitenskaplige forskningsråd 1973:6.

development of society as a whole. A relatively uncritical historiography, in the political sense, turning away from the large national and class controversies which the leading historians of earlier times addressed, can be a part of, and a precondition for, the relative harmony which has reigned in politics and social life for the bulk of the post-war period. The main features here are a common programme among the political parties in the immediate post-war years, the institutionalized peaceful solution of labour conflicts from 1935, full employment up to the 1980s, the fact that the national problem for Norway appeared to be definitively solved in 1905, and the generally moderate reform programme of the dominant Labour Party.

It could be said that the fragmented historical production of the post-war period was not in fact more distinct from social and economic interests, in the ranks of historians or in society, and was not more determined by "pure quest for knowledge" than was the case in earlier times. The connection simply became more subtle, and perhaps less recognized.

This impression is reinforced by the fact that harmony both among the ranks of historians and in society has lessened in the past two decades. The growing social divides from the "yuppie" period in the 1980s, with growing unemployment, is the main source of this on the social side.

On the professional side, the main aspect of the new unrest is critique of the empiricist research programme and of the fragmented activity which seems to follow from it. Several suggest that greater stress must again be placed on historical synthesis. This must go hand in hand with more energetic theoretical work, and with a renaissance in the importance of *values* as criteria of relevance.[68] Such a historiography will also have a greater critical potential.

One aspect of the new unrest in the historical profession is that some younger and older historians claim that the historical discipline has lost social prestige, and political, social, and intellectual importance, relatively and possibly absolutely, compared with the

68 Sejersted 1993; Nielsen 1994; Lunden 1991:91–141, 242–308; Kjeldstadli 1991:30–49.

situation one hundred years ago.[69] At the 125th anniversary of the Norwegian Historical Association in 1994, it was noted that the association had around 1,000 members in 1869, but only around 500 in 1994.[70] The former figure includes those interested in history, while the latter largely includes only professional, active historians; but precisely this distinction illustrates that historiography has become more a matter for the "specially interested". Among the membership in 1869 were half the government, 80 members of the Storting, and two-thirds of the district governors; from 1871 the king himself belonged. In 1994 there are few if any members of this kind.

A particular effect of the reduced political and social importance of the history discipline nowadays is that not even the most intense political conflict of the 1970s and the 1990s, that on EU membership, has gained any great deal of historical anchoring, in marked contrast to the situation in the last century during corresponding conflicts.[71] Here one might argue that it is *European* "state-building" which now corresponds to the nation-building of the nineteenth century. But *this* does not ameliorate the situation for Norwegian historiography; even "Europeanization" has not called forth activity which can in any way be placed on a par with that of Munch, Sars, or Koht.[72]

A possible remedy for the loss of social prestige and political importance should be the mentioned: growing emphasis on synthesis, once again. On the whole a remedy can lie in a return to Koht's view of what constitutes "living" or "useful" history: it cannot be guided by an abstract "pure quest for knowledge" (which indeed arguably does not exist), but must be part of a politically and morally committed debate about the society we have, and especially about that which we wish to have in the future.

69 Langholm 1994:41f.; Lunden 1991a:242ff.; Nielsen 1994:28ff.
70 Langholm 1994:41.
71 Lunden 1992 and Lunden 1993 are minor exceptions.
72 Førland 1993 is a minor exception. Professionally important work, which may be indirectly linked to European integration, is Riste 1973–8 and 1987, and other works on Norwegian foreign policy and military history. A large project on the history of Norwegian foreign policy is under way.

2. History as Science[1]
Knut Kjeldstadli

Professional historical research in Norway is not a very special case. From the 1830s to the present, Norwegian historians have been influenced by main currents of western thought – historism, evolutionism, historical materialism, functionalism, and critical theory. However, certain peculiarities have resulted from the timing of these impulses, their relative impact, and their specific adaptation:

1) An affinity to a kind of "history of society" can be traced from the very start.
2) A "common sense materialism" has been prominent in the twentieth century.
3) The intellectual climate has oscillated between two stances: the analytical and the synthetical approaches have coexisted, though they have been weighted differently in various periods.
4) Despite changes a certain quarrelsome unity has prevailed. This is most clearly seen in a common subject matter: national history. Continuity has been preserved both through straight lines of intellectual heritage *and* dialectically: predecessors are debated, not ignored.
5) Most historians have not worried about the scientific basis of history; they have sworn by a kind of "craftman's ideology" of research.

This presentation deals with some methodological and theoretical questions which have preoccupied successive generations of Norwegian historians. Accordingly several eminent empiricist "craft"

1 "One is carried by one's time." Munch 1853:16.

historians are omitted.[2] Four spheres will be considered in order to explain the development: the internal development of historical research, the adaptation of contemporary intellectual movements, the institutional framework, and finally the broader societal connections.

Historism – the "Norwegian historical school"

"Scientific" history arose in the early nineteenth century with the generation which matured after Norway acquired its own university in 1811.[3] Rudolf Keyser (1803–64) and Peter Andreas Munch (1810–63) were the most prominent historians.[4] They were branded the "Norwegian historical school" by contemporaries, although Munch himself wrote about the "so-called school". The name alludes to the "German historical school" of Leopold von Ranke, Georg Barthold Niebuhr, and others.[5] In some respects this is a valid parallel. They shared the same historist stress on historical individualities and the need to understand each people and each epoch on their own premises. In the history of ideas, Keyser and Munch were romantics, national romantics, in fact.

Their prime aim was to show that the original Norwegians immigrated from the north and east, not from the south. Thus they were not an offspring of the Danes or Swedes, but formed an original people in their own right. This interest in the genesis of a people, understood as an organic unity, dated from the Germans Herder, Fichte, and Schelling. It reached the Nordic countries at the beginning of the nineteenth century. The contemporary background for the special Norwegian interest in the matter is obvious: after Norway in 1814 seceded from the Danish *Helstat* (unified state), it con-

2 For general presentations of Norwegian historiography, see *Norsk historisk videnskap i femti år* 1869–1919; Dahl 1959 (new, expanded edition 1990). For the last period, see Dahl 1987.
3 "Scientific" should not be understood in the sense of being analogous to natural science, but in the more open sense used by Collingwood 1946/1960:9: "the forms of thought whereby we ask questions and try to answer them".
4 On Keyser, Andersen 1960; Dahl 1959. On Munch, Dahl 1959.
5 On the "German historical school", see Iggers 1984:12–24; Krogseth 1983:501–27.

sidered itself a separate country, although it was united with Sweden through having the same monarch and through a common foreign policy. Emphasizing the peculiarities of the Norwegians was considered important, in order to legitimize the new state and to resist what was called an "amalgamation" with Sweden.

The Norwegian historical school was more "ethnographic" than the German, partly because of their interest in prehistoric and early historic times. Furthermore, because of its historical position, the Norwegian state could not be the "hero" of the drama, or the embodiment of any central idea. The state was never very strong; in the Danish period from 1536 till 1814, it disappeared as an independent entity. An inner continuity had to found elsewhere – in the "people". Today one finds concepts such as "people", "tribe", and "nationality" problematic. They have connotations of essentialist, inherent qualities in a certain population. Nevertheless, they left an important legacy – a concept of history that went beyond political institutions and tended to deal with the basic social structures. *"Haupt- und Staatsaktionen"*, high politics and diplomatic manoeuvrings, were not regarded as the core of history. Thus the backwardness and smallness of Norway helped to produce an advanced concept of the subject matter of history.

The school's keen interest in migrations of peoples served to stress the ethnographic dimension also in the choice of material and methods. The Norwegians advocated and practised research which went beyond written sources and mere textual criticism, beyond philology. Their "historical–ethnographic science" (Munch) also drew on comparative linguistics (in order to see the interrelatedness of languages – and accordingly of different peoples), on archaeology and anatomy (to study variations in osteological material), and on geography.

Even so, disciplinary affinity to Ranke was clear; concentration on primary evidence and source criticism were common hallmarks. Munch gathered an impressive range of source material, particularly from the Vatican archives. He thus added much information to that contained in manuscripts previously known. Much of his effort went into editing, commenting, and publishing this material. In this work Keyser and Munch employed hermeneutic text criticism within each document and in comparing documents, such as different versions of the sagas. They concentrated more on narrative sources than on documentary sources. Here Keyser created much of the vocabulary later used in writing about Norwegian history.

An enthusiastic, almost naive scientific optimism permeated their work: "We have decisively experienced, that human knowledge always increases, and that the scientific level itself progresses through the times", Munch wrote.[6] Even the most brilliant among the older generation were bound to err because of their lack of information; they should not be reproached in this respect. But new materials and methods gave historical research a breakthrough, Keyser and Munch felt. In their view professional quality rested on "craft rules", i.e. primarily research techniques. Questions of ontology, epistemology, or metatheories of history and society were given little consideration. This formative period of Norwegian historiography thus left another legacy: most Norwegian historians since have upheld a craftman's ideology of historical research, or an impressionistic empiricism, and look upon "theory" as a necessary evil or even a nuisance.

Although Keyser showed a synthetic ambition in dealing with the early periods when formulating the immigration thesis, a total vision of Norwegian history in its full extent was not produced until 25 years later. University chairs in history were so few in the nineteenth century that changes in the discipline had to wait until the old men retired.

Evolutionism and one grand synthesis

While the generation of the 1830s was preoccupied with the genesis of the nation, the generation of the 1860s dealt with its continuity. Influenced by evolutionism they faced the following problem: how could one claim a coherence in history, since Norway was not an independent state from 1536 to 1814? Their task was to find, or construct, links between three distinct periods, seemingly divided from one another – old medieval Norway, the Danish period, and the new-born state.

6 Munch 1853:5.

One answer was given by conservative scholars, like Michael
Birkeland (1830–96) and Torkel H. Aschehoug (1822–1909): the
elite in the Danish period, mostly of Danish origin, represented a
positive factor in Norwegian history and contributed to a growth
that made it possible to function as state after 1814. Politically
Birkeland and consorts represented "Scandinavianism", an intellectual movement seeking a merger or a very close co-operation
between the Nordic states, at the expense of Norwegian nationality, according to the critics.[7]

Another answer was given by Johan Ernst Sars (1835–1917),
the most towering figure in Norwegian historiography. His *Udsigt
over den norske Historie* (Overview of Norwegian History) I–IV,
1873–91, is a grand story about the inner continuity of Norwegian nationality. It indeed remains the only single-handed effort at
a total synthesis of Norwegian history.[8] (See chapters by Lunden
and Nordby in this volume.) One main point was the relative personal freedom enjoyed by the peasants. According to Sars this
characteristic of the peasants and hence of the Norwegians could
not be explained in terms of material poverty or scattered topography, as the conservatives claimed. The motivating force was their
political credo. Political arrangements and institutions were manifestations of the deep ideas of a people.

When it comes to Sars's views on history, four catchwords are
often mentioned: evolution, progress, idealism, and laws. Like
Birkeland and Aschehoug, Sars conceived history as an "evolutionary process". He thus carried on the romantic idea about
organic growth – about human history as a gradual, step-by-step
development, with each step leading to the next. As with Keyser
and Munch, Sars's interest lay with the "people" or the "nation".
Continuity was evident, not only in Norwegian history, but in the
history of mankind. ("Mankind" turns out to be the West, as in the
thinking of most European historians at the time.)

Sars's evolutionism differs from the Darwinist idea of adaptation in a "blind", unpredictable universe. External forces, in the
sense of both "foreign" and "outside" (i.e. material) forces, were of

7 On Birkeland and Aschehoug and other conservatives, Dahl 1990:113–55.
8 On Sars, Worm-Müller 1935; Mykland 1955; Dahl 1990:156–94; Fulsås
  1990.

secondary importance. Evolution meant the gradual inner development of a principle inherent in a historic individuality to maturity, just as a seed containing an inner potential and "genetic" programming becomes a full-grown specimen. Thus there is a teleological flavour in Sars's way of thinking. History moves towards a *telos*, or a goal: freedom.

Development might be understood through "the law of organs", as he called it. An institution, practice, or *organ* might function well for a long time, but then regress into being a hindrance to development. It then needs to be superseded. He considered the fate of the Norwegian aristocracy to be a special case under this general law. His law of organs and his insistence on the priority of the internal workings of a system may be read as a precursor of functionalism. This version of functionalist reasoning is "dialectic"; it does not insist on the smooth reproduction of a system, but allows for a concept of dysfunctions leading to change.

For Sars, "change meant improvement, evolution implied progress" (Knut Mykland). In this respect he was a typical European liberal bourgeois. But what kind of progress was implied? Sars was a philosophical idealist. "It is not interests, but ideas, that tie the strongest bonds between men." He considered ideas to be the motivating force; he also held ideas in high esteem. The outcome of history should, could, and would be the increasing "emancipation of the individual" and the "growth of nationality", or national freedom.

How could he be sure about this? At this point a fourth notion became important: the idea of laws in history, analogous to natural laws. Sars was originally trained as a natural scientist. He read extensively in the works of thinkers like the positivist August Comte, the evolutionist Herbert Spencer, and also historians like the Englishman Henry Buckle. In his *History of Civilisation in England*, Buckle proclaimed that history should be a science, in the sense of establishing general laws ruling history and eschewing a loose amassing of facts.[9]

9 Sars's belief in the laws in history was matched only by rather simplistic versions of his epigons. Thus Worm-Müller 1935:22 calls Sars's stress on the internal forces in the Norwegian development "the Sarsian law". In a way this positivist belief in universal laws recalls the universalist pretensions of the Enlightenment; see Krogseth 1983:xi.

Sars was a historicist, not a historist.[10] (For an English-speaking public this can sound confusing, since the German *Historismus* is sometimes translated as "historicism".) The distinction is briefly as follows: the historists – Ranke and the romantics – insisted that *"jede Epoche ist unmittelbar zu Gott"*, i.e. each epoch had its own value. In their view it should neither be evaluated by universal standards, as the historians of the Enlightenment tended to do, nor be considered merely as a stepping stone towards a later goal, as the evolutionists were wont to do. On the other hand, the historicists – Comte, Spencer, Marx, and Hegel, as well as Sars – saw history as dynamic, moving, if not towards a definite goal, then at least in a certain direction. An epoch should be understood and appreciated according to its contribution to this general development.

This idea of laws presented Sars with a problem. How could one insist on determinism and yet maintain that a liberated, free individual was the outcome? He never really solved this problem, but over the years he tended to put more stress on "the great personality", or the genius, understood not as an isolated person, but as being "representative" of an age.

Sars has usually been characterized as an "organic thinker", using biological metaphors about "growth" etc. (Ottar Dahl). This does not, however, imply that Sars considered biology to be very important; he excluded race as an explanatory factor when trying to explain Norwegian "national character".[11] Narve Fulsås has proposed that Sars may be better understood through using drama metaphors in the manner suggested by Hayden White and Paul Ricoeur. In this view Sars has rendered a narrative which is constructed as a plot, thus securing the inner continuity of national history. Sars's *Udsigt* is a grand play where the *peripeteia* (dramatic reversal) took place in the thirteenth century, when the upstart King Sverre eradicated much of the old hereditary aristocracy. This paved the way for the later "decline" of the Norwegian state, a development which subsequently enabled Norway to be in the forefront of democratization in the nineteenth century.

If we turn from Sars's interpretation of history to his theoreti-

10 The concepts are borrowed from Fulsås – unpublished manuscript.
11 Moe and Sars 1914.

cal conception of the science of history, we may note his insistence on "coherence", "harmony", and "totality" – or synthesis – as the proper goal: "the scientist reckons that truth will first be given through the grand connection". He scorned those who simply amassed loose pieces of information. In his later years, however, he became more inclined to value details, and criticized Comte and others for being too mechanical.

Sars agreed that the historian should work empirically and inductively; a historian was not simply a philosopher of history. But the philosophical, deductive approach was also necessary. He once wrote that the mature historian combined three characters: the researcher or critical inquirer, who scrutinizes the material; the philosopher, who could link this material to a theoretical whole ("vues générales"); and finally the artist, who through his choice of literary form was able to convey to the reader a sense of synthesis, an intelligible picture.

This combination of empirical data and preconceived theory may, of course, imply tensions, and it is probably fair to say that Sars sometimes overlooked evidence that did not support his grand theses. He was more eager to verify his views than to disprove them. One might add that Sars obtained his synthesis through choosing one perspective: the political, judicial, and ideological perspective. The dominant historians of the next generation shared some of Sars's preoccupations, such as the questions of nation-building and continuity in history, but they looked for answers in other spheres of society.

Maverick Marxists

The intellectual and political development of Halvdan Koht (1873–1965) has been described as going "from Sars to Marx" (Ottar Dahl). Along with his younger colleague Edvard Bull sen. (1881–1932), Koht secured a predominance for Marxism as a point of reference among Norwegian historians for several decades. However, their version of Marxism was maverick; it did not follow the herd of orthodox "dialectic materialism".[12]

12 On Koht and Bull, see Den Norske Historiske Forening 1920; Steen 1935; Dahl 1974; and Dahl 1990.

If we first consider their concept of history as a science, we find a tension or bipolarity between the analytic and the synthetic approach in their work, most clearly in the case of Koht. On the one hand they carried to completion the source criticism started by Keyser and Munch and continued by Gustav Storm (1845–1903). Koht picked up the Rankean method of "laboratory" seminar work in 1897, while visiting the Danish historian Kristian Erslev. In their teaching Koht and Bull advocated close scrutiny of historical texts. Particularly the Icelandic and old Norse sagas were subjected to a devastating radical criticism, leaving the general public with a feeling of being thrown into a historical wasteland. Any idea of the sagas giving a true historical narrative was rejected. The sagas were treated as contemporary sources from the time of their production, and read with a keen eye for class, party, or faction viewpoints in the texts. Documentary evidence – such as laws – was given greater attention. True to this programme, both Koht and Bull undertook a large number of specialized, detailed studies.

On the other hand Koht rapidly developed a strong sense of "lines in history" (to paraphrase the title of one of his essays, from 1929). In his young days he had read Buckle, and the influence of Sars went parallel to this. Koht also strongly favoured a holistic position and wrote that "society itself" should be "the leading character" in historical writing.[13] He produced synthetic work, not in the grand, sweeping manner of Sars, but on an intermediate range. In *Norsk bondereising* (The insurrection of Norwegian peasants), he wrote on the history of the struggles between peasants, state bureaucrats, and bourgeoisie in the early modern period. Traces back to Sars are clearly evident.

When it came to theories of history and society, however, Sars and Koht parted company. Sars remained a philosophical idealist, seeking laws and continuity in the polity. Koht developed into a materialist, seeking the unity of history in society itself. Moving from a concept of "order of society", understood in political and legal terms, Koht came to emphasize class relations and conflicts as the axis of history. He also stressed societal production, the econ-

---

13 Koht, "Historieskrivinga i framtida" (1938), reprinted in Koht 1953.

omy, as society's decisive sector. In these respects Koht – and Bull – were historical materialists.

Yet their Marxism was undogmatic, or idiosyncratic. Bull advocated the study of "psychological social history". He understood "the material" also in the sense of nature, for instance, in climatic changes.[14] There is indeed a certain continuity from the conservative historians of the nineteenth century to Edvard Bull sen., in that both insisted that physical nature may shape or restrict social relations.

As for Koht, it can be said that he laboured with a non-Marxist notion of "two-class societies", insisting that there had always been an upper class and a subaltern class. He seems not to have grasped the distinction between "mode of production" as a theoretical concept (and involving two classes, one exploited, one exploitive) and "social formation", i.e. an actual historical society where several modes of production and hence several classes may coexist. Further, he strove to solve his own existential political problem: he started in his youth as a radical democrat and nationalist, and was an ardent member of Venstre (the Left), the radical liberal party. While he maintained his national attitude, he came to consider himself a socialist from 1896. (Bull, being younger, did not make this detour, but embraced socialism in his student days.) Thus Koht had to solve the problem of combining nationality and class in a historical analysis. (On Koht's "formula", see Nordby in this volume.)

Koht's solution allowed him to combine the notions of rupture *and* continuity. He kept up Sars's evolutionism – the insistence on a inner unity in the history of Norway. But for him this unity was obtained through revolutionary means. This solution also suited Koht's socialist views; although he stayed within the Labour Party when the right-wing social democrats left in 1921, he undoubtedly felt more at his ease when the party definitively turned reformist in the early 1930s. He served as foreign minister in the Labour government from 1935.[15]

14 Bull, "Klima og historie" (1913), reprinted in Bull 1933.
15 Koht also played an important role in international organizations; he served as president of the Comité international des sciences historiques from 1926 to 1933.

Why did the shift "from Sars to Marx" take place? First, it should be noted that other professors did not share Bull's and Koht's Marxism. These included people like Alexander Bugge (1870–1929), Oscar Albert Johnsen (1876–1954), who was close to the agrarian movement, and Jacob Worm-Müller (1894–1963), who belonged to the liberal left and saw himself as an heir to Sars. They did their best work in empirical studies, and did not leave strong marks on Norwegian historiography.

In the case of Koht, one inspiration came from foreign contacts. In 1898 he studied with Karl Lamprecht, and was impressed by Lamprecht's anti-Rankean programme of understanding cultural conditions and interconnections between cultural phenomena. As professorships were few, neither Koht nor others were employed at the university in this period. This deprived Norwegian professional history of the kind of "realist" intellectuals that dominated other university disciplines.[16] "Realism" should here be understood as a position abandoning political idealism *à la* Sars and maintaining a sober materialist realism, though without embracing a historical materialist position. In this period we did not get Lamprecht's brand of cultural history or the history of everyday life that the Dane Troels Lund represented, nor the kind of socio-economic history found in Werner Sombart's *Der moderne Kapitalismus* (1902).

When a "societal" interpretation of history re-emerged, it came in its Marxist version. The main reason for the breakthrough of Marxism probably did not lie in the realm of the discipline itself, understood as a purely intellectual activity. An external explanation seems apt in the case of Koht and Bull. After national independence in 1905, when Norway seceded from the union with Sweden, the question of nationalism and high politics lost their frontstage position. Economic and technical development were now on the agenda, and industrialization went into a new phase. The general "mental climate" of the period became more "materialist". Even Ernst Sars at the end of his life spoke in favour of economic history.

As a corollary, class struggle developed, in the shape of both an

16 The point is made by Bull in "Historiens opgaver" (1914), reprinted in Bull 1933.

urban–rural conflict and a labour–capital conflict. Koht and Bull became socialists. World War I had an epochal impact on other, younger historians. The times were confusing, and one possible reaction might have a kind of Dadaist–surrealist stance. Marxism offered an alternative: the possibility of making sense of history, and to construct an intellectual order in a world of chaos. An interpretation of history in terms of class and class struggles seemed to be confirmed by events. For Bull especially, historical interpretation went hand in hand with political activism; he was vice-chairman of the Labour Party from 1923 until his death in 1932.

We have claimed that Norwegian historiography may be described in terms of oscillations and tensions between analysis and synthesis. After Sars died no one took on the task of constructing a new overview of Norwegian history from A to Z. "Our researchers have been sharper in analyses than in syntheses, cleverer at studying singular phenomena than making overviews", Sverre Steen, later professor at the University of Oslo, stated in 1935. Bull was not particularly interested in this kind of enterprise. However, allowing for the possibilities of synthesis on an intermediate range, both Koht and Steen himself *were* in fact rather successful at presenting general interpretations, which dealt with more restricted epochs. If Keyser's synthesis was developed to defend the very existence of a Norwegian people, and if Sars strove to underpin parliamentary democracy and national independence, Koht's project may be seen as an answer to a pressing dilemma of the contemporary class struggle: full overthrow of the state or submissive integration into society? Synthetic endeavours seem to have been responses to contemporary situations, in which a need for understanding and meaning, but also for legitimization or guidance, was keenly felt.

Pragmatic materialists

Koht and Bull left a legacy. Even if their pupils may not be described as Marxists, nearly all had a certain common sense materialism and a concept of history as something going beyond the politics of the state. Several of them deserve attention, such as medievalist Johan Schreiner (1903–67) and the social historians Ingrid Semmingsen (b. 1910) and Edvard Bull jun. (1914–87). But the more general characteristics of the generation may be seen in the works of Sverre Steen and Andreas Holmsen.

Sverre Steen (1898–1983) was first and foremost a great history narrator.[17] Several volumes of *Det norske folks liv og historie* (The life and history of the Norwegian people) as well as *Det frie Norge* (The free Norway) on 1814 and its aftermath and a tremendously popular series of radio lectures on Norwegian history in the 1960s earned him the epithet "the history teacher of the Norwegian people". His work was guided by some fixed leitmotifs, which show how the Marxist heritage was managed by its inheritors in their analyses of history and society. Steen demonstrated great interest in the economy of societies, though without conceptualizing this as a base determined by the interplay between productive forces and productions relations. Steen's most important guiding notion was "type of society" (*samfunnstype*), a totality governed by a certain economic rationality (see Myhre in this volume). This concept was analogous to Max Weber's ideal types, both in the sense that the concept should be constructed by the historical scientist and in the sense that it should be understood as a "pure" notion which in varying degrees may correspond to "reality".

Steen developed a view of history as a succession of periods of stability, dominated by one "type of society", being superseded by "times of ruptures" (*brytningstider*), leading to the establishment of a new society. In these "times of rupture", the old and the new type of society coexisted, partly in isolation, partly in competition. Changes took place in several spheres of society, most importantly in economic mentality and practices. The interrelations between the two types of society were acted out as a struggle between the carriers of the old order and the representatives of the new. In the 1930s Steen considered "revolution" (in a broad sense) to be an apt term to describe these transformations. After World War II he tended to stress their developmental and evolutionary character, leading to their merger in a new social order.

This idea of stable systems being superseded or transformed

17 On Steen, see Edding 1983 and Dahl 1990:281–6.

through periods of competitive practices or even crisis definitely has a structural–functionalist flavour. At one point Steen professed interest in functionalism, citing Bronislaw Malinowski's theory of human needs as a prime mover or stabilizer of systems. This functionalist bent was equally prominent in Steen's contemporaries, Andreas Holmsen and the young Jens Arup Seip, particularly in the decades around World War II. While they retained the totalizing interest of the Marxists, their explanations tend to be multifactoral. Their view on what constituted the core of the totality became more empirical or pragmatic. Hence one may call both Steen and Andreas Holmsen pragmatic materialists.

Andreas Holmsen (1906–89) was trained as an agrarian historian, and was one among several prominent scholars in this field.[18] This subdiscipline probably received a particular impetus from the fact that the agrarian crisis in the wake of the Black Death was interpreted as a prime cause of "the Decline of Norway" as an independent state. Be this as it may, agrarian history was quickly developed to an advanced level. It had its own disciplinary profile, using a huge quantitative material trying to pinpoint economic and demographic changes, and to exploit the possibilities for retrospective deductions. It also sought to utilize topographic insights. "History without geography is nonsense", Holmsen wrote.

Important studies in agrarian history were conducted within the framework of local history. A practical reason for this was that almost every municipality in Norway has chosen to commission several volumes of local history. From the 1930s this offered a growing and important market to professional historians. Holmsen argued in favour of local studies also on scientific grounds. By limiting the area of study, you can illuminate your object from several angles, using a manifold of material. Moreover, in a local study you can show what Holmsen calls "topographic individualism" – the specificity of the object. Finally, these local studies may be linked through a comparative approach, which can reveal both similarities and more general characteristics and peculiarities.

18 On Holmsen, see Dahl 1990:274–6; Lunden, "Ein samfunnshistorikar: Andreas Holmsen 75 år", in Lunden 1985:215–19.

This school of agrarian historians may be seen as parallel to the first generation of Annales historians. Marc Bloch and the Austrian medievalist Alphons Dopsch stayed in Oslo in 1929 as guest lecturers, the occasion being the inauguration of a programme of "Comparative studies in the cultural relations of peasant society".

However, Holmsen's most important contribution was his *Norges Historie* (History of Norway), an instructive synthesis of Norwegian history from the earliest days to 1660 (the introduction of absolutism in Denmark–Norway). In the same way as Steen, he reached a huge public. The book has been reissued several times, only slightly revised, and is still used as textbook. Like Steen, Holmsen was a "historian of society", working from a scaffold constructed from below: material production/economy created a corresponding social structure, with classes and factions struggling to use the state apparatus. Like Steen, Holmsen wanted a synthesis where empirical evidence supported the particulars, while plausibility was the criterion of truth applicable to the totality. A strict analytic empiricism was not established until after World War II. Finally, as mentioned, Holmsen was attracted to the structuralist–functionalist approach. In a methodological article on agrarian history (1940), he stressed the importance of structural, stable phenomena, in a manner reminiscent of Fernand Braudel.[19] His functionalism may be seen in his development of Koht's concept of a medieval "popular monarchy" (*folkekongedømme*); in this the monarchy is not seen as repressive or exploitive, but as filling needs or functions in peasant society (such as securing civil peace).

Ambiguous analysis and critical empiricism

Jens Arup Seip (1905–92) also started as a pupil of the Marxists, and particularly of Edvard Bull sen.[20] Seip's early works showed the same general characteristics as Steen's and Holmsen's: a common sense materialism, loose ties – but still ties – to Marxism, an

19 Holmsen 1940.
20 On Seip, see his own theoretical contributions, collected in Seip 1983; Dahl 1990:276, 286–8; Ringdal 1981; Fure 1983; Fure 1984; Lunden, "Val for historia. Motsetnader hos Jens Arup Seip som metodolog og venstrepolitisk legitimator," in Lunden 1985:220–65.

emerging functionalism, and an insistence on studying the single fact in relation to the larger surroundings. He published his most important programmatic article in 1940, titled "Problems and methods in Norwegian research on the medieval age". This article was influenced and inspired by his teacher Bull, as well as by Marc Bloch and Max Weber.[21]

Nevertheless, Seip's later development, after the war, makes it natural to treat him along with his younger colleague Ottar Dahl (b. 1924), despite differences in age and research profile. Seip's development has been characterized as a development "from Marxism to Machiavellianism" (Ottar Dahl). After the war he switched his focus of research to the nineteenth century. He gave low priority to economic and social history, and instead concentrated on politics, power, and state relations. (He did, however, claim that studying the political was not an end in itself, but simply the most effective way to understand society at large.)

Methodologically, Seip came to advocate individualism: one should try to see events from the actor's point of view. Seip was a master of sketching psychological portraits. Probably his most outstanding work in this line is a book on the later phases of the old bureaucratic regime, before the parliamentary principle was established in 1884. The book was conceived as an Aristotelian drama; it presents the scene, the protagonists, the conflict, and the final tragic outcome from the point of view of the elite – the impossibility of stemming the tide.[22] His methodological individualism was linked to a scepticism about norms: men were guided more by self-interest than by general norms. While Steen tended to see man as fundamentally "socialized", being a "carrier" of society, Seip saw man (or at least powerful males) as creator, stressing self-interest, choices, and actions. Accordingly, arguments in debates should not be taken at face value; they should be suspected as being substitute arguments, chosen because they might effectively persuade or in order to cover motives that were not acceptable to the public. The task of the historian should be to "undress", not to "dress", as Seip put it.

This stance might have reduced Seip to an ordinary historian of

21 Reprinted in Seip 1983.
22 Seip 1945.

politics, or a mere student of *"Haupt- und Staatsaktionen"*. However, through the notion of *sequence*, i.e. linked chains of actions, and through understanding actors as having *relations* to other actors, Seip avoided this kind of atomism. Indeed, his portrayal of the Norwegian state in the nineteenth century as an *embetsmannsstat*, a "state of the bureaucrats", where the higher officials acted as rulers, does not show an individualistic approach. He focuses on the state's stable, systemic characteristics.

This kind of ambiguity or dualism may be found in other aspects of his work. One example is his views on sociology and particularly on the use of preconceived sociological models. He moved away from an initially positive attitude to a strongly critical position while debating the models of sociologists Stein Rokkan and Gudmund Hernes on different occasions.[23] Rokkan was a macrosociologist who earned international fame for seeking to compare social structure, history, and political systems in European countries. He tried to sum up the Norwegian development in terms of specific combinations of five different "cleavages": producers and consumers in the food market, labour and capital in the labour market, a religious cleavage between orthodox pietism and cultural radicalism, a territorial urban-rural split, and finally a political conflict between "centre and periphery". Hernes launched a general model for the study of power, drawing heavily on analogies to economics, and using terms like "transactions", "demand", and "change value"; the American sociologist James Coleman was his foremost influence.

Seip criticized both their models on empirical and theoretical grounds alike. In this context the latter is of most interest. He warned against models in general. They tended to "colour" the vision and block the mind; the alluring aesthetics of simple and sometimes geometric models were seductive; models often implied a certain unspoken ideological bias and implied illegitimate analogies from one sphere to another. Finally he regarded models as too general and too far removed from the empirical facts. He also

23 Seip, Modellens tyranni. "Analyse av Stein Rokkans anvendelse av en sentrum-periferi modell på norsk historie" (1975) and "Studiet av makt (med Ekskurs. Gudmund Hernes' maktmodell, En kritikk)" (1976), reprinted in Seip 1983.

found models clumsy from a stylistic point of view; when a house has been built, one should remove the scaffold. As an alternative he recommended "close combat" with the sources, meeting the evidence with an open mind, or with "several minds", as he put it. Models might be permitted, but *ex post facto*, springing from the empirical work, not in starting it.

Combatants and critics, like Rokkan, Hernes, and the historian Kåre Lunden,[24] retorted that having several open minds in fact implied the use of varying models. Clarifying the differences between these "minds" to oneself amounts pretty much to consciously using models "on probation", not as proved theories, but as heuristic devices. Seip missed the difference between a heuristic model and a proved (or non-refuted) theory.

Historiographers have with some relish pointed out that Jens Arup Seip himself was actually a strong constructivist, carrying an implied model to his material, at the same time as he warned against models. He is said to have worked from a model of society in which the state is seen as heavily politicized, i.e. governed by politicians and their actions. This alleged implied model has been labelled a kind of "perennialized medieval state".[25]

Seip's methodological remarks were often made *en passant*, in the course of book reviews and such. The generation that matured after World War II found its theoretical, systematic spokesman in Ottar Dahl.[26] Having finished his *hovedfag* thesis on Bull and Koht as historical materialists, he wrote a doctoral thesis on problems of causation in historical research. Thus far this is the only major purely theoretical work produced by a Norwegian historian.[27] Dahl participated in the intellectual circle around philosopher Arne Næss, who had been trained before the war in the logical empiricism developed in Vienna.[28] While the Vienna Circle insisted that valid science should be built exclusively on statements about elementary observations and logical combinations of or deductions from such elements, Næss found that philosophy should be

24 Rokkan 1967 and 1975; Hernes 1977; Lunden 1985.
25 Ringdal 1981:127.
26 On Dahl, see his own works; Fure 1993; Ødegaarden 1989.
27 Dahl 1956.
28 On Næss, see Thue 1992.

more genuinely empirical. It should undertake the task of investigating how people actually used words. Through empirical–semantical investigations of language, or "occurrence analysis", one should try to lay bare the implied logical structure in the use of words. Dahl took up this approach, using statements about causality from historians as his source material. In so doing, conceptual clarity, precision, and the subdivision of problems into treatable, operational questions became his hallmark.

Dahl demonstrated among other things how mechanistic, organic, and anthropomorphic ways of thinking are built into the terms that historians use in writing about causality ("start the ball rolling", "grow", or "create"). He also developed a set of criteria and distinctions whereby causality could be understood. These were as follows: chronological succession and a restricted distance in time as minimum requirements; the distinction between necessary and sufficient conditions; various ways of understanding the concepts of main cause and supplementary causes; and the distinction between causes that may be said to be favourable to a certain development and those actually precipitating a change.

Dahl went on to define the proper area of historical research as "socially relevant human behaviour in a context of definite time/space co-ordinates". He accepted that there might exist a type of historical entity which did not comprise short-term events or actions, but "limited regularities", such phenomena are quite extended in time and space without being universal. But he tended to favour an approach where the historian focused on objects that were not too extended. This was not because he denied the possible existence of more general classes of laws, but because he maintained that the individualizing perspective was more fertile.

In a typology of explanations, Dahl distinguished between causal, functional, and intentional explanations. He claimed, however, that "cause" and "motive" do not belong to different realms, to nature and man. On the contrary, one may treat motives as causes; it depends whether the chosen perspective on human actions is internalistic or externalistic, both being legitimate. Another distinction was drawn between "evolutionary" or "genetic" explanations and "contemporaneous" explanations, of which one subtype is a "field-theoretical", systemic approach.

On verification Dahl adopted the stance of Karl Popper. Science cannot prove theories in any definite way, but theories should be constructed in a manner where they may be tested and disproved, or falsified. Hypotheses that a priori cannot be disproved should be avoided.

In a widely read textbook on historical methodology, *Grunntrekk i historieforskningens metodelære* (Basic features in the methodology of historical research), he supplemented his views.[29] A new point was his treatment of objectivity in history. Science should – and could – be kept free from intrusions from political opinions and value judgements. Historical results were not valid as political arguments, because "drawing lessons from history" often implied an invalid use of analogies. In fact, the societal value of history was more aligned to the research process itself, and less to the outcome of the process. Its strict methodological demands, the need for argumentation, the reign of rationality, and the call for evidence may have beneficial effects in society at large, Dahl suggested.

A strong analytic impulse sprang from Dahl's work. His insistence on empirical evidence, his critical attitude towards speculation, his claim that problems should be avoided if they could not be disproved, his preference for the problem limited in time and space, and for the well-defined operational problem – all these messages coalesced and inoculated almost two generations of historians. The essence could be summed up in a quotation from Jens Arup Seip: "A historian should be myopic; his most important instrument is the magnifying glass."

From one point of view, Dahl was a creator of disciplinary norms. He was, however, not alone. From 1965 Nordic conferences on the methodology in history were arranged; to date more than twenty publications testify to this activity. In the first generation Dahl co-operated with his Norwegian colleague Sivert Langholm (b. 1926), who published a book on methodology (1967) along the same lines as Dahl's, though Langholm's was more accessible to the ordinary student.[30] Langholm went on to publish

29 Dahl 1967.
30 Langholm 1967.

profound articles on the methodology of social history. He argued that collecting information connected to individuals did not necessarily imply any ontological individualism. In Denmark H. P. Clausen wrote a similar book, inspired by Dahl, while Rolf Torstendahl from Sweden and Pentti Renvall from Finland produced introductions of their own.[31]

In the 1940s the theoretical basis of Norwegian historical research first shifted from Marxism to functionalism or at least a vague structural functionalism. Functionalism may, as we have mentioned, be traced in Steen, in Seip's programmatic article on medieval history from 1940, in Holmsen's views on the functions of the medieval monarchy, and in Dahl's insistence that the proper theme for historians should be human actions in a *social* context. Both Seip and Dahl read Talcott Parsons, Robert Merton, and Paul Lazarsfeld.

This change cannot be understood fully in internal terms.[32] The Marxist views of Bull and Koht had been connected to "the forward march of labour". When the Norwegian Labour Party came to terms with capitalism, stressing the class struggle was felt to be outdated also for scientific purposes. When the medieval monarchy was reinterpreted from being an instrument of repression to being an institution filling important needs among the peasants, this corresponded to a contemporary political situation in which a labour government was launching a reformist programme for a welfare state. The prestige of functionalism may also be understood in terms of a new American hegemony, in the social sciences as well in world politics. For several reasons (a large emigration, geopolitical location, etc.), Norwegians were predisposed to Americanism.

Functionalism still implied a kind of totalizing notion of society. Yet another step away from the old ideals should be taken. Many historians in the fifties and sixties worked in ways which implied an atomistic conception of society and kind of artisanal empiricism in their research. Why?

---

31 Clausen 1963; Renvall 1965; Torstendahl 1966.
32 The points made about the change from Marxism to functionalism and from holism to atomism are to a large extent drawn from Fure 1983 and Fure 1993.

Innovative as Dahl was, in some ways he conceptualized or codified experiences common to his generation. They had understood the pre-war period and the war even more so as a time when strong, totalitarian ideologies, total systems in thought as well in politics, had led the world into the abyss. Now they felt that the time had come for a clean slate, for facticity, for unveiling. It was important to know what was what, and to distinguish between true and false. "A matter-of-fact attitude (*saklighet*) is the very essence of science", Sverre Steen said in a speech to the new students of 1946. The "death of ideologies" was proclaimed. The generation after the war was anti-fascist, of course, and most of them became anti-communist. After the communists had been politically neutralized in the early fifties a kind of basic national consensus gained ground until around the late sixties.

The holistic, synthesizing ambition of Koht, Steen, and Holmsen was replaced by sectoral histories. Holism, in the megalomaniac version of Arnold Toynbee, but also in the form of Sars's grand narrative, Koht's "societal history", and the functionalist effort, fell into disrepute. The "departmentalization" of history may – somewhat speculatively – be interpreted as a response to contemporary politics; the order of the day was not total change, but sectoral reforms or "piecemeal engineering" in the spirit of Karl Popper.

A more limited concept of what history is about also corresponded to a new situation for historians. Their number had grown. They were more professionalized. In 1919, when the Norwegian Historical Association celebrated its fiftieth anniversary with an anthology on Norwegian historical research, the inclusion of archaeology, the history of art and culture, folkloristics, literary history, local history, and genealogy was self-evident. The corresponding publication, in 1969, only found room for contributions from historians in the narrow sense of the word. Historians were also more institutionalized. A well-organized historical institute was created in Oslo in 1953, primarily through the efforts of Sverre Steen. They had also become more specialized. Steen and Holmsen in particular represented the old brand of polyhistorians, dealing with all aspects of society. Those who matured after the war belonged more or less to a certain subdiscipline: the history of political institutions, social history, economic history, agrarian history, or the history of politics.

Critical theory, or the Art of Inheriting?

History as a scientific discipline has gone through phases, changing from historism to evolutionism, Marxism, functionalism, and empiricism. We have stressed the alternating emphasis laid on analyses and syntheses, on criticism and construction. Yet it does not seem apt to describe Norwegian historiography in terms of changing paradigms *à la* Thomas Kuhn, at least if one employs a more radical version of the concept. One cannot speak about successive starts from clean slates. Despite tensions, oscillations, and personal animosity between some important personalities, there has been a kind of common ground in the discipline. Predecessors have been criticized, but not ignored. Ruptures, in the way conceptualized by Michel Foucault, have not occurred. Tradition has not been indifferently abandoned and deemed totally irrelevant.

It is, of course, difficult to establish a valid measure of unity and consensus which could be used to prove this thesis, especially for transnational comparisons. Suffice it to make two observations.

First: Nuclei or spheres of influence have existed around important figures. The "Seipians", the pupils of the late Jens Arup Seip, are one example. This spans both the generation of historians who are now in retirement (though still active) – like Knut Mykland (b. 1920), Alf Kaartvedt (b. 1921), and Rolf Danielsen (b. 1922) – as well as those in their fifties and sixties.[33] Seip was active and influential to the very end, and was seen as a model *historien historisant*. Whether one speaks of a Seipian "school" is a matter of choice. He certainly represented an intellectual programme which viewed other approaches with some enmity. But Seip and the Seipians have not systematically *combined* this with organizational measures, such as close supervision of pupils and a consequent

---

33 See interview with Ottar Dahl in *HIFO-nytt* 12(2).

favouritism in university appointments, to the systematic exclusion of other approaches.[34]

A second observation: The fight against "positivism" and a myopic "empiricism" in favour of a "new", critical history, was so bitter in neighbouring Denmark during the late sixties and seventies that two generations of historians were hardly on speaking terms. One result was a plethora of competing historical periodicals. This debate might become sharp also in Norway. Adherents of critical theory and Marxism have stated the case for explicit use of theory, for a totalizing perspective, for the impossibility of completely value-free history, and for the legitimacy of societal and political use of history.[35] Yet the participants in this debate have kept up a dialogue, albeit a combative one. *Historisk tidsskrift* maintained its position. In fact, the neo-Marxists were not very far scientifically from established historians like Kåre Lunden (b. 1930) and Francis Sejersted (b. 1936). One outstanding historian inspired by Marxism, Trond Nordby (b. 1945), worked closely with Ottar Dahl in the use of roll-call analysis as a technique in political history.[36]

Why has Norwegian historiography kept this relative unity – at least until recently?

A fairly broad concept of history dates from Keyser and Munch, and there has existed a shared, implied common sense materialism

34 One probable reason for the absence of "schools" is that sociologically speaking a Norwegian professor is a rather humdrum – or democratic – social figure compared with the might and splendour radiating from German or even Swedish colleagues. There are comparatively many tenured full professors, while the formal mandate is so weak and the resources at the command of each individual professor are so scarce that to speak of university "chairs" in this respect would be rather misleading.

35 See, for instance, Berntsen 1969; Egge 1970; *Studier i historisk metode*, Vol. 8, 1972, with comments by Benito Scocozza, Jon Elster, and Knut Helle in *Historisk tidsskrift* 51:4 (1972); Fure 1976; Kjeldstadli 1980.

36 See Lunden 1985 and 1991, and the articles on theory and method in Sejersted 1993. A special case was philosopher Jon Elster, who was connected to the Department of History in Oslo from 1975 to 1986. He represented a kind of minimalist, analytical Marxism, which later developed into a defence of rationalism and methodological individualism. From Elster's huge *oeuvre*, Elster 1971, 1978, and 1979 probably had the greatest impact among Norwegian historians. Nordby 1983 and 1989.

since Bull and Koht, which underlines the general importance of societal production and the material interests of man. This intellectual heritage was shared by radicals and conservatives alike.[37] The one prolific conservative historian of the post-war period, Francis Sejersted, started his career as an economic historian. There has also been a moderation in the opposing intellectual positions which have been taken. Ottar Dahl has staunchly defended the empiricist stance. Yet he has never failed to emphasize that he understands himself as a *critical* empiricist: i.e., although "data" should have the final say, results depend upon the questions posed, and more generalized theory may be helpful in the interpretation of data. Historical method should not be reduced to "source criticism". Thus, young, critical Marxists of the seventies never found an ideal positivist opponent. A 1992 book on historical methodology which claims to present a "crossbreed of pragmatic Marxism from the 1970s and acritical eclecticism from the 1980s" is in debt to Dahl's work, although it differs in having a broader thematic scope, a new emphasis on the constructive importance of theory, and a stress on the societal and political implications of the discipline.[38] Nor have recent culturalist and feminist tendencies and some voices speaking, somewhat hesitatingly, in a "post-modernist" vocabulary in the nineties seriously doubted the relevance of empirical research and source criticism.[39]

This relative unity reflects a hegemony. Politically, Norwegian historians in the twentieth century represented an alliance between national democrats and socialists. Historians have served in prominent positions – chairmen, vice-chairmen, foreign ministers – in the radical liberal Venstre party, in the Labour Party, and also among the post-war leftist socialists. Articulate conservatives are definitely in a minority. Philosophically speaking, there has been a clear anti-idealistic strain among Norwegian historians in this century. When the history of ideas (*idéhistorie*) was established as a university discipline in 1953, this took place outside the Institute of History; it was an offshoot of the discipline of philosophy.

37 Myhre 1995 makes the same point.
38 Kjeldstadli 1992.
39 Hagemann 1994; Sandmo 1993; Kaldal 1994; Andersen 1994.

Relative internal unity and the predominance of social democratic and national radicalism should also be understood in the
context of Norwegian society, which has been *relatively* homogeneous and egalitarian. The nation–state has been conceived as the
relevant frame of action, even for those who have wanted to wreck
the state and build a new one. The country has maintained a
degree of social and political unity, even in times of high tension.
To give an example from the intellectual sphere of life: after World
War I there was a feeling that the neutral countries had a special
obligation to offer something to the world in order to rebuild international understanding. Thus Edvard Bull sen. co-operated with
Fredrik Stang, a law professor, to establish the Institute for Comparative Cultural Studies (Institutt for sammenlignende kultur-
gransking), which opened in 1927. Among other things it could
boast of publishing Marc Bloch's *Les caractères originaux de l'histoire
rurale française* (1931). This partnership was not hindered by the
fact that Bull was the vice-chairman of the still-revolutionary Labour Party, while Stang had been the chairman of the Conservative
Party.

"Norway" or "the people of this country" has served as a unifying point of reference. After the Venstre party took power in 1884,
Sarsian ideas were popularized and diffused through textbooks
and school teachers until they became almost self-evident. They
secured national-democratic ideological hegemony until recently.
"Building the nation" has somehow been an imperative, even if
the emphasis has changed. While Sars and his predecessors
wanted to (re)construct the Norwegianity of Norway in the struggle for national independence and for general political citizenship,
later generations have urged that ordinary men and women
should have "the right to a past" (Edvard Bull jun.) and should be
included in national history. A place in history for all could be seen
as a kind of a parallel to ideas about an extended social citizenship;
it was something of a welfare state programme within history, or a
fulfilment of Koht's insistence on classes growing into the nation
through struggle. Few have doubted that this place is to be found
within the framework of the national history. In this respect the
Norwegian intellectual climate has differed from, for example, the
American, where attacks on "the history of Dead White Males"

have been launched from ethnic, feminist, and gay positions.[40]

At present there is a feeling that the age of a relatively unified discipline may have come to an end. Obvious reasons may be found at the organizational or institutional level. The number of professional historians has grown; the Norwegian Historical Association now counts roughly 500 members, including some colleagues who work in archives, museums, and schools. Correspondingly there has been a proliferation of themes, an increased span within the discipline, indeed a veritable change in the concept of what history is about.[41] There has been an expansion in time; the history of antiquity has been invigorated by a successful infusion of social anthropology. There has been geographical expansion: several theses have been written on the Third World.[42] There has also been a widening of interest in regard to the social groups studied (working class history, women's history, the history of childhood) and to the spheres of human life that are found worthy of interest (work, domestic life). This thematic expansion has created problems, particularly for the content of basic university education. When "new history" enters the curriculum, other themes must be discarded or diluted, or students may have scope to pick and choose on an à la carte basis. The unity of the discipline is at stake.

Furthermore, from the beginning of the 1970s, subdisciplines connected to new techniques have emerged. Oral sources have contributed to "social history with a human face". Electronic data processing has opened new avenues, such as roll-call analysis, family reconstitution within historical demography, and prosopographic "microhistory" using "the individual as a combination unit for the variables" (Sivert Langholm) in order to reconstruct the life course of social groups. The microhistorical approach served as a basis for a large-scale project on social history in the last century; the social groups of the capital and of one rural community were "x-rayed" to the extent that the sources allowed. The ambition of the project leader, Sivert Langholm, was to understand individual agency *and* social structure.[43]

40 On this debate, see Appleby, Hunt, and Jacob 1994.
41 See Kjeldstadli 1993.
42 Hubbard 1992.
43 Langholm 1974 and 1976.

Most importantly, however, the concept of nation and national history has come under attack. When *Historisk tidsskrift* celebrated its fiftieth anniversary in 1919, the magazine took pride in having "hauled building stones to the history of Norway. Some may seem inconsequential and of little use, but at some time they will surely be inserted in their proper place in the building" (Wilhelm Munthe).[44] A new general "history of Norway" was launched in 1994, but one may doubt whether the nation will be the central subject of yet another grand narrative. If no building is to be built, hauling stones from the quarry may become meaningless. The cement that has kept Norwegian historians together may dissolve.

Dissolution – or a new totality?

In the early 1990s a discussion among leading historians like Sejersted, Lunden, and Dahl centred on the character, possibility, and usefulness of syntheses. It resulted in a relative consensus about the benefits of such endeavours. Symptomatic of the present situation is the fact that medievalist Knut Helle (b. 1930) has joined those who call for synthesis, whereas Helle in 1961 had stated programmatically that medieval history was stuffed to the gills with loosely grounded totalizing conceptions, and that specialized studies to produce more precise empirical knowledge should be on top on the research agenda.[45]

Some examples of quality synthetic work have been produced, among them several volumes of a series on general Norwegian history in the 1970s and a series on world history in the 1980s, where several contributors pursue a "history of society".[46] The editors of a new twelve-volume Norwegian history being pub-

44 Den Norske Historiske Forening 1919:352.
45 Sejersted 1989; Lunden, "Historisk syntese, særleg funksjon i forhold til offentlegheita", in Lunden 1991; Dahl 1991; Helle 1994. See also the contributions in Marthinsen and Winge 1992, particularly Ida Blom, "Kjønnssystem som et element i syntesedannelse"; Dahl, "Hva er syntese?"; Knut Kjeldstadli, "Synteser og språk"; Seip, "Om syntese i historieforskningen"; and Torstendahl, "Historisk syntes".
46 *Cappelens Norges Historie*, Vol. 1–15, 1976–80, *Aschehougs Verdenshistorie*, Vol. 1–15, 1982–7.

lished in the 1990s have proclaimed their intention to make ecology their unifying perspective.[47] But it remains to see whether the series as a whole will amount to more than a *"Buchbindersynthese"*, as the Germans sarcastically put it.

Why this interest in syntheses? One reason lies in the proliferation of historical research. Another reason is found in a change in the intellectual climate within the discipline itself. Seip and Dahl are still respected, but criticism of their methodological and theoretical programme has been launched. A cardinal point has been that their insistence on explicit evidence has constrained Norwegian historiography to dealing with rather circumscribed themes, pushing longer-term development or the society at large out of focus. Empiricism certainly cancels out loose speculation, and an actor's perspective serves as an injunction against that kind of functionalist slag, where one postulates simply that a certain institution exists because its serves an unintentional purpose. But there was a danger of throwing out the baby with the bath water: empiricism and methodological individualism also dampened imagination and hamstrung those who might have started on more courageous intellectual tours. Thus historians ended up as traders in details, in bits of knowledge that were not seen as all that pertinent by the general public, and perhaps not even by many of those within the profession itself. An illustration of this situation may be the fact that the number of subscribers to the national *Historisk tidsskrift* is on par with the number before World War II and lower than it was in 1873, although the number of professional historians has roughly quadrupled since the 1950s.

The claim that a need for syntheses exists may finally be regarded as a response to a change in society and in politics. The "end of the post-war period" has been proclaimed for some time by now; the reconstruction is now history. Opinion swings – to the left in the 1970s, towards an individualistic right-wing position in the 1980s – seem now to have rested for some time at point zero, with a tendency towards indifference. Some delight in an à la carte atti-

47 *Aschehougs Norges Historie*, 12 vols., 1994ff., eds. Knut Helle, Knut Kjeldstadli, Even Lange, and Sølvi Sogner. Along with ecology, there will be stress on the question of nationality, on analyses in terms of gender system, and on the history of culture and mentalities.

tude towards opinions and interpretations, claiming that to consume is actually a very creative and innovative act, whether they are intellectual or moral positions that one consumes. Some programmatically claim that "modernity" or "the post-modern condition" devaluate history, both as past experience and as a science. To many, the times are bewildering and senseless, and lack an intelligible pattern. There is a loss of faith and a loss of meaning.

Historical syntheses may create sense without abandoning understanding. They may create a meaning which is neither theological nor teleological, but which is secular and retrospective. They may represent an alternative to fundamentalist interpretations outside the discipline, and within the discipline to that kind of relativist, deconstructionist, new historism which paradoxically ends up close to the positivist position: only very small stories may be told, and only pieces of historical information may be gathered.

3. The Infrastructure of History
Sivert Langholm

This chapter concerns history as a profession, with its institutions and organizations. It considers how these came into being and how they have developed. It thereby also deals with the formation of a discipline.

In general, this book focuses on historical *research*. In the process of institutionalization and of the making of professions and disciplines, however, the role of *education* is perhaps even more fundamental. We therefore begin with an account of history in Norwegian education.

But first of all, a brief comment to put things into perspective. Basically, the human sense of history is not a product of either formal education or research, and certainly not a professional quality. The making of the academic discipline and the profession of history has to be understood against the background of a more original and spontaneous, popular sense of tradition, a thirst for knowledge about the ancestors, and a curiosity about the events and relics of the past. I do not know if this dimension of historical culture is stronger in Norway than in other countries, but it has certainly played a part in the development of the Norwegian academic discipline, both as a contrast, an opposition, and as a factor influencing it.

History in Norwegian education

In the present context, we have to concentrate on education at the university and college level. It should, however, be remembered that history education at lower levels is also highly relevant for the development of a historical culture, both in the popular and in the professional sense.

In primary school, history was not a common subject until 1860, when it was made obligatory by an important education act for the rural districts adopted in that year.[1] At the teachers' colleges, which were established from the 1830s on and which gained greater attendance after 1860, history was a compulsory subject, with particular emphasis on national history.[2] It is no accident that when the Norwegian Teachers' College (Norges Lærerhøgskole), an extension college for primary school teachers, was founded in 1922, history was one of the disciplines that got one of the first three teaching posts, the other two being pedagogy and Norwegian.[3] In the period from around 1850 to the inter-war years in particular, primary school teachers played an important part in local cultural life.[4] Among other things, they have been central in the development of local history and as writers. One of the pioneers of Norwegian local history research, Lorens Berg (1862–1924), was a primary school teacher.[5] The Norwegian folkehøgskoler (folk high schools), which were created from the 1860s onwards on the Danish Grundtvigian[6] model, reinforced this influence. National history was a fundamental element in the teachings of these schools, and they must have been important for the development of interest in local and national history, especially among the rural population.

The regular secondary schools, on the other hand, were of more direct importance for the development of history as an academic discipline, since teachers for secondary school were educated at the university. History was taught to an increasing degree during the eighteenth century, but for a long time the core of the curriculum in these schools, in Norway as elsewhere in Europe, was the study of Latin and Greek.

The first Norwegian university, Universitas Regia Fredericiana or Det Kongelige Frederiks Universitet (now Universitetet i Oslo,

1 Dahl 1959:62.
2 Dahl 1959:*passim*.
3 Kirkhusmo 1983:45ff.
4 Hagemann 1992:36ff., 53ff.
5 Johnsen 1920:284ff.
6 Grundtvig, Nikolai Frederik Severin (1783–1872), Danish clergyman and poet, founder of the Scandinavian folk high school movement.

the University of Oslo) was formally established in 1811. Teaching began in 1813, and history was one of its subjects from the start.[7] At the level of final examinations, history was compulsory as part of the "teacher's degree" in philology, which qualified persons to teach in secondary schools. However, the study of classics was for a long time predominant in this degree, as it was in secondary school itself. The same applied to the more advanced *Seminarium philologicum*, which existed from 1818 to 1841. In any event, rather few students opted for the philology degree in the early period.

Until 1845, however, history was also one of several compulsory subjects in the preliminary *examen (philologico-) philosophicum*, which had to be taken by all ordinary students, regardless of faculty. After this date, it became an optional subject.[8] Throughout the nineteenth century, therefore, much history teaching at the university was aimed primarily at these first-year students who were reading for the *examen philosophicum*, also called *anneneksamen* or "second examination" (*examen artium* being the first).[9]

The first small step towards a higher degree of specialization in history was taken with the 1871 law on the "teacher's degree in languages and history". This law made the subject group "History and Geography" one of four study options, of which students had to choose two. It was the consequence of a reform in Norwegian secondary school education that introduced science and modern languages as an alternative to Latin.

The next important step was the introduction of the "main subject" degree (*hovedfag*) in 1905. The "main subject" included a "thesis" (*hovedoppgave*), which was at first optional, but was made obligatory in 1915. Since 1920 the title of the degree has been *candidatus philologiae*, abbreviated as *cand. philol.* According to the present regulations, the *hovedfag* requires seven semesters of study, but many students take longer.

The 1905 system also had a lower level of study, the "secondary subject" (*bifag*), which required three semesters of preparation

7 Morgenstierne 1911:17.
8 Morgenstierne 1911:*passim,* and the respective regulations.
9 University of Oslo, Annual Report, various years.

(and of which the candidates had to choose two, in addition to the *hovedfag*, to obtain the *cand. philol.* degree). An important reform, with quite revolutionary consequences for student and teacher numbers, was the introduction of the 1-year "foundation course" (*grunnfag*) in 1957. In the present-day system, the 3-semester "intermediate subject" (*mellomfag*) corresponds to the former *bifag*.

In 1957–8 history was also introduced as a discipline at the University of Bergen (formally established in 1948), with studies being organized on the Oslo model. From 1958 university-level courses in history were also offered at the Norwegian Teachers' College, which was incorporated into the University of Trondheim in 1968. In 1972 the University of Tromsø (also established in 1968) followed suit.

The establishment of the so-called district colleges (*distriktshøy-skoler*) from 1969–70 was another step in the reform of higher education. In 1977 these were integrated into a wider system of "regional colleges", which in turn was reorganized in a compre-hensive university and college reform in 1994–5.[10] The district colleges were originally designed to provide academic instruction at lower levels, including the *grunnfag* level. Today seven of these institutions offer 1-year *grunnfag* courses in history.

A number of other educational institutions, including ad-vanced colleges such as the Norwegian College of Agriculture (Norges Landbrukshøyskole) and the Norwegian School of Eco-nomics and Business Administration (Norges Handelshøyskole), also include history in their curricula.

Student enrolment

The number of students enrolled in philology at the Norwegian university was for many years quite modest: 10 students were reg-istered in 1835, 22 in 1845, and 35 in 1861.[11] The 1871 law on teachers' examination became operative in 1874 and was super-seded in 1910. Over this period the subject combination History and Geography was chosen by a total of 115 candidates, which

10 NOU 1993:24.
11 Morgenstierne 1911:263.

represented an average of 36 percent of all candidates for a degree in the humanities. However, the percentage rose from less than a third of all graduates before the turn of the century to about 60 percent in last decade of the programme. In popularity History and Geography caught up with French and English, and later also with Norwegian (including Old Norwegian) and German. One reason for this shift was undoubtedly that enrolment in the fourth programme, Classical Philology, fell from about 50 percent of all students to less than 10 percent, after an education law in 1896 further reduced the teaching of these subjects in secondary school.[12]

Since the 1905 reform introducing the *hovedfag* degree, history has become one of the most popular subjects in the Faculty of Humanities, outnumbered generally only by Norwegian (Nordic) studies. History has also had a comparatively high proportion of degree-taking students. As in other disciplines, the number of students rose dramatically with the establishment of the mass university from around 1960. In 1968 the total number of history students at university level was 750. In 1975 the number at the four Norwegian universities totalled 2,171. After falling by more than half during the 1980s, the number rose in 1992 to 2,025 registered students, well ahead of the closest competitors (English, with 1,255 students, and Norwegian, with 1,102). In addition, several hundreds studied at the regional colleges. In 1992 about 48 percent of the university students were women – a lower percentage than in most other humanities disciplines.[13]

At the University of Oslo, an average of 9–10 candidates passed the *hovedfag* examination each year in the years 1920–40, and about 18 each year in the period 1946–60.[14] The figure then increased from about 25 per year in Oslo and Bergen together in the early 1960s to a national total (at the four universities) of more than 100 each year in 1974–8.[15] In the four-year period

12 Calculated on the basis of the examination registers in the university *matricul.*
13 *Educational Statistics* 1975, 1978, 1984, 1988. Data furnished by the Central Bureau of Statistics of Norway and the Institute for Studies in Research and Higher Education.
14 Amundsen 1961 II:67; Hubbard 1992:10.
15 Hubbard 1992:10.

1989–92, the total number for Norway averaged about 45 candidates per year, exceeded only – and by a very slight margin – by Norwegian studies. About 35 percent of the history degree candidates in this period were women.[16] In the years 1945–90, a total of 2,129 theses (*hovedoppgaver*) were accepted at Norwegian universities (including 14 in economic history from the Norwegian School of Economics and Business Administration).[17]

Training for research

Traditionally, Norwegian higher education has not had very much formalized training in historical research. The *cand. philol.* education was, and still is, intended primarily for teachers in advanced secondary schools. However, it has also functioned as the first level of training for professional research workers, at least for many of those students who choose history as their main subject degree. This education has mainly been in the form of tutorials – individual, critical guidance given to the students while they prepare their theses. Especially after World War II, the scholarly level of the *cand. philol.* theses tended to rise, and since the 1960s or 1970s the general quality has been quite high. Indeed, an important part of historical research in Norway over the last generation has appeared in this form. The best of these theses doubtless stand comparison with an international Ph.D. standard, and quite a few have subsequently appeared as monographs or as articles in scholarly journals.

Defining who is a professional historian is not an entirely straightforward issue. If Norwegian historians of today had to choose a single formal criterion for the delimitation of their profession, they would probably say "history as *hovedfag*". Thus, in 1983 the newly founded Norwegian Association of Historians (Norsk historikerforening, or HIFO), which defined itself as an association of professional historians (*yrkeshistorikere*, or *Berufshistoriker*), made this qualification a condition for membership.

16 Data furnished by the Central Bureau of Statistics and the Institute for Studies in Research and Higher Education.
17 Hubbard 1992:3.

A more specialized degree for prospective researchers was the degree of *magister artium*, introduced at the University of Oslo in 1921, and later at the other universities. However, few historians have preferred this alternative, which is now abolished in all but a few disciplines in Oslo.

The traditional doctor's degree in the humanities in Norway is the rather exclusive *doctor philosophiae*, established in its non-Latin form in the University Act of 1845. The first historian to be awarded this degree was the future professor Gustav Storm in 1874. The following 40 years saw only six or seven more (depending on how we define "history"); most of these also bestowed on future professors.[18] Even in the period of university expansion since the 1960s, this degree has still been relatively rare. In the years 1950–87, only 65 doctor's degrees in history were awarded at Norwegian universities, averaging one or two per year. In 1987, only one-third of the tenured historians in Norwegian universities and colleges possessed the Dr. philos. degree.[19] The proportion among full professors at the universities was higher, though still not 100 percent. Individuals tended to conduct their doctoral research in isolation and while holding down another job, often in teaching. A general complaint has been that the doctorates in the humanities, including history, are typically acquired at too advanced an age. In the period 1950–87, the average age of the new *doctores philosophiae* in history was 43.2 years. To obtain a more efficient system of education and accreditation of researchers in the humanities, including history, a new degree of *doctor artium* was established at the various universities from 1984 onwards (the last being the University of Oslo in 1991).[20] Containing a compulsory training component, it corresponds more closely to the international Ph.D. The results of this reform in history, however, remain to be seen. The relative rarity of the doctor's

18 University of Oslo, Annual Reports. Since these doctorates were awarded by faculty, not by department, assignment to a specific discipline is not always clear.
19 Skodvin 1989:37ff. According to the same source, a total of 99 doctor's degrees were acquired by Norwegian historians in the years 1874–1987; 16 of the doctors were women.
20 University of Oslo, Annual Report 1991.

degree among Norwegian historians should in part be interpreted in the light of the high standard of the better *hovedoppgaver* and of the time-honoured custom among historians of (partially) qualifying for academic posts through various kinds of commissioned research.

Academic staff at universities and colleges

Judged by the number of professorships,[21] history was given high priority as a subject at the new Norwegian university in the nineteenth century. In fact, a professor of history was one of the first

21 Some explanation has to be given of the Norwegian system of academic posts. A Norwegian *professor* corresponds to a professor in the usual European sense (in the USA: "full" professor). In the nineteenth century, the posts of *dosent* or reader were recruitment posts. Later they were transformed into posts ranking next to the professors and demanding almost the same level of qualifications. In 1985 the title of *dosent* was abolished (except in the district colleges), and all readers were made (full) professors. In the nineteenth century, the *universitetslektor* (university lecturer) ranked second to the professors mostly by seniority. The new posts of *universitetslektor* or *høyskolelektor* (college lecturer), created in large numbers in the expansion period from the late 1950s onwards, however, were predominantly teaching posts. They did not at first require research qualifications beyond a good *hovedfag* level. Since the late 1970s, the official and commonly used term for these posts is *amanuensis* (assistant professor); *førsteamanuensis* (associate professor) is used for those who have acquired academic qualifications judged equivalent to a doctor's degree. Today the doctorate or *førsteamanuensis* level is a minimum requirement for obtaining tenure. The qualifications level of this group has generally been rising over the years. The work obligations have correspondingly in many cases become more or less the same as those of the professors. During the 1980s, therefore, quite a few of the most competent in the *førsteamanuensis* group were promoted to professors on a personal basis. Since 1993 all holders of tenured academic posts at universities and colleges who are declared competent for professorships have the right to such promotion. This applies also to the regional colleges. As a consequence of these developments, the number of professors in disciplines such as history, where the general level of research qualifications is relatively high, has been rising quite steeply in recent years. The system also includes the part-time post of professor II and the recruitment posts *universitetsstipendiat*, *høyskolestipendiat*, and *forskningsstipendiat* (fellow/scholarship holder; research scholar). The last-mentioned are usually three- or four-year engagements financed respectively by a university or college or by the Norwegian Research Council (Norges Forskningsråd).

five professors to be appointed on 16 January 1813.[22] As early as 1816, another post was established. And in 1874 the Storting (Norwegian Parliament) created a third, extraordinary professorship for the Venstre historian Ernst Sars. By comparison, the university had a total of only 14 professors and 4 lecturers in 1817, 51 (full) professors in 1880, and 71 in 1911.[23]

The staff in Oslo stayed at 3 professors and 1 *dosent* or reader[24] until 1940. In addition, a *dosentur* (readership) existed at the Norwegian Teachers' College in Trondheim from 1922, and the holder was appointed professor in 1935.[25] In the early 1950s, academic personnel in history in Norway still numbered a mere 6 persons: 5 in Oslo and 1 in Trondheim. Then the growth started. In Bergen, the first 2 professors were appointed in 1957, and the following year the first 4 university or college lecturers[26] were engaged: 2 in Oslo, 1 in Bergen, and 1 in Trondheim. By 1961 the number of university teachers had risen to 20. The national total (which from 1972 on also included Tromsø) then soared to more than 60 in the late 1970s before it levelled out: there were 61 in 1977, 66 in 1983, and 66 in 1993.[27] Today almost three-quarters of these are full professors. If we also include research fellows, scholarship holders and such, the total number of historians working in the history departments of the four Norwegian universities in 1993 was 110. Of these, 21 percent were women; at the level of full professor, the percentage of women was 14.[28] The largest staff, representing about one-third of the total, is in the University of Oslo.

22 This ought to be interpreted in the light of the fact that the first task of the new professors was to organize *examen artium*, the final examination of secondary school. See Nielsen 1911:LIIIf.

23 Morgenstierne 1911:37, 287, 293, 357, 365ff.

24 See note 21.

25 Kirkhusmo 1983:213.

26 See note 21.

27 Data furnished by the Institute for Studies in Research and Higher Education. Includes persons engaged in posts of professor, reader, and *amanuensis/førsteamanuensis*.

28 Ibid. The percentage of women was 9 in 1961, 15 in 1977, and 17 in 1985; at the level of full professor, 8 in 1977 and 4 in 1985. The first woman to be appointed to a full professorship was Ingrid Semmingsen (b. 1910) in Oslo in 1963.

In addition, smaller teaching and research milieus have developed at some of the district colleges, where posts as *amanuensis* were established beginning in the 1970s. Some of these persons now hold personal professorships.[29]

Special chairs in history also have a long tradition at the Norwegian College of Agriculture (Norges Landbrukshøyskole), where a professorship including agricultural history was established as early as 1914 (specialized in agricultural history only, from 1921), and the Norwegian School of Economics and Business Administration (Norges Handelshøyskole).[30]

Institutionalization of education and discipline formation

As stated above, the context of history teaching at the university was initially the preliminary *examen philosophicum* and the traditional "teacher's degree" in philology. The first, half-way step towards specialization was taken in 1871 with the "teacher's degree in languages and history". In the combined subject group History and Geography in this degree, examination requirements in history were explicitly defined with reference partly to (secondary) school curricula and partly to textbooks written in the specific Nordic and Western European countries whose history had to be studied in particular depth. In addition, Greek and Roman antiquity was to be studied in textbooks which treated the subject "more fully". Implicitly, it appears that the core of the subject was the usual (political) history of nations and states. But candidates were also required to "acquaint themselves with the relevant auxiliary sciences, particularly chronology, the geography of earlier periods, and also the development of constitutions, of the Church, philosophy, literature, and culture".[31] In the revised regulation of 1905, the requirements remained more or less the same, adding at *hoved-*

---

29 See note 21.
30 Låg *et al.* 1959:471f. Jensen and Strømme Svendsen 1986:403.
31 Regulation of 15 July 1872. See also the unofficial syllabus, *Studieplan for alle Fakulteter* 1897:71ff.

fag level historical methods, archaeology, general ethnography, and "the basic elements of economics".[32]

Seen in relation to the textbook core of history, the first professors taught a wide range of subjects. Indeed, at first, the professorship was defined as "history and statistics".[33] Rudolf Keyser was from 1829 a lecturer and from 1837 a professor of "national history, Old Norse and archaeology". His teaching covered the history of constitutions, Old Norse language and literature, religion, and culture.[34] P. A. Munch, lecturer from 1837 and professor of history from 1841, at different times taught geography, historical ethnography, and even the history of Anglo-Saxon language.[35] Ludvig K. Daae, appointed lecturer in 1862 and professor of history in 1866, lectured on ethnography and geography.[36]

In the late nineteenth and early twentieth century, the subject became gradually narrower. Old Norse was separated from history with the appointment in 1866 of Sophus Bugge as extraordinary professor of comparative Indo-European linguistics and Old Norse. A professorship in Nordic archaeology was established in 1875, and its first occupant was the former professor of history Oluf Rygh.[37] In 1890 a chair in geography and ethnography was created; to judge from his research and writings, the first holder of this post, Yngvar Nielsen, was also a historian.[38]

As an examination subject, "geography with ethnography" was separated from history in 1905, and it was established at *hovedfag* level in 1920.[39] In 1921 the degree of *magister artium* was introduced in archaeology, art history, literary history, and the history of religions, as well as a number of other disciplines.[40]

Since the Second World War, a new process of diversification and specialization has taken place, corresponding to the develop-

32 Regulation of 21 October 1905. See also *Studieplan for Sproglig-Historisk Embedseksamen* (syllabus) 1907:29ff. and 1910:30ff.
33 Dahl 1990:20.
34 Bugge 1911:225ff; Dahl 1990:46; University Annual Reports.
35 Bugge 1911:237; University Annual Reports 1851, 1852, and others.
36 University Annual Reports, for instance, 1864, 1867, 1869.
37 Morgenstierne 1911:295.
38 Dahl 1990:137ff.
39 Regulation of 21 October 1905; Amundsen 1961:63, 81.
40 Amundsen 1961:67–8 and *passim*.

ments in historical research in this period.[41] In fact, history sylla-buses in this period seemed increasingly to be more influenced by research interests and perhaps less so by the needs of secondary school teaching. Particularly at the *hovedfag* level, studies have become quite specialized in the last generation. Nonetheless, the formal university degree remains a general one, in "history". More specialized examination subjects such as "contemporary history", "local history", "economic history", etc. are found only in some regional and other colleges, which enrol comparatively few students.

Administrative arrangements

At the first Norwegian university, history belonged to the Faculty of Philosophy from the beginning in 1813, and to the Faculty of Humanities after the Faculty of Philosophy was divided in 1861. In 1951 an external Institute of Norwegian Historical Research (Institutt for norsk historisk forskning) was founded on the initiative of Professor Sverre Steen, as a response to the establishment of the Norwegian Research Council for Science and the Humanities. This institute was transferred to the university as the Historisk institutt in 1953, and in 1965 it merged with Historieseksjonen, the section which organized educational matters, examinations, etc.[42] In Bergen, too, history was organized as a department (*institutt*) in the humanities faculty in 1957.[43]

In Trondheim and Tromsø, however, different solutions have been tried. In the Norwegian Teachers' College in Trondheim, history was at first organized as an institute in the Department of Social Studies (Avdeling for samfunnsfag), but it was later transferred to the Department of Philological Studies (Avdeling for filologiske fag, now called the Faculty of Humanities).[44] The University of Tromsø, by contrast, does not have separate faculties. There, history has been included from the beginning in a multidisciplinary Department of Social Studies (Institutt for samfunnsvitenskap).

41 Hubbard 1992:5–6.
42 Dahl 1978:51ff.
43 Bagge 1994:5ff.
44 Kirkhusmo 1983:216, 224ff.

The actual extent of interdisciplinary integration is said to be weak.[45] In Oslo a reform of faculty structures in 1990 placed history as a subdepartment in a multidisciplinary School of Cultural and Social Studies (Institutt for kultur- og samfunnsfag), along with subjects such as geography, ethnology, and others. But this did not gladden the historians of the 1990s, and the accustomed autonomy was re-established in 1995. Thus, although interdisciplinary collaboration in matters of education is probably gaining in importance, it is restricted mainly to the level of advanced seminars, postgraduate research training, and the like.

One may see from the above that formal organizational subdivisions according to historical specialities or periods are generally absent in Norwegian universities. For instance, separate departments for economic history do not exist, but there is a separate department for intellectual history (Idéhistorie) at the University of Oslo. At the national level, collaboration between history departments is organized in the National History Council (Nasjonalt fagråd for historie), but it does not have the power to make binding decisions.

Research institutions

The institution regarded as the first scientific institution in Norway, The Royal Norwegian Society of the Sciences (Det Kongelige Norske Videnskabers Selskab), was founded in Trondheim in 1760. Created on the model of the learned societies found in other European countries at the time, the Society was mainly a meeting-place for interested amateurs, but also had an important library and a museum of antiquities, and it supported the publication of historical writings. The historians Schøning and Suhm were among the founding members.[46] There is no space here to discuss the scholarly professionalism of Schøning and Suhm or their forerunners in Norwegian historiography.[47] In the first decades of the nineteenth century, the leading Norwegian historians were learned amateurs at

45 Fulsås 1993:190ff.
46 Midbøe 1960:13ff.; Dahl 1990:15.
47 Dahl 1990:13ff.

least in the sense that they made their living from other professions. Jens Christian Berg (1775–1852), for instance, was a judge. The first university professors of history were not very active as researchers, though Ludvig Stoud Platou (1778–1833) wrote a much-used textbook on Scandinavian history.[48]

In the generation of Keyser and Munch from the 1830s onwards, however, university professors took the lead in historical research. Yet throughout the nineteenth century, important contributions also came from other sources. Several major historians, among them Michael Birkeland (1830–96), worked as keepers of the National Archives.[49] The National Archives has also had an important role as a provider of jobs and as a training ground for historians in the earlier stages of their careers.[50] In addition, barriers between neighbouring disciplines were not insurmountable. Thus, T. H. Aschehoug (1822–1909), professor of law (and later of political economy and statistics), made valuable contributions both to constitutional and to economic and demographic history.[51] Conversely, nineteenth-century Norwegian professors of history conducted research in, among other things, Norse philology, archaeology, ethnography, geography, and toponymy.[52]

Teaching loads and, increasingly, administrative burdens are of course of decisive importance for the research opportunities of university staff. There does not appear to have been fixed, quantitative regulations of the teaching load in the nineteenth century.[53] At least in the early period, the number of weekly lectures could be high, up to 12.[54] However, exemptions for such purposes as to finish books or to visit foreign archives were apparently granted rather liberally.[55]

---

48 Dahl 1990:20ff.
49 Dahl 1990:270, 124ff.
50 Dahl 1990:137 (Yngvar Nielsen), 157 (J. E. Sars).
51 Dahl 1990:104f., 121ff.
52 Dahl 1990:49, 61, 80, 227.
53 The university law of 28 July 1824, § 21, states only that every university teacher is obliged to give each semester the public lectures which are his duty according to the syllabus, without extra remuneration.
54 Morgenstierne 1911:16. The cited example is not taken from history.
55 University Annual Reports. See also circular from the university senate of 28 January 1907, which announces restrictions.

An Order in Council (*kongelig resolusjon*) of 19 February 1907 set the general teaching load for university professors at five lectures per week, which could be reduced by a maximum of one weekly lecture in case of other demanding duties. This regulation applied at (full) professorial level until recently.[56] The university lecturers engaged in large numbers from the late 1950s onwards were not at first expected to be active researchers, and their teaching burdens were correspondingly heavy. Over the years, however, the work obligations of the two categories have been more or less equalized.[57]

In theory, after subtracting the time taken up by normal administrative duties, the working time of university academic staff is divided equally between teaching and research.[58] With the great increase in both student numbers and administrative tasks, however, this ratio has not proved realistic. A recent investigation found that in 1991 the professor, *førsteamanuensis*, and *amanuensis* groups[59] in the humanities at the four universities were able to spend on average only 29 percent of their total working time on research and "their own education" (*egenutdanning*). And this figure included both project planning and sabbaticals. The limited data available suggest that this distribution of work-time has been typical since the mid-1960s.[60] No data are available specifically for historians, but if we assume their working conditions are similar, then the professor and (*første*)*amanuensis* groups at the universities in the 1980s and early 1990s were able to invest annually around 20 "work-years" (*årsverk*) in historical research out of a total staff of some 65 work-years. This figure is rather modest compared to the 45–50 scholarship holders[61] who devote at least three-quarters of their time to research, and to the yearly output of about 45

56 Similar rules were adopted at the other universities. These traditional regulations were abolished with effect from 1993 only.

57 At the University of Oslo, they have been in principle identical since 1993.

58 In Oslo this is fixed as 47 percent of total working time each for research and for teaching. See circular from the Faculty of Humanities, University of Oslo, 25 June 1992.

59 See note 21.

60 Kyvik and Enoksen 1992:Tables 2.2, 3.5 and *passim*. Note that supervision of *hovedfag* and doctoral students was not counted as research. These tasks represented 8 percent of total working time.

61 See above, and note 28.

hovedfag candidates,[62] each of which represents at least one year of historical investigation.

Although departments of history at the Norwegian universities are combined research and educational units organizationally, the departmental contribution to research (beyond the actual manpower) usually consists only of office accommodation and rather meagre grants for equipment, assistance, and travel. Larger or more ambitious projects have to rely on external sources of funding. Departments as such have rarely taken on the role of initiating and organizing research projects.[63] Attempts to change this are perhaps now to be expected.[64]

Particularly since the 1980s, a number of interdisciplinary research centres have been established at the Norwegian universities, several of which employ historians. Important examples are the centres for women's research in Oslo and Trondheim, the Centre for the Study of European Culture (Senter for europeiske kulturstudier) in Bergen, the Centre for Technology and Human Values (Senter for teknologi og menneskelige verdier, TMV) in Oslo, and the Centre for Technology and Society (Senter for teknologi og samfunn) in Trondheim. In addition to the university staffs, quite a few historians work at various colleges, including about 20 at the district colleges, which have been increasingly involved in research since the 1970s.[65] Special mention is due the interdisciplinary Institute for Comparative Research in Human Culture (Instituttet for sammenlignende kulturforskning). In existence since 1922, it has among other things made valuable contributions to the history of Norwegian peasant society and culture.[66] Today a varying number of historians work for shorter or longer periods and sometimes hold permanent posts at interdisciplinary research institutions such as the Institute for Social Research (Institutt for samfunns-

62 See above, and note 16.
63 One early exception is the project *Norsk samfunnsutvikling 1860–1900* (Norwegian Societal Development 1860–1900) in Oslo, which was initiated by the Department of History in 1970, when Ottar Dahl was head of the department. See Langholm 1974:243.
64 This refers to certain plans at the University of Oslo.
65 Skodvin 1989: Table 2.2, gives 20 historians at the district colleges in 1987. See Skoie 1992:36ff.
66 Dahl 1990:272ff.

forskning), the International Peace Research Institute (Institutt for fredsforskning, PRIO), the Norwegian Institute of International Affairs (Norsk utenrikspolitisk institutt, NUPI), the Norwegian Institute for Defence Studies (Institutt for forsvarsstudier), and others. Of a somewhat different character is the Centre for Business History (Bedriftshistorisk senter), established in 1979 as a subdivision of the Norwegian Private Archives Institute (see below).[67] In 1989 it was transferred to the Norwegian School of Management (Handelshøyskolen BI) and reorganized as the Department of Economic History (Avdeling for økonomisk historie). It currently employs 10 historians who spend 80 percent of their working time on research.[68] Finally, a number of professional historians at any given time participate in individual or collective research projects without being attached to any research institution.

Complete statistical information about the financing of Norwegian historical research does not exist. Since its establishment in 1949, the Norwegian Research Council for Science and the Humanities (Norges almenvitenskapelige forskningsråd, NAVF) has been a main source of financing for both scholarships for postgraduate research training and other project types. Increasingly, it has also exerted influence on research priorities, particularly since the 1980s through the formulation of research programmes. In 1993 all the earlier Norwegian research councils were merged into a single Norwegian Research Council (Norges forskningsråd).[69] Under the heading "History", the Research Council in 1993 contributed to 55 research projects at a total cost of about NOK 10.6 million.[70]

This is a modest sum compared with the NOK 40 million invested in 1991 by Norwegian local authorities in the researching and writing of local history. No fewer than 199 authors worked on this in 1991, and about half of them (49 percent) had a degree in history.[71] This information comes from the Norwegian

67 Dahl 1990:270.
68 Information received from the Department of Economic History, Norwegian School of Management, October 1994.
69 See NOU 1991:24.
70 Norges forskningsråd. *Prosjektkatalog 1993. Humaniora.* The grants include both scholarships and other projects.
71 *Kringsjå,* nr. 21, May 1993:3ff.

Institute of Local History (Norsk lokalhistorisk institutt), a central service and advisory institution in local history founded in 1955. We do not have corresponding statistics for the other main areas of commissioned research, such as the history of business firms, of private organizations, or of state institutions. The Department of Economic History at the Norwegian School of Management, which conducts some of these projects, had a budget of about NOK 4 million in 1994, based on six projects financed by firms and five by the Research Council.[72]

A peculiar feature of Norwegian historical culture and historiography is the strength of multi-volume history works written by professional historians for a non-professional public and financed by publishing companies. At least five multi-volume histories of Norway or of the world, ranging in length from nine to twenty volumes, have appeared since the 1950s. Sales of the respective editions have totalled up to about 77,000 copies, with first printings as large as 44,500.[73] The initial run of the new twelve-volume history of Norway that began to appear in 1994 is projected at 30,000 copies with a budget of NOK 24–25 million, internal overhead excepted.[74]

Traditionally, historical research in Norway as elsewhere has been conducted on an individual basis. But increasingly since the late 1960s, larger, co-operative projects engaging several researchers under a common management have gained ground. Typically, a team comprises senior researchers, postgraduate research fellows, and *hovedfag* students. This development is encouraged both by the Norwegian Research Council and by the universities' governing bodies, and historians have been pioneers among the humanities. Some of these projects are also interdisciplinary and/or co-operate internationally; this was the case with one of the earliest examples, the so-called Scandinavian Deserted Farms Project (*nordiske ødegårdsprosjekt*) carried out in the years 1968–75.[75]

Finally, one should re-emphasize the fact that historical

---

72 See note 68.
73 Information received from Aschehoug, Cappelen, and De norske bokklubbene publishers, October/November 1994 and January 1995.
74 Information received from Aschehoug publishers, October 1994.
75 Dahl 1990:293, 297f. For another example of an early project, see note 63.

research is a wide field in which many disciplines are involved. An investigation covering the years 1981–9 found that among upwards of 400 projects identified as "historical", only about 70 percent were conducted by professional historians; the others were led by social scientists or researchers from other humanities disciplines.[76] An outstanding example of the contributions of the social sciences was the work of the political sociologist Stein Rokkan (1921–79). His theories on regional differences in Norway's economic and cultural structure and political development provoked controversy but also stimulated historical research.[77]

Archives, museums, and other institutions for documentation

As well as seeing the establishment of the university, the early nineteenth century was above all the period when institutions for the preservation and publication of national historical sources and monuments were created: the National Archive, the Museum of Bergen, the Museum of Antiquities at the University in Oslo, and the University Library.

The National Archive (Riksarkivet) of the new Norwegian state was created in 1817 as a subdivision of the Ministry of Finance. It gained in efficacy when the office of National Archivist was created in 1839 and again when it became an independent institution in 1875. Regional archives for the dioceses of Trondheim and Tromsø and of Bergen and Stavanger were created in 1850 and 1885 respectively. Since 1904 the State Archives System of Norway (Arkivverket, until 1935 Arkivvesenet) is directed by the National Archivist (Riksarkivaren) and includes the central National Archive in Oslo and a growing number of (as of 1994: eight) regional archives (statsarkiver). The latter are mainly responsible for documents from local and regional administrations. The storage capacity of the central National Archive in Oslo, opened in 1978,

76 Pryser 1989:463. The projects were identified through a computer search for "history" in the title, as a subject catchword, or as the discipline classification, in a database on research projects.
77 Rokkan 1970:passim; Dahl 1990:308f; see also Chapter 7.

is about 80,000 metres of shelves, which is now (1994) almost completely exploited; the necessary expansion is under planning.[78] As of 1994 the State Archives System employs a permanent staff of 166. Its 45 official archivists, all of whom have the university degree in history, have the right to devote one-seventh of their working time to research.[79]

Publication of primary sources for research use has been an important part of historians' activities since the early nineteenth century. In the 1840s *Norges Gamle Love* (The Old Laws of Norway) were published by the history professors Keyser and Munch. In 1847 the first volume of the *Diplomatarium Norvegicum* appeared. This and other important publication projects were for several decades organized by the keepers of the National Archive in collaboration with the university professor of Germanic and Romance philology, Carl Richard Unger.[80] In 1857 the Storting approved a grant to the Norwegian Historical Sources Fund (Det Norske Historiske Kildeskriftfond), at first led by the keeper of the National Archive, and from 1886 by a commission. The system was reorganized in 1934 with the establishment of the Norwegian Historical Sources Institute (Norsk Historisk Kjeldeskriftinstitutt), which in 1991 became a department within the National Archive. Likewise, the Private Archives Commission (Privatarkivkommisjonen), established in 1951, was reorganized into a state-owned institution, the Norwegian Private Archives Institute (Norsk Privatarkivinstitutt) in 1977, and then incorporated into the National Archive in 1987.[81]

There are, of course, many local archives, as well as archives for various, specific purposes.[82] Of particular interest is the Archive and Library of the Labour Movement (Arbeiderbevegelsens Arkiv og Bibliotek) in Oslo. Established in 1909, it is one the earliest insti-

---

78 Svalestuen 1992:13ff; Johannessen 1992:30f. Information received from National Archives Norway.
79 Information from National Archives Norway. Cf. also Svalestuen 1992:20.
80 Dahl 1990:26, 78, 227; Svalestuen 1992:24.
81 Dahl 1990:76, 130, 269f; Svalestuen 1992:16.
82 The booklet *Hvor er kildene? Institusjoner til hjelp for lokalhistorikere* (4th ed., 1994), for instance, lists a great number of archives, museums, and other collections that can be of help to local historians.

tutions of its kind in Europe and has played a central role in much modern historical research.

Along with the Royal Norwegian Society of the Sciences and the University (Oslo), the Museum of Bergen (Bergens Museum) was one of the most important institutions in the genesis of Norwegian science. The museum was founded in 1825 on the model of the British Museum by W. F. K. Christie, who was president of the Constituent Assembly in 1814. It built up important collections and contributed to research in archaeology and wide areas of cultural history (for example, ethnology and the history of art), as well as the natural sciences, until its incorporation in 1946 into the newly established University of Bergen. The museum's activity did not, however, include political history.[83]

In Christiania a collection of Nordic and mainly Norwegian antiquities was created by The Royal Society for the Benefit of Norway (Det Kongelige Selskab for Norges Vel) in 1810 and donated to the university in 1817. From 1829 the responsibility for this institution, still known as The University Museum of Antiquities (Universitetets Oldsaksamling), was assigned to the professors of history Rudolf Keyser and (after him) Oluf Rygh, until the professorship was divided and Scandinavia's first chair in archaeology was created in 1875.[84] However, the collaboration and overlapping research interests of historians and archaeologists have in many cases been important also in the twentieth century.[85]

The allotted space does not permit specific mention of the several other museums of interest particularly with regard to local, social, and cultural history. Valuable collections are, of course, also to be found in the university libraries and in the recently established National Library Division in Rana (Nasjonalbibliotekavdelinga i Rana).[86] Many of these, and other institutions, including university departments of ethnology, folklore, or history, have collections of manuscripts, photographs, or oral information.

The Norwegian Central Bureau of Statistics (Statistisk sentral-

83 Thue 1994:Chapter 1.
84 Gjessing 1920:161ff.
85 Dahl 1990:242.
86 See note 83. The Norwegian National Library was not formally separated from the University Library of Oslo until 1989.

byrå) was established as a separate institution in 1876. Norwegian official statistics, however, have a much longer tradition; for instance, the first national census in the new Norwegian state was arranged as early as 1815. The still-earlier nominative census of 1801 was registered in machine-readable form by the Department of History in Bergen in the 1970s, and its data are available online. A special service institution, the Registration Centre for Historical Data (Registreringssentral for historiske data, RHD) at the Department of Social Studies, University of Tromsø, was set up in 1981. The RHD processes and stores census and parish register information for use in demographic, social, and local history.[87] The Norwegian Social Science Data Service (Norsk samfunnsvitenskapelig datatjeneste, NSD) in Bergen provides valuable computerized information on nineteenth- and twentieth-century societal developments, particularly at regional levels.

Journals, associations, and international collaboration

The preoccupation with national history in the new Norwegian state manifested itself in early attempts at organizing journals and associations, both in Christiania (Oslo) and in the milieu around the Museum of Bergen.[88]

The first Norwegian historical association, the Society for the Language and History of the Norwegian People (Samfundet for det Norske Folks Sprog og Historie), was founded in Christiania in 1831–2 by a group consisting mainly of learned amateurs. The purpose was to publish a historical journal, which appeared in the years 1833–9 and which at one time had more than 500 subscribers. The association did not survive the 1830s, however, and a new attempt from the late 1840s was also short-lived.[89]

A generation later the project proved viable. The Norwegian Historical Association (Den norske historiske forening) was

87 RHD, Årsrapport 1993 1994: passim.
88 Dahl 1990:37f; Thue 1994:7.
89 Munthe 1920:322f; Dahl 1990:22, 35ff., 76.

founded on 22 December 1869 and started its activities on 1 January 1870. The purpose of the association was to "further the study and knowledge of history, particularly with regard to the fatherland (*Fædrelandet*) and its literature". This was to be achieved mainly through the publication of a journal, covering "not only actual (*egentlige*) historical accounts", but also works in "Nordic philology and archaeology, and ethnographic, topographical or statistical descriptions of the land and the people".[90] Foremost among the founders was the historian and keeper of the National Archive, Michael Birkeland, who also became the first president (until 1879). The board included other central representatives of the historical professions and institutions in a wide sense.[91]

The new association met with great response. The first annual report records 1,180 members, among them half the Cabinet, two-thirds of the *amtmenn* (regional commissioners), about 80 Storting representatives, and a number of other prominent figures from the Norwegian establishment. In 1871 the association could register His Majesty the King as a member.[92] Membership reached 1,242 in 1873. A long decline then set in which did not end until 1903, when there were only 547 members. The decline is partly explained by the fact that the leaders were mostly on the conservative side in the deep political conflicts dividing Norway in this period. The national democratic historian Ernst Sars, for instance, was never on the board and rarely published anything in the journal.[93] In 1912, however, a new generation took over, with Halvdan Koht as a particularly active president until 1927. Among other things the board now organized public lectures, which had hitherto been rare.[94] In 1927, membership was about 850. After another slight decline, it reached more than 1,300 in 1980.[95]

In 1913 the Historical Association appointed a standing commit-

90 Statutes of 22 December 1869, §§ 1 and 2. In actual fact, the editorial policies tended to be somewhat more restrictive; cf. Munthe 1920:333.
91 Munthe 1920:324 ff.; Dahl 1990:111f., 125.
92 *Historisk tidsskrift* 1871:XIIIff.; cf. Langholm 1994.
93 Munthe 1920:335ff; cf. Dahl 1990:121.
94 Munthe 1920:338, 348, 349ff; Dahl 1990:234.
95 The Norwegian Historical Association, Annual Reports in *Historisk tidsskrift*.

tee for local history, and in 1920 this resulted in the establishment of the National Organization for Local History (originally Landslaget for bygde- og byhistorie, now Landslaget for lokalhistorie). Its first president (until 1945) was the professor of history, Oscar Albert Johnsen. This organization has published the journal *Heimen* since 1922.[96] The membership of the some 300 local divisions of the Organization for Local History is now (1994) about 50,000.[97]

The further development of Norwegian historical organizations at the national level may be briefly summarized. In 1926, the Comité International des Sciences Historiques was founded in Geneva and Halvdan Koht elected its first president (serving until 1933). In 1928 the Sixth International Congress of Historical Sciences was held in Oslo.[98] To arrange this meeting and, subsequently, to handle the relations with the Comité International, the Norwegian Historical Association appointed an internal committee, the Norwegian Committee for Historical Science (Norsk komité for historisk vitskap). Under the leadership of Koht until 1957, the committee gradually developed an autonomous position. Particularly after the Second World War, it also took up other functions on behalf of the profession. Membership was enlarged by co-option and by *ex officio* admittance of the staff of the history departments of the universities; in 1988 it totalled 90.[99]

This organizational framework, however, failed to meet the needs of the growing historical profession. In 1983 a new organization, the Norwegian Association of Historians (Norsk historikerforening, or HIFO), was created. This was an "association for professional historians *(yrkeshistorikere)"*. A *hovedfag* or *magister artium* degree in history was made the normal minimum condition

96 Dahl 1990:234, 245f.; cf. Chapter 9.
97 Information received from the National Organization for Local History, December 1994.
98 Comité International des Sciences Historiques. *Bulletin d'Information*, Vol. 1:1-5.
99 Den norske historiske forening and Norsk komité for historisk vitskap, Annual Reports in *Historisk tidsskrift*. The archives of Norsk komité for historisk vitskap, temporarily at the Department of History, University of Oslo, will be transferred to the National Archive. Cf. "Norske historikeres organisasjonsforhold", *Historisk tidsskrift* 1989:113ff.

for membership. In addition to publishing the journal *HIFO-nytt*, the association operated an employment service for historians and held seminars on research methods and historiographical approaches.[100] In 1988–9 it had nearly 200 members, 40 or 50 of whom conducted full-time commissioned research.[101]

The coexistence of three national historical associations was not considered satisfactory, and in 1990 a reorganized Norwegian Historical Association, Den norske historiske forening (HIFO), was established through the merger of the three bodies. The reorganized association combines the functions of the three predecessors, including the publication of *Historisk tidsskrift* and *HIFO-nytt*. Unlike the original Historical Association of 1869, the 1990 version is an organization for professionals, but membership conditions are somewhat more liberal than in the 1983 HIFO statutes; among others, secondary school history teachers are admitted.[102] In 1994 the membership was about 530, including about 115 *hovedfag* students. About one-third of the members were women.[103]

Public conferences for the exchange and debate of new research have a considerable tradition in the historical profession in Norway as in other countries. The first national historical conference in Norway was held in Bergen in 1910 on the initiative of the literary historian and keeper of the Regional Archives of Bergen, Just Bing (1866–1954), and other members of the milieu around the Museum of Bergen. The second and third Norwegian conferences took place in Christiania in 1912 and 1914. A fourth conference planned for 1917 had to be postponed because of the war. Such national conferences in general history (De Norske Historikerdagene) began again in the 1980s; the last was held in Tromsø in 1992; the next will be in Bergen in 1996.

During this long hiatus, Scandinavian-wide historical meetings took the place of national ones in Norway. The first Nordic Histori-

100 Statutes and archives of Den norske historiske forening (HIFO); see note 99.
101 "Norske historikeres organisasjonsforhold", *Historisk tidsskrift* 1989:116f.
102 Annual Reports for the years 1989 and 1990, Den norske historiske forening, *Historisk tidsskrift* 1990:Iff. Minutes of the constituent assembly, Den norske historiske forening (HIFO), *Historisk tidsskrift* 1991:141ff.
103 Information received from the treasurer, December 1994.

cal Conference (Nordiske historikermøte) was held in Christiania in 1920.[104] Since then, Nordic conferences have been arranged usually every third year, rotating among the Nordic countries. The 22nd and most recent one took place in Oslo in 1994, and drew more than 400 historians from Denmark, Finland, Iceland, Sweden, and the Baltic states, besides Norway. Archivists from the Nordic countries have also held regular conferences since 1945. Another Nordic co-operative undertaking is the Nordic Conferences on Historical Method (De nordiske fagkonferanser om historisk metodelære), which have been held regularly since 1965, initially every year, and lately every second year.[105] Norwegian historians also collaborate with Nordic colleagues in the publication of the *Scandinavian Economic History Review* (since 1953) and the *Scandinavian Journal of History* (since 1976).

Conclusion

In Norway today, perhaps the most significant general characteristic of the history discipline as a profession is the tension between, on the one hand, centrifugal forces represented by specialization and, on the other, a strong feeling of a common professional identity. The latter builds on a common basic education in the discipline and on a view of what the science of history is, as distinct from other disciplines – a view which in the final analysis is relatively cohesive.

In Norwegian society generally, the profession appears to inspire confidence and to have a comparatively strong position: "amidst all the words and all the noise, the history discipline has a credible voice".[106] Yet Norwegian historians in general could achieve a greater international profile than they currently enjoy, even if there are considerable differences in this regard according to subdiscipline. Arguably, the still-evident tendency towards introversion is an after-effect of preoccupation with our own national history, for so long a dominant feature of the profession.

104 Reports of the conferences in the respective annual volumes of *Historisk tidsskrift*. See Dahl 1990:235.
105 Langholm 1970 b:68 ff; Simensen and Helland 1984:239ff. The reports of the conferences are published as *Studier i historisk metode*.
106 Nielsen 1994:33.

Part II
Major Eras

4. The Middle Ages

Sverre Bagge

As in many countries, historiography and the nation have been closely linked in Norway since the beginning of the last century. The connection differs from that in more established nations like England or France, or, within Scandinavia, Sweden and Denmark. First, the transition from greatness in the Middle Ages to loss of independence and then to liberation in the early nineteenth century created a special need for an overall narrative, to explain the *"grandeur et décadence"* of the country.[1] Second, national history has been closely linked to the political left, corresponding to the political constellation of most of the period after 1814. The great syntheses of Norwegian history have mainly been created by historians of the left. The Middle Ages hold a particular importance in these syntheses. The period was regarded as the age of greatness, and might serve as a source of inspiration for building the new Norway of the nineteenth century, as a clue to the country's subsequent development, or as a particular intellectual challenge, to explain the birth as well as the death of a state in a period of a few centuries.

It seems natural to divide a survey of the historiography of the Middle Ages[2] according to the great syntheses, although there are a number of works that cannot be classified in this way. Such a division gives the following five periods: 1) The Norwegian historical school, *c.* 1830–60, 2) Evolutionism and source criticism, *c.* 1860–1910, 3) The Marxist period, *c.* 1910–45, 4) The new empiricism, 1945–*c.* 1980, and 5) Social sciences and the history of mentalities, since *c.* 1980.

1 The expression comes from Ernst Sars; see Mykland 1955:47.
2 The standard work on the development of Norwegian historiography, including that of the Middle Ages, is still Dahl 1959 (new, enlarged edition 1990), which has been extensively used in the following.

The Norwegian historical school, 1830–1860

Interest in Norway's medieval past was growing already before 1814, and some work was done during the first generation after that date. But the real breakthrough for the study of medieval history came in the 1830s and 1840s, thanks to the founders of "the Norwegian historical school", Rudolf Keyser and Peter Andreas Munch. The special importance of the study of the Middle Ages was pointed out shortly after 1814: The "real" past of the country was to be sought in the period before the loss of independence and submission to Denmark in the early sixteenth century, and preferably before 1319, when the first union was formed with another neighbouring country, Sweden. The new Norway should continue where the old age of greatness had been broken off, discarding the dark period in between. Keyser and Munch were more moderate in their attitude to the "Danish" period than some of the most patriotic writers immediately after 1814, but they nevertheless considered it their special duty to rescue the past greatness of the country from oblivion.

Keyser and Munch belong to the movement of romanticism and historicism, which had its origin and centre in Germany. They were no doubt influenced by contemporary German scholarship – for example, Munch uses a quotation from Niebuhr as a motto for his work – but the extent and character of this influence have never been the subject of detailed study. One obvious parallel is the systematic attempt to trace and publish all extant sources and to use them to reconstruct national history. This programme resulted in new and better editions of sagas and other sources, and in the two great series, *Norges gamle Love* (The Old Laws of Norway) and *Diplomatarium Norvegicum*, the Norwegian equivalents of *Monumenta Germaniae Historica*. The two series began to appear in 1846 and 1849 respectively and are still unfinished. Munch spent several years in the Vatican Archives to find material for the latter series and was one of the first foreign scholars to work there.[3]

The result of this work with sources was narrative history

3 Chadwick 1978.

which gave a far more detailed and exact picture of the past than earlier works. Munch's history of Norway, of which he managed to finish eight large volumes before his death, covering the period until 1397, is the most important work of this school.[4] As in Germany, there was a strong connection between detailed research, narrative, and national history. The aim of historiography was not generalization, as during the Enlightenment, but the exact description of a unique national past. This description was most adequately presented in a narrative form. Thus Munch, in his preface, explained that he did not intend to write a separate social and cultural history, but rather to present the events in their full detail, so that readers could draw their own conclusions about such conditions. Further, the narrative was to be based on critical research. All extant sources should be used and carefully compared, and earlier sources should be preferred to later ones. The use of these sources must be based on a theory of their origin, attitudes, and validity as sources of information. Like Niebuhr and the German romantics, Munch and Keyser believed that the narrative sources derived their information from a continuous oral tradition going back to the events themselves; the sagas, for instance, could be trusted regarding events that took place several centuries before they were written down.

The idea of the uniqueness of the national past served to distinguish Norway from the other Scandinavian countries. Keyser and Munch rejected the then-current idea of a common Scandinavian cultural heritage, claiming that the great literary monuments such as the sagas and Eddic and Scaldic poetry were specifically Norwegian. They also maintained that Norwegian society in the Middle Ages differed from the neighbouring countries in being based on a free peasantry, whereas Denmark and Sweden were feudalized; they sought to explain this difference by the different ways the countries had been settled. While the Norwegians had immigrated from the north to an empty country, the Danes and the Swedes had arrived from the south, subduing an indigenous population.

To some extent, the origin of Norwegian society explained the

4 Munch 1852–63.

later history of the country. In their more specific explanation of the *grandeur et décadence* of the country in the Middle Ages, Keyser and Munch were above all concerned with constitutional issues. The initial unification of the country was carried out by a monarchy from "outside", based on military power and wealth accumulated on Viking expeditions. Gradually, however, this monarchy entered into co-operation with the peasantry and the aristocracy, and eventually with the Church. The following history of the country was one of the relationship between these powers. During the century of internal peace (1030–1130), Norway had a balanced constitution in which no single power dominated. In the following period, the Church in alliance with the aristocracy tried to take control over the country, and this led to a monarchic reaction under Sverre (1177–1202), who allied himself with the peasants. The result was the victory of the monarchy under Sverre's successors and the establishment of an almost absolute monarchy in the thirteenth century. This absolute monarchy created internal peace and stability and strengthened the position of Norway among the powers of the north, but it proved disastrous during the unions following 1319, when the Danish king was able to use his strong position to abolish Norwegian independence. The strong emphasis on constitutional issues and the ideal of a balance between the internal powers may be part of the heritage of the Enlightenment, which was prominent in the Norwegian constitution of 1814. Keyser and Munch's ideals on this point can also largely be explained by reference to contemporary conditions, and specifically to the attempts of intellectuals, civil servants, and politicians to defend the Norwegian constitution against encroachments from the Swedish king.

Evolutionism and source criticism, 1860–1910

The deaths of Munch and Keyser in the 1860s and the emergence of a new generation inaugurated the second phase in our chronological division. The new generation was influenced by current ideas of evolution and historical progress and by the emerging social sciences, particularly in England and France. In accordance with their ideas of organic development, and under the influence of Scandinavianism, this generation gave a more positive evaluation of the period under Danish rule and modified the idea of the Middle Ages as the period of Norwegian greatness. Typically, these historians, who were mostly conservatives, explained Norway's loss of independence in the Later Middle Ages by the poverty of the country, thus implying that even the earlier age of greatness was less glorious than assumed by their predecessors.

The greatest historian of the new generation, Ernst Sars was not a conservative, however, but a liberal. He continued the national tradition of Keyser and Munch and actively used history in the contemporary struggle for popular government and for greater equality for Norway in the union with Sweden. Sars, who was influenced by Comte and Buckle, was one of the great evolutionists of the nineteenth century, trying to explain the history of Norway by general laws. In contrast to Keyser and Munch, who focused on constitutional arrangements, Sars regarded social groups or classes as the driving forces in history.[5] These classes were not the result of the forces of production, as in Marxist thought, but were formed through culture and emotional ties. Sars accepted the main outlines of the historical narrative of Keyser and Munch. However, he tried to show that the shifting phases of Norwegian history were not the results of sudden or dramatic events, exaggerated demands by prelates, or more or less adequate "social engineering" on the part of the leaders of society, but were caused by social laws, so that one step in the development inevitably led to the next. Norway was originally the most aristocratic of the three Nordic kingdoms; therefore, it eventually became the most democratic. After the initial unification of the kingdom, the king had to seek close co-operation with the aristocracy in order to rule. The aristocracy, which had originally consisted of local leaders, thus developed into an exclusive class, an aristocracy of the realm, which ruled in co-operation with the king and eventually assumed the real power in the country. By so doing, however, the aristocrats undermined their own position, losing touch with the

5 Sars 1873–91.

ordinary population. This development then led to the monarchic revolution under Sverre and his successors, who created an absolute monarchy based on the support of the peasant population. The social structure resulting from this revolution became a weakness for Norway in the Later Middle Ages and the Early Modern Period, during which a strong state had to be based on a strong aristocracy. In Sars's own, democratic age, however, this weakness became a strength. The people were now ready to take over the government, through Sars's own liberal party, which was based on the farmers and led by liberal intellectuals, and which fought a conservative government of civil servants increasingly seeking the support of the king.

While Sars gives a typical example of a nineteenth-century evolutionary synthesis of history, his contemporary, Gustav Storm, represents another trend, that which became the dominant one at most European universities towards the end of the century: the learned, technical tradition. Storm continued the work of Keyser and Munch in editing the sources. His historical writings usually deal with very specific problems and are based on close reading of the sources, thus having a far more technical character than Sars's synthesis. In his attitude to the trustworthiness of the narrative sources, he follows in the footsteps of Munch, although with greater exactness and consistency, taking a more critical attitude to the saga tradition. As a university teacher, Storm was the most influential of his generation, introducing the new methods of seminar exercises, developed in Germany, in the same way as his Danish contemporary and colleague, Kristian Erslev.

In entirely different ways, Sars and Storm exerted a lasting influence on historical thinking and writing in Norway. Sars's great synthesis was widely read and formed the basis of the education of new generations in national history through textbooks and popular works until well after the Second World War. Storm contributed greatly to the formation of a small but important milieu of professional historians at the University of Oslo, who continued his critical study of the sources in a more radical way.

The Marxist period, 1910–1940

Despite Sars's and Storm's lasting influence, the most prominent among the next generation of historians, Halvdan Koht and Edvard Bull sen., largely developed their historical interpretation in opposition to their teachers. This marked the transition to the third, Marxist phase of Norwegian historiography. While Sars's historical synthesis was formed in close contact with the liberal party and the farmers' movement, Koht and Bull both belonged to the new, great political movement of the twentieth century, the labour movement. Both were active as politicians. Bull was one of the leaders of the Labour Party in its radical phase in the 1920s and was its first foreign minister (1928). Koht was foreign minister during its more moderate phase in the 1930s (1935–41).

As well as a new narrative of Norwegian history, Koht presented a radically new view of the sagas as sources. In a famous article, originally presented as a lecture in 1913, Koht maintained that the saga writers were real historians, in the same sense as Koht himself and his contemporaries.[6] Admittedly, previous scholars, and Storm in particular, increasingly stressed the saga writers' deliberate effort to reconstruct past events, analysing their use of sources and way of organizing the narrative. Koht went further, and attributed to the saga writers an overall interpretation of history, based on their experience of struggles and social conditions in their own age, and influenced by their attitude to the contemporary conflicts between the king, the aristocracy, and the Church. To some extent Koht's new approach may be regarded as a Norwegian parallel to the attempt of the Swedish historians Lauritz and Curt Weibull to make history really scientific by introducing rigorous rules of source criticism; these rules caused the Weibulls to almost completely reject the sagas as sources for early medieval history.[7] Koht was less critical of the sagas than the Weibulls, and his re-evaluation had a different purpose. First and foremost, he wanted to replace an old synthesis of Norwegian history with a new one. In the long run, however, Koht's and the Weibulls' con-

6 Koht 1921.
7 L. Weibull 1911 etc. See also Torstendahl 1964 and Odén 1975.

tributions had similar effects, making historians more reluctant to use the sagas as sources, and more inclined to prefer documentary evidence.

Koht's reinterpretation of the sagas was influenced by the Marxist view of intellectual life being determined by political, social, and economic conditions. It was also intimately linked to Koht's Marxist revision of the main lines of conflict in Norwegian history. Although there were at times violent conflicts between the king, the aristocracy, and the Church, particularly during the age of Sverre at the end of the twelfth century, the main thread in the country's history was co-operation and alliance between these powers. The picture Sars and his predecessors had found in the sagas of an almost continuous struggle between the king and the magnates was the saga writers' own construction, based on their experience from an exceptional period of conflict between the king and the aristocracy, the age of Sverre (1177–1202).

In a number of works, Koht as well as Bull brought forward a new synthesis, which later received its most systematic expression in Andreas Holmsen's survey of Norwegian history until 1660, which combined the Marxist ideas of his teachers with his own research on settlement and agrarian history.[8] This book remains the starting-point for a general interpretation of Norway in the Middle Ages, despite frequent criticism. For Holmsen, demographic growth from the eleventh century until the Black Death in 1349 gives the key to the social, economic, and political history of the country. Considering the relation between population and resources, Norway was already overpopulated by the twelfth century. This situation forced the peasants to become tenants under great landowners, and this in turn created increasing social divisions. Antagonism between classes produced the internal struggles of the twelfth and the early thirteenth century; the main line of division was between the great landowners on the one hand, and the ordinary peasants together with pauperized proletarians on the other. The latter won a temporary victory with Sverre at the end of the twelfth century. However, this victory merely resulted in the formation of a new aristocracy of upstarts, which eventually

8 Holmsen 1939.

made peace with their adversaries in the period after Sverre's death. This united aristocracy took over political power during the age of greatness in the thirteenth century, using the king as their puppet. Thus there was no victory of the monarchy over the aristocracy in the thirteenth century. Nor could the subsequent decline of the country be explained by royal absolutism. Its real cause was the Black Death, which all of a sudden changed the relationship between land and population. When the plague cut the population by half, land became abundant. A large number of farms were deserted and land rents dropped to about one-fifth of the pre-1349 level. A large proportion of the landowners were reduced to poverty, and the material basis for an independent Norwegian state disappeared.

This interpretation of Norwegian history conforms to Marxist thought, in which social classes and their conflicts and alliances are seen as determined by economic conditions. Agriculture was the foundation of the Norwegian economy in the Middle Ages, with land the most important source of wealth. Hence landowners had fundamental common interests against the workers, the peasants. In its attitude to the state and the ages of greatness and decline, as well as in its narrative of Norwegian history, this synthesis seems to be in sharp opposition to that of Sars and his predecessors. This divergence is not as great as it may appear at first glance. Both Koht and Holmsen – though not Bull – shared the national attitude of their predecessors. They were quite positive to the strong state of the thirteenth century and they lamented the decline of the following period, despite the "liberation" of the peasants. To Koht, the class basis of the Norwegian state of the thirteenth century did not prevent it from being the first step towards the strong, democratic state of Koht's own age. Koht regarded the development of the state as a process of gradual integration, including the aristocracy in the Middle Ages, the bourgeoisie in the Early Modern Period, the peasants in the nineteenth century, and the workers in the twentieth century. Koht's and Holmsen's work also bears resemblance to Sars's great synthesis in other ways, in their definition of the classes, and in their way of finding general lines and continuity during periods of apparently revolutionary change.

Unlike Koht, Bull stood in opposition to the national interpretation of Norwegian history. He was not particularly interested in the state, which he regarded as only one of several factors in the history of society. Politically, Bull was the more radical and probably more "orthodox" Marxist. On the other hand, he was first and foremost engaged in concrete, empirical studies, often without great relevance to Marxist theory. In this way he continued Storm's critical work with the sources. Although he made important contributions to the Marxist synthesis of Norway's history, Bull's main achievement lies in his work on economic, social, and institutional history. In his first book, his doctoral dissertation, he dealt with popular religion and with the Church and its relationship to the people in Norway in the Middle Ages.[9] Bull's main thesis was that the ordinary population was not really converted to Christianity and that there was an antagonistic relationship between the peasants and the clergy. This conclusion was based on general assumptions about the character of peasant religion rather than on specific Norwegian evidence, and has generally not been accepted by later historians. The main importance of this book rests with its detailed examination of various institutional aspects of the Church and religion and of their relationship to the peasant population. Bull subsequently became a pioneer in a field that is still very important for Norwegian medievalists, namely agrarian history and the history of settlement.

Norwegian development at this point seems to parallel the rise of the French Annales school. There is indeed some direct connection. Bull met Marc Bloch at the International Congress of Historians in Oslo in 1928 and invited him to a longer stay there. Bloch then spent four or five months in Oslo in 1931 and also published his book *Les caractères originaux* there. The most specific parallel between Bloch and the Norwegian school is the use of the retrospective method: the idea of immobile or slowly changing institutions and structures allows the scholar to draw conclusions on the past from far later sources. This method was developed in Norway well before Bloch's visit and was used with considerable success by Asgaut Steinnes in his book on taxation in the Middle Ages.[10]

9 Bull 1912.
10 Steinnes 1928–31.

Whether Bloch was inspired by his Norwegian hosts, and the nature of the exchange of ideas which took place, is still to be determined: there are no detailed studies on Bloch's stay in Oslo or on the connection between Norwegian and French scholarship during this period.[11] Apparently, however, such contacts as were established in 1931 were short-lived; this may in part be due to Bull's death in 1932. The pattern seems to have been of a parallel development in two historical milieux rather than of direct interconnection. Significantly, the position of agrarian history differs in the two countries. The Annales school was originally strongly opposed both to the established historiographical tradition and to the centralization of French political and intellectual life in Paris. By contemporary French standards, the historians of this school took an almost revolutionary step by rejecting studies on the state, the nation, and central institutions in favour of research on the peasants and the countryside. By contrast, the Norwegian school of agrarian history – with Bull as an exception – continued the national tradition of the last century. Peasant studies were clearly compatible with national history in a country where the nation had largely been identified with the peasants. One of the particular attractions of agrarian history was that it helped resolve the crucial problem of Norwegian medieval history: the country's decline and loss of independence in the Later Middle Ages.

The new empiricism, 1940–1975

After Bull's death, and particularly after the Second World War, the leading agrarian historian was his pupil Andreas Holmsen. Holmsen made several important contributions to the field, and together with a number of pupils made agrarian history the main field of medieval historiography until well into the 1970s. The importance of the Marxist interpretation gradually declined within Holmsen's school. This development can be interpreted as the result of political changes – the socialist party became less radical – but also as a new paradigm becoming "normal science", in

11 For a comparison of the two schools, with a short comment on the question of influence, see Sandnes 1981.

Kuhn's terminology.[12] Holmsen and his pupils conducted often very technical empirical studies, on the extent of settlement and cultivated land and on the distribution of landownership. Above all they studied the demographic and agrarian crisis of the Later Middle Ages. This crisis also became the theme of the largest enterprise of the school, the Nordic project on deserted farms, involving scholars from the five Nordic countries. This work began in the 1960s and concluded in 1981 with the publication of a common report in English.[13] Agrarian history continued to play a central role in following years, and larger areas of the country became the subject of detailed research on settlement, economic conditions, distribution of property, and social structure. The founding of the University of Tromsø in 1968 brought a revival of such studies of Northern Norway.

Not all of Bull's pupils became agrarian historians. Johan Schreiner dealt with a variety of historical problems but took a great interest in political history. He sought in the beginning of his career to understand political conflicts through the Marxist theory of the class struggle. Later on he focused more directly on conflicts within elite groups. A third pupil – and no doubt the most important – Jens Arup Seip is now known chiefly for his work on the nineteenth century. But he started as a medieval historian, producing several brilliant studies on this epoch. In one of his early works, he attacked the Marxist interpretation of Norwegian history, while at the same time adhering to what he considered "the fundamental ideas of this theory".[14] His criticism was mainly directed against the idea of the king as an instrument of the landowning aristocracy. Seip argued for the relative independence of the individual kings, as well as of the monarchy as an institution, in balancing the various classes of society. The general implications of these arguments were, firstly, that the evidence of the sources should be used to modify theories to a greater extent than Marxists had done in Seip's opinion, and, secondly, that the politi-

12 For an account of this development, together with an excellent presentation of the school, see Salvesen 1982.
13 Gissel *et al.* 1981.
14 Seip 1940.

cal sphere was not as directly determined by social and economic conditions as Marxists assumed. Rather than acting according to their position within the Marxist social division, as landowners or peasants, people identified themselves with more limited group interests, i.e. as members of the clerical or lay aristocracy, as royal servants, and so forth. Nor were such group interests incompatible. Consequently, some interests were common to society as a whole. This meant that society needed to be studied as a system of functions, in accordance with the ideas of the English constitutional historians of the beginning of our century, such as Maitland, and possibly also in accordance with the ideas of the social sciences of the inter-war period. This conclusion contradicted not only the Marxist view but also the nineteenth-century Norwegian tradition of legal and constitutional history, which mainly focused on formal arrangements and constitutional issues in the study of political institutions.

Seip's article had few immediate consequences, probably because of the dominance of agrarian history. Twenty years later, however, a young historian at the new University of Bergen, Knut Helle, developed Seip's criticism of the Marxist school.[15] Helle attacked the idea of the king as an "instrument" of the agrarian aristocracy and concluded by expressing a general scepticism about "the grand theories of Norwegian history". He considered that there were at the time too many theories and too little empirical research. Detailed studies were urgently needed to find out "what we know and what we do not know". This message corresponded to an attitude widespread among younger historians, even those belonging to the agrarian school. Specialization and empiricism were the dominant ideas. Generally, after the Second World War, in Norway as elsewhere, there was a strong belief in objective research and in the duty of the scholar to refrain from allowing religious, political, or other convictions to interfere with his or her work. This attitude, a reaction to the totalitarian movements of the pre-war period, was critical not only of Marxist thought but also of the use of history in the formation of a national identity.

15 Helle 1960.

The 1960s were a period of expansion for medieval history, as they were for research and universities in general. With the expansion of the University of Bergen (founded in 1946) and the foundation in 1968 of two new universities, Trondheim and Tromsø, and with the rise of regional colleges during the 1970s, the number of medievalists rose considerably. The combination of more scholars in the discipline with stronger specialization produced a number of articles and monographs on various problems in medieval history from the 1960s onwards. A significant proportion of this work was conducted by graduate students in the form of theses. While agrarian history had dominated during the period before 1960, the field of study now widened considerably.

Helle's own book on the royal government from 1150 to 1319 may be regarded as the fulfilment of Seip's programme from 1940.[16] It examines in detail the various groups of men the king consulted when ruling the country ("the good men", "wise men", etc.) and their organization in assemblies and councils. Helle convincingly demonstrated that these counsellors were too loosely organized to form a real government, dominating the king. However, he did not examine the wider question of the function of the monarchy within society as a whole; he confined himself to the forms of political decision-making rather than dealing with the interests served by government policy. Though she did not address these general questions, Grethe Authén Blom studied an important part of the content of the monarchy's political decisions over a long time scale in her book on royal privileges from the beginning until 1387.[17]

The study of *political thought* was initiated by Johan Schreiner in the 1950s and continued by Torfinn Tobiassen, Erik Gunnes, and Sverre Bagge.[18] Some of these studies also treated *Church history*. In addition Arne Odd Johnsen, Vegard Skånland, and Lars Hamre have dealt with various, mainly political, aspects of ecclesiastical history. There is a strong tradition in Norway for studying the Church mainly insofar as it was in conflict with the state or in other

16 Helle 1972.
17 Blom 1967.
18 For this and the following, see Helle 1981 and Bagge 1987.

ways relevant to it. *Urban history* became a prominent field during this period, partly because of excavations in medieval towns like Bergen, Oslo, Trondheim, and Tønsberg, and partly as the result of towns celebrating anniversaries. In the period 1956–91 the history of the medieval towns of Trondheim, Bergen, Stavanger, and Oslo were written. The *history of trade*, and particularly of the dominance of the Hanseatic League in the Later Middle Ages, was treated by Schreiner in several works from the 1930s onward. Schreiner wrote mainly from an anti-Hanseatic point of view, as a contribution to the understanding of the decline of the country. Urban history, and especially the history of Bergen, greatly stimulated Hanseatic studies. In accordance with the prevailing ideal of objectivity, the new generation of scholars sought a more balanced understanding of the role of the Hanseatic merchants. They stressed the merchants' positive contribution to the economic development of Norway, though without neglecting the old question of the important role they played in the political decline of the country by preventing the rise of a Norwegian merchant class. The most important study was Arnved Nedkvitne's research on Norwegian trade in the Later Middle Ages and the sixteenth century, which presented a new picture of the subject. Through systematic quantification, admittedly based on fairly meagre source material, Nedkvitne assessed the relative importance of trade for the Norwegian economy, its changing volume and value, and Norway's position in the Hanseatic trade network.[19]

Chronologically, the period of Norwegian greatness – the High Middle Ages – attracted more interest than the periods before or after, and was certainly the subject of more varied studies. The Later Middle Ages were a central interest of agrarian and Hanseatic historians, but there were few studies of the political history of the period. The main exception to this is Lars Hamre's work on political, legal, and ecclesiastical history. His pupil Steinar Imsen has also contributed to the study of late medieval political history. Recently Imsen and Grethe Authén Blom have extensively studied the central and local government of the Later Middle Ages. They discern considerable continuity in this field from the High Middle

19 Nedkvitne 1983.

Ages, and thus reject the view widespread among agrarian historians of an almost total breakdown in the second half of the fourteenth century, resulting from the Black Death and the agrarian crisis.[20] The Early Middle Ages and the Viking Age remain the most neglected field within medieval history in Norway. This probably results from the difficulties involved in using the sources from this period, following the devastating attack on the trustworthiness of the sagas at the beginning of this century. Remaining sources, such as Scaldic poetry, the law codes, and archaeological sources, for the most part demand highly technical skills. The period has therefore been studied more by archaeologists, and by philologists, than by historians. The most prominent scholars in this field in recent decades have been Per Sveaas Andersen and Claus Krag.[21]

Despite the historians' reluctance towards getting involved in the technicalities necessary to study early medieval history, contact with disciplines like philology and archaeology has undoubtedly increased during the period of empiricism. Contact with archaeology has been stimulated notably by the study of urban history. Greater emphasis on thorough and accurate reading of sources has encouraged historians to seek greater acquaintance with philology and languages, which has led to joint efforts by historians and philologists to continue the nineteenth-century tradition of editing and making available source material.

Compared with the periods before and after, the period of empiricism was relatively uninterested in connections between Norway and other countries in the Middle Ages, and in comparative international research. Both Koht and Bull systematically tried to develop international contacts, but a certain isolation of Norwegian historical research seems to have begun around 1930, after Bull's death. Seip gave a theoretical justification for this, in accordance with his functionalist point of view: foreign influences were less important than local conditions in understanding social phenomena.[22] The emphasis on detailed empirical research gener-

20 Imsen 1990; Blom 1992.
21 Anderson 1977; Krag 1991.
22 Seip 1940.

ally did not stimulate comparison or the search for new theoretical insight abroad. There are, however, some exceptions. Johan Schreiner and Arne Odd Johnsen studied the relationship between Norway and other countries in several areas. The agrarian historians eventually developed contacts with scholars in Germany, Great Britain, and elsewhere, who also studied deserted farms and villages and the crisis of the Later Middle Ages. Knut Helle's study of the royal government incorporates a detailed comparison with other countries, while studies of political thought often sought to trace the European origin of the ideas occurring in Norwegian sources, and to compare Norwegian political thought with that of other countries.

The period of empiricism was above all a period of extensive research, during which our knowledge of medieval Norway was widened in several fields. It is difficult to identify a general interpretation of Norwegian history common to this generation of scholars, but a few trends may be indicated. On the one hand, there was a widespread reaction against the Marxist synthesis of the previous period, and notably against seeing politics exclusively as the consequence of economic conditions and the class struggle. This reaction resulted in a modification of the Marxist theory on specific points, rather than an alternative theory. On the other hand, the extensive research carried out by the school of agrarian historians led to increased emphasis on the economic factors influencing the history of the country, and particularly on the agrarian crisis as the cause of its decline in the Later Middle Ages.

The social sciences and the history of mentalities, c. 1980–

According to the empiricist tradition, dominant in the post-war period, it is sufficient to study sources carefully, without being influenced by prejudices or ideological attitudes, in order to reach an adequate understanding of the past. Such studies can then draw conclusions on the basis of common sense. Implicitly, this entails an assumption that medieval people were governed by a similar common sense, and that their institutions, ideas, and actions could be understood either as an adaptation to practical conditions or as the expression of individual or group interests.

Opposition to this interpretation started in the 1970s and grew in the 1980s and 1990s. Kåre Lunden's volume on the period 1177–1319, which appeared in the general history of Norway published by Cappelen in the 1970s, forms an early example. Here he contended that the mentality of the period was completely different from our own, as were the material and social conditions.[23] In practice, however, his work was above all a renaissance of Marxist historiography. According to Lunden, the suppression of the majority of the population by the dominant class was even worse than Holmsen and his teachers had maintained. In stressing the importance of military dominance in establishing this suppression, Lunden departed from the idea of the older generation of Marxists, who had held that social and political conditions were determined by the forces of production. Lunden regarded the political system at least partly as an independent variable. He also differed from the earlier Marxists in interpreting the internal struggles as struggles within the aristocracy, and in seeing the strong aristocratic government of the thirteenth century as the solution to this internal crisis.

Despite the "students' revolution" starting in 1968, which took a more moderate form in Norway than in countries like Germany, France, and the United States, this Marxist renaissance remained a fairly isolated phenomenon. Another political movement of the 1970s, the women's movement, had important consequences for Norwegian historiography as a whole. It was somewhat less significant for the study of medieval history, although some articles and theses on medieval women in Norway have appeared since the 1970s.[24] In general, new impulses in medieval history have come from other scholarly disciplines rather than political movements. The most important of these has been social anthropology. Kåre Lunden made an early attempt to analyse medieval Norway through social anthropological theories, principally those of Polanyi.[25] Lunden's

23 Lunden 1977.
24 See the surveys by Øye 1990 and Fløystad 1990.
25 Lunden 1972.

book was not very influential at the time of its publication. Since the 1980s, however, Norwegian medievalists have been increasingly influenced by social anthropology. At approximately the same time, the French Annales school was "discovered" by Norwegian historians. Without leading to a total change, these influences forced Norwegian historians to pose the fundamental questions of the relationship between a "universal human nature" and the particular mentality of a given society, and in particular, to consider religion, political thought, economy, and institutions in a different way. The sources and the Norwegian historiographical tradition are no longer sufficient; international and comparative studies have become necessary.

Several examples of these new trends can be mentioned. In another volume of Cappelen's general history of Norway, Ole Jørgen Benedictow commented on popular and aristocratic mentalities of the Later Middle Ages, seeking among other things to depict the psychological effects of the plagues and other crises of the epoch.[26] His most recent works deal with demography and the plague, and encompass both the contemporary attitudes to these phenomena and the customs and social relationships which serve to explain the spread of the disease in a sparsely populated country.[27] Lunden has applied the theories of Polanyi and Chayanov to Norwegian conditions in his studies on the peasant economy.[28] Jørn Sandnes from Trondheim, the former leader of the project on deserted farms, has published a short book on violence and crime in the Later Middle Ages and the Early Modern Period.[29] In the 1980s Sverre Bagge started work, mainly based on the sagas, on "political mentality". He examines political behaviour and the relationship between norms of loyalty and self-interest in a society governed by concepts of honour and shame, as well as changing concepts of society and social norms caused by the formation of a state in the thirteenth century.[30] Somewhat later Arnved Nedkvitne paid great attention to mentality and popular attitudes

26 Benedictow 1977.
27 Benedictow 1992.
28 Lunden 1974; Lunden 1978.
29 Sandnes 1990.
30 Bagge 1991; Bagge 1995.

in his history of Oslo.[31] Here he gives a vivid and detailed account of popular religion, inspired by the work of French historians like Jacques Le Goff, Jean-Claude Schmitt, and André Vauchez, and includes numerous comparisons with conditions in other European countries. During recent years studies of slavery and of Icelandic society during the Free State period have appeared, in which theories from social anthropology as well as from the history of mentality have been integrated.[32] Recent times have thus seen a renewal of social, religious, cultural, and political history. For political history the influence of social anthropology and the history of mentality seems to have led to a further movement away from the Marxist theory of the class struggle and its economic basis. Early Norwegian society is now increasingly understood as based on kinship, friendship, and personal loyalty, and historians try to trace how these ties were gradually replaced by more impersonal ones from the late twelfth century onwards. In this way, a new synthesis of the political system of Norway in the Middle Ages may be under way.

Greater interest in general social theory and in new impulses from the historiography of other countries has also led to a greater *internationalization* of medieval studies in Norway. Although the majority of Norwegian historians, of the Middle Ages as of other periods, still publish mainly in Norwegian, publications in other languages, notably English, have become more frequent. Younger historians more often go abroad to conduct comparative research, and there are a few examples of Norwegian medieval historians dealing with the history of countries other than Norway.

Conclusion

The story told on the preceding pages can be taken as one of a pendulum movement between periods of great syntheses and general theories, and periods of specialized research. This is no doubt an oversimplification. A more detailed examination of how various historians have treated particular problems shows a cumulative

31 Nedkvitne and Norseng 1991.
32 Sigurdsson 1993; Iversen 1994.

process, resulting in new knowledge and more refined methods and principles of interpretation. If we confine ourselves to the pendulum perspective, however, a certain parallel appears between the Norwegian historical school of the first half of the nineteenth century and the empiricism of the post-war period, with the period between standing apart. In the latest period, the influence from the social sciences and the history of mentality may be an indication that a new synthesis is under way. Such a synthesis must, of course, take into account the results of existing and future studies of the history of mentality, and also the work accomplished during the period of empiricism on agrarian, urban, and institutional history. In the present situation we can reverse Helle's statement from 1960: What we need most is not more detailed empirical studies, but rather new ideas and works of synthesis. And last but not least, medieval studies in Norway have to become more international. Not only will more systematic comparison with other countries produce new insight into Norwegian history, but a comparison with Norway and other countries in Scandinavia and the periphery of Europe generally will be an important contribution to the understanding of the Middle Ages in Europe. In this context we have not fully developed the implications of Seip's remark from 1940 – that the history of medieval Norway allows us to observe the birth as well as the death of a state. How can the observations from this laboratory be applied to the study of the emergence the state in Europe?

5. Norway in Union with Denmark[1]
Øystein Rian

This period in Norwegian history stretches from 1380, when the kingdoms of Norway and Denmark were united in a personal union under Olav IV. After his death the union was strengthened by his mother, Queen Margareta. Sweden joined in the 1390s, but it re-established its independence in the period 1448–1523, while the duchies of Slesvig and Holstein were firmly tied to the Danish–Norwegian polity. As the most sparsely populated of the kingdoms, Norway came to play a reduced role in government especially from 1536, when the Norwegian council of state became defunct, and Norway assumed the status of a dependent kingdom under the Oldenbourg dynasty. In 1660 the Danish council of state was also abolished, and Norway and Denmark were formally placed on equal footing in a single kingdom with Copenhagen as the seat of government. The union with Denmark was dissolved in 1814, when Sweden with the help of the Great Powers forced Frederik VI to concede Norway to the king of Sweden. The Norwegians set up their own Norwegian state in a loose personal union with Sweden.

National democrats and conservatives

Before 1814 historians were obviously unable to treat the period of union with Denmark as a completed whole. Moreover, most of the early historical research concentrated on the Early Middle Ages. The most important exception was Ludvig Holberg (1684–1754), who looked at recent Danish–Norwegian history in the seventeenth century and emphasized Norway's economic importance

---

1 Translated by Eamonn Noonan.

for the monarchy.[2] After 1814 it was important to show that Norway had deep historical roots down to Viking times and to the Norwegian state of the High Middle Ages. The period of union with Denmark came to be described negatively as a Danish oppression of Norway. The period was neglected in an era when historians concentrated on showing that which was genuinely Norwegian. An effort was, however, made to take account of archives from the Danish period, and in this connection some special studies closely based on sources appeared.

A new generation of historians in the 1860s were unhappy about the one-sided interest in the Middle Ages. They wished to integrate the period of union with Denmark into a complete picture of Norwegian history and to show how social conditions had developed right up to their own times. One of the most influential of this generation, the later national archivist Michael Birkeland (1830–96), stated in a lecture to Oslo students in 1866 that it was not the Vikings, but the men of the seventeenth and eighteenth centuries who were their fathers.[3] The idea that Norwegian history interacted with the rest of Scandinavia and Europe grew stronger. It arose from a Scandinavian student movement which favoured deeper co-operation between the Nordic countries.

Initially this was a uniform reaction against an earlier negligence. But the reaction split into a right-wing and a left-wing history, a Norwegian parallel to similar splits in other European countries. Right-wing history included a circle of historians who belonged to the class of senior officials which at the time provided Norway's political and economic leaders. The ancestral roots of this elite lay in the bureaucratic and mercantile upper class of the period of union. They sympathized with the existing regime and had a sober attitude towards the union with Denmark.

The conservative historians mainly concentrated on specialist studies. Before Birkeland the most prominent studies of the union period were by T. H. Aschehoug (1822–1909), Ludvig Daae (1834–1910), and Yngvar Nielsen (1843–1916). They emphasized the economic and demographic conditions which helped

2 Holberg 1732–35.
3 Birkeland 1919:101–13.

explain how Norway came as the subordinate partner into union with a neighbouring country. The population was so small, the aristocracy so sparse and weak, and the crown's income so low that a separate polity could not be maintained.[4]

The conservatives were not especially interested in distinguishing between Norwegian and non-Norwegian elements, and they researched the history of the nobility, officials, and burghers – all immigrant-dominated groups as they developed in Norway from the sixteenth century. They stressed the importance of foreign trade for the Norwegian economy and for the development of the administration towards a modern state. They took an interest in cultural history, often in miniature, especially with insights into urban and official circles,[5] though also with sympathy for agrarian culture.

This provided an important impulse for work with folklore, ethnology, and museums. The more practical part of this work, notably the establishment of museums, was able to unite right and left wings in a joint endeavour. Both sides stimulated local history research, which for a long time focused mainly on the seventeenth and eighteenth centuries, where sources were richer than from earlier centuries. The conservative historical school in Norway was not one in favour of agitation; the tendency was to seek harmony. The relation of authorities to the general population, for instance, was generally seen as administrative rather than political.

The split among historians occurred during the strong politicization of Norway from around 1870. The left conquered political power in 1884 and propounded a national democratic view of society and history. Influenced by Darwinism, Johan Ernst Sars (1835–1917) furnished the left with a teaching of historical development which resembled Whig history in England.[6] When the kingdom and a denationalized nobility organized a Scandinavian union, this was marked by external, non-Norwegian forces. The officials and burghers who established themselves in Norway in the sixteenth and seventeenth centuries were in the main foreigners and were influenced by a foreign culture. That which came to save Norway from eradication was the farmers, who kept the national

4 Aschehoug 1866; Nielsen 1880.
5 Daae 1871.
6 Sars 1873–91; Butterfield 1931.

genius alive from the Middle Ages to modern times. They were the constant factor in Norwegian history. They were strong, while the upper class was weaker than in other countries. When the new elite put down roots in Norway, ideals of freedom and equality induced in them an enthusiasm for the free Norwegian farmer, in a reawakened patriotism in the second half of the eighteenth century. On this basis the elite carried out the work of liberation in 1814. In the following generations the left-wing movement bore forward the heritage of 1814 by democratizing all social institutions.

Sars's interpretation had a strong general influence, particularly through school textbooks. While Sars allowed the new elite quite a positive role in nation-building, his socialist heir as the ideologue of national democracy, Halvdan Koht (1873–1965), was more negative. In Koht's version of Norwegian history from 1380 to 1814, the farmers were exploited and struggled stubbornly against a more uncomprehending ascendancy.[7] But in some of his specialist studies, we find more nuanced accounts, which show that Koht stressed the importance of the economic, bureaucratic, and cultural growth which laid the basis for the later building of the Norwegian nation. He also wrote many perceptive biographical articles about historical protagonists.[8]

Pragmatic approaches

The Labour Party won power in 1935. In spite of ideological kinship, however, the national democratic interpretation lost ground from the 1920s and 1930s. Leading historians embraced historical materialism, and on that basis they came to carry forward the conservatives' emphasis on economic studies. This contributed to a much shorter distance in research than in politics to men who sympathized with the right. Foremost among these was Oscar Albert Johnsen (1876–1954), who mainly worked on economic and administrative history, and who did much for local history research.[9]

7 Koht 1926.
8 *Norsk bibliografisk leksikon* (Dictionary of Norwegian Bibliography).
9 Johnsen 1939.

The Marxist Edvard Bull sen. (1881–1932) also involved himself in local history research, with the emphasis on the agrarian economy and the growth of capitalism.[10] Although he was politically more radical than Koht, he was less politicizing as a historian and concentrated on critical analyses of sources. He encouraged comparative research in the history of the old agrarian society, with an international perspective. His students dominated the research of the next generation.

Sverre Steen (1898–1983) was the one who most regarded society as an organic whole. Like Sars he stressed long lines. Changes resulted from collective movements, not from individuals or sudden impulses. Steen elucidated this in the 1930s when he wrote no fewer than four volumes on the period 1500–1814 in a new history of Norway.[11] For Bull and Steen it was evident that the conservatives were right, in that union with Denmark resulted from inadequate resources for the maintenance of a separate Norwegian state. For the period from 1500 to 1814, Steen accorded much space to the growth of trade and the transition from tenant status to freeholding. He laid the main emphasis on two lines of development. A new social class, whose ancestors were foreigners, established a new business life geared to a steadily increasing foreign trade. This class raised a stronger state authority, which intervened in an increasing number of areas. At the same time conflicts appeared between agrarian society and capitalist urban society.

Studies in the economic history of agrarian society came to dominate from the inter-war period up to the first generation after 1945. Andreas Holmsen (1906–89) led this research milieu, in which Asgaut Steinnes (1892–1973), Halvard Bjørkvik (b. 1924), and Jørn Sandnes (b. 1926) were also important contributors to the Norwegian agrarian historical paradigm.[12] This involved in part studies of the development of various settlements, inspired by the old national problem: why did Norway cease to be a separate state in the Late Middle Ages? Retrospective studies of land registers and tax lists from the sixteenth and seventeenth centuries

10 Bull 1922–36.
11 Steen 1930–5.
12 Salvesen 1982:75–133.

indicated a marked reduction in the number of farms in the Late Middle Ages, and a strong expansion in settlement from the beginning of the sixteenth century and through the subsequent centuries.[13]

Studies in the history of land ownership were also central. Up to the eighteenth century, the practice of tenancy dominated, and researchers used the retrospective method in analyses of ownership registers from the seventeenth century to determine the distribution of ownership many centuries back.[14] They stressed the peculiar characteristics of the Norwegian system of dispersed holdings, and studied relations between owners and tenants. The transition to freeholding from the 1680s and the growth of the cotter class from around the same time was researched less systematically. Both these themes were, however, examined at the microscopic level, partly in local history works and partly in dissertations. In relation to settlement and ownership patterns, studies were made of agrarian society's production conditions, covering both farmers' activity in itself and their dealings with merchants.

Research of the history of the union period was increasingly marked by empiricism, with the strong conviction that it was possible to map out demographic and economic structures. This optimism was inspired by the modern social sciences, with their affinity for the methods of the natural sciences. Researchers examined extensive public accounts and quantified important economic and social conditions.

From the end of the 1960s, demographic studies grew naturally from this research strategy, attracted by the rich source material on population matters from the mid-seventeenth century onwards. Led by Sølvi Sogner (b. 1932) and Ståle Dyrvik (b. 1943), this research has shown how families organized their existence by adapting marriages to possibilities for a livelihood,[15] analysed demographic crises,[16] and demonstrated migration patterns in advance of industrialization and emigration to America.[17] Demog-

13 Sandnes and Salvesen 1978.
14 Bjørkvik and Holmsen 1972.
15 Dyrvik 1978.
16 Dyrvik et al. 1976.
17 Sogner 1979.

raphy of the seventeenth and eighteenth centuries in Norway has in later years combined empiricism with an increasingly qualitative approach to the sources. This has occurred in work on women's history, children's history, and family history. Women's history has to a large extent taken up legal historical issues, such as women's legal status in marriage and in society, their liability to accusation and punishment in sexual matters, and so on. Research in recent years has drawn an optimistic picture of the social position of Norwegian women in the Early Modern Period.

A blossoming of the number of both teaching and research institutions in the last twenty years has stimulated a regionalization of history research. The University of Tromsø, for example, has led the way in the investigation of the history of Northern Norway. Some of the earliest regional histories in the 1970s and 1980s concerned counties or smaller districts. One chose to examine the Early Modern Period, partly because many local histories have been completed for this period, and partly because the source material was favourable for such a project. The results showed that the regional histories of the period give us a sharper and more nuanced picture of economic and political relations between differing social strata.[18]

In the period up to the 1970s, there was a growing trend to tone down interest in the significance of nationality in Norwegian history. Interest for political history in this period was already weak. Both Norwegian and Danish historians regarded the common capital, Copenhagen, as a purely Danish city. Danish historians included the government in their research, though generally under the misleading impression that this involved a purely Danish political system also before 1814. Edvard Holm, professor at Copenhagen University in the decades around 1900, was the most important exception.[19] Norwegian historians interested themselves unsystematically in the interaction between the government apparatus in Copenhagen and the various interest groups in Norway.

From the 1960s this began to change. In his studies of administration, Rolf Fladby (b. 1918) carried out the inheritance of O. A.

18 Lindbekk 1978; Rian 1980; Døssland 1990.
19 Holm 1891–1912.

Johnsen.[20] Many examinations of county administration led by Lars Hamre (b. 1912) drew a picture of Danish district officials who were far more integrated in Norwegian society than earlier research had indicated.[21] In the 1970s Knut Mykland (b. 1920) took the initiative for a research project which mapped out in a Nordic comparison the influence of population groups on the government under absolutism.[22] The project showed in the 1980s that Norwegian social strata below the nobility exercised more influence on the government than the corresponding Danish groups. In their contributions to the general Norwegian histories written in the 1970s and 1980s, Mykland and Dyrvik drew an optimistic picture of the development of Norwegian society.[23] In an economic history produced in 1979 to which Dyrvik and Stein Tveite (b. 1930) were the leading contributors, this interpretation was further strengthened.[24]

Tax and the nature of government

The nature of the rule Norwegians lived under in the Danish period has been a central theme through two centuries. The question of how heavy taxation was has been central in the debate. The tax burden has been difficult to evaluate, largely because our knowledge of production is based on schematic tax assessment material.

In the first generation after 1814, the broad consensus was that Norwegians were exploited economically. The conservative historians of the nineteenth century disagreed with this interpretation. In Sars's national democratic synthesis, the picture was one of moderate exploitation, while this was markedly more serious in Koht's version. Empiricists from the 1930s to the 1960s concentrated on measuring taxation, and hardly addressed how much of a burden it was. In the 1970s Mykland, Dyrvik, and Tveite reached

20 Fladby 1963.
21 Rian 1975.
22 The Nordic research project "Central power and local society – the decision-making process in the eighteenth century". Publ. 1-6, Oslo 1982–5, Malmö 1994.
23 Dyrvik 1978; Mykland 1978; Mykland 1987.
24 Dyrvik et al. 1979.

the conclusion that the pressure of taxation was light. Kåre Lunden (b. 1930) contested this view.[25] He claimed that economic growth in the period was not related to the union, but was due to demand for Norwegian goods on European markets. Growth in Norway was inhibited because of steadily increasing taxation pressure, and because well over half of these taxes were used in Denmark. Debate continued through the 1980s, with more nuanced contributions as the participants gradually refined their interpretations.[26] I stressed the need to divide the long time-span into periods, since the pressure of taxation varied greatly, and also the need to distinguish the varying impact of taxation between geographical areas and taxpayer groups.[27]

In recent years a certain consensus has emerged with regard to the chronology of the question. The great escalation of taxation took place from the 1620s, and ebbed away at the conclusion of the Great Northern War in 1720. Young researchers have in recent years devoted increased attention to the impositions policy of the nobility in regard to tenant farmers. They have shown that such impositions were higher than earlier assumed.[28] On the other hand, a number of historians have also shown that public accounts and registers do not cover the entirety of actual production in Norway. Johan Schreiner (1903–67) showed in the 1930s that the export of lumber from Norway was significantly underestimated, a point which was later confirmed by other researchers. Indications were also supplied to the effect that farmers paid much less than complete tithes, and that the tax registers underestimated the potential of agriculture and forestry. This was related to the fact that the officials in charge of registration and taxation themselves participated in business life; they were not interested in letting the central authorities know its full extent.[29]

A counterfactual approach is implicit in the discussion on tax levels: to what extent would conditions have been significantly different if Norway had been a separate state? But the chief trend in

25 Lunden 1980.
26 *Heimen* 1/1981:67–114.
27 Rian 1992.
28 Hosar 1981.
29 Schreiner 1934; Kjærheim 1958; Jørgensen 1969; Rian 1992.

research has clearly been to show that the union was materially unavoidable, in the light of Norway's limited and dispersed resources at the start of the Early Modern Period. That the capital remained Copenhagen has generally been taken as an indication that the monarchy was Danish, and those who interpreted the union negatively have stressed the draining of Norwegian resources to Denmark. This is an irrefutable point, since between one-half and two-thirds of recorded state revenues in Norway were transferred to the government in Copenhagen, which used these funds in the city and in its immediate hinterland. Those who have most emphasized this point have drawn a picture of Norway as a Danish colony.

Historiographically, Norway's status in this joint polity has been more explicitly discussed in relation to the question whether the Norwegian kingdom was abolished in the Danish period. Christian III's Danish coronation charter of 1536 stated that Norway should no longer be a realm, but a part of Denmark. The debate about the paragraph on Norway has in part revolved around the intention of this resolution. Historians of all shades have always agreed that the main issue for the king and for the Danish aristocracy was to create a common state and to secure Norway for the regime.

Considerable disagreement has, however, arisen about the extent to which the paragraph on Norway was implemented. It was never proclaimed to Norwegians or to foreign powers, and was never subsequently repeated. But the first generation of historians after 1814 emphasized that it was in the main implemented, in that a unified state was established under Danish dominance. No one has disagreed completely with this, but significant differences have ever since persisted among both Norwegian and Danish historians in the interpretation of the administrative, judicial, and civil law consequences of the change of regime in 1536. Curiously, historians of both the conservative and national democratic schools (Aschehoug, Birkeland, Nielsen, Sars, and Koht) agreed that Norway continued as a separate realm, with its own social order within the framework of the common state. Koht, however, laid more stress than Sars on the central point that the Norway paragraph was intended to clear a path for the Danish nobility to gain access to Norwegian fiefs.

In the 1930s there was a growing inclination to focus attention on the king's motives. Historians laid particular emphasis on his relation to leading princes, to the Emperor Charles V and his relatives (who saw Christian III as a usurper), and to the Swedish ruler Gustav Vasa, who wanted to expand his dominion westwards.[30] The debate on the status of the Norwegian realm has paralleled that on the position of the royal house in the polity. It is, of course, undisputed that the king made himself absolute ruler in 1660, but there have been differences about the power balance between the king and the Danish council of state in the period 1536–1660. Norwegian historians have generally accepted that the king was the supreme head of the administration, but they have taken it as given that his legitimacy was based on election by the council of state. Helge Kongsrud (b. 1946) has, however, shown that the royal house emphasized Norway's original succession law, and thus implied that Norway was a hereditary kingdom.[31] On this basis Lunden claimed that the constitutional position before 1660 was less clear than has generally been assumed. In his view the royal house's pretensions to succession rights is so significant that one cannot say definitively that Denmark–Norway was an elective monarchy. Both Kongsrud and Steinar Imsen (b. 1944) have challenged this conclusion. The latter has shown how the drift towards election occurred in the fifteenth century. Both Imsen and Kongsrud insist that the electoral order was valid in civil law until 1660, even though Kongsrud does accord the royal pretensions some political significance.[32]

This debate has also cast light on the fact that the king's interests were not identical with what we may, for the sake of simplicity, call Danish interests. For the dynasty it sufficed that Norway was a realm alongside Denmark. After the elimination of the Norwegian aristocracy, the royal house had a special position in Norway, and was thereby strengthened. In a little-noticed study of foreign policy, the Dane L. Laursen showed how Frederik III fought like a lion in the peace negotiations of the years 1657–60, in order to retain

30 Thowsen 1981.
31 Kongsrud 1984.
32 Lunden 1986; Imsen 1987; Kongsrud 1987.

as much of Norway as possible. At the same time he ceded nobility-dominated East Denmark to Sweden, without opposition.[33] Historians have been influenced by the fact that Denmark and Norway developed as democratic nation–states after 1814. Denmark, with Copenhagen as capital, was seen as the continuation of the state which before 1814, in abbreviated form, was also called Denmark and was described as Danish. Knut Mykland has stressed that Denmark–Norway was a princely ruled conglomerate state, similar to the one ruled from Vienna and Madrid by the Habsburg monarchs. He suggests that there is good reason to emphasize this even more than Danish and Norwegian historians have done to date. For the prince, the national identity of the subjects was of secondary importance. If we consider the three main population groups over whom the Oldenbourgs ruled, the capital was in this sense not Danish, but Danish–Norwegian–German.

The role of the people

The conservative and national democratic schools have in a curious way concurred on the question of how authority was managed in Norway. The king was in part a kind of people's tribune, receiving complaints and punishing officials who maltreated farmers. The difference rests in that national democrats, especially Koht and Lunden, have been pessimistic in regard to the king's possibilities to intercede against malpractice. Critique of the government's Danish character has meant that the king has indeed been regarded as the most Norwegian element in the government. This interpretation was arguably influenced to some extent by the patriotic tone of the regime's rhetoric, which flattered Norwegians by continually reminding them that they were the bravest and the most steadfast for both king and fatherland.

On the other hand, the central responsibility of a partly Norwegian royal power for the development of a strong and demanding state power has not been adequately emphasized. The king pushed forward the building up of the taxation regime and the military

33 Laursen 1920:215–43, 297–313, 345–76.

state against the opposition of the Danish council of state, which in 1660 was eliminated from the government because it stood in the way of the expansion of the state. In the 1980s a Scandinavian project, "State power/military state in the north in the sixteenth and seventeenth centuries", presented this development as part of the general strengthening of state power in Europe; the two Nordic countries went further than most others in mobilizing society's resources to their own ends.[34]

There is a paradox in the national democratic view that the people were accorded an apparently strong role in the life of society, though they were pushed aside from participation in government. The unceasing opposition of the peasantry ensured that its tormentors did not get away with exploitation without considerable discomfort. How such an exploited general populace could remain so stubbornly effective generation after generation is an unsolved problem, especially in Koht. Sars found an acceptable formula, in that the complaints of the farmers increasingly caused the authorities to correct disparities. Lunden also has more logic on his side than Koht: in Lunden's account exploitation plays a stronger part than the peasantry's attempts to oppose it.

Compared with the national democratic school, the conservatives had an easy time of it: the peasantry's great social activity was evidence of their favourable position. In their interpretation, the authorities took even greater account of complaints than in Sars. Historians of Holmsen's agrarian history school have concluded that the conflicts were small. This is most explicitly stated by Jørn Sandnes. Compared with resistance in neighbouring countries and in Norwegian history in the period 1150–1250, he suggests, "Norwegian peasants' resistance in the sixteenth century [was] little more than a ripple on an otherwise calm surface.... The most important reason [was] probably that the Norwegian peasant made good use of a strong and free position in the Danish period."[35]

Many historians of the eighteenth century, notably Mykland and Steinar Supphellan (b. 1939), have renewed and provided jus-

34 Rian 1985.
35 Sandnes 1990:92–118.

tifications for the conservative interpretation. The general populace achieved influence on the decision-making process through the petition procedure. This largely restrained the authoritarian character implied by the system's outer form. The Nordic project on relations between central power and local society in the eighteenth century showed that, through petitions, the population attained an influence which resembled that of the Swedes in the Riksdag system.[36]

One should, however, acknowledge that the time, place, protagonists, and issues involved were all of importance for the outcome. In Norway, too, those with greater resources found it much easier to provide for their interests. Many generations of historians stress this point in relation to the elaboration of the privileges of the higher estates. Production and trade privileges were of the greatest importance for those heavily involved in business. At the end of the 1950s, Lars Reinton (b. 1896) demonstrated, moreover, that in the eighteenth century the established farmers gained the support of local officials in their struggle against settlers disputing the farmers' rights in outlying areas and in commonage.[37] Other researchers later showed how the central authorities repeatedly had to adapt their regulations on forestry and the lumber trade to the main business actors: merchants, local officials, and timber-selling farmers.[38]

Research concentrating mainly on spectacular cases remains relevant, even though the trend of research in the 1970s and 1980s was towards the study of more mundane, everyday matters. The peasants' resistance to the supplementary tax in the 1760s, Christian Lofthus's peasant movement against the merchants' advances and against officials' fees in the 1780s, and Hans Nilsen Hauge's pietist movement after 1796 have all been thoroughly researched through the nineteenth and twentieth centuries. New studies in the 1970s about the history of the supplementary tax, led by Gudmund Sandvik (b. 1925), suggest that the farmers' pressure on the government to abolish this tax was suc-

36 Supphellen 1978.
37 Reinton 1955–61.
38 Eliassen 1972; Rian 1984:129–78.

cessful because it was supported by the Norwegian elite.[39] The Lofthus movement and the followers of Hauge met with much greater resistance, with tragic consequences for the two leaders, because large parts of the Norwegian elite turned against them. In relation to the government, I have in addition argued that cases can be seen as hierarchical. The government gave some cases such high priority that it brushed aside all resistance and implemented its wishes. This was so for the military cases from the mid-seventeenth century. It was so little concerned with other cases that the population attained considerable influence on what was done. This happened in cases about poverty or schools. Business cases stood in an intermediate position; compromises were worked out between the government's fiscal interests and the economic interests of social groups.

Legal history research has been amazingly weak in Norway, especially considering the dominant position law assumed from the start of the nineteenth century as a university discipline and in the education of senior officials. In the 1930s Jens Arup Seip (1905–92) showed how jurors acquired the task of passing sentences in the Late Middle Ages.[40] Steinar Imsen, inspired by German research in the history of agrarian communalism, later stressed that Norwegian farmers participated actively in local government in the Late Middle Ages, especially in legal functions such as juror and constable.[41]

It has, however, been usual to emphasize that from the end of the sixteenth century the authorities pushed the general populace aside and entirely took over the administration of justice. In the national democratic interpretation, this has been assumed into the picture of officials misusing their power to impose arbitrary and severe punishments, an interpretation accepted to some degree by all schools in relation to the seventeenth century. But many have stressed that the authorities answered the farmers' complaints with constitutional efforts, which started in the sixteenth century and which had growing effect from the end of the seventeenth

39 Sandvik 1975.
40 Seip 1934.
41 Imsen 1990.

century. This was initially accompanied by a sharpening of punishments, and from the 1730s by a liberalization.

The period in which punishments were becoming more severe poses a problem for historians, who have debated whether this was a development in the direction of a constitutional state. It has been shown how the authorities raked in fines, often after a purely arbitrary confrontation between constable and accused. An increasing number of activities were criminalized, notably sexual transgressions. The Church developed a system for controlling the moral conduct of the population. Hans Eyvind Næss (b. 1943) has shown that the persecution of witches ran riot from 1610 to 1670, and that torture was used as an interrogation method.[42]

On the other hand, the extent to which Church discipline and the application of criminal law changed the population's behaviour patterns is questionable. Traditionally – and most recently by Næss – it has been claimed that the violent criminality revealed by the sources from the sixteenth and seventeenth centuries indicates that the Reformation and accompanying social changes led to a dissolution of norms. On the other hand, it has been suggested, especially by Jørn Sandnes, that an evaluation of source material shows that the frequency of violence fell strongly from the start of the seventeenth century.[43] This may indicate that severe punishments and increased control caused people to restrain themselves more, a development which led to a later relaxation in interpersonal relations and thereby laid the foundation for a liberalization of the legal punishment regime.

There is broad agreement that the legal system developed towards a qualitatively higher standard in the last generations of the period of union with Denmark. Among other things a thorough and clear body of laws was compiled in understandable language, as Gudmund Sandvik sees Christian V's Norwegian law of 1687.[44] Stress has also been laid on the standardizing effect of the higher courts and the institution of pardon, combined with a raising of the educational level of judges: the office of judge in Nor-

42 Næss 1982.
43 Sandnes 1990.
44 Sandvik 1987.

way was attractive because of high fee income. Moreover, inspired by comparisons with the practices of modern dictatorships, a very positive significance has been accorded in recent years to the fact that court sessions took place completely in public, with jurors as assessors and with many villagers in attendance.

The view of 1814, when a separate Norwegian state was re-created, is relevant to the manner in which one regards the results of the union with Denmark. Some historians, especially Steen and Seip, lay the greatest emphasis on the idea that external forces forced through the transformation.[45] Others, notably Sars and Mykland, stress that the foundation of the state would not have been possible if a material and cultural basis had not been laid in the past.

Sars and other national democrats have stressed the advance of patriotic opinion in Norway from the 1760s and 1770s, with demands for a separate Norwegian bank, a separate university, and an end to the favouring of the Danish elite. The latter had greater opportunities for influencing the organs of government in the capital. The conservative nineteenth-century historians did not dispute that these were important matters, but they did not interpret them as expressions of a general discontent with the system. Steen and Mykland have adopted a similar position in this century. They have emphasized that the discontent of the elite was assuaged by periods of booming business, and that the farmers had very little grounds for dissatisfaction since the pressure of tax-ation was dampened by inflation. In Mykland's view the whole system had become so liberal that he finds the commentary of Mary Wollstonecraft, the English radical, accurate. She visited Norway in the 1790s and concluded that the Norwegians were the world's freest people.

Though there is disagreement on how deep dissatisfaction was in peacetime, there is a general consensus that Denmark–Nor-way's joining Napoleon's war against Britain in 1807 brought such great suffering and economic damage to Norway through the English blockade that Frederik VI's popularity was severely shaken, and Norwegian patriotism developed towards separatism.

45 Steen 1951; Seip 1974:15–60.

Economic and social conditions

In relation to purely non-political themes, it has not been so easy to distinguish the Danish period from the periods before and after, or to find evidence that its social conditions either gave rise to or arose from the political system. But the fall-and-rise theme has been politically coloured, and this has continually interested historians. This is particularly seen in settlement and population history. The desire to quantify these developments is linked to the fact that they have been regarded as fundamental for the fate of the whole nation. This theme has also aroused interest because it concerns the living conditions of ordinary people, an important point in the historical–materialistic tradition. The two perspectives have, however, been difficult to combine. The Late Middle Ages have been presented as a period of decline, a depiction inspired by the national perspective. As data have gradually been gathered showing how much feudal dues actually fell in this period, it has become necessary to stress that the development entailed an economic easing for the population.

Research has especially focused on settlement history. With the aid of this specialized discipline, we have come to a deeper understanding about basic production conditions in older times and about social development on the microscopic level. Although the retrospective method has so painstakingly quantified the development of settlement, it has been increasingly difficult to evaluate the numbers and to explain the changes they indicate. This has prompted a debate on methods.[46] Interest in quantifying developments in settlement has been linked to the fact that it was believed that relatively reliable indications of population size would thereby emerge. But in recent years there has been growing uncertainty about how many individuals were involved in each registered farm up to the start of the seventeenth century.[47]

There has also been uncertainty about why the expansion of settlement in the sixteenth century occurred and about what it entailed. This has in part led to its being described without an

46 Lunden 1979; Sandnes 1979; Lunden 1981.
47 Fladby 1986:68–83.

explicit discussion of its causes. When causes have been discussed, it has been usual to limit oneself to stating that this was due to a rise in population. Where attempts have been made to go further, one points to the probability that illness, and especially plague, was less devastating than in the Late Middle Ages. This has given rise to deeper research on plagues in recent years, with Ole Jørgen Benedictow (b. 1941) as the central figure.[48]

It has also been usual to point to the growth in supplementary occupations as a contributory factor in population growth: new trade possibilities in timber, mining, and fisheries gave many people a livelihood. None of this is particularly controversial. In recent years the main disagreement has concerned the role of the authorities in this expansion. Helge Salvesen (b. 1947) has claimed that they played an important role in stimulating and organizing the establishment of new farms, while Halvard Bjørkvik has objected that the rate of growth was alike in both mainly tenant farming districts and mainly freeholding districts.[49]

In the Norwegian historiographical tradition, there has been a fairly strong view that society comprised relatively homogeneous social strata, and that there were no more than four or five social strata. In the nineteenth century one generally operated with these simple distinctions, and many have carried them forward to the present century. This has applied especially to farmers, although the trend in the research of recent years is towards a perception of many levels within the farm sector. Local history works have contributed to this view in no small measure; Anna Tranberg's (b. 1939) work on the rich East Norwegian district of Ringsaker, for instance, shows that large farmers emerged as shrewd traders and conducted business almost according to capitalist principles right from the seventeenth century.[50] It is typical that more social distinctions within local societies have emerged as studies have analysed matters more closely. In latter years those who have commissioned local history research in specific municipalities have had a strong desire to uncover the living conditions of

48 Benedictow 1992.
49 Salvesen 1979; Bjørkvik 1983.
50 Tranberg 1993.

the ordinary people. This has also helped to develop a more nuanced picture of the social system of the old agrarian society. Local history research has further shown how varied and complex economic activities were. And this underpins the point that the greater the resources, the greater the influence people had on the authorities' implementation of legislation.

The trend towards more nuance has also emerged in the research on the history of the upper classes. The burghers have traditionally been regarded as a fairly homogeneous group, in that the bourgeoisie adopted a common position *vis-à-vis* other estates. Urban historians ever since Edvard Bull sen. have indicated how the grander bourgeoisie dominated trade. A series of new urban histories in recent years has deepened this picture of a grand bourgeoisie which took the lion's share of trade and especially of exports.[51] This has also increasingly been seen in the light of their contacts with the authorities. It has emerged that the greater part of those who made a career as merchants and property owners did so in combination with an office of state.[52] Interest in the Norwegian nobility has also grown in recent times. It seems that they were more dynamic than was earlier assumed, and that the Norwegian character of the nobility was more prominent than has traditionally been suggested.[53]

Economic history in this period has been marked by dominant interpretations, but also by debate on what kind of economy was involved, and notably on the extent to which subsistence and self-sufficiency were prominent characteristics. There has been tension between the view that trade was of great importance and the view that agrarian life generally was quite stable and untouched by this international economy. The Holmsen school reinforced the dominant trend from the last century, which was to suggest that farmers strove to produce as much as possible for their own consumption. They traded principally to gain the means to pay taxes, dues, debt repayments, and interest, as well as to meet their need for goods by the purchase of basic necessities. The great transition to

51 Fossen 1979; Sprauten 1992.
52 Reksten 1985; Rian 1985:337–63.
53 Weidling 1988.

trade-oriented production, according to this teaching, came around the mid-nineteenth century.[54]

Stein Tveite was the first to challenge this interpretation. Since the end of the 1950s, he has claimed that farmers produced that which did best, and he pointed to their considerable participation in trade.[55] Tveite and a growing band of followers have emphasized the great importance of additional occupations alongside agriculture. They have also been able to demonstrate that farmers in certain districts specialized in certain types of production for trade.[56]

The dominating historiographical tendency has been anti-capitalist. Trade was regarded with suspicion and it was felt that farmers were cheated by merchants. Even the nineteenth-century conservative historians were inclined to believe this. They belonged to the world of the officials who had long before distanced themselves from the merchants. It goes without saying that the socialist impulses of the twentieth century did not weaken anti-capitalism. Here too Tveite, together with Axel Coldevin (1900–92),[57] stood in the first rank of those challenging this interpretation. In their view, farmers were in the main strengthened by the growth of trade.

The view of commercial credit can be seen as the leading indicator of attitudes towards commerce. Traditionally it has been felt that farmers were pressed into a subordinate position in relation to merchants by this instrument; merchants used this leverage on farmers to force them to supply goods cheaply and to accept dear goods in payment, a process which could end in complete indebtedness. The alternative interpretation suggests a certain reciprocity between merchant and farmer, with the latter, moreover, being protected by the landowner, especially in Northern Norway. Credit was often a positive factor, in that it secured for the farmer necessary supplies in crisis years when agriculture failed, while the merchants did not exploit their debt leverage to dictate conditions more unfavorable than the usual.

54 Steen 1957; Holmsen 1982.
55 Tveite 1959.
56 Tranberg 1992:172–9.
57 Coldevin 1938; Dahl Bratrein 1972.

This interpretation has found support especially in research on commercial relations between merchants in Bergen and fisher–farmers in Northern Norway, most recently in a dissertation written by Arnved Nedkvitne (b. 1947).[58] The degree of traditionalism was probably significant: older commercial businesses had balanced relations to a greater degree than newer commercial business. Research has in any case shown that the new timber and mining businesses in the seventeenth century were more characterized by the dominance of merchants than the fisheries trade, and that the timber and mining trades developed towards more balance between merchant and farmer in the eighteenth century.[59]

The role of foreigners

The national democratic tradition has put a negative interpretation on the fact that such a large part of the upper class – both noble and bourgeois – was foreign. In Marxist analyses this has been seen as confirmation that what was happening was the faceless exploitation of the indigenous population by capitalism. The conservative historical school of the nineteenth century saw this as a lesser problem, an attitude which is rather akin to a prominent view of recent years, namely that immigrants also brought expertise into the country and thus gave positive impulses. This blends into the discussion of other problems. In purely economic terms, the question is whether one regards society as static or dynamic – whether the foreigners came and appropriated for themselves that which Norwegians would otherwise have had, or whether they as entrepreneurs created more economic activity, so that there was more to share.

In the history of mentalities, it is especially interesting to see to what extent the immigrants remained foreigners or became Norwegian. Some have placed strict conditions on who may be called Norwegian. Others have been more open to a broader definition of Norwegianness which allows a mixing of foreign and Norwegian

58 Nedkvitne 1988.
59 Holmsen 1946–71; Sejersted and Schou 1972.

influences. For Sars it was an important point that officials and merchants became Norwegian in that their families settled here, and that sons and daughters followed in their fathers' footsteps and became Norwegian patriots. He was therefore more disposed to accept the originally foreign upper class as Norwegian than the majority of his national democratic disciples. While empiricism in the 1930s contributed to a lessening of interest in this question among historians, there has been a renewed interest in recent years. Younger researchers have emphasized more than before that there were gradual transitions between the Norwegian and the foreign, first and foremost in that many foreigners married into Norwegian families and settled permanently in one district, where the family accordingly had all its business interests and where their children established themselves.[60]

Interest in people's national identity hangs together with a general renaissance or cultural history, inspired by the French Annales school. A cultural history tradition from the nineteenth century manifested itself. Up to the 1960s this was increasingly channelled into local history works. Sverre Steen was his generation's most important cultural historian, and this bent also marked his works on national history. Many community books contain a wealth of cultural historical material, some based on traditional material, notably from the eighteenth century. Community books have also drawn on court records, the foremost being Lars Reinton's book on Hol in Hallingdal.[61] With a reorientation towards history of mentalities, the use of court records has become more systematic in a project led by Sølvi Sogner.[62]

Conclusion

Norwegian history in this period has posed a particular problem, in that researchers have applied themselves to such a long period in which the kingdom's capital lay outside the country's borders. This has led partly to their giving a local anchoring to their inter-

60 Rian 1990.
61 Reinton 1938.
62 Marthinsen 1990; *Historisk tidskrift* 2–3/1991:149–351; publications of the Court Records Project 1992–4.

pretation, with links to economic and social history themes. In part the meeting of the Norwegian and the foreign has become an important theme. Relations between the centre and the periphery have been of major interest, in the relation between subjects and authority, between farmers and merchants, or indeed between the weak and the strong. That Norway was part of a larger whole, in commerce, economy, and politics, is a point of growing relevance to our own times, when European integration seems to be breaching the barriers between nation–states. This will perhaps lead to increased interest in Norway's long period of union.

6. Approaches to Modern Norwegian History[1]

Francis Sejersted

A confrontation

One may justly regard a confrontation with historicism as an important milestone in the development of the history discipline. Historicism entails that teleological elements of a metaphysical character are inserted in historical explanation. It is presumed that historical developments are predetermined, and that they have a purpose or meaning.[2] The actual historical explanation is thus given with reference to the future, rather than to the past, as is usual when explaining causality. Such teleological elements of predetermination have been very common and have been closely linked to a generally optimistic view of developments. In historical research in Norway, Ernst Sars is an outstanding example. He has been a dominant figure in Norwegian historiography. In his work, historical evolution points inexorably towards the accomplishment of a national democracy.

Teleological presentations of this kind were undermined by the influence of positivism as a scientific ideal from around the turn of

---

1 Translated by Eamonn Noonan. This chapter is a revised version of "Den truende idyll. Om de vekslende perspektiver i studiet av moderne norsk historie", in Langholm *et al.* 1994:229–49. The main difference is that the section "Syntheses and the perspective of genre" is new. The earlier version, furthermore, has more detailed notes and references. I wish to thank Jorunn Bjørgum and Kjetil Jakobsen for particularly valuable comments and contributions.

2 The concept "historicism" here is taken from Popper 1957, Norwegian ed. 1971. Popper distinguished this from "historism", which is associated with the historical school's rejection of general laws in history. Popper's critique of historicism is directed against Hegel and Marx in particular.

the century.[3] It is nevertheless accurate to state that clear evidence of this kind of thinking is to be found in the work of a historian such as Halvdan Koht, the dominant historian in Norwegian circles in the inter-war period. He could in this context draw on both Sars and Marx, in that the analysis is extended beyond Sars's idealism and into Marx's materialism. The most prominent international representative of historicism in modern times is Arnold Toynbee, who produced his great twelve-volume work, *The Study of History*, in the period 1934–61. A confrontation with historicism to some degree will be directed against Toynbee. The best-known critics of historicism internationally are Karl Popper and Pieter Geyl. In Norway a critique was formulated by Jens Arup Seip.[4] Ottar Dahl also comments on this type of history. In his doctoral dissertation he disputes that such a "metaphysical anticipation of an ideal condition" can have any meaning in an empirical context. One can talk of teleology and intentionality only in connection with the analysis of motivation on the individual level.[5] This is our starting point: with the dethroning of metaphysical teleology, the stage was cleared; but what replaced it? Teleological elements gave an overarching structure and a direction to history. What characterized the newer and – let us say – more modern perspectives? We shall limit ourselves to an examination of the writings of a few selected historians on recent Norwegian history.

What happened in the first place was that works with grand syntheses were removed from the agenda. There was in the 1950s a common opinion that the discipline of history should be – or to a

3 Sars was known to be a "positivist" in the Comtian sense. He had a positivistic notion of history as an organic process. He was, however, not a positivist in the modern sense, by which positivism is a scientific ideal stating that history should be based only on "objective facts". See Fulsås 1994.

4 Popper 1957; Geyl 1955. See Francis Sejersted, "Norsk historisk forskning ved inngangen til 1990-årene", in Sejersted 1993:311. Seip places the political scientist Stein Rokkan alongside Sars and Koht: "Rokkan, like Sars and Koht, is capable of foreseeing the future." Seip 1983:221.

5 Dahl 1956:172–3. In his evaluation of this dissertation, Seip made a reference to Dahl's failure to treat "the nineteenth century's development-deterministic historical research. Nor is there any representative of the twentieth century's quasi-historians of Toynbee's ilk." Seip 1983:182. Dahl, however, had a justification for not including them in his analysis.

large extent already was – separated from the various social ideologies. Grand syntheses were rejected not only because they represented a metaphysical teleology, but also because they contributed to the misuse of history for political purposes. The researcher should concentrate on thorough individual investigations. The history discipline acquired an empiricist aspect.[6]

It is ironic that the very rejection of evolution-optimistic historiography was itself based on evolution-optimism: i.e. that one had at last come to the stage where one could contemplate the possibility of a more scientific, value-free historiography, with the history researcher placed outside or over the society which was to be analyzed. The progress of the discipline made it possible to reveal the fiction of the idea of progress! A critical look at the self-image of this research seems appropriate.

In the first place, it can be convincingly argued that a confrontation with historicism – as well as the greater theoretical consciousness which came to mark the history profession in Norway from the 1950s – represented a huge gain. Professional activities were also expanding, with the development of new subdisciplines. In time this came to mark the general orientation of the discipline; we will return to some examples later. On the other hand there were indications that the discipline was running into problems of legitimacy. This was firstly because the scientific standard of the historical sciences did not appear to measure up to that of the burgeoning social sciences.[7] Secondly, the legitimacy conferred on the discipline by the old identity-creating function was now lost; clearing away the old synthesizers meant that the connection between past and future was played down. The past was, by definition, something concluded. The evolution perspective, which had been so important among the elders, was removed.[8]

---

6 Sejersted 1993:311–3; Fure 1993:54; Kjeldstadli 1992:63.
7 Sejersted 1993:305f, 343f.
8 Fure 1993:44. He underlines this as a typical element of Ottar Dahl's history theory, and suggests that Dahl's methodology therefore becomes unhistorical.

Sverre Steen and the inheritance from Sars and Koht

It did not, however, entirely disappear. Sverre Steen, who with Jens Arup Seip was the dominant figure in professional circles in the 1950s and 1960s, continued to write in the evolution-optimist tradition. In his large, six-volume work *Det frie Norge* (The Free Norway), which appeared in the 1950s and 1960s, he describes the birth of modern Norway in the first half of the last century. But Steen also wrote an overview of Norway's history up to the post-war era in four small volumes which were published in the 1970s. We can see the underlying evolution-optimism in the titles: *The country slowly becomes our own, The dream of freedom, By ourselves,* and *Freedom and life are one.* A broad historical development is portrayed which ends in modern, pragmatic social democracy. To an even greater degree than Halvdan Koht, Steen became the historian of this social democracy. The two lines which dominate his ideas of development, material progress and the advance towards political freedom, are united in a national kind of social democracy, where conflicts are to a large extent reconciled. The last volume includes a central chapter he entitled "The Remarkable Year" ("Merkeåret"); this was 1935, the year the Labour Party came to power, inaugurating the period of social democratic hegemony:

> With Nygaardsvold's government at the forefront and supported by the young farmers' party, the Norwegian people returned to its old society. This society was not to be destroyed, but stabilized and reformed. The political structure remained standing as the fathers at Eidsvoll had planned it, and as the men of later times had rearranged it. All political parties of importance closed ranks around the king and democratic majority rule, and wished that this should continue.[9]

The 1940–5 war is given much attention, and here the main point is that it "created solidarity among the people, more strongly than ever before in Norway". After the war Einar Gerhardsen, social

---

9 Steen 1977:86. "The fathers at Eidsvoll" refers to the constituent assembly in 1814.

democracy's leading figure and prime minister from 1945 to 1965 (with two minor interruptions), was able to realize a "bourgeois socialism": "Political conflicts did not appear frightening, and nor did the social ones."[10] Here there is a quiet evolution-optimism, even if Steen himself hardly saw the attainment of the social democratic state as determined by fate, or as the end of history, as one could perhaps interpret Koht.

Steen would not have been Steen if he had not also looked at the reverse side of the coin. He was a man of ambivalence, in contrast to Koht. He explicitly turned away from the general evolution-optimism found before the First World War, when the "so-called civilized countries" experienced a "development intoxication" and characterized "all changes as development, and all development as progress". The world war and the atom bomb had in the meantime made fear "a dominating emotion".[11] Steen thus draws a picture of a relatively peaceful Norwegian social democracy in a threatening world. The line through history ends with entry into NATO, which stands out as a reasonable response to this situation: "On behalf of Norway, Halvard Lange (the social democratic foreign minister) signed the Atlantic Pact in Washington on 4 April 1949."[12]

The threat had the function in his synthesis of opening up the future. This is in contrast to the great syntheses with sprinklings of metaphysical teleology, implicitly or explicitly postulating an end to history, which also entails the possibility of seeing into the future. The situation as described by Steen is not an end, but rather a happy moment. It is therefore typical that even if the above quotation is the last sentence in this drawing of a historical line, it is not the book's last sentence. Steen adds a short concluding chapter where he gives vent to his ambivalence, and the book's definitive last sentence is: "for humanity, the future will always remain the great unknown."

Steen left an impression found in, among others, Magne Skodvin, and in the group somewhat loosely called the Skodvin school. This school researches in part the wartime period, in part the

10 Steen 1977:180, 200.
11 Steen 1977:184, 222.
12 Steen 1977:219.

international situation and in part the development of the social democratic state after 1945. It represents pragmatic historical research with limited thematization and with a solid foundation in sources, as is appropriate for modern historical research after the removal of syntheses from the agenda. The original evolution perspective is absent.

Significantly, however, this perspective's influence is clear in the mildly apologetic tone which characterizes much of the group's writing, in which the social democratic state is also described as a "happy moment". This is history written with great stress on empathy, as regards understanding the motives of political actors. It is therefore no coincidence that Geir Lundestad, reviewing Skodvin's book on Norway's entry into NATO, can comment that it is difficult to separate Skodvin's valuations from those of Foreign Minister Halvard Lange. In some of these writings, critical distance to the object can be extremely short.[13] The large, collectively written volume *Vekst og velstand* (Growth and Prosperity) is in many ways the central contribution of this empathic school. Lundestad, who himself must be reckoned to belong to this tradition, writes in the concluding chapter:

> Ideological principle from the past had to make way for an acceptance of the steps which can create maximum growth within the given international framework. The policy brought good results. It meant that the need to implement fundamental economic policy reforms was reduced. For the Labour Party the decisive factor had to be that economic growth combined with the social welfare venture appeared to be the main basis of the uniquely strong position the party managed to achieve and maintain.[14]

The tone is sober, but we recognize basic elements of that which we have seen as characteristic of the Steen tradition: a fundamental empathy and a sense of social democratic Norway as a happy moment in historical development. This profile becomes clearer if one views it against the background of the more critically minded tendency.

13 Lundestad 1972:221–4.
14 Bergh and Pharo 1977:475.

Jens Arup Seip and the inheritance from Sars and Koht

Jens Arup Seip was, as suggested, the man behind the confrontation with Sars and Koht and with historicism, warning against syntheses. Nonetheless, he himself appeared as a synthesizer. In what he himself called "a formalized and comprehensive description", he drew a line through Norway's modern history in his well-known lecture "From civil servant state to one party state", given to the Student Association in 1963.[15] He indeed linked with the great synthesizers, opening with a reference to the fact that it was 100 years since Sars had put forward his theory of history, and 50 years since Koht had done the same; now Seip would put forward his theory. But his purpose was different from theirs.

Sars and Koht had both marked out "lines of development which ended in a future ideal society, united, content, liberating for that which was valuable in human life." Seip's line of evolution ended at another point. Where Sverre Steen, in the Koht tradition, had seen a realization of freedom, Seip saw a loss of freedom in the bureaucratic "one party state":

> That which is called "the free Norway", to use Sverre Steen's expression – and I add, the not entirely content Norway – was granted a fleeting life, suspended as if on a swing between the old bureaucracy and the new, between civil servant state and one party state.[16]

In clear opposition to Steen, he saw Gerhardsen's social democracy as a perversion of "the free Norway", which had never really been all that free. Halvard Lange, for Steen the man who guided Norway into the sensible NATO alliance, was for Seip the man with "the pompously presented platitudes from the government benches".[17]

Whatever one may say about the new ideal of "the freedom of research from social engagement", it is clear that Seip, like Steen, was on a political errand. It is fair to say that the lecture shows that for Seip historical research and writing are a political and moral project. He explicitly asserts that lines into the future should help us

15 Seip 1963:8.
16 Seip 1963:42.
17 Seip 1963:22.

understand where we find ourselves today. Seip, however, like
Steen, avoids the kind of determinism we find in Sars and Koht. The
future is open. Understanding should call forth action.[18] Nor is it
the case that this lecture was a casual divergence from his actual
research. On the contrary, there is complete agreement between the
viewpoints in the lecture and the viewpoints in the two volumes of
Utsikt over Norges historie.[19] It is fair to regard the lecture as a synop-
sis of the great project he was sadly never able to complete.

Seip's confrontation with his predecessors was not least a confrontation with evolution-optimism. According to Seip, history has
not brought us forward to a particularly happy society. Here,
indeed, he stands in opposition to Sverre Steen too. On the other
hand, he can hardly be described as an evolution-*pessimist*. He
rejected Oswald Spengler's *Untergang des Abendlandes* as firmly as
he rejected the optimists' viewpoint.[20] While Steen with his characteristic ambivalence draws elements from both evolution-optimism and -pessimism (or critiques of civilization), Seip is more
consistently dismissive of every kind of development theory
coloured by determinism. Nevertheless, there is an undertone of
pessimism which relates more to human nature than to society.[21]
Seip cannot easily be pigeon-holed. Nonetheless, one can say that
his teaching on "substitute motives" (*"vikarierende motiver"*) and
his message that a "historian's task is not to clothe, but to
unclothe", correspond to what we may call a *realism*. There is an a
priori notion that the individual's motives can normally be
reduced to a wish for power, profit, etc., and that it is the historian's
task to reveal these "real" (and indeed bad) motives.[22]

18 Seip 1963:42.
19 Seip 1974 and 1981. The two volumes cover the period 1814–84.
20 *Dagbladet*, 11 October 1980. Interview: "Historikere i kamp om Høyre".
21 It is important to distinguish between the view on development and the
    view on human nature. It is accordingly possible to combine a pessimistic
    view of human nature with an optimistic view of social development. This
    was usual within the liberal tradition; for example, both Immanuel Kant
    and Adam Smith shared this outlook. See Sejersted 1993:17f.
22 Seip 1963:78f; Seip 1968:117. Dahl 1975:10, where Seip's "urge to 're-
    veal'" is stressed. The realism concept is as in White 1973:33. For White this
    becomes a genre built on satire, which is no more "objective" than other
    genres (comedy, tragedy) within history writing; it only pretends to be so.
    See Chapters 10 and 11 in Sejersted 1993.

It is no accident that Seip presented a major lecture, "From civil servant state to one party state" in 1963, the year before the jubilee year of the 1814 Constitution. He opened by saying that we "stand before the time of the great jubilee, a time for moving words, and the tight, tight bonds.... Let us seize the opportunity, before the flood is upon us. Today we will weep dry tears."[23] He introduced his major 1980 lecture, "Trends in Høyre [the Conservative Party] over the last century 1880–1980", with the following formulation: "We must therefore, here and now, anticipate Høyre's centenary. We shall put the party in its place, before it puts itself on a pedestal in its coming historical writings."[24] Seip placed himself political-strategically in advance of the great jubilees in order to fight for his revealment perspective. "The dry tears" represent in a way his political programme. It should be added that Seip hesitated to assume the role of synthesizer and politician. This is perhaps not surprising in view of his initial activism in favour of scientific historiography and against syntheses. However, he let himself be persuaded to hold the famous lecture of 1963. Nor is there any doubt that from that year he thrived as a normative synthesizer.

In his realism, Seip transmitted fundamental tendencies from modern legal sciences and the social sciences generally into the history discipline.[25] His influence on this point has probably been substantial. In much of the political history written in recent decades, one discerns a tendency towards "revealing". In his more synthesizing contributions, the ironic or satirical form is especially noticeable. In broad terms, he assigns the history discipline a political position; it should assume a critical function in society. As has been stated, he came to justify the left-wing political opposition in post-war Norway.[26] On the other hand, by adopting this ironic–critical position, Seip became a strong defender of the profession's independence.

It is characteristic of Norwegian political historiography since 1945 that we see relatively clear tendencies towards two schools.

23 Seip 1963:8.
24 Seip 1980:9.
25 Slagstad 1987.
26 Dahl 1980.

One, in the tradition of Sverre Steen, has much more empathy for the object of its studies; the other, in the tradition of Jens Arup Seip, has much more distance. Historical analysis must always locate itself between empathy and distance. It is indeed fair to say that precisely this tension between empathy and distance is, or should be, fundamental for the profession, while at the same time there are hardly objective criteria for balancing them.[27]

Edvard Bull jun. and the inheritance from Sars and Koht

There are few explicit attempts to capture Norway's recent history or the Norwegian modernization process in "a formalized and comprehensive description". As mentioned, syntheses were largely removed from the agenda with the turn towards empiricism. Edvard Bull jun. has, however, launched such a formula, in direct contrast to that of Seip.[28] Seip had placed politics or "looking at the state" in the centre of attention. Bull attacks this: "the actual changes in the period lay outside 'the political process'". Like Sars and Koht, to whom he refers directly, Bull wishes to begin from the social perspective. The programme of "history from the bottom up" he formulated was to be understood as an indication of the most important cause-and-effect linkage. On this basis he sketches three phases in development. First comes "agrarian society", then "capitalism's liberating phase" from *c.* 1860 to *c.* 1920, when the agricultural society's underclass was liberated in that capitalism opened alternatives for them. The last phase he calls "organized capitalism". In this phase capitalism is perfected under the Labour Party's period in government.[29]

Bull's approach is in fact not as fundamentally different from Seip's as it might at first appear. Seip's justification for putting politics at the centre is not that politics in itself is important as a kind

27 The tension between empathy and distance is characteristic of the German *"Historikerstreit"*. In Norway there is a parallel though more muted discussion about the history of the occupation.
28 Bull 1975:225–38.
29 Bull 1975:228, 233.

of first mover. Seip could largely share Bull's (and also Steen's) view of social development in one or other form as the most important. Political development is first and foremost a reflection of this; politics is the form in which social forces appear. Seip himself had not moved further from Sars and Koht than this.

It is reasonable to emphasize that the idea of the fundamental character of socio-cultural conditions has been extremely strong in Norwegian historiography right up to the present. It was, however, not obvious that this should be the case. Reflecting on this point in his review of Ottar Dahl's *Grunntrekk i historieforskningens metodelære*, Odd-Bjørn Fure characterizes the idea as a thoroughly modern feature. He explains it by way of continuity from the Marxist-inspired generation of historians of the inter-war period and by the influence of the Annales school.[30]

Against this background it is paradoxical that political history came to assume such a strong position, in both the empathic and the distanced variant. One might perhaps have expected a clearing out of socially determined history, but this did not happen. There was no real attempt to assert the primacy of politics, not even by Seip, as we have seen. Politics was analyzed more as an effect than as a cause.

One can justifiably emphasize Bull's central position both in the historical treatment of the process of modernization in Norway and for the generation of historians which stepped forward in the 1960s and 1970s. While Seip took on the Koht tradition in Norwegian history by attacking its weaknesses, Bull further developed the stronger aspects of the same tradition. He thus becomes a transitional figure between the old synthesizers and modern social history research. His formalized and comprehensive description reflects and clarifies the primacy of the social factor, in many ways the most important underlying concept in Norwegian historiography, better than the political syntheses. At the same time his book

30 Fure 1993:46. Concerning the transmission of viewpoints from the Annales school, and the writing of synthetical presentations, Andreas Holmsen should be named, even if he did not write about the modern period. His views are summed up in Holmsen 1938.

about the labour movement became fundamental for social history research.[31] In one important way Bull's view of the history discipline varies from Seip's and from Seip's confrontation with historicism. This concerns the positive view of the role of history in creating identity, concisely formulated in one of his book's titles: *Retten til en fortid* (The Right to a Past).[32] The programme of "history from the bottom up" also draws inspiration from this idea of a political function. The role of history in creating identity is a central theme in modern historiography. Modern history research is intimately linked to rendering national identity conscious. This was dominant in Sars and Koht, and continued in a modified form in Steen and in what we have identified as the tradition following him. But while Steen was conciliatory and saw identity in a national context, Bull preserves a strong idea of a continuing class struggle and links his project to the emancipation of the working class. When Steen characterizes post-war Norwegian society by the concept "bourgeois socialism", this is intended positively; but when Bull speaks of the Labour Party's "organized capitalism", the tone is negative.

Bull inspired the new social history research. We may talk of a *history of classes*, or in this context of a history of the underclass. But he was also an inspiration behind that which we can call a *history of the class struggle*, or in this context, the history of the labour movement. The two developments formed two relatively independent circles. The history of the labour movement was more politically oriented and became a very large circle, even having its own periodical.[33]

31 Bull 1958. The book was strongly criticized when it appeared, but it has stood as a central work in Norwegian historiography. Ingrid Semmingsen and Sivert Langholm were central in the expansive social history research which followed; among others see Langholm's project *Norsk samfunnsutvikling i det 19. århundre.*
32 Bull 1981.
33 *Tidsskrift for arbeiderbevegelsens historie* has appeared since 1976. The results of its research were collected in the six-volume *Arbeiderbevegelsens historie i Norge*, of which Bull wrote the first, which came out in 1990. This work seeks to unify the history of classes with the history of the class struggle.

The most striking thing about Bull's explicit attempt to sum up the recent history of Norway in a simple formal alternative to that of Seip is the similarity of their conclusions. Both end with a political criticism of the society of the day, or of "social democrats' treachery", to use Bull's term; he links this to Seip's theory about the eternal treachery of politicians. (Bull, however, chooses his words somewhat cautiously, in that the expression "treachery" comes in a question to which the answer is open.)[34] Here we discern an irony: politics is not supposed to be that important. This is, however, a poor starting point for a historian who has embarked on a political errand. It is easy to slip into the view that politics is quite important after all, at least in the society in which we now live. Seip too slips the reins a little when he concludes his lecture by saying that treachery is, of course, not inevitable. Understanding should, as suggested, lead to political action.

In relation to the two schools we sketched, Bull assumes a somewhat particular intermediary position between Steen and Seip. His political involvement caused him to vary between the empathic and the distanced. It should also be noted that neither Seip nor Bull considered modern society generally to be bad. Like Steen, they saw a positive aspect in material progress, but in contrast to Steen they also saw an anti-democratic feature in modern social democracy.

Sars and Koht lie like shadows over the generation from which we have presented three of the most important actors. Earlier Norwegian historical research seems to be largely identified with Sars and Koht. It is therefore important to respond to them. The programme of the new generation was to write, if not an objective history, then at least a nearly objective history, independent of social involvement. Syntheses were to be deliberately removed from the agenda. The history discipline was to become empirical and scientific.

One can, of course, discuss the extent to which this actually was a programme. We have presented these three precisely because they did not (or at least partly did not) follow this programme. All three were emphatically empirically oriented

34 See Sejersted 1993:141f.

researchers who did not fear close combat with sources. But they also attempted to formulate, in a formalized description, that which they regarded as the quintessential in the process of modernization in Norway. The idea of the primacy of the social aspect is never seriously challenged. Evolution-optimism and elements of metaphysical teleology are indeed absent, but the ambition to construct hibernated, as did political engagement. They dared to give vent to their idiosyncrasies, and largely because of that, they came to blaze a trail.

Syntheses and the perspective of genre

The theme of the three synthesizers discussed was social democracy, or the deep historical process which led to social democracy. To a striking degree the three fit into Hayden White's three categories of synthetic presentations of history. Steen's genre is *comedy*. An initial harmony is disturbed by a series of intrigues and misunderstandings. When these were cleared up, "the Norwegian people was able to turn back to its old society". We thus find the obligatory "happy end" of comedy. But that which above all gives away the plot of the comedy is the expression "back to". Steen includes a picture of an actual or initial harmony. There is probably a connection between the plot of the comedy and Steen's characteristic ambivalence. The latter creates a particular kind of distance to the material. Steen is an observer who writes with a sympathetic understanding of mankind's foibles.

Seip's genre is *satire*. This appears clearly in his fundamental concepts of "substitute motives" and "politicians' treachery". From his "realistic" viewpoint one should never have expected anything other than treachery. Bull's genre is also clear: *tragedy*. Initially Bull was close to the Koht and Steen line in the sense that earlier developments had borne so many promises. But these were not kept. Precisely because of this, "the social democrats' treachery" was not something which had to come, but rather an unhappy deviation – a tragedy.

We have now seen that all three placed themselves in relation to an older and dominant tradition which we have linked to the names Sars and Koht. Sars and Koht can be seen as representatives of the mainstream in modern historiography as it grew in the last century. It was an evolution-optimistic historiography with a strong metaphysical and teleological character, in which the nation–state and liberal democracy were seen as the finest fruits of history. The dominant genre within this tradition was White's last genre: *romance*. Romance is "a favourite self-portrayal of a modern, secularized, individualized culture which believes in evolution", as Svante Beckman writes.[35] The confrontation we sketched in our introduction was above all a confrontation with this type of teleological understanding of history. It is in many ways typical that when one strives again for synthetic presentations after a confrontation, one fumbles with various, less evolution-optimistic genres. It is indeed also questionable whether the romance form was entirely dead.

A noticeable feature of Norwegian historiography is that a large number of extensive, multi-volume histories of Norway have been published, from the middle of the last century and up to the present. These are usually written by the most representative academic historians, for the general reader, and appear at more or less regular intervals. It is reasonable to say that the tradition began with P. A. Munch's *Det Norske Folks Historie*, which appeared in the years 1852–63. Munch is in many ways the founder of modern Norwegian historical science. As a historian he became one of the central contributors to nation-building in the development of Norway into a modern nation–state. The next great history of Norway was written by Ole A. Øverland and appeared in the years 1887–98. While Munch's history ended in 1400, with the decline of the old free Norway, Øverland's ended in 1814, with the birth of the new free Norway. Øverland was not a university historian. The next great work was *Norges Historie fremstillet for det norske Folk*, which appeared between 1909 and 1917. This was a joint project of the country's leading historians. Sars wrote the last, large volume. The 1930s saw *Det norske folkets liv og historie*, of which Sverre Steen wrote four volumes. *Vårt folks historie* followed in the 1950s. The 15-volume *Norges Historie* of the 1970s was written mainly by academic historians; Bull wrote the last two volumes. A

35 Beckman 1990:189.

corresponding work is in progress in the mid-1990s. Sweden has no similar tradition. In Denmark there is a tendency towards this, but even there one cannot speak of a corresponding collusion of the country's leading historians to regularly present new summaries of the nation's history intended for the general reader. It is fair to see this as connected to the fact that the history of Norwegian nation-building is particular, among other things in that Norway achieved full national independence only in 1905.

Broad presentations of this kind, written by many hands, easily assume an eclectic appearance; one can hardly talk of syntheses. Ottar Dahl is thus correct in his presentation of Norwegian historiography; he writes that Øverland's Norwegian history was "without any clear, organizing overview"; that the version by Sars and others was "without a common basis"; and that the 1930s history, though intended to have a common approach, did not succeed in this respect.[36] One can undoubtedly make similar comments about the subsequent histories. But even if these are not fully formed syntheses, something in the basic concept gives the tradition a certain unity. In the introduction to his work, Munch writes:

I have deliberately called the work "the history of the Norwegian people", not that of Norway, of the Norwegian Kingdom, or of the Norwegian kings. It was my intention to furnish as true and complete a presentation as possible not only of the country's political or external history, but also of the people's inner history, of popular life in its development and progression; not only of the overlords', but also of the people's own affairs.[37]

This is the romance form – the history of a people which takes control of its own history and creates its own, good, national society. Evolution-optimism naturally weakened over time, and the eclectic element became more evident. Yet it is striking that this programme formulation could maintain its validity for the whole tradition. As a genre this tradition has never entirely broken from the romance form.

Illustrative of the weight of the tradition is the fact that at one

36 Dahl 1990:228, 230.
37 Munch 1852:iv.

stage it appeared to have been broken, but that this proved to be merely a parenthesis. This occurred not unexpectedly in the 1950s, the period of the great confrontation with historicism. At the time two Norwegian histories were planned. The first was *Vårt folks historie*, as mentioned above, which was intended for a general readership. The remarkable point about this was that it was not written by academic historians, but by schoolteachers and journalists. Secondly, a scientific *Handbok i Norges historie* was planned, to be written by academics for professional circles. This was to give a "summation of established results of research".[38] In the confrontation with historicism with which we began, where syntheses were removed from the agenda (at least initially), it was clearly intended that professional historians should be freed from the need to write for the general reader. A distinction was made between presentations within the history discipline and popular histories. Novick has noted the same tendency in American historiography: "historical work was increasingly, and less apologetically, directed to a 'strictly academic' audience." Further, with reference to the scientific ideal of objectivity: "to write solely for one's fellow historians could be a kind of liberation, allowing a less contaminated pursuit of the old ideal."[39] The new demand for being scientific thus threatened the old national history tradition.

Neither of the two Norwegian histories launched in the 1950s proved a success. The one intended for the general reader sold poorly, and the scientific one was never finished. That is to say, a few volumes of high quality appeared, but the project then ran into the sand. Perhaps this was partly because the ambition of the scientific work was too great a departure from established norms of the discipline. It was to be a "compendium of Norwegian historians' knowledge about Norwegian history". But how was the problem of differing interpretations to be tackled? It should give an account of "different historians' opinions on central problems."[40] The author should thus present other people's interpretations of history, but without interpreting him- or herself. This might be regarded as a quasi-objective way to present history. One retains

38 Helle 1964. Quote from the preface by the editor, Knut Mykland.
39 Novick 1988:373f.
40 Helle 1974. Mykland's preface.

one's scientific virtue, yet makes concessions to the necessity of perspectives which are inevitably somewhat subjective. Books of this kind are also found as textbooks for undergraduates. They can be said to *present* the discipline, rather than to *represent* it. The type of presentation may be somewhat unclear. It tends to become a hybrid of a real historical presentation, a historiographical study, and a historical lexicon. The point is that if this great project remained incomplete, it was perhaps because it was very difficult, if not actually impossible, in the form in which it was conceived. To present a fairly coherent retelling of Norway's history demands elements of perspectives which inevitably go beyond the inter-subjectively valid, not to mention the objectively stated. The Norwegian history of the 1970s reverted to the traditional concept, and with great success. The romance form was not entirely dead.

Of our three synthesizers, Steen and Bull are found as central writers in their respective great histories of Norway. This shows that we must be careful not to take the genre-perspective too far. They break with the romance form principally in that evolution-optimism is dampened. In the Marxist-inspired Bull, the break is perhaps most obvious, in that he in a certain way questions whether we have come so far in nation-building. Yet neither of them completely breaks out of the great tradition. This becomes clear from a comparison with the last of our synthesizers, Seip, who took the lead in the assault on historicism and who genuinely broke with the great national history tradition. He was involved in the initiative behind the writing of a "scientific" handbook, but he was not involved in any of the great works for the general reader. Satire, which was Seip's genre, stands in diametric opposition to the romance form. It is therefore difficult to imagine Seip as a contributor to any of the great histories of Norway. He had to write his own. As we have seen, he managed to write two volumes of his *Utsikt* before he died. The two volumes cover large parts of the nineteenth century.

Some recent trends

Modern Norwegian historical research is characterized by an emphasis on the fundamental significance of social factors, as we have seen. Even if Norway was precocious in this regard, the devaluation of the political was perhaps not so remarkable when seen in the international context. It is perhaps more unusual that the technology-deterministic tendency is so weak. In the international context there is a strong tradition which regards technological development as the most important mover, and as that which leads to the changes in social structures which in turn dictate politics. There is also an element of such an approach in Norway, but it is not strong. The explanation may indeed lie in the tradition of the dominant position of social factors. This in turn depends on the fact that the capitalist paradigm has been relatively strong, compared with the industrialism paradigm, as the theory behind the process of modernization. One might also suspect that the reality in Norway tended to contradict the concept of technology-determinism. A main point in presentations of this kind is the technological imperative embodied in the growth of the large industrial corporation; but precisely this was absent in Norway.

The original Marxist-inspired emphasis on social factors has been challenged in recent times by what we might term institutional history, and perhaps also by a certain effort to give a new justification for the central position of political history, a movement towards the primacy of politics. We also observe a new interest in the middle classes, as compared with farmers or workers. Some feel that we are in a period in which syntheses are again tempting, and constructive ambitions thrive.[41] There are therefore signs of a confrontation with the confrontation, which as we have seen was not a complete clearing out. Or should we perhaps view some of the more recent trends as the completion of the confrontation? We shall now discuss some of the challenges mentioned.

Many institutional histories have been written in recent decades, such as the history of the Storting and the history of central administration, to name the most prominent. Many of these works display

---

41 See Seip 1983:283, "We are again on the road to a period in which syntheses are tempting". One of those to argue most strongly for putting syntheses back on the agenda is Kåre Lunden, "Historisk syntese, særleg funksjon i forhold til offentligheita", in Lunden 1991:91–106, originally a lecture held in 1989. See also Sejersted 1993:305f; this was also a 1989 lecture. See also Martinsen and Winge 1992.

a tendency to analyze institutions in the light of social factors as their actual driving force, and this fits in with the realist programme. Institutions are seen as instruments for social groups or as arenas for conflicts between social groups. An institutional perspective entails, on the other hand, that the institutions are seen as more autonomous. As March and Olsen write in a book tellingly entitled *Rediscovering Institutions*: "In the institutional state, government agencies are not neutral instruments. They are carriers of cultures, missions, values, and identities."[42] A more institutional perspective thus entails a critical attitude to the reduction of motives to desire for power, profit, etc., as found in realism. The significance of social factors is also strongly moderated in that "bureaucratic biography" is emphasized at the expense of "social biography".[43]

It is all but inevitable that the many institutional histories also develop clear elements of what we have called an institutional perspective. It is apparent in, for instance, Alf Kaartvedt and Rolf Danielsen's volume of the history of the Storting, and also, quite clearly, in Anne-Lise Seip's history of nineteenth-century social policy, *Sosialhjelpstaten blir til* (The Emergence of the Social-Service State). The question is thus when we can talk of a more systematic shaping of the perspective.

The debate between Jens Arup Seip and the author of this chapter about the formation of the state in the 1800s reflects among other things this difference in views on institutions. Quite typically, Seip refers to a social group to characterize the state, which he calls the "state of the officials" (*"embetsmannsstat"*), while the present writer refers to a particular institutional order, in calling it a "liberal constitutional state".[44] It is also characteristic that the present writer emphasizes the importance of "bureaucratic biography"; in connection with the role of the judge, for instance, this is the tendency among judges to behave precisely as one would expect judges to behave, irrespective of their own interests or their social biography. The institutional perspective is further developed in the 1993 book *Demokratisk kapitalisme* (Democratic Capitalism). Here it is

42 March and Olsen 1989:113–4.
43 Lægereid and Olsen 1978.
44 Sejersted 1984.

attempted to describe the genesis of some of the central modern social institutions, stressing the interaction between organizational development and normative development. This applies to phenomena such as the market, the relation of the market to civil society, the legal system in relation to the political, and so on. On this basis an attempt is made to develop a synthesis or comprehensive description of modernization in Norway – "the Norwegian *Sonderweg*". The essential element in this is a strong petit bourgeoisie, which was established both organizationally and in the normative-cultural sense in the last century. A strong local orientation and strong democratic norms are characteristic. The most remarkable point about this development, however, is that this structure has persisted to the present day. This comprehensive description ends with a picture of today's society which borrows many elements of Steen's concluding description (the empathic school or the comedy variety), although there are also clear differences. In general one can characterize today's situation as "the threatening idyll".

The institutional perspective departs from the strong emphasis on social factors and from the tendency in realism to reduce genuine motives to a desire for power, profit, and so on. In this regard it modifies a tradition which goes back at least as far as Koht. Institutions are analyzed in their dual function of determining actions *and* facilitating actions; this entails an attempt to create a space for politics as a moving force. This is not a total novelty. Just as the institutional perspective has grown up partly through the many institutional histories, the idea of political room to manoeuvre and the primacy of politics grew through extensive research in political history, of both the empathic and the distanced variety. This is evident, for instance, in Rolf Danielsen's *Borgerlig oppdemmingspolitikk*.[45] This writer's *Demokratisk kapitalisme* thus emphasizes, with reference to Rune Slagstad, that the new society which grew up in Norway in the 1800s was "a capitalism staged by the state".[46] Quite simply, this development was to a large extent wanted and planned.

It is fair to underline here that this kind of institutional perspec-

---

45 Danielsen 1984:378. This is a long footnote in which he modifies his basic position on determining interests.
46 Slagstad 1992:145f.

tive and the new stress on the primacy of politics restores the teleological element as regards larger developments; it does so not,
however, as metaphysical teleology, but as a precondition for the
explanation of developments by reference to human intentions co-
ordinated in institutions and through political processes. Intended
consequences must be acknowledged. Political guidance is possible; history gives us examples. This may be seen as a return to a
moderate version of the romance form.

The new attention given to the bourgeoisie is also worth noting.
The new focus on norms and the importance of politics strengthens the necessity to study the bourgeoisie. This is because we find
important keys to an understanding of the modernization process
in this group's modernizing ideology and in their institutions in
the broad sense. There is thus a tendency to turn away from a
strong focus on farmers and especially on the working class. This
focus also had its own specific, political basis, as we have seen. Significantly, the social democrat Sverre Steen underlined the importance of devoting more attention to the bourgeoisie in his comprehensive history. He wrote a chapter called simply: "The forgotten
social class and the new system". This is the middle class.[47] Here
too we find an internal development within the profession which
points to the new trend, parallel to that which we noted in connection with the institutional perspective and the new view on the
possibilities of politics. In recent decades, for instance, a number of
extensive town histories have been written, in which the middle
classes have naturally been treated broadly. It is hardly coinciden-
tal that one of the strongest proponents of a larger project on
the middle classes has been a leading urban historian, Jan Eivind
Myhre.

Syntheses are once more on the agenda. It seems to be legitimate to attempt more comprehensive, constructive presentations,
and there are further examples of interesting developments in this
direction besides those mentioned above.[48] In general, however,

47 Steen 1973:132–43.
48 E.g. Olstad 1990 and Nordby 1991. Tellingly, the starting-point for these is
the old-style workers and farmers, perhaps because an established empirical
basis for synthesis exists in these areas.

there has not been any marked change in attitude towards the time when programmatic synthesizing disappeared from the agenda, but in which, ironically, some of the most powerful examples of synthesis emerged. In addition we may discern a new irony: now that grand constructions are once more topical, there is a simultaneous blossoming of the deconstructionist tendency, in the form of narratives, biographies, and so on.[49]

49 See Kjeldstadli 1992:65.

Part III
Central Themes

7. State- and Nation-building[1]

Trond Nordby

As early as the Middle Ages, Norway was a state in the sense of an administrative unit. During the 400-year union with Denmark up to 1814, the country was treated like a province, and was ruled for long periods by a Danish governor. The legitimacy of the union rested on the *dynastic* principle. The peace treaty of Kiel ceded Norway to the Swedish king, because Denmark–Norway had been on France's side in the Napoleonic wars. *National* identity was at that time little developed in Norway, but a political elite comprising officials and merchants demanded full independence and a separate constitution. An uprising whose ideological force was drawn from the revolutionary ideas of the time, mainly American and French, brought only limited progress. In the face of Sweden's military supremacy, the new union was impossible to prevent. The constitution, markedly democratic by contemporary standards, was also shelved.

In this constitution lay the seed of a sovereign *nation–state*, legitimized by an elective democracy, where decisions ultimately lay with free citizens in an election. But in order for this system to work, those granted the right to vote had to be willing to use this right. In other words it was a precondition that citizens regarded themselves as members of a national community. Only in the second half of the nineteenth century did a national identity take root in broad sections of the population, chiefly as a consequence of modern communications and of the social changes brought by industrialization. The struggle about the union with Sweden also helped strengthen national identity, through the agitation and conflicts it induced. A high point in this process came in 1905.

---

1 Translated by Eamonn Noonan.

When the question of Norway's secession was put to a referendum on 13 August 1905, 386,208 people voted in favour, and just 184 against. The high level of participation in the referendum and the broad unanimity achieved confirmed that state and nation had merged into a symbiosis.

The national preconditions for the dissolution of the union drew the attention of historians relatively early. From the middle of the 1800s, historians were involved in the cementing of the view that Norway was a separate nation, with all the rights this must imply in relation to the partner in union, Sweden. Themes such as the development of the state and of national identity also occupied historians after 1905, though to date there has not been a thorough analysis of the genesis of either *state* or *nation*. This chapter deals with Norwegian historical research on these themes. To look at all contributions by historians would go too far; there is a huge number of specific studies, especially on the development of the state. I concentrate on the most important works, and particularly on those which provide the most overarching perspectives. The model developed by sociologist Stein Rokkan (1921–79) serves as an appropriate frame of reference.[2] He had the synthesizing ambition needed in order to treat the complex matters we are dealing with. He attempted to integrate basic preconditions, such as cultural variations, political traditions, and socio-economic systems, with the ongoing social conflicts. He was also concerned that his model assumed a form which allowed for systematic comparison.

For Rokkan, state-building was about how the state's political power was consolidated; nation-building concerned the national standardization of language and culture, the clarification of the state authority's role in the religious practices of the people, and the way in which the population to an increasing degree participated in national decisions. He proposed a number of central research areas.[3] One concerned how the state penetrated into the

2 For the sake of simplicity, I speak of Rokkan's "model" without elaborating on the many forms it gradually assumed. This approach is fully justifiable as long as I am dealing only with the basic features of the model. See especially Rokkan 1970.
3 Rokkan 1970:65ff.

surrounding society. A second regarded how the population was integrated into the state community: this encompassed recruitment to state bodies, the school system, and the linking of the various districts which came from the expansion of the communications network. Another was the growth of a national "identity", which was in the first place linked to the spread of mass literacy, the organization of teacher training, and the creation of state-guided religious observance. Further research areas were how the population accepted the established political order (legitimacy), as well as participation in elections, membership of parties and organizations, newspaper readership, and so on. Rokkan linked the actual historical substance in nation-building to tension between centre and periphery on the one hand, and a functional integration on the other.[4]

Measured against Rokkan's comprehensive model, many of the historians discussed here consider only partial aspects. On the other hand, the historical literature treats many subsidiary subjects in much greater detail than Rokkan. His contribution was to create a relatively abstract model, and he did not manage to build this up empirically in an adequate manner. He may also be criticized for not dealing with the deliberate nation-building conducted by politicians, academics, and artists. He ignored too the nationalist activist ideology and the political actions which this gave rise to in the period up to 1905. It was the determined nationalists who created the conflicts with Sweden. These conflicts in turn served to meld the nation even closer together than was the case before they started. In any event, many of the historians' contributions may be used to amend and supplement Rokkan.

Shifting historical traditions
What distinguishes traditions?

The writers relevant to this historiographical review are anchored in a wide variety of disciplines and traditions. Three criteria help to encapsulate their differences: breadth of theme, theoretical position, and attitude towards the object of investigation.

4 A standard work here is Lipset and Rokkan 1967. For a broad interpretation
 of Rokkan's concept of dividing lines, see Aardal 1994.

One can in the first place report large variations in thematic breadth. The narrowest perspective is maintained by historians who devote attention chiefly to the relation between motive and action. The question for analysis is this: what motivations led the protagonists of the past to act as they did? Much of this research has been solely *individual-oriented*. Other historians raised the analysis to what we might call the *sectoral level*, in that they took on only limited areas of the life of the society, such as party history, parliamentary history, and economic history. Even if the themes are geared towards collective actions, the emphasis of the investigations is nevertheless on the protagonists' motives. The broadest perspective is found among a group of historians who practice what we may call *multi-level analyses*. Here connections are made across the limits of sectors such as economy and politics, so that one can talk of what may be termed a synthesizing historiography.

Secondly, historians may base their work of reconstruction on differing theoretical platforms. It is impossible to cover more than 150 years of research in an analysis without a unified classification scheme. Research ranges over such conflicting directions as classical positivism, Norwegian variations of Marxist theory, and purely common sense observations. The most near-sighted within the source-critical tradition appear hostile to theory, and give at best neat reconstructions of easily documented connections.

Thirdly, historians have assumed differing attitudes towards the object of study, and especially towards the cultural aspects of nation-building. In some presentations we find a positive attitude, often with a specifically national partisanship. Other writers have been critical especially towards anything which they regard as redolent of nationalism. Between these two extremes lies an expressly neutral attitude.

Historical research has never been monolithic; rather, differing and at times opposing tendencies have always coexisted. We can, however, say that research since the middle of the last century has tended to move away from synthesizing evolution theories, with a teleological orientation, and towards narrow sectoral analyses. A continuous characteristic among the older historians was that they made value judgements, and often played an active part in politics. The first post-war generation stayed close to sources, and were not really oriented towards syntheses. Historians deliberately assumed a neutral attitude towards the subjects they took up. In recent years, however, historians have again gained more constructive ambitions. At the same time they have been more open to normative question-setting.

In the service of nation-building[5]

Many nineteenth-century historians were concerned with legitimizing the new nation–state with presentations on ethnicity, community of language, and common history. This involvement was not unique. In a number of countries, intellectuals, and particularly historians, took active parts in the shaping of their land's national identity. A common starting-point was the "Young Europe" association, founded by Guiseppe Mazzini in 1834. Mazzini built on the idea of the right of "nations" to have a "state". Seen in this manner, national identification was a construction. The historians involved were thus co-creators of that which Benedict Anderson has called "imagined communities".[6] In Norway the breakthrough came with what is called "the historical school". A characteristic of this school was the downplaying of the period of union with Denmark as a subject and a corresponding upgrading of Norwegian Middle Ages history, and above all of the oldest times. In terms of the history of ideas, those who belonged here were close to German romanticism, where Johann Gottfried Herder among others stressed that the nation was a cultural community which had its roots far back in the past. In Norway a breakthrough for nationalistic thinking among writers and artists came in the 1840s.

Norwegian historians had an explicit goal, formulated as early as 1832: to show that the population was "one of Europe's oldest, most historically renowned peoples, not just a puny offshoot of the fermentations of the current times".[7] These historians applied the idea of a "people's individuality", and cast about terms of honour

5 Analysis of nation-building in Norwegian historical research largely rests on Dahl 1990.
6 Anderson 1983.
7 Gregers Fougner Lundh, cited after Dahl 1990:44.

such as "people", "tribe", and "nationality". They were concerned above all with mapping the first immigrations into the region. A widespread view was that Norwegians were the indigenous Nordic people and therefore had author's rights to the rich literature of the saga period. The first to launch this view was Rudolf Keyser (1803–64), who wrote the pathbreaking dissertation "Nordmænddenes Herkomst og Folkeslegtskab".[8] Another major figure was Peter A. Munch (1810–63), who sought to show "the significance of Norwegian nationality in ancient times", and on that basis that Norwegians were entitled to be placed on equal footing with the other Nordic peoples.[9]

The most influential historian of the 1800s was Ernst Sars (1835–1917). His critical approach was markedly "socially dynamic", in that he saw politics as the reflection of underlying social circumstances. In his philosophy of history, he was influenced by French developmental ideas, particularly those of Auguste Comte and Fustel de Coulanges. In Sars's conception the peasants took the place of the bourgeoisie as bearers of freedom and democracy.[10] Sars thought he could show an inner relationship between events which might superficially appear unconnected: independence in 1905 was the result of a slow, organic growth. In this regard he endorsed what one might call a teleological view of history: history showed a "progressive evolution" towards steadily higher levels, of which the democratic nation–state was a historic ultimate goal. The germ of both democracy and national independence lay hidden in the freedom of the peasant of the Middle Ages, which was considerable if compared with that of Central European countries. Sars also felt that the national viewpoint gradually strengthened within the population, and that the union *of necessity* would dissolve.

Sars stressed that there had been favourable and less favourable periods of growth, according to external circumstances. He

---

8 Printed in *Samlinger til det norske Folks Sprog og Historie* VI (1939); Dahl 1990:47.

9 Ibid.

10 I consider the term "peasant" more appropriate as a translation of the Norwegian *bonde* in this period the alternative term "farmer"; most holdings were small and family-run.

emphasized that it was the "external events" which in 1814 gave "an opportunity for the awakened desire for freedom to near its goal before it had become strong enough to force a change on it own".[11] He therefore accorded the union with Sweden a positive function: "it has played a very important role in our inner development in waking and encouraging national independence, and this role was completed only when the entire Norwegian people stood together behind the demand for full and unlimited political sovereignty."[12] In this perspective, according to Sars, two central lines of development – the *national* and the *democratic* – culminated in the unanimity of the vote in 1905.

Sars had a normative purpose in much of his writing, and he treated "nationality", "national independence", and "fatherland" as supreme values. Through his attempts to scientifically underpin the view that Norway's population was a "nation" and that the nation was grounded in a cultural and historical community, Sars himself stood out as an important protagonist in the service of nation-building. Many of his writings gained a large readership. In addition he was involved in politics, both in the constitutional struggle which led to the breakthrough of parliamentarianism in 1884, and thereafter in the dispute over the union.

Halvdan Koht (1873–1965) took over hegemony from Sars. He was concerned with making syntheses upon what he himself regarded as a *Marxist* basis. He accordingly emphasized that history was driven forward by the class struggle. First the peasants revolted, and then the working class. He saw independence in 1905 as the result of the peasants' long struggle for more democracy. In other words he viewed the dissolution of the union and the breakthrough of parliamentarianism, which in Norway's case came around 1884, in the same perspective. After the peasants' struggle was brought to a conclusion, according to Koht, workers won themselves civil rights. Gradually they were also able to take over the governing of society, and this occurred from 1935 on.

Despite Koht's explicitly Marxist starting-point, the influence of

11 This idea was put forward, for instance, in the pamphlet *Historisk Indledning til Grundloven;* Mykland 1967:177ff.
12 Sars 1906.

Sars was striking. In contrast to classical Marxism, Koht underlined that the ultimate goal was *cultural* integration. This view is
summarized in the article "Peasants against burghers in modern
Norwegian history" ("Bonde mot borgar i nynorsk historie"):
"each time new classes fought their way in the work of society, the
whole nation became broader and richer. Progress for democracy
was basically the same as an ever stronger national unity."[13]

Historical development was thus set in a cultural framework,
where the nation became the highest unit of analysis. This value
judgement marked Koht's analysis of the politics of the union:
Norway and Sweden had very different starting-points: "We were
strangers to each other. We had no mental inheritance in common."[14] He expressed his own attitude towards the national community of values as follows: "The rich heritage we have from our
fathers and forefathers is that which binds us together mentally."[15]
Koht, like Sars, announced clearly that his research had a political
purpose. While Sars was a member of the bourgeois Venstre party,
Koht was an active socialist. In 1935 he became foreign minister
in the Labour Party government.

Sars's viewpoint was carried forward in the first instance by
Arne Bergsgård (1886–1954) and Jacob S. Worm-Müller (1884–
1963), who helped uphold Venstre's national democratic tradition
– a tradition which played a leading role in Norwegian politics right
up to the Second World War. Like Sars, these two historians were
active in the Venstre party. But as historians they were much less
original than Sars. Bergsgård emphasized that "national growth"
had been strong between 1814 and 1905, and wrote enthusiasti-
cally about how in 1905 it rose "like a powerful wave within the
Norwegian people that we must get out of the union".[16] He further
stressed "the vital forces which lay hidden in the soul of the Norwegian people, an ancient sense of freedom, respect for law, sense of
responsibility, demand for justice and law which have followed the
people from time immemorial".[17] This was like an echo of Sars.

13 Koht 1910:225.
14 Koht 1955:2.
15 Koht 1977 (1920):12.
16 Bergsgård 1958:258.
17 Cited after Mykland 1967:199.

According to Bergsgård it was the peasants who pressed forward demands for political and individual freedom in Norway. This view was expressed in his biography of one of the nineteenth century's leading agrarian politicians, Ole Gabriel Ueland:

> Nothing could better suit the conditions and attitudes of the Norwegian peasant. His whole attitude towards life was and is individualistic and had to remain so, given the conditions for him on the isolated farms. Individual force characterizes our people.[18]

Bergsgård also thought that agrarian politics superseded class interests: "All European liberalism sought the general, that which can apply for all individuals and social classes; so it was also with Norwegian agrarian policy."[19] Nevertheless, in his great work on the principle of nationality, he showed an understanding which was more in keeping with then-contemporary European research.[20]

Worm-Müller accepted without reservation Sars's teaching about evolution: "Sars's law has gone the way of many other revolutionary ideas: today it is self-evident."[21] The great overviews hardly materialized in Worm-Müller's own research on the politics of the union. He mainly collected sources and wrote rough sketches, as well as articles which dealt with relatively limited subjects. He was also preoccupied by great men, in a very different way from the other historians involved in Venstre. He strewed out labels like "the bravest" (polar explorer Fridtjof Nansen) and "the powerful will" (the poet Bjørnstjerne Bjørnson). On the role played by the ultra-radicals in 1905, he wrote: "they were the driving ones, they were ones who encouraged, they were the most fiery ... they were like wild horses." Worm-Müller in other words regarded the strong men as the *unleashers* of inherent national forces. This emphasis on the unleashing aspect marks the transition to a concentration on politics at the elite level which came to characterize much of historical research after the Second World War.[22]

18 Bergsgård 1932:78.
19 Ibid.:79.
20 Bergsgård 1946.
21 Worm-Müller 1954:187.
22 See below.

With Bergsgård and Worm-Müller, the direct heritage of Sars expired. Subsequently it is easy to dismiss that which this tradition stood for as ideological production. The idea that the Norwegian peasant ever since the Middle Ages had been a bearer of democracy and national consciousness does not tally with empirical research. Furthermore Sars's dichotomy between Norwegian and foreign culture obscured differences which went deep in agrarian society and which divided the population both before and after 1905. Differences between classes, moreover, deepened in the period up to the First World War, when the first modern heavy industries were established in Norway. The historians thus far discussed did not make any satisfactory suggestions as to stages in nation-building, and they did not consider many of the "forces" which influenced this process. Koht should, however, be credited for having seen that the establishment of an agrarian class also sprang from the wish for greater participation in the government of the society in order to gain control over the activities of the central authorities. His coupling of the struggle for democracy and national sovereignty also seems to be a fruitful approach.[23]

"Neutral" studies of cause and effect

Bergsgård's continuation of Sars's view of the Norwegian peasant was first criticized by Sverre Steen (1898–1983).[24] In complete contradiction of Bergsgård, Steen claimed that the peasants of the 1800s conducted a "clear and deliberate class politics", and that the peasants' struggle against the official class could be traced back to the way in which the agrarian economy was organized. Steen's starting-point was the idea that "the whole agrarian society in Norway" in Ueland's times enjoyed a high degree of *self-sufficiency*. Consequently all expenditure by the state authority was a source of unrest in the day-to-day business of the farm: "Agrarian society first met the state authority in officials and civil servants, with whom

23 In this point Koht's analysis, like Sars's, coincides with one of the central points in Rokkan's model. Everything suggests that Rokkan was directly influenced by the two historians. This point has earlier been made by Sejersted 1984.
24 Steen 1930–3.

peasants were continually in conflict because there was a natural antagonism between agrarian society and the modern state."

According to Steen, that which knitted peasants together behind a common political line was the demand for "savings in the state budget". Otherwise peasants had diverging interests, depending on what part of the country they came from. On the question of a protective tariff, for instance, corn growers in East Norway opposed the West Norwegian peasants, who were mainly occupied with livestock. Steen therefore denied that peasants were individualist. On the contrary, he believed that "the common peasants hung together in families, clans, settlements, neighbourhoods, districts." In Ueland's time peasants fought for the greatest possible number of matters to be removed from state control and handed over to local authorities. Steen here cited the so-called peasant communalism which developed in the 1830s. This political tendency was strongly anti-bureaucratic, and demanded public savings, less taxes, and the transfer of authority to popularly elected institutions. In his own research Steen carried out thorough empirical studies of agrarian society, in its economic, social, and cultural aspects.[25]

The central concept in Steen's analysis of pre-industrial society was the *self-contained society* – in contrast to the subsequent money society. In this there are clear similarities with the German Karl Bücher's 1893 work, *Die Entstehung der Volkswirtschaft*, which put forward a development theory for agriculture in the transition between a closed economy and an integrated national economy. It is difficult to say conclusively whether this work influenced Steen directly.[26] In other works Steen presented an evolutionary, "slowly the country became our own" perspective.[27] Here he seems to

25 This applies especially to Steen 1957.
26 The Institute for Comparative Research on Human Culture was a workshop for such viewpoints. Here in 1928 Edvard Bull sen. started a project called "Comparative studies on cultural conditions in agrarian society" (Dahl 1990:272). Bücher's social historical works (both the work mentioned and its later editions) are well represented in the University Library in Oslo. The Institute did not have its own library; it stored its books in the University Library, where the project also borrowed offices.
27 Sverre Steen wrote a presentation of Norwegian history, from the Middle Ages up to around 1950; this was the title of the first of four volumes; Steen 1967.

revert to some extent to Fustel de Coulanges, whom Sars had introduced to historical circles in Norway.[28]

Jens Arup Seip (1905–92) and Ottar Dahl (b. 1924) represent the most consistent breach with previous research traditions. Seip began the reorientation with a 1940 article entitled "Problems and methods in Norwegian medieval research" ("Problemer og metode i norsk middelalderforskning"),[29] in which he swept away much of what Marxist historians, including Koht, stood for. In the 1950s he encouraged his student, Ottar Dahl, to strengthen the discipline's theoretical and methodological aspect, breaking with earlier thinking on systems. In spite of the age difference, this was not so much a patron–client relationship as a simple case in which two researchers began to think similarly about a series of issues at about the same time.[30] The central concepts in Dahl's methodological thinking gradually became a markedly individualized problematization, combined with strong demand for empirical testing.[31] He himself characterized his position as *critical empiricism*. His theoretical inspiration came in the first instance from Karl Popper and the Norwegian philosopher Arne Næss, who laid the basis for a strongly analytical tendency within Norwegian philosophy. Dahl additionally built on the history discipline's tradition of source criticism.[32]

While Koht stressed that "all things in a society hang together", Dahl denied that everything in what we call society is of necessity interlinked. He added that if some things do indeed hang together, it must still be legitimate to separate out certain parts for closer study.[33] With this he contributed to the demise of the synthesizing

28 There are as yet no complete analyses of Sverre Steen as a historian. Suggestions on who may have influenced him must therefore remain hypotheses.
29 Seip 1940.
30 Seip gave clear signs of his admiration as an examiner of Dahl's doctoral dissertation, which concerned problems of cause in historical research: "this little book gives the world in a nutshell". Later Seip allowed his assessment appear in a collection of theoretical articles; Seip 1983.
31 See especially Dahl 1956 and Dahl 1967. He later produced a revised version of his methodological teaching in Dahl 1986.
32 An important starting-point was the Danish historian Erslev 1961:73.
33 Dahl 1956:87ff.

STATE- AND NATION-BUILDING 193

ambition, as found in Sars and Koht. Dahl furthermore emphasized that it should be possible to align all kinds of utterances,
including cognitive utterances, with intentional actions. There is
much to suggest that the source of this idea was modern linguistic
philosophy, and in the first instance John L. Austin's concept of
"performative utterances".[34] While earlier source criticism was
mainly concerned with testing the reliability of handed-down
accounts, Dahl's contribution helped towards greater attention
being paid to the question of what induced the protagonists of the
past to say what they said. In a more refined theoretical form,
therefore, he supported the search for *hidden motives*, which was a
main characteristic of Jens Arup Seip's work.[35]

Seip established himself first as a medievalist, where he applied
a structural perspective. As late as 1940 he displayed a positive
attitude towards functionalist thinking, on a more principled basis.[36] That also indicated an interest in what I have called multi-
level analyses. Gradually, however, as he worked through the history of the nineteenth century, he narrowed the perspective and
directed attention towards political activities and the formation of
associations, parties, and political institutions, without extensively
going into functional contexts.[37] As an alternative to Sars and
Koht's orientation to systems, he made it his purpose to study limited "sequences".[38] While his two predecessors interpreted politics
as a reflection of deeper movements in society, Seip went a long
way towards regarding politics as primary. In addition he rejected
Stein Rokkan's use of general models.[39]

34 Dahl's book on methodology (Dahl 1967) uses the concept of the performa-
    tive aspect of utterances, but without referring explicitly to Austin. Ref-
    erence is, however, made in Torstendahl 1966. Torstendahl's and Dahl's
    arguments are very similar, and the two historians had close contacts when
    they were developing their methodological positions.
35 Dahl talks of the performative aspect of utterances; he thereby allows that
    the utterance may be treated as more than a strategic action (e.g. as a cul-
    turally determined linguistic convention).
36 See especially Seip 1940.
37 Dahl 1992.
38 Seip 1974:7–12. Seip was thus also influenced by American sociology as it
    appeared in the 1950s. Seip was involved in the introduction of sociology as
    a university discipline in Norway.
39 Seip 1975.

A central theme in much of Seip's post-war writings was how political leaders used institutions as instruments with which to govern. In a 1963 essay he directed attention to four apparatuses of power:[40] the state powers of Storting and government, the parties, the associations, and the bureaucracy. On this basis he produced a series of pathbreaking works on politics and political institutions, as they had developed after 1814. In this context Seip underlined that which was typically Norwegian in the events and institutions he described.[41]

Seip's view of politics had obviously Machiavellian aspects: the politician's goal is power; power is gained through manipulation; politicians keep their real motives hidden. In line with this view, Seip defined politics as "trading behind closed doors". Among other things he lay great weight in his analysis of the events of 1814 on the power struggle within the political elite around the Danish crown prince, Christian Frederik.[42] Seip was critical of ideology in the sense that he sought "interests" behind ideological utterances.[43] This *realistic* viewpoint[44] also marked his view of nationalism as an ideology:

> National feelings are a typical substitute motive. They have characteristics which make them suitable for such a role. They are easy to admit, easy to find expression for. They have a stimulating effect on one's activities. They take root easily and easily become determining motives, especially among young people.[45]

These qualities, Seip argued, made national sentiments "a good means by which a politician can guide others whither he wishes".[46] Within this "top down" perspective the political elite

40 Seip 1963.
41 E.g. Seip 1959.
42 Seip 1974.
43 On this point he carried on the tradition of his Marxist teacher at the University of Oslo, Edvard Bull sen. (1881–1932). If Bull is not included in this analysis, it is because he hardly touched the subjects discussed in this chapter.
44 On the realistic tendency in recent Norwegian historiography, see Slagstad 1987.
45 Seip 1963:78.
46 Ibid.:79.

appear, if we understand Seip correctly, as ideology-free, while other members of society are a wax which the elite can shape in any way they wish. A consequence of this analysis is that neither Seip nor his students have taken nationalism seriously enough as a driving force in Norwegian politics.

Seip introduced a "golden age" in close empirical studies of politics and political institutions. A relatively large group of historians gradually came to work to a greater or lesser degree within his paradigm.[47] One of Seip's students, Knut Mykland (b. 1920), became in many ways a transitional figure, in that he both continued and revised Seip's view of 1814. He showed himself to be open to the idea of national preconditions for the unrest in 1814, while he too accorded great importance to the power struggle at the top. Within the more conspiratorial framework of interpretation, Mykland also greatly stressed how the Norwegian opposition was led by the Danish crown prince. The tactic according to Mykland was to prevent the new union, in order to then re-establish the monarchical union with Denmark.[48] But Mykland also examined in detail the question of which groups were politically active in the period before 1814. He showed, for instance, that peasants were in general favourable to the union with Denmark – as long as the union lasted. Those who expressed dissatisfaction belonged mainly to the ranks of the bourgeoisie and the officials. Motivations for resistance were mixed, in Mykland's view. Some were opposed to a continued union with Denmark and wished instead a constitutional union with Sweden. Others whole-heartedly backed Christian Frederik's strategy.

Mykland's colleagues at the University of Bergen, Rolf Danielsen (b. 1922), Alf Kaartvedt (b. 1921), and Leiv Mjeldheim (b. 1929) have provided valuable studies of central political institutions and parties. Danielsen and Kaartvedt, for example, have perceptively analyzed the role of the Storting in the system of governance between 1814 and 1908,[49] in which period the parlia-

---

47 The central viewpoints in Seip's many writings about the nineteenth century are summarized in Seip 1974 and Seip 1981.
48 Mykland 1978.
49 Kaartvedt 1964; Danielsen 1964. The period after 1908 receives a less stringent treatment in Greve 1964.

mentary principle won through.[50] In Oslo, Per Maurseth (b. 1932), Edgeir Benum (b. 1939), and Kåre D. Tønnesson (b. 1926), of whom the first two were students of Seip, wrote correspondingly broad surveys of the history of central administration in the periods 1814–44, 1845–84, and 1914–40.[51] A prominent element of these analyses is the close empirical treatment of the subjects considered. The research strategy is overwhelmingly inductive. To that extent they follow Ottar Dahl's strong demand for empirical testing.

Danielsen and Kaartvedt especially were close to Seip's train of thought. It is natural to link these two historians to Seip in that they strongly emphasize tactical considerations within the political elite. Danielsen, for example, suggested that Venstre's leaders in 1891 radicalized the politics of the union in order to outmanoeuvre Høyre and because they believed that a national policy could help mend differences within Venstre, especially over social policy issues. For Danielsen, however, Prime Minister Christian Michelsen, head of the Norwegian government in 1905, chose to act on political party grounds, since he thought at that point that the union stood in the way of a broad bourgeois coalition against the rising tide of socialism.[52] Danielsen sought merely, in his own words, to explain "the timing and the circumstances" of Venstre's radicalization in 1891. The linking of Michelsen's motives of strengthening the party to his persistence in the union question was expressly intended as a partial explanation of why the union had to fail. By tailoring his subject so narrowly, Danielsen avoided the question of the role played by nationalist ideology. He preferred not to draw into his argumentation the implications of nation-building, which had been proceeding for many decades, for the choice of political course.

In a detailed study of the conservative Francis Hagerup (Høyre), prime minister between 1903 and 1905,[53] Kaartvedt

---

50 A standard work about the deep conflicts in Norwegian politics up to 1884 is Kaartvedt 1956.
51 Maurseth 1979; Benum 1979; Tønnesson 1979.
52 Danielsen 1961–2.
53 He was replaced by Christian Michelsen when the conflict about the union intensified in 1905.

supported the thesis that the union had to be ended because it stood in the way of a bourgeois coalition.[54] But Kaartvedt also raised the question of the anchoring of nationalism within the society. He considered, for instance, the connection between nationalism and economic interests as follows:

> The socio-economic basis of the nationalist movement was a rural society in the process of transforming itself from a subsistence to a cash economy, lacking any significant foreign export markets, and a lower middle class preoccupied with local economic problems. For these groups the Union could have little economic appeal.[55]

The "upper class", by contrast, had according to Kaartvedt profited economically from the union. But the so-called Bilateral Law (*mellomriksloven*), which secured free trade between Sweden and Norway, was revoked in 1897, and this cementing factor disappeared. Thus Kaartvedt limits the basis of nationalism: it applies merely to economic interests in the strict sense. He prefers to explain Norwegian nationalism in the period by pointing to the *removal* of positive bonds with Sweden.

In essence it remained for Seip and his students to explain the growth of this ideology and to show its political effects. By way of critique of this research tradition, I would underline that political actions first and foremost acquire *meaning* when they are interpreted in the light of a social and economic context; at a given time, forms of mentality, *interpretations of reality* and *attitudes*, exist which are linked to social groups and classes, and which are marked by the economic and social situation. Faced with complex contexts, research of motivations falls short. This applies particularly to the focus on individual motives, which are of little worth when the task is to explain the growth of mass movements covering the whole country. We should also seek to benefit from the results of comparative social research to a much greater extent than historians have done so far.

---

54 Kaartvedt 1980b.
55 Kaartvedt 1950a:15f.

A new constructivism[56]

Edvard Bull jun. (1914–86) was one of the first to indicate a change of course, when he criticized Seip's preoccupation with the political elite. Bull belonged to a social history tradition which throughout ran parallel to Seip's paradigm. Now Bull sought to draw on his career experience in the study of politics. While Seip took refuge in the leading politicians, and saw history from the top down, Bull proceeded to study history from below – a "from the bottom up" perspective: "My main goal concerns to what extent and in what ways people have usually been able to decide over their daily lives, and especially their working lives."[57] Bull thus underlined that there were other power factors than the political apparatus.

To supplement Bull it must be noted that Seip's focus on politics at the elite level easily leads to the granting of too great an explanatory power to the power motive and to tactical manoeuvres. On the other hand one gets a distorted picture if one studies social reactions in isolation, as was Bull's wont. In other words Bull's analysis is as narrow as Seip's, in that consideration of *interaction* between politics and social movements is easily omitted. Bull's demand that history was to be studied from the bottom up nevertheless marked a step in the direction of a renewed interest in a sociological approach.

This constructive ambition receives perhaps its strongest expression in Francis Sejersted (b. 1936). Sejersted has throughout been close to the conservative party, Høyre.[58] Yet he has become the one established historian who has shown the closest kinship with the theoretical positions assumed by the neo-Marxists of the 1970s. That is to say that Sejersted has made more energetic attempts to capture the interaction between various social strata than many historians who are politically more radical.[59] More precisely, his key concepts for understanding how politics happens are "traditional ideas, internalized norms, and ritual actions".[60] An

56 On the concept of constructivism, see Sejersted 1994.
57 Bull 1975.
58 See Sejersted 1989.
59 See below.
60 Sejersted 1993:337.

interest in politicians' tactical manoeuvres thus recedes into the background. Sejersted's view is expressed, for example, in a series of works on the nineteenth century's *liberal norm structure*, upon which he builds an ideal type summed up as the bourgeois "constitutional state".[61] Sejersted was thus the first to provide a basis for a synthesis of the evolution of the Norwegian state in the nineteenth century. While Seip emphasized that leading officials aimed at a wide-ranging guidance of the society, Sejersted argues that the bureaucracy, on the contrary, tried to rescind *creative* policies in favour of a *routine* governance.[62] Creative activity was to be left to private initiative, in accordance with the ideology of the times. Thus, in Sejersted's view, the corps of officials lined up behind the expanding bourgeoisie. In this interpretation of the nineteenth-century Norwegian state, Sejersted was clearly influenced by Jürgen Habermas's analysis of private and public spheres in modern society.[63]

To the extent that Sejersted interprets the norms of politics in the light of forces outside the political institutions, he assumes the mantle of Sars and Koht. Yet there are evident differences. While the two predecessors stressed cultural conflicts and conflicts about political participation, Sejersted draws attention to constitutional norms and economic interests. The orientation towards more universal principles at the same time breaks with the idea of Norway as a historical curiosity. Sejersted thus views Norwegian history in the light of more general developmental trends, and uses it as a basis for systematic cross-national comparisons.

Nation-building has not hitherto been a central theme in Sejersted's writings; nor has he furnished empirical analyses of nationalism. On the other hand he has sketched an interesting perspective of the union with Sweden, in which he pays homage to the syntheses of Sars and Koht. At the same time he stresses that nationalism was a real driving force up to 1905. Breaking with, among others, Jens Arup Seip and Rolf Danielsen, he writes: "Even

---

61 Sejersted 1978, and elsewhere.
62 Sejersted's viewpoint was criticized by the Seip school; see e.g. Maurseth 1987.
63 Sejersted referred to Habermas's *Strukturwandel der Öffentlichkeit* (1962).

if those who appealed to nationalism did so for tactical reasons, the nationalism to which they appealed must have existed, in order for the tactic to work."[64]

Sejersted has hitherto stood almost alone in his inclination to change the paradigm. In the 1970s interest in the history of the labour movement did indeed grow among Norwegian historians. This undoubtedly owed something to the political radicalization of university circles which occurred at the end of the 1960s in Norway as in many western countries. Despite the preoccupation with Marxist theory, however, much of the new research which sprang from these projects was not particularly oriented towards the connections between politics and society. The focus was rather on the theoretical and strategic considerations of the socialist leadership. In short, these historians wrote more about centralized debates on theses than about workers themselves and the attitudes prevailing in lower social strata. They largely ignored Koht's overall perspective on the integration of the working class. There are some signs of this kind of approach in the contributions of Per Maurseth, Tore Pryser (b. 1945), and Trond Bergh (b. 1946) to a major work on the history of the labour movement.[65] Finally it should be mentioned that Knut Kjeldstadli (b. 1948), a student radical in the 1970s, presented in 1994 a wide-ranging survey of Norway's history in the years 1905 to 1935 in which he describes the Labour Party's path to government in 1935 with the help of superficial labels such as "class compromise" and "tactical alliance".[66] An overarching historical–sociological grip is lacking. A party which a few years earlier had talked of revolution and the state's appropriation of the means of production now assumed the responsibility of power within a capitalist society; Kjeldstadli's explanation for this remarkable shift is a long, à la carte list of more or less equally important moments.

Within the subject area of nation-building, Øyvind Østerud

64 Sejersted 1984:115.
65 Maurseth 1987 (on the years up to the Labour Party's accession to power in 1935); Pryser 1988 (on the crucial years 1935 to 1945); Bergh 1987 (on what he calls the Labour Party's golden age, when the party attempted to implement its project of a social democratic modernization).
66 Kjeldstadli 1994.

(b. 1944) has worked in a far more pathbreaking manner than most historians, particularly by bringing in theoretical positions developed within international comparative research.[67] He has in addition brought nationalist ideology and deliberate nation-building into Rokkan's model. Østerud points out among other things how nationalist arguments were used to legitimize the foundation of the Norwegian state, and how the school system spread ideas of a common history and a common language. He also stresses that Norwegian patriotism fulfilled a general need to belong during the growth of mass society, when traditional social bonds were torn apart.[68]

Trond Nordby (b. 1943) has attempted to show in more detail how national identification and an active nationalism interacted in the years before 1905.[69] One must distinguish analytically between these two phenomena. The former basically involves consciousness of belonging to a community which is created by history, and which is characterized by a certain similarity in customs and forms of believe. One may value this community, or at least parts of it, without necessarily being a nationalist. Nationalism for its part involves both an ideology and a programme of action. The ideology endorses ideas about the people (folket), the ethnic group, or indeed the race having special qualities. The political goals will be either to conquer territory or to defend oneself against conquest, or in some cases to break away from a larger state.

As for national identification, Nordby's historical analysis emphasizes the cultural gathering which occurred from the 1870s, as roads and railways opened up more or less isolated districts to the outside world. At the same time people generally received a better education, and there were ever more newspapers and periodicals. In addition people joined country-wide organizations in far greater numbers than before. This led to a process of consolidation in opinions and attitudes. Market integration came later; for agriculture this was linked to investment in new

67 See e.g. Østerud 1978b and 1994.
68 Østerud 1984.
69 Nordby 1991. In order to finally be able to draw a picture of the most important phases in Norwegian nation-building up to 1905, I shall briefly state the central arguments of this book.

machines. This led to credit obligations and dependence on buying and selling. The latter process started in the 1860s, but began to accelerate only after the turn of the century, and especially in the years around the First World War.

The analysis of the *political* aspects of integration rests on Rokkan's four stages:[70] allocation of rights (formal incorporation), use of rights (mobilization), own representation (activation), and nationalization of lines of conflict in society (politicization).[71] The first stage came in 1814, when all owner–occupier peasants (including those who leased land registered for taxation), officials, and urban bourgeoisie gained the franchise.[72] The peasants dominated in terms of numbers within this electorate. At the same time they became eligible for election to the Storting. But a long time passed before the broad range of these voter groups made use of their rights. Instead they allowed the officials to dominate, not just administratively, but also in politics. The transition to communal self-government (1837) meant that peasants began to get better schooling as politicians, and from the middle of the century, more and more of them dared to let themselves be nominated for parliamentary elections. Participation in elections also boomed, first during the struggles about the constitution which led to the breakthrough of parliamentarianism (1884), and later during the referendum of 1905. As soon as independence had been won, new differences quickly arose, particularly between socialist and bourgeois parties. This fact, however, does not invalidate Rokkan's scheme of development. The point is that the parties, the first of which was established in 1884, functioned as national parties and presented the same programme all over the country, and at the same time entered in municipal elections.

Despite the fact that national identification was strengthened in the course of the 1880s, it was still not sufficiently aggressive to tear Norway out of the union. Only in the very last phase of the union did a spontaneous tide of opinion rise to embrace the entire nation: the fatherland must tear itself free! National identification

70 I here disregard other elements of the model, such as territorial integration and socio-cultural standardization.
71 Rokkan 1970:227.
72 At the time, of course, this applied only to men.

thus at the time bore nationalism in its womb. But for the majority of Norwegian voters, this involved a temporary ideology of action, which grew only when the Swedes displayed their arrogance, and which receded after the dissolution of the union.

The politics which created conflicts and drove developments towards the break with Sweden sprang in the first instance from a nationalist movement whose socio-economic roots lay in certain parts of agrarian society. The movement manifested itself in the 1880s in shooting associations, which constituted a popular militia of the radicals in the constitutional struggle up to 1884. It was prominent again in the language question (the campaign for the use of New Norwegian – *nynorsk*), and in a nationalist youth movement which was consolidated in 1896 into the organization Norigs Ungdomslag. Around 1905 this youth movement comprised almost 50,000 members, distributed among *c.* 800 local groups, while there were fewer than 70 local language associations.

The growth of a nationalist ideology must be seen in the context of the changes society underwent during industrialization, from the middle of the nineteenth century up to the outbreak of the First World War.[73] The economic–historical part of this interpretation is based, as is Øyvind Østerud's, on the anthropological tradition established by A. V. Chayanov's classic work *The Theory of Peasant Economy*,[74] whereas the political–historical part is in the first instance inspired by the British historian Eric J. Hobsbawm.[75] The form of agrarian nationalism encountered here is evidently not a specifically Norwegian phenomenon. Drawing on comparative studies by the Czech scholar Miroslav Hroch,[76] Hobsbawm shows that such movements often occurred when peasants came

73 Nordby 1991.
74 Øyvind Østerud was the first to develop Sverre Steen's view of the relation between agrarian politics and the way agriculture was conducted in pre-industrial Norway. Peasants were not necessarily, as Steen suggested, concerned with supporting themselves. In contrast to modern farmers, their economic horizon was to meet the household's economic needs for a year at a time. Østerud 1978a. Bjørn Qviller, a historian of antiquity, has contributed strongly to my orientation towards social–anthropological theories; see Qviller 1981.
75 See e.g. Hobsbawm 1990.
76 Hroch 1985.

in contact with industrial society. Nationalism became a part of a defensive ideology, directed against the social and economic transformations set in motion by industrialization and the development of the market. As a general trait, Hobsbawm suggests, nationalism had its greatest appeal in areas which were not yet fully integrated, but where industrial society was sufficiently near at hand for the inhabitants, and especially peasants, to feel threatened. This pattern suits Norway well. The core areas of nationalism in the last part of the nineteenth century covered a central belt of the country, which included the valleys and the inner fjord areas ("mountain and fjord Norway").

Occupations in these cultural areas corresponded in many ways to the transitional society described by Hobsbawm. Specifically, *subsistence agriculture* was practiced; the farm constituted a social and economic unit, and the goal was to secure the livelihood of the household for a year at a time. Socially, politically, and culturally, the individual district communities constituted relatively stable and closed units. In terms of business activity, "mountain and fjord Norway" differed from both the fisheries districts along the coast, which were strongly linked to the market economy from early on, and the most industrialized areas around the Oslo fjord. In large parts of "mountain and fjord Norway", the numbers involved in secondary activities were relatively small as late as the census of 1900.[77] This observation applies especially to areas where the first shooting associations and the later youth movement had the bulk of their members. The same areas belonged to the strongest bastions of the New Norwegian language. Furthermore, Venstre regularly received around three-quarters of the votes here in the Storting elections around the turn of the century.

Towards the end of the nineteenth century, the new industrial society encroached more closely on the relatively backward areas. Inhabitants felt the pressure on traditional occupations. They feared that new social groups would assume control, and regarded the new urban lifestyle with deep suspicion. Against this background nationalism developed as a defence ideology against the

77 Done using the municipal database at the Norwegian Social Science Data Services (NSD) in Bergen. See Nordby 1989:116.

modernization of society. Teacher training colleges with a specifically nationalist profile were established. Those who were trained
at these schools contributed to the spread of national and democratic attitudes which marked large parts of agrarian society
within this region.

The suggestion that nationalism was a defensive ideology is
underpinned by expressed beliefs. The youth movement gathered
poets, journalists, and other writers. The nature of their arguments was marked by its origins in a transitional society. The stress
on the national community can be traced back to the social organization of agrarian society around the neighbourhood; nationalism merely added a broader perspective: from district to
nation–state. Nationalism accordingly assumed agrarian society's
mistrust of people from outside. Attacks were especially directed at
the official class, many of whose ancestors were of German or
Danish origin. As is also evident from comparative research, leaders of the national movement often had an agricultural background. They had themselves risen in social terms, but they saw
clear differences between old and new kinds of production, and
they tended to idealize the idyll of the old agrarian society as a contrast to the new industrial surroundings.

In the period up to 1905, politicians linked to the nationalist
movement played an active role in Venstre. They pushed forward
the great conflicts with Sweden, partly by rejecting all attempts to
make the union closer, and partly by demanding greater independence. It could seem that the nationalists were driven by a need to
outbid each other in national fervour. The revision of the party
programme in 1891, dealt with by Rolf Danielsen, for example,
resulted from pressure by a "noisy" opposition.[78] At the party's
national conference, this managed to press through a vague proposal about "an arrangement of the treatment of the diplomatic
question, which introduces significant constitutional responsibility for the Norwegian state authorities", which also meant Norway
nominating its own foreign minister. The latter was a radical
demand, which few if any Swedish politicians could have accepted
at this point without declaring war.

78 Including the poet Bjørnstjerne Bjørnson.

The fact that the proposal for a separate Norwegian consular service came from representatives of local associations refutes Danielsen's model of tactical manoeuvres. It must be added that the Venstre government did not follow up this radicalism on the union until well into 1892. If the persistent nationalists succeeded in establishing their views within Venstre, it was because this radicalism fitted into the party's strong democratic tradition. In the last phase of the union, the conflict with Sweden come to centre on the matter of separate Norwegian consular representatives (both a symbol and a lever), autonomy in foreign affairs, and the nation's right to change the nature of co-operation within the union. The most radical within Venstre began to call for full independence in the 1890s. Høyre, however, showed great respect for the union's existing institutions. On the question of revising the relationship within the union, Høyre opted for negotiation rather than unilateral Norwegian actions, right up to the very last phase.

Before the dissolution of the union in 1905, the Storting approved a law providing for a separate Norwegian consular service. The king refused to sanction it. Christian Michelsen's coalition government for its part refused to sign it, and left office. The situation was deadlocked, as no other party could take over. On 7 June 1905 the Storting responded by declaring the union dissolved. Broad support for this decision proved that Venstre's activism had also won through on the national level. Even Høyre, which in the 1890s was prepared to accept the extension of the union's institutions, accepted the separatist solution. Later in the year, in the August 13 referendum, the voters unanimously endorsed the decree of June 7.

The background to the unanimity in 1905 is worth recapping. In 1902 negotiations with Sweden began. The following year the two countries' governments issued a communiqué which proposed a separate consular service. The declaration was vaguely formulated, but it created great expectations in Norway. Especially the conservatives looked forward to a solution of this issue. In autumn 1904 the Swedish prime minister, Erik Gustav Boström, torpedoed all these hopes. He stated that the Swedish negotiators had gone too far, and gave the declaration an interpretation which underlined Swedish supremacy in the union. This interpretation was

later called the Swedish "point of dependency" ("*lydrikepunktene*").
This demonstration of power ignited a patriotism which can only
be explained by reference to that which I call national identification. Even those hitherto friendly towards the union reacted vio-
lently.

The relation between nation-building and nationalism merits
more research. The former has mainly been treated in political
terms; we still lack an account of how Norwegian culture, in a
broader historical perspective, became unified through a common
written language, through the building up of the education
system, and through the state organization of religious observance.[79] In view of the role of nationalism, the agitation of the
various groups which were gathered within Venstre should be
studied more thoroughly than hitherto. There should also be more
detailed studies of precisely how the contacts between nationalist
organizations and rural people came about.[80] If the goal is to give
the most complete analysis possible, my own investigations have
been too biased towards a focus on agrarian nationalism. While it
is true that Norway was largely an agrarian society well into the
twentieth century, active nationalism also drew strength from
other sources. An important theme is therefore the relationship
between agrarian nationalism and the nationalism which developed in the towns and in intellectual circles.

In recent years historians and other social scientists have
shown increasing interest in nation-building and nationalism, and
this will undoubtedly lead to new interpretations. The medievalist
Kåre Lunden (b. 1930) has lately attempted to unite "old" syntheses with more recent research on nationalism. He became especially involved in the debate within the discipline about the origins
of the unrest of 1814.[81] Lunden also intervened in the contemporary debate on Norway's relation to the European Union (EU) on a
nationalist basis.[82] The head of the Norwegian organization

79 This would help to fill out empirically one of the main points in Rokkan's
   model. The same criterion was put forward as central in more recent years
   by Gellner 1983.
80 My investigation is mainly based on ecological data.
81 Lunden 1992.
82 Lunden 1993.

opposing Norwegian membership of the EU said that he did not
wish to have anything to do with nationalists. Lunden nevertheless argued before the autumn 1994 referendum that the "No"
side would "need all the 'nationalists' it can mobilize". Lunden's
goal was to build further on Norwegian traditions, politically and
culturally. In this context he regarded membership of the EU as
threatening the annihilation of the nation. The heritage of Sars
and Koht, in other words, has been taken up again, at least by one
important historian.

What will the future show?

The debate on whether Norway should join the EU enables one to
test the strength of national identification and to find out how
great a potential for nationalist movements exists in today's Norway. These questions were raised during the first referendum in
1972, when the majority voted against membership of the EEC, as
it was then called. The opposition comprised a broad alliance, and
there was little to suggest that traditional nationalism was especially active at the time. Some indeed thought along nationalist
lines, believing that Norway should be kept for Norwegians and
that Norwegian culture should be protected behind closed cur-
tains. But these were not many. Others spoke about how poorly a
small nation would be treated within a larger union. Another
group was most concerned with democracy and the distance to
where decisions would be taken ("Brussels is further away than
Oslo"); democracy was felt to work better within small units.
Groups of urban radicals wanted as much as possible to maintain
national controls over capital. To an extent, much of this represented a nationalist tendency. National symbols were also used,
and symbols occasionally played on many levels. This was the case
with the badge "No to the sale of Norway", with the flag in the
background. But the bulk of the opposition comprised people concerned with defending their own livelihood.

In recent years, as the question of membership was reopened,
protectionists once again dominated the opposition to the EU,
demanding protection of agriculture, fisheries, and North Sea oil
resources. Many sceptics also revived the democracy argument. As

in 1972, opposition embraced an unspecified "fear of the unknown" in addition to the motivations just mentioned; no one knew what EU membership entailed, much less what the union would look like in the future. Such an amorphous threat could mean that many seek a mental "reinforcement" in the use of national symbols. One of the country's leading handicrafts stores, at Bø in Telemark, reported that the sale of traditional costumes rose in advance of the referendum of 1972, and that the same was happening in 1994.

It is an open question whether national identification is so strong that it can again transform itself into nationalism, as in 1905. We will have a new opportunity to address this question if the elite again on some future occasion seek to manoeuvre Norway into the EU. The answer is probably no, because large parts of the political elite have long practiced a kind of national deconstruction – to turn Rokkan's concept on its head – with the intention of clearing the way for Norwegian membership of the EU. Leading politicians, especially within the Labour Party and Høyre, have in recent years spread the idea that steadily fewer problems can be solved within the framework of the nation–state. At the same time Norway, like many other countries, has undergone a cultural assimilation which crosses national frontiers. Perhaps the historians of the future will write not just of the rise of the Norwegian nation–state, but also of its fall.

8. Social History
Jan Eivind Myhre

The birth of modern Norwegian social history took place around 1970, according to many contemporaries as well as later historians. Speaking at the centenary celebration of the Norwegian Historical Association, Edvard Bull jun. and Sivert Langholm launched a programme for the future direction of Norwegian historical research.[1] Their appeal for a social history was heeded by the large post–World War II generation which inundated the universities from the late 1960s. They envisioned a history of powerless people, of the small societal units, of relations between age groups (Bull); in other words a history from below, "micro-history", studied with theories and methods borrowed from the social sciences (Langholm).[2]

In 1970 Langholm, on behalf of the Department of History at the University of Oslo, initiated a large social history project.[3] Graduate students rushed to the project, as well as to the offices of Bull and other historians providing supervision of social history theses. The intellectual climate of the 1970s provided a fertile soil in which the seeds of social history could grow. The number of Norwegian social history dissertations climbed from fewer than five per year in the 1950s and slightly more than five in the 1960s to an annual average of almost thirty in the peak years 1974–83. Their share of all history theses rose from 10–20 percent in the 1950s and 1960s to a peak of more than 40 percent in the early 1980s.[4]

---

1 Bull 1970 and Langholm 1970. The Association was actually founded in December 1869, but the centenary celebration did not take place until January 1970.
2 Particularly evident in Langholm 1972, 1974, 1976a, and 1976b.
3 Langholm 1976a; Langholm 1974; Myhre 1978a.
4 Hubbard 1992. Of all social history theses, working-class studies, women's history, and historical demography (mobility and family history) loomed particularly large. "Theses" refers to the *cand. philol.* (*hovedfag*) degree. The theses may be placed somewhere between an American M.A. and a Ph.D. In length they are between 100 and 400 pages. See also Chapter 3.

Seen from a distance of twenty-five years, however, the upsurge of social history from around 1970 was in some respects a *rebirth* of the discipline. Social topics and social viewpoints had a long-standing tradition in Norwegian historiography. Norwegian *society* and the *people* of Norway had often been the focus of the classical works; the *state* was not allowed to dominate the historical field.[5] This may help to explain the relative absence of resistance to the new trend from the old regime of the Norwegian historical establishment. Yet Langholm had interpreted Bull's view as a revolutionary clarion call, intending to "liberate social history from the dominance of political history." In a sense, there was not that much to conquer. I intend to show, however, that there were several undeniably new themes and approaches. They were significant enough to make the years around 1970 a watershed in Norwegian historiography, despite the fact that the new social history was slow to become institutionalized in the Norwegian university system.

A major theme in this chapter is the comparison of the older social historical tradition with the new movement of the last short generation. The salient points in this discussion of the development of Norwegian social history are the following:

1) The *societal background* and social relevance of Norwegian historiography have always been important. Three aspects in particular concern us here: Modern nationalism pointed to the epochs, societal strata, and social groups relevant to the formation of Norwegian national identity. The labour movement, and the radical thrust of the 1970s, inspired much of the work identified as social history. Finally, where social history and political history intersect, we find the history of social policy, or welfare state history, a subdiscipline on the rise from about 1970, albeit with scattered predecessors.[6]

2) Norwegian historians have long had a commitment to *total his-*

---

5 Dahl 1990; Maurseth 1984; and Sejersted 1994 have made this point with varying emphasis.

6 A.-L. Seip 1981. See also Myhre 1986 for a review of the historiography of Norwegian living conditions.

tory, in this connection denoting *local history* and general works on *national history*. Local history has a long tradition as a scholarly endeavour, the ambitions regarding total history being directed towards social rather than political history. Large-scale commissioned works of national history (ranging in length from eight to fifteen volumes) have been published roughly every twenty years throughout the twentieth century. In addition, there are textbooks and smaller works of national syntheses.

3) Although a fairly strong current of social history has existed in Norwegian historiography for more than a century, the *theoretical foundations* have changed considerably. Generally speaking, social history has become more theoretical over time, with greater refinement and a higher level of consciousness concerning *method*. Inspiration from the social sciences and the humanities has been increasingly common, and foreign impulses have become more pronounced.

4) The writing of social history has been a means of coming to grips with *larger societal processes*, such as urbanization, industrialization, democratization, modernization, and the emergence of welfare states and societies. The competing approaches are economic and, in particular, political. Langholm's project "defines itself as *social historical*, and aims in particular at studying changes in social structure during the process of *industrialization.*"[7]

I have so far deliberately avoided any attempt at defining "social history". Defining the concept has its own history which is itself a part of the historiography. Historians have at various times perceived social history in different ways. One is its subject matter: powerless people, the working classes, or social groups in general. The subject is also seen as a moral or political project ("from below"), by the level or sphere of society in question ("social conditions", everyday life, work conditions, private life, social relations, social occasions, and the like) and by the approach it offers to history in general (the social structure as the basic grasp in under-

7 Langholm 1974:244.

standing society as a whole). These various perceptions have guided my identification of social history where authors offer no explicit views as to what kind of history they were writing. Depending on the definition employed, social history may overlap with other historical subdisciplines dealt with in this volume, such as economic history, local history, and women's history. In one instance, the borderline is particularly hard to draw. *Social policy* originates in social conditions and the perceptions of these conditions. The history of social policy also shares with social history the ambition to offer a synthesizing perspective of history. The Norwegian version of this perspective may be labelled "the rise of the welfare state" and will be included in the present account.

The primacy of society

Nationalism and Marxism as social history: Koht and Bull

In 1915 the Christiania newspaper *Tidens Tegn* published an obituary of the German historian Karl Lamprecht. The author was Edvard Bull sen. (1881–1932), later to become professor at the University of Christiania (Oslo). He endorsed Lamprecht's historical perspective, and in particular his broad conception of what history was about. For Lamprecht, history was not confined to the politics of the national state: it should deal with "culture in the very widest sense of the word, all manifestations of human lives, spiritual, material and social."[8]

Bull's colleague and contemporary Halvdan Koht (1873–1965) shared Bull's viewpoints in many respects.[9] Koht also advocated a historical science focusing on economic and social problems, dealing with ordinary people as well as statesmen, and approaching society in a structural way. Neither Bull nor Koht aimed to carry out the full consequences of Lamprecht's programme, but both departed clearly from the ethnographic orientation of many nineteenth-century Norwegian historians. The Rankean brand of political history had never dominated Norwegian historiography.[10]

8 Bull 1933 (1915):17. All translations are by the present author.
9 On Bull and Koht, see Dahl 1990 and 1974; and Skobba 1994.
10 See Chapter 2.

Bull and Koht drew inspiration from Sombart and Marx as well as Lamprecht. Both grew up in a nationalist radical–liberal environment. Bull moved in a Marxist direction quite early, while Koht had a rather loose relationship to Marxism. From a Marxist standpoint, they took slightly different courses. Bull, a medievalist and local historian, undertook detailed and almost rigidly empirical studies of economic structure in medieval Norway and of religious orientation among ordinary Norwegians. The influence of Sombart is most apparent in his three-volume study of the town of Oslo from the eleventh to the eighteenth century. Here he follows the German in dividing the inhabitants into two groups: people exercising economic functions for the surrounding world and therefore serving as founders of the town (*Städtegründer*), and people filling purely local functions, the town occupiers (*Städtefüller*).

Koht seemed less close to the sources than Bull. His best-known social historical interpretation is given in the title of a long article from 1910: "Peasant against burgher in modern Norwegian history".[11] This applied the Marxist theory of class struggle to preindustrial Norwegian society in the nineteenth-century nationalist Norwegian tradition. The burghers, predecessors of the bourgeoisie, were alien to Norwegian society in early modern times, being of mainly Danish and German extraction. The most eminent historian of this nationalist tradition was Johan Ernst Sars (1835–1917), whose name, like those of Bull and Koht, appears frequently on the pages of this book. Sars's famous synthesis of Norwegian history from the Middle Ages through the nineteenth century was that the (freeholding) peasants were the bearers of Norwegian identity through centuries under foreign masters (nobles, burghers, civil servants). The decline of the indigenous nobility in the Late Middle Ages, which left the country open to foreign dominance, was turned into a democratic advantage in the nineteenth century when a degree of political independence was achieved. Norway had no aristocracy, and the leading class of higher civil servants, which had by then become native, ruled in the name of the people, that is, the peasants. In the second half of the century, the peasants themselves seized political power,

11 Koht 1910.

through the liberal–national coalition whose institutional expression was the Venstre party.

Sars cannot reasonably be labelled a social historian. His prime interest was in political institutions and ideas; the common people are viewed at a safe distance. His synthesis, however, built on the development of social structure, and social groups formed the major categories. Bull and especially Koht rearranged the groups and their relationships in a Marxist direction. Furthermore, their knowledge of the everyday life of Norwegians in the past was both wider and deeper than that of Sars and other nineteenth-century historians, even though economic conditions and mentalities were much more prevalent in their works than other "social" conditions.

What the three had in common was a structural view of history, and this separated them from several earlier and contemporary historians. Sars was the first self-acclaimed positivist of the Norwegian historical profession. Koht was more oriented towards classes than Bull, while the reverse was the case with other structural phenomena. Bull explicitly endorsed comparisons in historical research. Jens Arup Seip, a proponent of actor-oriented history, in 1940 criticized both Koht and Bull for leaving individual actors out of history.[12] In the case of Koht, this charge was rather unjustified.

All three were also evolutionists, with clearly discernible teleological traits. Sars showed more than an element of Whiggery in that he saw the Norwegian peasant-based liberal democratic movement as the zenith of history. Koht and Bull were prominent Labour politicians, and both became foreign ministers in the interwar years. They regarded the attainment of socialism or social democracy as the goal and meaning of history. This is much more apparent in the scholarly works of Koht than those of Bull.

Social narratives and social structures: Steen and Holmsen

The next generations of social historians, still *avant la lettre*, disposed of teleological elements, whether nationalist or socialist, while keeping the structural viewpoints. Clearly visible from

12 Seip 1940.

around 1930, the new tendencies involved a preoccupation with larger social configurations (such as types of societies), yet were at the same time firmly empirical. In a sense, the new approach was sociological, though without most of the concepts used by sociologists.

The principal figures were Sverre Steen (1898–1983), whose writings mainly cover the sixteenth to the nineteenth century, and Andreas Holmsen (1905–89), a historian of medieval and early modern times. Both produced general Norwegian national history as well as works of local history and monographs and articles devoted to more specific problems. Although they differed in some respects, Steen being the great narrator and Holmsen the more analytic researcher, they both believed that structure, or large categories, must have priority over actors in historical explanation.

In a review of Jens Arup Seip's 1945 book on the crisis of the civil servant regime in the 1870s (*Et regime foran undergangen*), Steen noted that the problem seems to boil down to a conflict between two men, Stang and Broch, and doubts that it is historically correct to pose the problem this way. Individuals "mirror" systems rather than make them, insisted Steen, who then criticized Seip for placing too much emphasis on individual actors.[13]

In a programmatic article of 1940, Holmsen attempted to pin down what was new as follows: an "essentially direct study of the continuous historical reality arising from and around the lives and activities of social groups and whole societies."[14] A key word is "direct". Interest in structural phenomena was nothing new, Holmsen admitted, but these had mainly been studied indirectly, through events and individuals, as in the cases of Sars and Koht. A direct study, he asserted, involved the scrutiny of structure-registering sources like tax records, censuses, fine records, property registers, military files, and the like. Holmsen wanted to study reality as "historical structure", concentrating on the stable factors in history. For this he found local studies particularly suitable.[15]

Holmsen distinguished between three structural elements: the

13 After Edding 1983:108.
14 Holmsen 1940:27–8.
15 Fagerbakk 1989.

structural *function*, satisfying societal needs; the structural *matter* (*stoff*), e.g. institutions; and finally the set of *attitudes* towards function or matter adopted by social groups or the society at large. All three elements contribute to structural continuity but in different ways and at different speeds. Holmsen makes the point that social institutions, for instance, may persist even when the social needs which gave rise to them cease to exist.

These lines of thought were presented to support what Holmsen called the *retrospective* method: the procedure of extrapolating backwards into ages devoid of sources. Holmsen and several older contemporaries such as Asgaut Steinnes (1892–1973) were interested in economic and social aspects of Norwegian agrarian society in the Middle Ages, particularly as seen through settlement history. While neither agrarian studies nor structural studies were new to Norwegian historical research in the 1930s,[16] it is not difficult to identify the origins of some of Holmsen's ideas. Marc Bloch had attended the Sixth International Congress of the Historical Sciences in Oslo in 1928. He was also invited (with Alfons Dopsch) to the Institute for Comparative Research in Human Culture in 1929, to help launch the Institute's new programme Comparative Studies in the Cultural Conditions of Rural Society. Bloch's Oslo lectures were later revised and published as *Les caractères originaux de l'histoire rurale française*, published by the Institute.[17]

The influence of the Annales school on Norwegian historiography before the 1970s was felt mainly through Holmsen and was restricted to the field of pre-modern history. Holmsen acquired many followers through his settlement studies and particularly through the Nordic Deserted Farms Projects of the 1960s and 1970s. Major figures here were Jørn Sandnes (b. 1926) and Helge Salvesen (b. 1947). The Institute of Comparative Cultural Research initiated research on the mountain dairy farm institution (the *seter*) and on the farmstead and social institutions in rural Norway in general. Most results were of economic rather than social historical interest, however.

16 The Institute for Comparative Research in Human Culture (Institutt for sammenlignende kulturforskning) was established in 1922. Edvard Bull sen. was one of the main initiators.

17 Dahl 1990:272.

Steen's endeavours were rooted in a somewhat diluted Marxist tradition. He was well versed in a wide variety of quantitative sources such as censuses and land registers, and often employed them, but he never did so in a large-scale or systematic fashion. He certainly shared with his teachers Bull and Koht the broad view of what history was about. Neither Steen nor his contemporaries harboured the contempt for political history felt by so many foreign colleagues of the "new history" school. The same was true of his predecessors, although Bull once spoke rather condescendingly of the "great man" view of history, and Holmsen was criticized for playing down the role of politics in his textbook on Norwegian history before 1660. These inter-war Norwegian historians were masters of synthesis, even without the teleological element. Steen's major syntheses are his four volumes of Norwegian history from 1500 to 1814, a couple of local histories, and several books on early nineteenth-century Norway.[18]

Steen broke with the nationalist tradition. In his account of the 1814 liberation, forces outside Norway (Great Power politics) played a more important role than nationalistic sentiments and the efforts of the Norwegians. The concept of class, on the other hand, was important in his 1930s account of Norwegian history in the sixteenth, seventeenth and eighteenth centuries. This relates how Denmark–Norway developed a capitalist economy led by the town burghers. The king, whose source of income changed from land returns to customs and taxation of commerce, allied with the emerging bourgeoisie to brush the nobility aside and make himself an absolute monarch (1660). "Towards the end of the sixteenth century", Steen writes, "we can clearly discern the structure of the capitalist society where economic class divisions conquer social estate divisions." Towards the end of the seventeenth century, according to Steen, "the old estate society turned into a class society".[19] The main criteria are clearly economic, although Steen is well aware that social structure is also constituted by non-economic factors. The estate society/class society for-

18 Steen 1930, 1932, 1933, 1935, 1948a, and 1957.
19 Steen 1935:248 and 1930:171. In Norwegian: "økonomisk klassedeling seirer over social standsdeling" (1935) and "Det gamle stendersamfunn var blitt et klassesamfund" (1930).

mula was to prove influential in the social historiography of the 1950s and 1970s, albeit in a different version.

Steen's most lasting concept, however, is the dual one of "the self-contained society" and "the money(ed) society" (*selvforsyningssamfunnet* and *pengesamfunnet*). These two societal forms co-existed in the early decades of nineteenth-century Norway. The moneyed society referred to the towns and a small sector of rural Norway; the self-contained society, to the rest. Obviously, economic criteria played an important part in defining the two societies, but the essence of the two societal forms was as much social and mental, or indeed cultural, as economic. The concepts were introduced in a 1957 book which triggered a debate on the nature of pre-industrial Norwegian rural society (see below). At the same time it gave the whole pre-modern and pre-industrial Norway a designation: "The Old Society" (*Det gamle samfunn*), identical with the title of the book.

Steen was above all interested in the larger forms of society or culture. His narrative structure, however, was not as ambitious as his concepts may indicate. At times the concepts seem to serve as pictures of momentary descriptions rather than as help towards larger theoretical constructions.[20] On the other hand he traced well-defined historical problems more analytically and systematically in some shorter articles. In an article about "times of rupture" (*brytningstider*) in history, he discusses problems of continuity and change. In a classic piece on voluntary associations and Norwegian democracy in the nineteenth century, he launched the so-called vacuum-hypothesis (*tomromshypotesen*) that suggests the associations arose mainly as a consequence of the tearing up of older social bonds.[21]

The 1950s: A social historical thrust

Steen's book on the old society was published towards the end of a fertile decade for Norwegian social history. A new generation, born mainly between 1910 and 1920, produced a number of path-

20 Dahl 1970:17.
21 Steen 1958 and 1948b.

breaking books and articles in the 1950s. In the small Norwegian academic community, they had all been students of Steen or, to a lesser degree, of Koht or Holmsen. Yet other influences led them away from the broad narrative style of Steen and towards narrower and more specific problems. Their inspiration came from the social sciences, mainly of the American brand, and their offshoots in Anglo-Saxon historiography. The task was not to offer a broad narrative of Norwegian societal development, but to explain phenomena like emigration to the United States (Semmingsen), the rise of the Norwegian industrial working class (Bull), the changing character of Norwegian social structure and social relations during the nineteenth century (Mykland, Mannsåker), and even the nature of the historians' endeavours in dealing with these problems (Dahl, Bull).

Ingrid Semmingsen's (b. 1910) major contribution to historiography is her account of Norwegian emigration to overseas in the period from 1825 to 1915 through a number of monographs and articles.[22] Her two volumes on emigration published in 1941 and 1950, and especially the second volume on the period of mass emigration (1865–1915), offer a blend of old-style narrative account (when describing the phenomenon) and analysis (where the historical variations are explained structurally). The analytical part was moderately quantitative. She relied solely on public statistics, but her approach was to become a model for a number of quantitative studies in the 1970s and 1980s.

Semmingsen's account of the causes of emigration necessarily involved an analysis of various demographic, economic, and social traits characterizing Norwegian society in the second half of the nineteenth century. A more synthetic version of the development of the Norwegian social structure was presented in 1954 in a long article entitled "The Dissolution of Estate Society in Norway".[23] The title was given in advance and not chosen by Semmingsen herself. As there were no estates in nineteenth-century Norway in the socio-political meaning of the term, she was compelled to reject the assumption inherent in the title, but she took the oppor-

22 Semmingsen 1938, 1941–50, 1972, 1978a, and 1978b.
23 Semmingsen 1954.

tunity to analyze the nature of Norwegian social change during this epoch.

The concept of an "estate society" might by understood in purely sociological terms, as a society where vertical social ties of loyalty and dependence prevailed, and where social mobility was severely restricted in practice, though not in theory. Steen described this structure in his book *Det gamle samfunn* (The Old Society), without using the term. He summed it up with the phrase: "Everyone looked upwards, as far as the eye could see."[24] Knut Mykland's (b. 1920) monograph on Trondheim in the nineteenth century traces the history of the dissolution of estate society in the above-mentioned sense of the word, and relates that the contours of a class society were clearly discernible by 1880.[25]

In his eloquent narrative of Norway's third largest urban society, Mykland is silent about the source of his theoretical inspiration. This is not the case with Dagfinn Mannsåker's (1916–94) dissertation on the Norwegian clergy in the nineteenth century, subtitled "Studies in Social History".[26] In the core of the book, which treats the social origins of the clergymen, he draws widely on contemporary literature on social stratification. This was a fairly new phenomenon, and it prompted the young historical methodologist Ottar Dahl (b. 1924) to reflect upon the nature and scope of social history in a well-known article. "Social history", Dahl writes, "will attempt to treat all relevant aspects of human social life in context, and especially the way it manifests itself in larger units or 'social groups' and in their mutual relationship."[27]

The social group which interested the younger Edvard Bull (1914–86) was the Norwegian working class and its multifarious subgroups. He began his career as a historian of labour politics in both the labour parties and the trade unions. Through labour pro-

24 Steen 1957:275.
25 Mykland 1955. Danielsen 1958 takes the Trondheim society into the twentieth century (1880–1914) with a similar emphasis on the social make-up of urban society.
26 Mannsåker 1954.
27 Dahl 1955:185. In the original: "Sosialhistorien ... vil behandle såvidt mulig alle relevante sider av menneskenes felleskapsliv i sammenheng, først og fremst slik som dette manifesteres i større enheter eller 'sosiale grupper' og deres innbyrdes forhold."

tection policies, he soon moved to the conditions of the workers themselves, whether at work, at home, or at leisure. In the years following 1950, he led a large-scale project which collected workers' biographies. The outcome was 2,700 interviews or written autobiographies from c. 1,700 workers, mainly factory hands, construction workers, and cottars. The cottars' biographies were collected by Ingrid Semmingsen.[28] Bull's crowning effort was his 1958 book, *Workers' Communities during the Industrial Breakthrough*, in which he compared the workers' environments in three different industrial towns during the last decades of the nineteenth century. He particularly looked at the workers' social and geographic background, their age, their housing conditions, and the leadership of the factories (e.g. whether paternalistic or not). He was especially interested in investigating whether an element of displacement (recent migration, renting instead of owning a house, unmarried status, rational non-paternalistic management, general unsettled environment) predisposed workers to antagonistic behaviour towards the management. This indeed seemed to be the case.[29]

By the end of the 1950s, quite a few of the characteristics normally associated with social history had been taken up by Norwegian historians. Whole societies or communities had been given a *social* designation, i.e. they were defined generally in social terms (Steen, Mykland, Danielsen). Systematic (quantitative) studies of social structure as both means and ends of analysis had been employed (Dahl, Semmingsen, Mannsåker, Bull). History was increasingly seen from below (Bull, Semmingsen).

The 1960s: Dominance of political history

Parallel to this social historical thrust, however, ran a strong line of more traditional political history, represented above all by Jens Arup Seip (1905–92) and some of his students. It must be remembered that Steen's *Det gamle samfunn* was one of six volumes in a series on early nineteenth-century Norwegian history which he

---

28 A selection of autobiographies were edited by Bull and Semmingsen in a series of volumes entitled *Arbeidsfolk forteller* (Workers Tell).
29 Bull 1958.

called *Det frie Norge* (The Free Norway). The other five volumes were political in a rather narrow sense. In the decade or so after 1958, political history seemed decidedly to hold the upper hand in Norwegian historiography. One of the big projects was the history of the Norwegian parliament, the Storting, prepared for its 150th anniversary in 1964. A new nine-volume *History of Norway* was traditionally political in its main perspective.[30] Some of the pioneers of the 1950s turned to political history, and the new generation of promising historians started their careers in political history. In medieval history the structural school of Holmsen was challenged by Knut Helle. In 1964 Holmsen remarked, not without a certain resignation, that "it is political history – the history of political thoughts and actions – which is the subject of historians harbouring full self-respect". He states, indirectly referring to Seip, that his preoccupation with structures did not imply a disparagement of the action perspective. The two ought to cohabit peacefully.[31] As late as 1970, in a collection of articles from *Historisk tidsskrift* to celebrate its hundred years of existence, social history was poorly represented. Steen and Semmingsen (!) were represented by essays on political history.[32]

The reversion to political history in the 1960s is hard to explain adequately. Bull was in 1958 severely criticized for uncritical use of sociological "content analysis" in an otherwise pioneering book. He turned to African history and published little social history during the decade. Seip's influence was strongly felt throughout the profession, not as an anti-social history pressure, but as an invitation to political history. Seip's agenda for historical research in the future was published in 1970, alongside those of Bull and Langholm.[33] He acknowledged a long-term tendency in the historical profession towards interest in mass phenomena and historical regularities. He pointed to the expansion of sociology and political science (which, under Stein Rokkan's leadership, experienced a golden age in Norway in the 1960s), and he hinted at a new ten-

---

30 None of the most renowned historians joined the project, however, and this made it different from all four similar projects in the twentieth century.
31 Holmsen 1966:331, 337. The article is based on a lecture from 1964.
32 *Hundre års historisk forskning.*
33 Seip 1970.

dency among history graduates to study past electoral behaviour quantitatively. Yet Seip predicted (and indeed wished) another direction for the future of history. Economic and social mass phenomena, he wrote, have since the nineteenth century tended to petrify (*stivne*) into institutional arrangements, parties, associations, companies, and the like. The study of these arrangements, Seip held, might shed light on the underlying phenomena and thus act as a peep-hole. However, institutions do much more than merely reflect underlying economic and social realities; they influence these realities, to produce norms and ideologies and to exercise *political control*, a central concern of Seip's. From this perspective, Seip predicted a shifting in interest from the social and economic to the political, from the peripheral to the central, and from the study of the many to the study of the few. His words did not fall on fertile ground. In the following two decades, the programme of Bull and Langholm, focusing on the social field of study, preferring the many to the few and concentrating on the peripheral in terms of power, made considerable gains within the profession.

Social history becomes a discipline: 1970 and beyond

Signs of the times

In 1974 and 1981 Jens Arup Seip published the first two volumes of *Utsikt over Norges Historie*, his masterly synthesis of Norwegian history in the nineteenth century. Although this was essentially an institutional and political history, the influence of recent works in social history was quite evident, particularly in the sections on popular movements and the social basis of different interest groups. In his outline of Volume III, in informal circulation from 1985 and published posthumously, the social historical inspiration was even more pronounced.[34]

Between 1976 and 1979 a fifteen-volume history of Norway was published by Cappelen under the general editorship of Knut

34 Seip 1994.

Mykland. We face the task, Mykland stated in the introduction, of "writing history as a history of society (*samfunnshistorie*) in the widest sense of the word", including "politics and administration, population development and economic development, social structure and cultural forms."[35] The editor stressed the importance of local variations (the geographical periphery being included by employing local historical works as sources), the necessity of giving ample space to ethnic minorities (Sami and Finns), and the necessity of seeing history from below (the viewpoint of the suppressed, the poor, the nameless). The emphasis on population history is justified by the global population problem. Mykland proclaimed the demise of the idea of progress in history, and as a consequence, perhaps, the work was founded in "no particular philosophy of history" (*historieoppfatning*). If nothing else, this was a token of the fall of teleology in Norwegian social historiography. The grand old man of social history, Edvard Bull jun., wrote the last two volumes, covering the years since 1919. His account of Norwegian history since World War II was divided into two parts. The first, covering the 1950s and 1960s, was entitled *Den tillitsfulle vekst* (The Confident Growth), while the second, on the 1970s, was less confidently named *Den nye utryggheten* (The New Insecurity).[36]

The two publications just mentioned were strong proof of the social historical turn taken by much of the Norwegian historical profession in the 1970s. Its hallmarks were many: The practitioners of social history were the first generation to actually name themselves *social* historians. The approach to the study of social phenomena was decidedly structural, and often quantitative, going far beyond their predecessors in the 1950s. There was a much more deliberate and varied use of social theory than two decades earlier; sociology was the main supplier,[37] with political science, economics, and geography as minor contributors (anthropology came later). As late as 1966, only one practising historian in Norway had studied sociology.[38]

35 Mykland 1976:7.
36 Bull 1979.
37 Langholm 1972.
38 Hernes 1966. To earn a degree, Norwegian students have to study three subjects of at least one year's duration each.

There was a considerable importation of inspiration from historians abroad, and in particular from Great Britain, the United States, France, and Sweden. Some research was organized in projects (in itself a new phenomenon), favouring case studies and employing micro-historical methods.[39] As in many other countries, the rise of social history was tied to a social and political commitment on behalf of the hitherto "invisible" in history.[40] The study of particular social groups and small geographical units soon spilled over to the study of larger socio-economic processes, such as urbanization, economic modernization, the rise of class society, and the foundations of a welfare state.

Langholm, Bull, and the new generation of historians which followed them recognized their indebtedness to Steen and the other representatives of the "history of society" tradition. Steen's interest in the social aspects of society, however, went hand in hand with a strong commitment to political history, as in his six-volume account of Norway between 1814 and 1840. One may go as far as to claim that the crowning product of the historical narrative was to describe the government. With the new generation, the *social historians*, social perspectives and issues were allowed to stand on their own feet, or even to predominate in a general historical account. They represented a historiographical break with the past, quantitatively and qualitatively.

The Ullensaker and Christiania projects

A striking feature of Norwegian historiography is how variations in access to sources, in relations to neighbouring disciplines, and in traditions within the discipline tend to bring forth different problems in different eras. The social history of the Middle Ages has tended to become the history of settlement patterns. In the Early Modern Period, efforts outside the spheres of politics and economy have to a large degree been directed towards demographic history. The twentieth century has been almost exclusively the domain of political and economic history, particularly after

39 Langholm 1974 and 1976b.
40 See e.g. *Studier i historisk metode* 1981; Bull 1981; Myhre 1977a; and Langholm's preface to Myhre and Østberg 1979.

World War II. The golden epoch for social historians, therefore, has been the nineteenth century. Following Steen's call to study periods of disruption, scholars and graduate students embarked on studies of social change in town and country during the most intensive period of Norwegian industrialization, modernization, and urbanization – that is, in the two generations from 1850 to 1914, and in some cases even a bit longer.

"The development of Norwegian society, c. 1860–1900" was the formal title of a project initiated at the Department of History in Oslo in 1970, led by Sivert Langholm (b. 1927). The project had two parts, nicknamed "The Ullensaker project" and "The Christiania project" after the two localities investigated, one rural and one urban.[41] These projects produced four books,[42] a number of articles, around thirty unpublished Master's theses on the two localities, and around another twenty on related topics in other municipalities. Organizing historical research as a collective endeavour was in itself a novelty. Students prepared sources for common use and supervised each other. Having the sense of engaging in a genuinely new, *social historical* effort, the project's participants developed an *esprit de corps* that found response in wider professional circles.

Four distinguishing traits of the project should be mentioned. Firstly, the theses were mainly case studies. Ullensaker, a parish around fifty kilometres north-east of Oslo, was chosen because it was thought to be fairly representative of a larger number of local municipalities in the south-east of Norway, and not because the parish itself was of particular interest. This could not, of course, guarantee the general application of the findings, so a number of comparative studies were undertaken for other parishes. They concentrated mainly on two problems: overseas emigration and the popular Thranite movement around 1850.

Secondly, the project focused on large societal processes such as the proletarianization of the countryside, the intrusion of the market into agriculture and rural social relations, the two exoduses leading from country to city and from both country *and* city to

41 The original title of the project: *Norsk samfunnsutvikling c. 1860–1900.* Langholm 1974 and 1976a.
42 Pryser 1977a; Myhre 1978; Myhre and Østberg 1979; Langholm 1984.

America,[43] industrialization in the cities, and the rise of class society.

A third trait was that Christiania (today Oslo), Norway's leading city in size and importance, was not chosen for its representativeness, but as the presumed locale for new tendencies in social structure. These were investigated through a number of studies on the rise (and fall) of social groups, but also by study of new institutional tendencies and urban topographical structure.

The fourth and last trait concerns method. To a large degree, this research took the form of collective biographies, ensuring that the individual became the combination unit of the different variables, a main characteristic of "micro-history", as defined by Langholm.[44] Prosopography entailed handling large amounts of data taken from censuses, church records, and the like. The Ullensaker and Christiania projects were among the first in Norway to employ computers in historical analysis, but larger, non-quantifiable historical questions remained of dominant concern.

Although the main thematic objective of the two projects was "to study, in particular, changes in *social structure* during the industrialization process", they are more aptly described as a "micro-historical experiment".[45] To answer larger societal and structural questions, Langholm wanted to turn to the *individual historical actors*, the common men and women of the past, and to investigate their contribution. Although these actors seldom speak to us through the sources, their actions and other details are available through a multitude of scattered documents: births, marriages, deaths, migrations, work, tax, crime, association membership, and the like. To combine these properties (or variables) at the level of the individual offers several advantages.

First, a more accurate description of social processes is possible.

---

43 Ingrid Semmingsen created another social historical stronghold in close cooperation with the Ullensaker and Christiania projects. Emigration studies were intimately interwoven with studies of social and economic structure in both town and countryside. Among Semmingsen's students combining demography with social history are Svalestuen 1972; Niemi 1977; and Engen 1978.

44 Langholm 1976b.

45 Langholm 1974:243–4.

One avoids, for instance, the so-called ecological fallacy. Second, the reconstruction of complete life courses may show how larger social processes interfered with individual actors' lives, and how these processes are connected in these lives. Third, tracing individuals with names may yield a sense of identification with the common actors of the past. Langholm held that micro-history was necessary in order to, among other things, "rescue the common people of the past, their conditions and choices, strategies and fates, from the grey and contourless anonymity of macro-correlations and split aggregates (*spaltede aggregater*)".[46] In this statement there was an implicit critique of some contemporary, mainly international, social science history. At the same time Langholm anticipated the accusations of remoteness made in the 1980s and 1990s against what passed as social history in the preceding decades.

Other centres of social history

Edvard Bull and his students at the University of Trondheim constituted another centre of social history. Between 1974 and 1977 they undertook a large-scale collection of oral history from Trondheim and the surrounding counties, interviewing farmers, fishermen, workers, and even some middle-class representatives. From this source emanated a kind of *"Alltagsgeschichte"*, as in Dagfinn Slettan's (b. 1941) book on domestic servants and farmhands in Verdal, a locality in Trøndelag.[47] The approach was not as much structural as empathetic, using oral evidence as the main source. The project "Rural society in dissolution" (*Bondesamfunn i oppløsning*), led by Bull, Slettan, and Kjell Haarstad (b. 1935) between 1980 and 1986, carried the study of the modernization process in the Norwegian countryside through inter-war years and well into the post–World War II period, using oral evidence as well as a host of other sources.[48] Bull and his followers carried social history in a more anthropological direction, influenced by E. P. Thompson, continental historians of mentalities, and the

46 Langholm 1974:258.
47 Slettan 1978.
48 Slettan 1989.

international oral history movement. However, there were no polemical exchanges with the somewhat more structurally oriented students in other quarters.[49]

The social historical surge was by no means restricted to these projects or indeed to Oslo and Trondheim. Bergen became a stronghold of demographic history. The new University of Tromsø (1972) in Northern Norway was populated by young historians graduating from the southern universities, as were the six or seven district colleges which taught history from the mid-1970s. In fact, the two oldest and biggest universities proved to be the weakest links in the Norwegian social history network in the 1980s, as tenured university jobs in Oslo and Bergen became very scarce after around 1973.

The large number of graduates from social history and related subdisciplines instead turned to the market for commissioned historical research, a market they took advantage of and helped to expand.[50] Commissioned local history was by no means a novelty to the profession. Some of the country's most prominent historians, including the elder and the younger Bull, Steen, Holmsen, Mykland, Rolf Danielsen (b. 1922), Kåre Lunden (b. 1930), and Knut Helle (b. 1930), first qualified as professional historians through local history.

Resorting to local history and other commissioned work became commonplace for the generations graduating in the 1970s and 1980s. Towns, rural parishes, public and private institutions, businesses, trade unions, private associations – the market seemed to be almost insatiable, with employers willing to pay historians one, two, or even five years' salaries to have histories written, and usually leaving the authors quite free to approach the task as they chose. And many chose to do social history, or general history with a social bent. Particularly evident in local history works, this is also clearly discernible elsewhere. The history of the Housewives' Association became the history of housework, while the history of the Teachers' Union became the story of the teaching profession.[51]

49 Sandnes 1981; Slettan 1994; Kaldal 1994a and 1994b; Andersen 1994.
50 See Chapters 3, 9, and 10 in this volume.
51 Avdem and Melby 1985; Hagemann 1992.

Social historical approaches, therefore, formed a considerable part of the total output of historical research at a time when the subdiscipline was poorly institutionalized in the two largest of Norway's four universities.

"The Big Change" and other themes and controversies

In 1942 the novelist and cultural critic Inge Krokann wrote an essay called "Shedding of skin in rural society" (*"Det store hamskiftet i bondesamfunnet"*), known in English as "The Big Change".[52] An earlier attempt by Holmsen to open a debate had come to nothing.[53] Krokann's essay, together with Steen's *The Old Society* from 1957 and Stein Tveite's (b. 1930) critique of Steen in 1959, formed the basis of the debate itself. It lasted about a decade, from the late 1960s on. The main protagonists were Kjell Haarstad, the political scientist Øyvind Østerud (b. 1944), Jørn Sandnes, Tore Pryser (b. 1945), and Hans Try (1934–90), with Steen's and Tveite's works looming in the background.[54] The starting-point was Steen's contention that Norwegian peasants, before 1850, aimed at being self-sufficient, while Tveite held that they simply stuck to what was most profitable. Østerud, following Chayanov's theory of the peasant economy, claimed that while Norwegian peasants might be quite market-oriented, their primary goal was to serve the needs of the farm household. They aimed to keep the farm safe for the heir and future generations; in other words they had a "subsistence-orientation". The debate became a social historical one because questions of mentality, household structure, social organization, etc. entered into the question of how Norwegian peasants coped with economic, social, and cultural challenges from around 1850. A pertinent question arose: if a farmer is an agricultural capitalist, when did Norwegian peasants become farmers?

The Trondheim project of the 1980s on the dissolution of rural society addressed this question. Slettan concluded that Norwegian rural society, despite considerable changes in technology and

---

52 Krokann 1976 (1942), with an afterword by Tore Pryser.
53 Holmsen 1933.
54 Østerud 1975 and 1978; Haarstad 1976a and 1976b; Try 1969 and 1977; Holmsen 1982; *Heimen* 1/1977 (Sandnes, Try, Pryser, and Haarstad).

organization, remained very much the same in its "way of life" until as late as about 1960. The small family farm was the basic unit, unspecialized production continued, and the familial organization of work was stable. In short, a definite rural way of life persisted.[55] This way of life has been much cherished by Norwegian historians, politicians, and the public in general since the early nineteenth century. It may well account for the importance attached by the profession to the debate on the nature of the Norwegian peasant–farmer, which forms the core of the "Big Change" discussion.

The discussion of how rural Norway shed its skin in the generations following 1850 was based almost solely on evidence from the southern part of the country. The northern parallel was the debate about the fisherman–peasant household and its place in Northern Norwegian society. This controversy, too, was related to contemporary political questions from the 1960s. It revolved around the thesis put forward by the anthropologist Ottar Brox (b. 1932) that 1) the household combination of fisherman and peasant has long been a backbone of society in Northern Norway, and that 2) it remains a viable adaptation in contemporary society, and thus deserves to be protected from many of the excesses of economic modernization.[56]

Edvard Bull's pioneering monograph on the rise of the working class in the wood-processing industries of Østfold – "Norway's most industrialized county"[57] – continued to inspire social historical research in at least three directions more than half a generation after its publication. The first question concerned the physical formation of the industrial working class. Even in a predominantly rural country like Norway, factories were to a considerable degree staffed by town-dwellers, contrary to earlier opinion, while other working-class jobs were left to the migrants from the countryside.[58]

Langholm's students placed the formation of classes, professions, and other social groups at the core of the social processes they wished to study and therefore of social history itself. This

55 Slettan 1989.
56 Aarsæter, Nilsen, and Reiersen 1982; Brox 1984; Drivenes 1985.
57 Bull 1972 (1958):15.
58 Myhre 1978b; Myhre and Østberg 1979.

entailed extensive studies in social and geographic mobility, a theme particularly suited to the methods of micro-history. The changing of both rural and urban society in nineteenth-century Norway was thus explored through the formation and dissolution of groups such as manufacturing workers (both men and women), artisans, domestic workers, landowners, freeholders, cottars, telegraphers, industrial entrepreneurs, prostitutes, and members of various organizations.[59]

The second direction this research took concerned the living conditions of the members of the new working class. Bull's view was quite optimistic. Industrialization improved the living conditions of Norwegian workers, in both the long and the short run. The only exceptions to the long-term improvement of living conditions in Norwegian society may have been the dreadful conditions prevailing in the east side of Christiania (Oslo) for a couple of decades around the middle of the nineteenth century, before industrialization reached any proportions in the city,[60] and the situation of the unemployed section of the population between the two world wars. Several detailed studies, mainly by economic historians, have supported Bull's view.[61] Even when factors other than real wages and housing conditions are taken into account, the general picture of improvement stands firm. Bull did not doubt that the movement from cottar or servant to factory-operative meant a step upwards in living conditions. This may have been because Norway did not urbanize too fast; Norwegians perhaps enjoyed the benefits of being second-round (or third-round) industrializers but first-round creators of welfare provisions.

The third direction of social historical scholarship deriving from Bull examined levels of consciousness. Under which circumstances did the physical aggregation of workers turn into a conscious collective of workers? What kind of consciousness can we talk about? Bull himself tested his father's hypothesis that the rad-

59 E.g. Myhre and Østberg 1979; Gjerdåker 1974 and 1981; Øhren 1977; Thue 1977; Strømberg 1977; Schiøtz 1977; Schrumpf 1978; Olstad 1978; and E. Myhre 1990.
60 Housing conditions in particular were bad. J. E. Myhre 1990.
61 Ramstad 1982; Minde and Ramstad 1986; Minde 1987. For overviews see Bruland 1992 and Myhre 1986.

icalism of the Norwegian labour movement from about 1911 reflected the uprootedness of Norwegian workers, which in turn came from a particularly rapid industrialization in the preceding decades.[62] After comparing three different towns, the younger Bull concluded that factors such as migration (and especially long-distance migration), single marital status, and a newly built environment predisposed workers to radicalism.

Other scholars have looked more closely at the conditions and processes of work, particularly those associated with the Bergen-based Centre for the Study of Working Conditions. These historians blend technological and other conditions at the work-place with more traditional sociological variables and produce important findings about working-class culture.[63] Studying working-class culture in a factory setting necessarily involves touching upon industrial relations and therefore contributing to the history of the labour movement. Quite a few historians of the working class have gone one step further and written books on the labour movement, the chief examples being Bull, Pryser, Øyvind Bjørnson (b. 1950), Finn Olstad (b. 1950), and Knut Kjeldstadli (b. 1948).

In general, social history in Norway has not suffered from the tendency of its counterpart in other countries to isolate itself from political history. The merging of the two is evident not only in the field of labour history (c. 1880–1940). It also occurs in the many studies of the social bases of the pre-industrial and early socialist Thranite movement of around 1850,[64] in Langholm's study of the urban electorate of 1868,[65] and in a number of syntheses of local and national history.

The connection between social and political history in the historiography of the welfare state is ambiguous. In Norwegian social science there has traditionally been a close connection between social surveying, the study of social conditions, and social policy. Relations between social history and the history of social policy, however, have not been that close. Most studies of social relations or social conditions are not conducted with their relevance for

62 Bull sen. 1976 (1922).
63 Kjeldstadli 1989; Bjørnson 1987.
64 Pryser 1977a and 1977b.
65 Langholm 1984.

actual social policy in mind; they tend instead to refer vaguely to some contemporary political issues. Anne-Lise Seip's (b. 1933) impressive one-woman effort in delineating Norwegian social policy from 1740 until the present, on the other hand, is not so much an account of social problems, as a history of how contemporary problems were perceived and how attempted remedies lay within the existing political and ideological framework. It is in other words an intellectual and institutional history. Yet Seip's political scope is wide; the political areas related to social policy are many, particularly in the 1984 volume on the rise up to 1920 of the Norwegian "social services state" (*sosialhjelpstaten*, as distinct from the succeeding welfare state).[66] Historically oriented sociologists and political scientists take a different approach. They work from models and compare larger categories of political systems and social structures.[67]

The study of societal processes

It would certainly be an exaggeration to state that Norwegian history has fragmented into parochial discourses about very limited subjects, the fate attributed to much American social history. There is, however, some distance between the broad societal scope of Sverre Steen's narratives and the relatively limited topics taken up by historians in the 1970s and 1980s. Yet the level of precision, in constructing concepts and in the framing of questions, has increased vastly. On the other hand, most social historians in recent decades have placed their research within the framework of larger societal processes. Some of the central questions on the character of Norwegian modernization, industrialization, and "The Big Change" have already been mentioned.

A central problem in the transition from "the old society" to a modern one has been the nature of social relations and indeed of social structure itself. What were the characteristics of the estate society as opposed to its successor, the class society? Quite a few of the historians mentioned above have contributed, directly or indirectly, including Steen, Semmingsen, Dahl, Mykland, Langholm,

66 A.-L. Seip 1981, 1984a, 1984b, 1986, and 1994.
67 A good example is Kuhnle 1983.

Pryser, and Myhre. Around 1980 Kjeldstadli and Olstad summarized the various positions taken, while at the same time expressing their own views.[68] Kjeldstadli elegantly summed up the main attributes of estate society (*standssamfunnet*) as "standstill", "distance", and "household" (*stillstand, avstand, husstand*). He called for a more Marxist-inspired analysis of modes of production, with more specific investigations of work relations and of the uses of capital. Olstad, like most of Langholm's students, maintained the primacy of social relations (e.g. "vertical" or "horizontal" relations), and held that social factors may have strong explanatory power even in economic matters.

The study of urbanization is another field, represented mainly by the present author.[69] Whereas much research has been devoted to rural settlement studies, "The Big Change" and related agrarian problems, overseas emigration, and industrialization and its problems, the societal process of urbanization has received scant attention, at least regarding the modern period. This may be because towns and urban societies have not been considered genuinely Norwegian in the same way as their rural counterpart. Anti-urbanism has occasionally pervaded sections of Norwegian intellectual life, with the towns being seen as the seat of the political elite and of imported culture. This attitude was reinforced by the strong centralization of urban Norway – and indeed of Norway in general – in the capital of Christiania (Oslo). An important goal for the late nineteenth-century rural-based political opposition, with its associated so-called counter-cultures, was therefore to conquer the capital and the other major towns – politically, socially, and culturally. The venture proved fairly successful.[70]

A considerable proportion of urban history in Norway has accordingly been produced as a by-product of industrialization studies.[71] The major contribution, however, takes the form of town biographies, written as commissioned local histories. The most valuable include the multi-volumed histories of Oslo, Bergen, Trondheim,

68 Kjeldstadli 1978; Olstad 1980.
69 Myhre 1977, 1983, 1987, and 1993. See also Blom 1977; Lorange and Myhre 1991; Niemi and Tjelmeland 1992.
70 J. E. Myhre 1990; Kjeldstadli 1990.
71 Myhre 1978b and Myhre and Østberg 1979 are good examples.

and Tromsø. They tend to be rather social historical in character and to view their respective cities as particular kinds of social entities, to be compared with other cities. Mykland's account of Trondheim's transition from an estate society to a class society in the nineteenth century is one example. Another is Kjeldstadli's history of how two deep social cleavages of early twentieth-century Oslo – between employers and workers and between natives and migrants (the urban and the rural) – were partly overcome by mid-century.

In a certain respect the debate on the rise of class society is Norwegian history seen through its social structure; urbanization studies are Norwegian history from a spatial and topographical point of view, leading to a more urban society; and the history of social policy is the history of Norway seen through the quest for social justice, pointing towards the welfare state and the welfare society. Anne-Lise Seip characterizes the hundred-year march from *c.* 1870 to the 1970s as a development towards "collectivism" (*kollektivisme*), or a concept of social responsibility. It was a success story, and its historiography is not without "Whiggish" traits. The growing perception of crisis in the welfare society, however, has begun to leave its mark: Seip's latest work betrays a certain air of scepticism or resignation.[72]

Critiques of social history

Around 1970 modern Norwegian social history had a comparatively easy rebirth. Social viewpoints had a solid tradition in Norwegian historiography. Social history did not raise a barrier between itself and traditional political history, and the social historical enterprise was endorsed or even initiated by some of the profession's major figures.

Yet critiques arose, partly from within and partly from outside the discipline. They revolved around the question of the *autonomy* of social history, and posed the question whether the discipline had (or needed) a clear *focus*. They asked whether the *structural* domination should prevail.

In an article published in the *Festschrift* to Edvard Bull jun. in

72 A.-L. Seip 1994.

1984, Per Maurseth (b. 1932), a student of Seip, who had assumed Bull's professorship in Trondheim, reviewed the Bull–Langholm–Seip debate from 1970.[73] He criticized the programme of Bull and Langholm for striving for autonomy, particularly from the political sphere. This was both undesirable and unworkable, Maurseth held, for at least two reasons. Autonomy would create isolated "social" subfields, and it would reduce our capacity for explanation by separating cause and effect when social phenomena are isolated. Yet the record of Norwegian social history since 1970 shows that such an isolation did not in fact take place. Advances in the empirical approach in the social sphere have not led Norwegian historians to look only for "social" causes. Rather, an important improvement has been the identification of social causes of political phenomena. Maurseth advocated, following Eric J. Hobsbawm's and Jacques Le Goff's articles in *Daedalus* in 1971, that political history be seen as a social historical field, which was exactly what Langholm did in his 1984 book, as did many others. No one wished to rule out political history. The problem to the generation of the 1970s was that the ultimate questions in history seemed to be defined as political. Why should they not be social?

Many social historians claim that historical syntheses may be constructed on a social basis. However, except for a few syntheses in local history, modern Norwegian social history has not managed to become a history of society. Its centrifugal effects on Norwegian historical writing have perhaps been stronger than its centripetal effects.

One explanation for this may be a lack of focus in the field. If social history is characterized by using a certain set of methods, or by being an empirical field, or by employing a specific approach, what is the core of social history? Francis Sejersted (b. 1936) has criticized social history for failing to give history meaning through a concentration on unplanned consequences of uncoordinated mass behaviour and on writing about people as victims of historical forces.[74] In order to put meaning back into history, Sejersted recommends focusing on institutions, particularly political ones.

---

73 Maurseth 1984.
74 Sejersted 1993 and 1994.

While these critiques may have some substance, they overlook the tremendous engagement on behalf of invisible and oppressed social groups that has pervaded much social history in recent decades. However, such engagement can never become a definitional aspect of the field. The critiques perhaps also overlook social history's capacity for studying social institutions in the widest sense, thereby making the historian's endeavour meaningful, through a focus on the struggle for social identity fought by all people in the past.[75]

The last critical note concerns the social historians' alleged propensity to study structures more than actors. Some Norwegian social history in the 1970s was clearly quantitative and structurally inclined, but it is very debatable whether historians lost sight of individuals. The record tends to show that this was not the case, as indicated above.[76] Indeed, the tendency of the 1980s, and particularly of the 1990s, has been to play down the quantitative aspect and to put meaningful actions in the forefront.[77] The agenda for Norwegian social historians in the coming years seems to be to reconcile the actor-oriented and the structural approaches: the active and the passive aspects of human behaviour.

---

75 Myhre 1994.
76 Myhre 1977a; Langholm 1974 and 1976a.
77 Slettan 1994; Andersen 1994; Kjeldstadli 1991.

9. Local History[1]
Harald Winge

It is often said – in Norway – that local history is strong in Norway. This statement can be developed in many directions. Purely in *quantitative terms*, it may be accepted; local history in Norway interests and activates many people on an amateur basis, and occupies a relatively large number of researchers. To the extent that one can describe local history produced by researchers as research, one can say that a relatively high proportion of the funding devoted to historical research in Norway goes to local historical projects.

The *qualitative content* of the above statement is worth reflecting upon. Local history is clearly a respected branch of the discipline of history in Norway. Contracted research in local history is regarded as worthwhile, and it therefore attracts competent researchers, notably young academics seeking to establish themselves. Local history is also a recognized discipline in most university and research circles.

Nevertheless, local history in Norway occupies a dual position. On the one hand, there exists a popular movement rooted in Norwegian history and Norwegian social conditions. This popular component is especially manifested in the form of local and regional history associations, the driving force behind a large part of the corpus of literature on local history; there is also a widespread interest in ancestral research. On the other hand, local history research, including works directed at a larger public, is an academic profession, located within the general discipline of history and exposed to the influence of the currents affecting that discipline.[2]

1 Translated by Eamonn Noonan.
2 Niemi 1987; Niemi 1991; Niemi and Winge 1993:1–5; Alsvik 1993:3.

Both the interest of professional historians in working with certain types of local history, and the relatively close contacts between the popular movement and academic circles, are characteristic of Norway. In the contacts between the two groups, however, there is also a constant possibility of friction, a subject I will return to below.

The growth of local history in Norway

Today there are local history associations in practically all parts of Norway. Most administrative districts have had their history written, in whole or in part, and Norwegian municipalities devote at least NOK 40 million annually to the production of local historical literature. Substantial additional sums come from private institutions and enterprises. The quantitative level is higher today than ever, but it has taken nearly one hundred years to advance this far.

One can seek the origins of local historical research in Norway even further back in time, in the strong topographic and antiquarian interest found among the country's civil servants in the age of the Enlightenment in the second half of the eighteenth and the beginning of the nineteenth century. This period brought an extensive series of local and regional descriptions, whose main purpose was to map out the country's actual economic potential; but the historical dimension was occasionally quite prominent. The topographical wave peaked in the course of the 1800s, with the production of large-scale compendiums covering the entire kingdom.[3]

The modern local history movement in Norway is about as old as this century. The first local and regional history associations were established around 1900 or slightly later, and the main branches of local historical literature, as we still recognize them today, developed from 1900 to 1920. Certain fundamental circumstances in contemporary society account for the breakthrough of local history coming in this particular period. The preconditions were economic and social, as well as political, cultural, and intellectual.

The background may be summarized briefly. Norwegian society experienced marked changes from the second half of the nine-

3 Kraft 1820–35; Helland 1898–1921; see also Sandnes 1970:13–31.

teenth century onwards, characterized by among other things industrialization and the growth of towns, mechanization, and, in agriculture, increased dependence on the market. In parallel a political consciousness and a certain polarization developed. This occurred partly in relation to conflict on the question of the union – the union with Sweden was dissolved peaceably in 1905 – and partly in that new social groups demanded a role in social decision-making. Important in this context were the introduction of a parliamentary system in 1884, the growth of political parties from around the same time, and the introduction of universal suffrage for men in 1898 and for women in 1913.

Local historical interest manifested itself in the dividing lines between two differing interests, represented by the peasantry and the historians.[4] The background for their respective positions may roughly be described as follows:

Norwegian farmers became owner–occupiers quite early and gained a relatively strong political position in the country through the 1814 constitution. They predominated in the local politics of the countryside in the second half of the last century. The rapid social changes of the latter part of the century threatened the farmers' traditional economic, social, and political hegemony in the countryside, and created in many rural communities a desire to preserve that which seemed to be disappearing. At the same time, national sentiments created a growing interest in the past. This led to the foundation of a series of local and regional history associations, in which farmers were strongly represented. In many cases farmers took the initiative in larger local historical works. Norwegian farmers also had the economic and political resources necessary to initiate such projects.

Around 1900, and especially after the struggle about union with Sweden had been successfully concluded, Norwegian historians turned their attention towards the country's internal history, and particularly towards economic and social conditions. This lent itself readily to studies at the local level. Many historians either conducted such studies themselves or directed amateur researchers, often local intellectuals (such as teachers) of an agricultural background.

4 Alsvik 1993:5–7.

One should emphasize that the historians, unlike the farmers, were not primarily interested in the individual local community's history *per se*. Their intention was to establish empirical foundations for a larger project, concerning the *nation's* internal history. The view that the main task of local history is to form "building blocks towards a national history" has always been present to a greater or lesser degree in research circles, although arguably less so in Norway than in other countries.

Despite an apparent community of interests, in that both farmers and historians wished to investigate the local society's history, their purposes and premises were not identical. This duality has been noticeable in local historical activities throughout the century. It has been said that local history in Norway is somewhat Janus-faced.[5]

In the course of the century, amateur historians have become more scholarly. This has occurred both individually, in that historians have had "clients" whom they have supervised, and in more organized ways – among others, through *Heimen*, Norway's only nationally circulated local historical periodical.[6] In 1956 the Norwegian Institute of Local History (NLI) was set up. This state institution was designed to improve conditions for local historical research, and offers guidance to local historians all over the country.

The point of intersection between the popular and the academic is in local historical literature, particularly in its main genres. Both disagreements and common interests are apparent.

Local historical genres

Norwegian local historical literature comprises to a considerable extent traditionally shaped genres, established in connection with the blossoming of interest in local history in the first decades of this century. Especially characteristic is the "community book" (*bygdebok*), which in its traditional form is a particularly Norwegian phenomenon. In the following we shall look more closely at this genre, and also at town and district histories and at local history yearbooks.

5 Niemi and Winge 1993:1.
6 Published by the National Organization for Local History (Landslaget for lokalhistorie), 1922–.

The remaining local historical literature will be treated only briefly. The typical community book has two parts. The first is the *farm and family history*, or simply the *farm history*. This concerns the history of settlements on an individual basis. Each individual farm or residence and its occupants are traced from as far back as sources permit and usually right up to the present. The second part concerns the *general history of the community*, dealing with the local society as a whole. For towns, however, the norm is solely the general history, and the same applies to districts.

It is probably correct to regard farm histories as a particularly Norwegian genre. It does not seem that other countries have local historical publications of this kind, and certainly not on the scale found in Norway. Here there has been a general view in recent generations that each community should have both a farm history and a general community history. The combination is the precondition for a complete community book. On the part of researchers, attitudes towards the farm history genre are more ambivalent.

The existence of the farm history genre in Norway can be attributed to actual circumstances and to the availability of sources. The dominant form of settlement in Norway has been the individual farm rather than the village. This farm could indeed be divided, but in its typical form it comprised just a small number of families and holdings. A Norwegian farm, subdivided or not, is as a rule clearly marked out from other farms by some kind of visible natural border, often forests or streams. Its bounds can be easily distinguished and mapped out. In spite of a number of revisions, particularly in connection with desertion after the Black Death, Norwegian estates have on the whole had stable boundaries through their entire period of settlement. Each farm area has preserved its own name, of corresponding vintage – the same today as a thousand years ago, apart from the orthographic changes linked to the general development of the language.

The typical Norwegian farm must therefore be characterized as a stable topographical and nominal entity, and it may be studied individually through written material in public archives. The same entity is to be found under the same name in written sources from the Middle Ages to the present day. It appears in medieval charters as in more recent records such as tax rolls, land registers, and so on. The people who have lived in the farms through the centuries are linked in the sources to the same named farms, for example, in church registers, court books, and probate registers.

As a consequence it is possible in Norway to study each farm's history more or less in detail, certainly for the last three or four hundred years. Records from the Middle Ages are less profuse, but some basic facts about the individual estates can be established even for that period. It is also possible to identify each estate's occupants in the last three or four hundred years, and to draw up the main outlines of each individual family's life.

The works on farm and family histories dating from the first three or four decades of this century are quite brief and have an element of cataloguing about them. Data from tax lists, registrations, and other sources are often reproduced without commentary, and little emphasis is placed on giving a coherent presentation of the farm's economic and demographic history. Works of this kind still appear today.

An innovative and exemplary work appeared through Andreas Holmsen's influential activity in the field of Norwegian local historical research. His farm and family history for Eidsvoll municipality became a standard, especially in relation to its comprehensive and skilful treatment of farm history, inspired and made possible by Holmsen's own basic studies in older Norwegian agrarian history. He showed that it was possible to write a coherent economic historical account of each individual farm, in which the farm could be portrayed as a resource area, a unit of production, a tax basis, and a unit of settlement; as a social system, a community in miniature comprising farmers, crofters, and others. He also set the farm in a larger cultural pattern, as the basis for neighbourhood, parish, district, and nation.[7]

Many of the farm histories to appear since the Second World War have followed Holmsen's pattern, at least to some extent. Their contents often include themes such as the following:

About the farm/residence: This includes the farm's name, what the name means, the farm's bounds and its layout, soil, eventual his-

7 Holmsen 1941–50.

torical relics, its probable age, to what extent it was deserted in the Late Middle Ages, how long any desertion lasted, to what extent the farm's area has been divided into individual holdings in medieval and later times, information on corn production or crops at specific times during the last 400 years, details of ancillary activities such as forestry, pastures, summer mountain dairying, fishing, hunting, tar-making, charcoal-burning, the extent to which the farm has had cotters' holdings, where these were situated, what they were called and how large they were, who owned the farm in the centuries when the farmers were tenants, the population in the area at the times of the various censuses, and whether there was co-operation with neighbouring farms in connection with milling, sawmills, road-building, exploitation of the outlying areas, and collective work.

About the inhabitants: Personal history material is always arranged so that each domicile within the farm area is treated in its own right. Beginning with the oldest known resident or resident family, families are presented one by one in chronological order down to the present, before moving on to the next domicile. Details given on each family generally include the following: name and year or date of birth for each spouse, when they married, where the non-native spouse came from, year or date of birth (and if possible year of death) for children, and where they moved to in the event of marriage. The presentation may additionally include information from probate registers, court books, and other records about the family.

A survey by the NLI in 1992 revealed that 46 percent of Norway's 439 municipalities had at that stage published farm histories for their entire geographical areas. Another 24 percent of municipalities had similar work in progress.[8] Considering that twenty to thirty municipalities are almost entirely urban, without significant rural areas, and are therefore unlikely to ever prepare farm histories, one can conclude that around one-half of the existing municipalities already have such a corpus of work, and that at least another quarter are in the process of creating one.

8 Løyland 1993:277.

These works are, of course, of variable quality. One can generally say that the oldest books, from the first half of the century, are much less comprehensive than the works which appear nowadays. As the traditional designation "farm history" suggests, the genre from the outset covers only the actual farms, and therefore passes over other types of settlement and their inhabitants. Particularly since 1970 this has changed to a considerable extent. Farm and family histories which now appear emphasize that no group in rural society should be discriminated against. The purpose is to present all on the same level, regardless of social status. This approach is a natural consequence of the general wish for non-discrimination, and is as a rule also needed in order to achieve a municipality's approval for a study.

Because of this approach, work on farm and family histories today absorbs more time and resources than before. New studies tend to be more voluminous than older ones. Works of up to six volumes and 3,000 pages for a municipality are no rarity – and three-quarters of Norwegian communes have fewer than 10,000 inhabitants.

General local history, or the history of the *local society as a whole* from the oldest times to the present day, is the second main component of a complete community book. For towns, as stated, only general histories are written, and not the history of the individual settlements. The same applies to the larger districts. The concept of general local history therefore includes all broad social history presentations of town, parishe, and district history.

General local history as written at the beginning of the century is characterized by its descriptive form and sober presentation of facts. It is always organized by subject. The author treats themes from the local community's history one by one, giving an account of each subject from as far back as sources or knowledge permit, up to the present day. Certain traditions as to the choice of themes were quickly established. A hallmark is that one almost always dealt with what one might call unanalytical subjects – obvious themes such as the most important occupations in the area, communications, schools, churches and ministers, municipal administration (from 1837), and so on. In addition there has always been a relatively free choice of a broad spectrum of lesser themes, often

particular to each parish. These may include important circum-
stances/events in the locality's history, or other special features.
Presentations arranged by theme continue to appear nowadays,
but are mainly written by amateur historians. Books of this kind
often have many authors, each writing about their own speciality.

The most usual alternative to a presentation organized strictly
by subject is a chronological, problem-driven account, which
divides the local community's history into periods, and which
seeks to identify main lines of development. Andreas Holmsen's
above-mentioned study of Eidsvoll was the pathbreaking work in
this genre too.[9] He conducted a broad social historical analysis of
the local society's development in a chronological framework.
Since the Second World War, it has been this kind of general local
history which professionals have recommended, and have themselves practised when commissioned to write town, parish, or district histories.

There has been a virtually continuous discussion about these
alternatives for many decades. The discussion has been of such
duration because the question of the manner of presentation is
closely linked to more fundamental aspects of local history.

Among historians the theme-driven format is regarded as inadequate because this makes it impossible to address all-embracing
questions which involve many themes. Such questions enable us
to trace hidden, more fundamental structures and processes in local society, in order that the reader may come to the best possible
understanding of the locality's past.

Supporters of the theme-driven format emphasize that the division by themes makes history more accessible to the average
reader, and that the chronological presentations written by historians are often so weighed down by question-setting and analysis
that the main readership can appreciate them only to a limited
extent. They also suggest that the most important point about general local history is that it can serve as a reference work; in this
context, a theme-by-theme presentation is much more functional
than a chronological one.

In the post-war period, the chronological form has been on the

9 Holmsen 1936–41.

advance, and in the 1980s almost 60 percent of the general local histories to appear were of this kind. Practically all of these were written by historians. Cases where the division by themes is still preferred may reflect local traditions, but also economic circumstances: it costs more to employ specialists (as is necessary if one wants a mainly chronological account) than to organize a local group of enthusiasts.[10]

The traditional and strict division between theme-driven and chronological presentations is hardly satisfactory. The reality is more ambiguous. Some works which at first glance appear to be chronological are in fact largely organized by themes and are analytical only to a small extent. This occurs when an author divides the history into periods, but writes of each period in such a way that the presentation is marked by the characteristic of theme-driven approaches, that is, an absence of an inter-thematic approach to problems.

A more adequate subdivision requires a more refined categorization: the first, purely theme-driven type does not pretend to be anything else. Each of the chosen themes is treated in isolation; the presentation is in the main fact-oriented and shows little interest in analysis. The second and third types occupy an interim position: (a) theme-driven presentation with a certain level of *infra*-thematic analysis and problem-setting; and (b) apparently chronologically arranged presentations, but with thematic divisions, as mentioned above. Fourthly, we have presentations which are in fact chronologically arranged, and are characterized by problem-setting and *inter*-thematic analysis; a certain number of these will also strive for synthesis and an overall grasp of the local community's history.

Synthesis is an ambiguous concept in relation to local history.[11] It is probably correct to say that all serious works in general local history today have ambitions to synthesize to the extent that they emphasize inter-thematic analysis. A few works go further and try to sum up historical diversity entirely in one formula, or one main story.[12] For this to succeed, the author must consciously stress the

10 Løyland 1993:284.
11 Niemi 1992.
12 Dahl 1992; Kjeldstadli 1992; Myhre 1994.

aspects of the local history which may be naturally grouped around the main perspective. The purpose must even then be to draw all the most important aspects of social life into the larger picture. The recognition that the "definitive" history of a society can never be written means that it is absolutely legitimate to present personally coloured versions; to do otherwise is, of course, impossible.[13]

The survey conducted by NLI in 1992 showed that almost one-third of the country's municipalities can be said to have their whole general history written up to at least around 1940. Around another fifth of municipalities had such works under way in 1992. The extent of coverage in relation to general history is thus weaker than in relation to farm history.

Farm, community, town, and district histories come into being, almost without exception, on the initiative of the public administration, and all expenditure is usually part of the municipal budget. Surveys have showed that total public allocations for such works have risen from around NOK 20 million annually in the first half of the 1980s to around twice that in the early 1990s. Some of this increase is due to inflation, but the figures do indicate a considerable real increase. If we assume that all local history works of the named types represent historical research, we may conclude that municipal funding constitutes a significant and growing part of public allocations to historical research in Norway. This applies even if we make a slight deduction in the municipal total to take account of the less serious works which the municipal budgets also cover. In any event the current NOK 40 million per annum – about NOK 10 per inhabitant – is a measure of the emphasis that has been put on this kind of local historical work in Norway for some years now.

Other notable kinds of local history literature include, above all, the local historical *yearbooks*. Like community books, these are about as old as the century. The first publications of this kind concerned entire regions rather than individual parishes, and they concerned especially the larger towns. Since the Second World War the entirely local yearbook has proliferated, i.e. yearbooks for individual municipalities or corresponding areas. Especially since the 1970s a large number of new yearbooks of this kind have been

13 Niemi and Winge 1993.

established. Around 250 local and regional history yearbooks now appear regularly in Norway.

The strong growth in the number of yearbooks in recent decades has many reasons. Local history generally has experienced an upswing, and this in turn reflects trends over time which have brought a greater interest in local culture. This has been particularly notable in Northern Norway, where local history was relatively weak right up to the mid 1970s.

The number of yearbooks is also related to the steadily stronger monopolization of the major local history works by professional historians. Whereas the threshold of expertise has risen for authors of community books, it has fallen for contributors to yearbooks. There is much to suggest that in recent decades there has been a further democratization of local history, in line with changes in the content of the history discipline. From the perspective of the local society, these changes have meant among other things that the everyday and the near-at-hand (in both time and space) have become more important. Population groups which had hitherto been silent have become vocal, particularly through the emphasis in later years on "oral history". The general level of education in the country has also risen in recent decades, and this has increased the number of potential contributors to yearbooks.

There is, furthermore, an extensive range of *miscellaneous local historical literature*, in the form of histories of churches, schools, companies, associations, families, communications, and so on. An estimate for the period 1971–90 suggests that around 650 titles of this kind appeared each year. The corresponding estimate for the period 1946–70 is around 400 titles a year.[14] These figures strengthen the impression that the level of activity within Norwegian local history has never been greater than today.

Who writes local history in Norway?

There are no surveys of the composition of the pool of writers who contribute articles to yearbooks and other small works of the "mis-

14 Bibliographical basis: *Norwegian local historical literature 1946–70 and 1971–90*, published by the University Library, Oslo.

cellaneous local history" type. Yet we can safely say that in Norway these have always been the domain of amateurs.

There have been studies of the authorship of the larger local history works, the corpus of town, parish, and district histories. The NLI determined in 1991 that 199 writers were working on either farm histories or general local histories. Only 22 were women, a strikingly small proportion. Almost 65 percent of the 199 had completed university education, mostly with a Master's degree in history. The rest were of mixed background, though most were relatively well educated.

The corresponding figures for writers with a completed university education in 1984 and 1970 were 58 percent and 35 percent respectively.[15] This shows that since 1970 there has been a noticeable increase in the proportion of professional historians. Historians and academics from related disciplines (such as ethnology and archaeology) have increasingly taken over the work on these main branches of local historical literature. In relation to town histories (an internationally recognized historical field), it is well known that this has always been the domain of professional historians, in Norway as elsewhere.

That historians have always played a significant role also within rural local history is probably more specific to Norway. An important element in connection with the growth of the local history movement in the beginning of the century was that historians both supervised amateurs and themselves showed an interest in working on local history. Right through the century it has been regarded as legitimate for Norwegian historians to concern themselves not just with the internationally recognized urban history discipline, but also with general rural community history. Interest in farm and family history has perhaps been less; many historians have regarded particularly the family history part of such studies with scepticism. Nevertheless, even local history of this kind is nowadays often written by historians.

Professional historians in Norway have worked extensively on local history tasks. This may reflect the relatively strong popular tradition in the discipline of history in Norway generally. Through

15 Marthinsen 1993:3–6.

the century the country has always had influential historians who have been favourably disposed towards writing for a wider public, without thereby abandoning academic standards.

Local history and history as an academic discipline

Local history has quite a strong position at most of Norway's higher education facilities, in practice if not always in formal terms. Very few posts are explicitly dedicated to local history – currently, only a professorship at the University of Trondheim and an associate professorship at the University of Tromsø. In reality almost all third-level colleges engage in teaching and research related to local history, whether continually or occasionally. At present, for example, researchers attached to the universities in Trondheim and Tromsø are working on those towns' history. Town histories for Bergen and Oslo, the two other university towns, have appeared in recent years in the same fashion.

The majority of the eight regional colleges with history on the curriculum accord local history a strong and clearly defined position, often with regular instruction within the discipline. Hitherto the regional colleges have had teaching only at a lower university level, but in recent times individual colleges have opened up towards co-operation with the universities, and their students can thus continue right through to a Master's degree.

A large number of the students who take a Master's degree in history or a related discipline write theses on local or regional history subjects. There are probably about 3,000 such works to date.[16] The number is rapidly increasing, partly because the country has more students than ever before, and mainly because there has been a trend among Master's students in recent decades to choose subjects of this kind.

Candidates who come from the universities and who thereafter take on work in local history are therefore as a rule familiar with research within a local or regional history framework. But they

16 Løberg 1987.

also encounter new challenges. Firstly, they must direct themselves to a broader public. Secondly, general local history of the modern kind, with ambitions towards synthesis, undoubtedly presents different demands in relation to research and analysis than a relatively narrow Master's thesis.

What is local history?

In Norway discussion of this subject has been conducted particularly in the journal *Heimen*. Corresponding debates have no doubt taken place in many countries. Well known in Norway are the various debates in Denmark, principally in the journal *Fortid og Nutid*,[17] in England in *The Local Historian*,[18] and in other contexts.[19] The perspective of French historians has also been communicated to Norway to some degree.[20] Generally, however, the Norwegian discussion has been relatively inward-looking. One indeed gets the impression that this has also been the case in other countries.

In this context we will limit the concept of "local history" to what we have termed the main branches within local historical literature in Norway. This involves the larger historical monographs with a more or less "total history" purpose, dealing with rural and urban local society or with larger districts, usually comprising established administrative units. We have given such works the common designation of general local history. To this is added farm and family history. Discussions about local history generally concern these genres. This does not, however, preclude the application of most of the viewpoints to other types of writing on local history.

The following general definition of the concept can serve as a starting-point for a consideration of what local history is: *local history is the presentation of the local past with the local population as the primary intended readership*. A brief commentary on this proposed

17 *Fortid og Nutid,* 1914–, ed. Danish Historical Association.
18 Originally *The Amateur Historian,* but since 1968 with the present title; ed. Standing Conference for Local History, London.
19 See e.g. Finberg 1954; Higgs 1960–2; Munby 1969; Hoskins 1972; Finberg and Skipp 1973; Schurer 1991.
20 Leuilliot 1967.

definition furnishes an opportunity to approach the most important issues concerning local history and its specific character.

Firstly, it seems clear that local history must by definition treat the past of the *local community*, rather than that of other possible entities. This applies whether one is concerned with a broad, "total history" presentation of the local society as a whole, or with a single or a few selected aspects of the local society's past, or with particular phenomena which are primarily localized in the specific community (events, individuals, farms, enterprises, associations, institutions, etc.).

The concept "local society" can be defined with the help of social–anthropological and sociological theory,[21] but in practice these definitions have little significance for local history research in Norway. Instead, a pragmatic attitude is prevalent. This derives from the fact that practically all the works to appear within the main branches named above are commissioned works, usually with the municipality as the initiator. As a rule these have the express precondition that the respective municipalities' boundaries should constitute the geographical framework. Yet these boundaries have been, for the most part, determined by political-administrative reasoning; thus, most Norwegian municipalities comprise a series of more or less distinct local societies. However, no one would protest about histories of such administrative entities being called local histories.

Co-operation between two or more municipalities on local history projects may also occur, and one may ask how large an area can be before it becomes misleading to talk of local history. One may claim that there should be an upper limit, towards regional history; a region in this context may be defined as from three or four up to twenty or thirty municipalities. Academic tradition within district history is, however, very similar to that of historical writing on smaller entities. We may therefore include district history in the concept of local history.

A second point is that there will be a certain (if not a complete) consensus that the *local aspect* is indeed a *necessary* characteristic of local history, though it is not a *sufficient* characteristic. A good

21 See e.g. Dyrvik 1981:10.

deal of written history with a local character does not claim to be local history in the generally understood sense of the term and does not function as such in the local society. This applies especially to academic treatises on various levels, which can be given the common designation of case studies. These works do not come about primarily from an interest in a particular local society *per se*, but use empirical data from the local community in order to illuminate general structures or processes. Case studies therefore do not have the local society as their ultimate subject.[22] They are not primarily intended for a local readership, are not commissioned by local agents, and usually do not come to the attention of the local population at all.

Many, both in Norway and elsewhere, will therefore deny that these works can be considered local history in the proper sense. Among Norwegian historians there is a widespread, though not universal, opinion that a work which is to be classified as local history should fulfil criteria other than having a local character. It must also consciously or explicitly be aimed at the local population as the primary readership. Such presentations have been dubbed "genuine" or "functional" local history (local history proper), while works which do not meet this demand are described, for instance, as "imitation" local history (localized general history).[23] Especially when discussing commissioned work, with local or regional public representative organs as initiators on behalf of the local population, the demand for a work to be accessible to the local people is impossible to ignore.

The above definition of local history thus excludes a very large number of purely academic works of local or regional character. This applies to, among other things, many of the two or three thousand Master's theses in history and related disciplines written in the course of this century. A long series of journal articles and treatises with locally linked themes are also excluded, since they are written for a purely specialist audience. There is, of course, no doubt that such works also benefit so-called genuine local history, in that the results of such research will permeate down to the pop-

---

22 See Langholm 1982.
23 Sandnes 1975:165.

ular literature. This should indeed happen more rapidly today than formerly, given that historians now account for a larger proportion of the writing within the various main genres of local history than they did a few decades ago.

A division between "actual" or "genuine" local history on the one hand and purely academic works with a local aspect on the other can therefore not be regarded as absolute. If we take the viewpoint of the profession, all presentations with local society as their theme will be relevant. But if we look at this question from the point of view of the local readership, "local history" will, of course, include only presentations which in one way or another are accessible to them. Only this kind of work will they call "their" local history.

The next question must be what it means to write with the local readership in mind. What consequences can or should this have in regard to form, content, approach, level of analysis, degree of problematization, ambitions of synthesis, and so on?

When the purpose is to write a presentation directed primarily towards a public without particular academic preconditions, one must accept that this inevitably has to affect the *form* of the presentation in relation to, for example, use of language, organization, perspective, and form of analysis. But there is no unanimity on which consequences one should consider, nor on the extent to which such a purpose should also influence the *content*, e.g. concerning which subjects one should address or which problems may be approached.

In the 1970s a possible guideline launched on the part of Norwegian historians was that local history must be written "on the local society's premises". Behind this formulation lay the demands on both form and content of functional local history that it should be accessible and that it take up "questions which arise as interesting for large sections of the local society".[24] This formulation can be interpreted variously. It should not be taken to mean that the historian should limit himself or herself to questions which are from the start seen as interesting to the local community; normally there will not be any consensus within the local society

24 Sandnes 1983:11.

about what aspects of the past are worth knowing, nor will one necessarily know in advance which questions and subjects it is *possible* to take up. It must therefore be at least as important for the historian to set new questions about the local society's past.[25] However, it must in any case be the task of the researcher engaged in local history to do his or her best to approach all issues and questions such that they may *become* interesting for the members of the local society.

When a local society, through its public bodies, engages a historian to investigate and present the local past, this must imply the recognition of a specialist expertise on the historian's part, and that the local society wishes to hire this expertise. The party commissioning the work may lay down more or less precise stipulations as to what the finished product should be. This usually obliges the historian to meet these wishes, as far as is professionally defensible. But in the final analysis, the work is the historian's responsibility, in regard to content and presentation, and therefore he or she must in any event have the ultimate authority over both form and content.

It is a considerable challenge for a historian to write a "functional" work on local history. The task imposes more demands than work on an academic thesis. On the one hand, the subject itself will be considerably broader. It usually concerns general local history with pretensions to total history, in that all important aspects of an entire local community (or a few communities) are to be treated over a long period of time, and a coherent picture of the society's past is to be presented. On the other hand, the presentation may also demand more communicative ability than an academic thesis written for colleagues.

Given this dual background of professional and pedagogical demands, one may perhaps say that functional local history must be written on the combined premises of the historians and the local society. The demands of the profession can certainly not be ignored, but neither can the demand for accessibility and a convincing local relevance in the work's contents.

There have been individual instances of attempts to combine

25 See Lunden 1980.

categories, in that academic theses have simultaneously been launched on the local market as local history.[26] The results cannot be said to have been satisfactory from the viewpoint of the local readership, and a central question is to what extent, and how, the above-mentioned "combined premises" can be met in practice.

There are no doubt differing opinions about this. However, most will probably accept that presentations must in any event have the actual local society as its ultimate object.[27] This must imply that the presentation must consistently see things from the perspective of the local society, and have the local society as its basis and starting-point – in sum, as its undisputed main interest. This further implies that the choice of themes, problems to be addressed, chronology, and so on shall not be guided primarily by, for example, national historical perspectives or the interests of research circles. The choice should arise from the actual local community's own history. On the other hand, this does not place an obstacle to emphasizing the importance of impulses from outside or from "above", or stressing the interaction between the local society and the surrounding world. Nor does this represent a barrier to introducing comparative aspects, something which is, of course, necessary especially in order to reveal the particular nature of the actual local society.

In short, an approach along these lines will by no means stand in the way of a professionally valid treatment of the local society's history. But for the main readership, it is of decisive significance that the presentation does not allow room for doubt that its primary interest is the local society *per se*.

The local reader will usually also prefer that the presentation opts for individualization where this is possible, displays intimate local knowledge, has an unmistakable local colouring, and is throughout marked by a empathetic attitude to the local past and the actors therein.

The essence of the main demand on functional local history may be formulated as follows: it must stand as a practical rather than a theoretical work; it must be characterized as much by a

26 Lunden 1965; Rian 1980.
27 Langholm 1982.

qualitative as a quantitative approach; and it should probably be centred on actors rather than on structures.[28]

Conclusion

Is local history strong in Norway? The question can hardly be definitively answered, in that comparative material is so weak. Only from the Nordic area do we have individual surveys which can furnish the basis for an answer. These suggest that in relation to local support for local historical ventures and organizations, Norway can hardly pretend to have a leading position. But the surveys do indicate that local history has a stronger position in university and research circles in Norway than in neighbouring countries. It can also be said that local historical literature receives stronger economic support from the public purse in Norway than elsewhere in Scandinavia. It is perhaps also the case that this literature, or at least certain branches of it, is greater in extent in Norway.

It thus seems fair to claim that local history is in many ways relatively strong in Norway. It can certainly not be unreservedly called, as in England, the profession's "poor relation",[29] in either the academic or the economic context.

28 See Leuilliot 1967; Winge 1992.
29 Schurer 1991:99. "Like it or not, it is the case that there is and always has been a gap between the study of local history and the study of what might be termed 'history proper', with the former always being looked upon as the poor relation to the latter."

10. Economic History
Even Lange and Helge W. Nordvik

Economic history is a latecomer to Norwegian academic life. It was established as a subject in its own right only a generation ago. The first full professor in the discipline at the University of Oslo was appointed as recently as 1972. In fact, there are still no separate departments of economic history at Norwegian universities, and business schools are the only institutions of higher learning where the subject is formally established as an independent discipline. Economic historians have found a room of their own at the Norwegian School of Economics and Business Administration in Bergen (NHH) and at the Norwegian School of Management in Oslo. Elsewhere most academic practitioners in the field are to be found inside history departments.

In Norway, then, economic history has developed as a subdiscipline of history – a path somewhat different from that followed in larger countries like Great Britain and the USA, but also different from Sweden, where a separate discipline with strong links to economics emerged in the inter-war years. This particular development has heavily influenced the historiography of the subject and the way it is conceived in Norway. The choice of themes rather than the methodologies employed still largely defines who is an economic historian, and by implication what constitutes economic history. Belonging to a well-established historical culture, the discipline has been slow to develop an identity of its own. This means that the boundaries with other historical disciplines have become blurred.[1]

1 This survey focuses on the historiography of modern economic development after roughly 1830, when the distinction between economic history and general history became reasonably clear in Norway. The many historians who have written on changes in agricultural society before that time are thus not included.

The background of this development is twofold: On the one hand, the study of social phenomena and processes became an integral part of political history very early in Norwegian historiography. Throughout this century the literature has shown a pronounced interest in the social consequences of economic development. By the broad scope of their writings, general historians largely appropriated what was elsewhere labelled "economic and social history". On the other hand, Norwegian economists of the last fifty years have largely ignored economic history. The dominant position of mathematical economics, starting with Nobel laureate Ragnar Frisch in the early 1930s, meant that economic history as an academic discipline has since mainly been "left to the historians".

Mainstream historical tradition thus shaped the field of economic history as it developed in Norway from the end of World War II up to the present. Since the middle of the nineteenth century, however, a strong tradition of descriptive statistics related to social development has also contributed to the foundations of the present discipline. Running parallel to general historical writing, though without seeking much dialogue with it, this tradition has mainly been represented by economists and other social scientists.

The nineteenth-century tradition

Just as general historical writing in the nineteenth century had an important function in building national consciousness, the early studies on economic structures and development must be seen as an intellectual aspect of the modernization of Norwegian society. The effort to develop a national identity encompassed the description and analysis of economic and social structures over time. Such writings were also part of the effort to formulate policies promoting economic development and tackling social problems associated with rapid population growth and structural economic changes. Intellectuals who joined forces with high-ranking officials in a common endeavour to further the social process of nation-building thus became pioneers of economic historical studies.

Eilert Sundt (1817–75), whose influence on social science and social history can scarcely be overrated, should in this perspective be counted as a father of economic history in Norway. Sundt was profoundly interested in the forces of technological change and economic development, especially for their effect on the daily life of the population. He was the pioneer of social-statistical investigations in nineteenth-century Norway. His many demographic and ethnological studies of Norwegian society published in the third quarter of the century combined a keen analytical mind with a critical sense of quantification – essential elements in the craft of economic history.[2]

The other major influence on the early development of the subject was the brilliant law professor, economist, and prominent politician Anton Martin Schweigaard (1808–70). A champion of economic liberalism, he also founded the tradition of historical statistics in Norway. His 1840 book, somewhat misleadingly titled *Norges Statistik*, did not confine itself to mere statistical description. Schweigaard offered incisive analytical comments on the various sectors of the Norwegian economy, as well as the first attempts to estimate the value of capital invested and the value of production.[3]

This tradition was carried on through the Norwegian Central Bureau of Statistics, founded in 1876 to continue the work previously conducted in the statistical office of the Department of the Interior. The Bureau's first director, A. N. Kiær (1838–1919), organized the collection and analysis of statistics. His many articles on topics as diverse as the development of Norwegian shipping, foreign trade, and income growth and distribution were of fundamental importance in establishing a firm quantitative foundation for subsequent research on the nineteenth-century economy.

Another influential academic was Torkel H. Aschehoug (1822–1909), a pupil of Schweigaard and his successor as professor of law, political economy, and statistics in 1870. Aschehoug exhibited an early interest in population studies and social issues, and published studies on the economic and social development of Norwegian agricultural society in the seventeenth and eighteenth cen-

---

2 For a survey of Sundt's work, see Seip 1986.
3 Schweigaard 1840. Schweigaard's work was carried on by Braun Tvethe, who worked in the statistical section of the Department of the Interior (Tvethe 1848). These two works are even today sources widely cited by historians writing on the pre-1850 Norwegian economy. Bergh and Hanisch 1984:26–49 contains a thorough discussion of Schweigaard's work.

turies and the economic crises and depressions of the nineteenth century. His approach to political economy was inspired by the German historical school, although firmly rooted in classical economics.[4]

Ebbe Hertzberg (1847–1912), who won the competition for a new chair in economics at the University of Christiania (Oslo) in 1876, also contributed to the emerging field, publishing several studies on Norwegian monetary history. With Nicolai Rygg (1872–1957), he wrote a fifty-year history of Den norske Creditbank in 1907, thus initiating an important trend in the development of the subject of economic history in Norway: the writing of commissioned business histories.[5]

The subject of economic history thus developed in a close relationship to disciplines like descriptive social statistics, sociology, and legal studies, which played an important role in the development of economics as a separate academic discipline in Norway. Throughout the century and up to the First World War, there was no clear dividing line between academic economists, civil servants, and laymen interested in social and economic development and associated issues. They regularly met and debated issues relevant to economic development and social modernization in clubs and societies such as the Polytechnic Society (Polyteknisk forening), established in 1852, and the Norwegian Political Economy Club (Statsøkonomisk Forening), founded in 1883. The shared values of logical positivism and a firm belief in progress based on modern science formed the methodological foundation of this tradition.[6]

On the other hand, general historical writings of the nineteenth century focused very much on political history and left little room for description and analysis of economic issues. For both political historians and the somewhat heterogeneous group of civil servants, social investigators, and academics such as Sundt and

4 For an analysis of Aschehoug as a scholar and politician, see Seip 1975. Cf. Bergh and Hanisch 1984:50–8.
5 Hertzberg 1882. For details on Hertzberg's publications, see Bergh and Hanisch 1984.
6 Bergh and Hanisch 1984. Einarsen 1904 is another valuable example of the work generated in this tradition, providing a descriptive and analytical survey of nineteenth-century business cycles.

Aschehoug, economic history was at best a peripheral activity. Their work resulted in scattered and partial accounts of selected sectors of the economy together with studies carried out in connection with economic policy issues, like taxation and the fiscal question, or free trade versus protection, and also with social policy questions. Although this literature has considerable value as source material, most of it does not constitute economic history in the modern sense of the term.

The early practitioners, 1920–c. 1950

A more substantial literature explicitly dealing with economic history topics is first evident in the years after the First World War. It had two sources: a broadening of the existing social-statistical tradition and a new interest in economic issues on the part of academic historians.

A generation of historically interested economists and social statisticians who were pupils of Kiær and Aschehoug further advanced the subject. Nicolai Rygg, professor of social statistics at the Faculty of Law in 1910, later director of the Central Bureau of Statistics, and from 1920 governor of the Bank of Norway, was the leading figure. His publications included several studies in banking history and important investigations of social issues. Rygg's two volumes on the history of the Bank of Norway up to 1918 are valuable accounts of the bank and the economy in the nineteenth century. They are based largely on published source material, occasionally supplemented by primary source material. However, they are stronger on description than on analysis, and lack the historian's willingness to pose challenging questions and to conduct analysis based on a judicious weighing of the evidence.[7]

---

7 Rygg 1918 and 1954. See also Nordvik 1994 for a discussion of Rygg's contribution to economic history. Rygg's successor as director of the Central Bureau of Statistics and as governor of the Bank of Norway was Gunnar Jahn (1883–1971). His contribution to economic history was neither as voluminous nor as wide-ranging as Rygg's, but he did play a role in integrating the topic of historical demography into economic history. After his retirement Jahn covered the period 1816 to 1940 in a commemorative volume on the Bank of Norway; Jahn, Eriksen, and Munthe 1966.

Another major figure among economists contributing to economic history in this generation was Wilhelm Keilhau (1888–1954), a professor of economics. Keilhau was a flamboyant personality who has suffered a fate not uncommon to economic historians: he was disrespected by his peers in the economics profession, and was considered an amateur and a non-professional by historians. In retrospect Keilhau emerges as an important figure in the building of economic history as an academic discipline in Norway. He was the first professional writer on economic history to make more than incidental use of economic theory in his works. Although certainly opinionated, and not always careful in his treatment of sources, he made seminal contributions in the fields of monetary history, general economic development, maritime history, and the history of commerce. His first major historical work (and perhaps the best) was the volume on Norway in the Carnegie Peace Endowment's series on the social and economic history of World War I. Keilhau also functioned as joint editor and wrote the three final volumes in the eleven-volume general *History of Norway* published in the 1930s. Covering the period from 1840 to the 1930s, he was the first to provide a coherent and well-written account of the modernization of the Norwegian economy for the general public.[8]

By integrating the study of economic processes into general history, the generation of historians who began their career at the beginning of the twentieth century developed economic history as an academic discipline. The understanding of central national issues, like the "revolution" of 1814, was for the first time intimately linked to economic factors. A prominent representative of this new trend is Jacob S. Worm-Müller (1864–1963), appointed professor of history at the University of Oslo in 1928, who produced studies on both the Norwegian economy in the crucial years before 1814 and the subsequent crisis period after the Napoleonic Wars. Worm-Müller subsequently went on to edit and co-author a monumental six-volume history of Norwegian shipping, employing several young historians as assistants. He thus became the founder of a tradition of professional maritime history in Norwe-

8 Keilhau 1927 and 1935–8.

gian historiography. A political historian by temperament as well as by training, Worm-Müller was more interested in people than in processes. Although he dealt extensively with topics of economic history, he invariably focused on personalities. In his writings centre stage was held by the activity of individual entrepreneurs, rather than by the workings of the economic system.[9]

During the inter-war years and the 1940s, several examples of what was to become a more important feature of Norwegian economic history also emerged: commissioned histories on firms and institutions written by prominent academic historians. Among these were a history of Aker Savings Bank written by Johan Schreiner (1903–64), a history of the Norwegian postal system written by Sverre Steen (1898–1983), and the first volume of a grandly conceived history of the family-owned Mathiesen–Eidsvold Værk forest enterprise, written by Andreas Holmsen (1906–89).[10] All three authors were appointed professors of history at the University of Oslo. None of them was an economic historian, but the fact that they dealt professionally with themes that are central to economic history contributed towards setting a higher standard for the emerging discipline. Furthermore, their writings gave added prestige to the study of economic processes and institutions in a dynamic setting. They also managed to integrate economic subjects into a wider historical context, thereby establishing an alternative to the more static and structural tradition of economic history writing deriving from the statistical tradition.

The situation by the mid-twentieth century was thus essentially dualistic. On the one hand, the nineteenth-century tradition based on what we have called the social-statistical school retained considerable influence. On the other hand, the role of academic historians was considerably enhanced, particularly by the fact that historians gave added weight to dynamic economic processes and variables in both their general writings and in their choice of topics. The net result was that the relative importance of economists and social scientists in the writing of economic history was reduced, while that of the professional historian was strength-

9 Worm-Müller 1922 and 1923–51.
10 Schreiner 1944; Steen 1923; Holmsen 1946. Cf. Schreiner 1963.

ened. Over the next generation, historians took over the subject and made it a subspecies of general history. As we shall see, this meant that Norwegian economic history primarily came to focus on themes that were of concern to historians. The practitioners of economic history also came to rely more on the historian's skills than those of the economist. Economic processes were analyzed from a decision-making perspective, focusing to a large extent on the choices faced by individuals and firms.

A historical discipline emerges, 1950–1970

In the post–World War II period, economists generally turned even further from economic history than before. However, a number of researchers associated with the Central Bureau of Statistics continued the tradition of quantitative, mainly descriptive studies of macro-economic and sectoral Norwegian economic development. Most of this work was directly or indirectly inspired by the compilation of historical national accounts, building on a Norwegian tradition going back to the work of A. N. Kiær.

Four names stand out. Odd Aukrust led the work on national accounts for many years. Gerhard Stoltz wrote a very useful survey of the Norwegian economy in the first half of the twentieth century. Juul Bjerke produced a study of Norwegian long-term economic development based on the historical national accounts covering the period 1865–1965. Finally, Hermod Skånland published a comprehensive analysis of the Norwegian credit market since 1900. Their work represented the culmination of a long tradition in Norwegian social science, namely the statistically based analysis of major economic trends. With the publication of long-term real growth series in the 1950s and 1960s, Norwegian economic historians for the first time had a consistent macro-economic quantitative basis for specialized, sectoral, and micro-oriented studies of firms, industries, and structural changes.[11]

The economists' focus on quantitative data and on relationships between macro variables was not matched by a corresponding interest in the micro-economic causal factors driving the pro-

11 Aukrust 1990; Bjerke 1966; Skånland 1967; Stoltz 1955.

cess of economic change. This meant that these studies had limited influence on the direction of economic history and the emerging economic history profession. Economic historians and economists rarely asked the same questions, although they often used the same sources of information: quantitative data generated by firms and public institutions.

During the late 1950s and the early 1960s, economic history became a recognized university subject for the first time. This institutional development occurred in Bergen, outside the national academic centre in Oslo. Posts at the associate professor level were created both at the recently established University of Bergen and at the Norwegian School of Economics and Business Administration (NHH). Stein Tveite, who had spent two years studying economic history at the London School of Economics and Political Science, defended his doctoral thesis on the Anglo-Norwegian timber trade of the seventeenth century at the University of Oslo in 1961. He was subsequently appointed associate professor in Bergen, where a teaching position in economic history already existed at the NHH. Originating from Anton Mohr's personal chair in commercial history and colonial policy, the early development of the subject was the work of Thorolf Rafto, who made economic history an optional subject for business students in the 1960s.[12]

Tveite exerted pioneering efforts in the areas of research and of supervision. His reputation as a scholar was cemented by a prolific output of books and articles covering a wide variety of topics, ranging from the Middle Ages to contemporary issues. Although specializing in agriculture and forest industries, he also wrote on trade, shipping, and financial history as well as manufacturing.[13]

The fact that for the first time full-time academics were devoting their time exclusively to teaching and researching economic history had a long-term positive effect on the subject. Others were stimulated to follow. This did not mean that the subject changed

12 From 1957 Rafto had occupied a post as research fellow and subsequently as lecturer in economic history at the NHH. He rapidly established a reputation at the NHH as an inspiring lecturer.
13 Tveite 1959 and 1962. Hovland, Lange, and Rysstad 1990 contains a full bibliography of his writings.

fundamentally in character. Although early practitioners like Tveite used concepts from economic theory in their writing, they were basically historians who chose to specialize in economic history. In their choice of themes as well as in their methodology, they prolonged the tradition of sectoral and industrial analysis. Though strongly influenced by national research topics, they also dealt with internationally debated issues.

In intense debates with other historians, both at home and abroad, Tveite in particular made a strong plea for the use of economic theory in analyzing the transition from an agricultural to a commercial society, and from a static to a dynamic economy. Tveite attacked the view of Sverre Steen, who argued that economic rationality and production for the market were new features of Norwegian agricultural society around the middle of the nineteenth century. Tveite maintained that economic rationality was not a temporal concept, and that Norwegian farmers had always been guided by market considerations in their investment and production decisions.[14] The debate between Steen and Tveite and their respective followers was significant in many respects: it concerned issues that were of general European interest, it raised the issue of economic theory in economic history, and it stimulated research and debate on an important topic in Norwegian economic history.

The 1950s and 1960s were also characterized by a more consistent output of commissioned studies and monographs dealing with the business histories of central firms, established during the early industrialization of the 1850s and 1860s or during the boom years between 1905 and 1920. Among the authors of these commissioned histories, some economists made important contributions by linking the development of specific firms to issues of economic policy. Erling Petersen published a substantial volume for the centenary of the leading Norwegian commercial bank. Petersen's book dealt with the years 1907–57. It was particularly good in its analysis of the crisis years after World War I, and of the bank's performance and problems in the context of economic policy-making during the inter-war period.[15] Another academic

14 Steen 1957; Tveite 1959.
15 Petersen 1957.

economist, Arnljot Strømme Svendsen, was a specialist in maritime economics with a strong interest in industrial history. He wrote extensively on business and economic history. Clearly inspired by Joseph Schumpeter and his Swedish disciple Erik Dahmén, Strømme Svendsen produced studies of firms in the metallurgic and wood-processing sector as well as a general survey of the Norwegian manufacturing industry in the twentieth century.[16] These authors had one great strength: a sound grasp of economic theory which enriched their writing; they also had one great weakness: a lack of professional training as historians, which was evident in their somewhat haphazard use of sources.

Another group of authors comprised trained historians who worked outside academia and wrote commissioned histories of firms and industries. Their work varied greatly in quality, but includes several valuable contributions to the knowledge base of Norwegian economic history. J. N. Tønnessen's three massive volumes of the four-volume history of the modern Norwegian whaling industry in an international context constitute a work of particularly impressive scholarship. Although not an economic historian in the strict sense, Tønnessen must be considered with Worm-Müller and Schreiner to be among the founding fathers of Norwegian maritime history.[17]

The last group which contributed to the growing tide of company history consists of authors with a background in journalism or other professions who made part of their living by writing commissioned histories. Some of these, like K. Anker Olsen, had a genuine flair for business history. Several of his books are of great merit. Anker Olsen's significant contribution to the volume on the history of Norsk Hydro, published in 1955, is a good example. He also wrote solid business histories of the shipping firm Wilhelm Wilhelmsen and the pulp and paper and mechanical engineering industries.[18]

16 Strømme Svendsen 1961 and 1972; Wasberg and Strømme Svendsen 1969.
17 Tønnessen 1967, 1969, and 1970. Bernt Lorentzen, another highly qualified non-academic writer, concentrated on firms and industries around his native Bergen; Lorentzen 1952 and 1954.
18 Olsen 1953, 1955, and 1961.

Most of these commissioned histories were confined to individual firms or branches of industry, and seldom placed their subject-matter in a context of historical enquiry and debate. In this way they may be said to reflect the general status of the emerging discipline. Although many individual pieces of the puzzle forming economic history were in place by the end of this period, they had not yet been put together to constitute a coherent whole.

Economic history comes of age, 1970–1985

The definitive breakthrough for economic history as an academic discipline in Norway occurred in the 1970s. By 1985 there existed a body of historians almost exclusively occupied in the teaching and writing of economic and business history on a fully professional basis. Both in Bergen and Oslo a growing circle of academics defined themselves as historians practising economic and business history. At the beginning of the 1970s, the subject was also recognized on its own terms, through the first full professorships at institutions of higher learning.

In 1972 the University of Oslo established a chair in economic and social history. Illustrating the difficult birth of a new subject within established academic settings, the chair was sponsored by employers and unions for an initial five-year period. Only after that was it financed by the regular university budget. Francis Sejersted, who was appointed to the chair, rapidly established a graduate seminar and teaching programme on an intermediate level in economic history within the Department of History. He also initiated a research programme on the Norwegian economy in the 1930s, and thereby recruited young historians who chose to specialize in economic and business history instead of general political history.

One important result of the approach taken by Sejersted was a widening of the definition of economic history. He represented a transition from the sector-oriented perspective towards an explicitly synthetical view of the discipline. Sejersted wanted to reinterpret established views on Norwegian national development on the basis of an economic historical approach. Methodically he and his followers were firmly planted in good old-fashioned economic history, and were explicitly critical of the contemporary phenomenon of "new economic history", which found very little response in Norway.[19]

However, Sejersted stressed the general importance of theoretical frameworks and eagerly embraced two other related approaches emanating from US academics, viz. the history of technology and business history. At the same time, he developed an old established field: economic policy and the history of economic ideas. His main contribution in this field consisted of integrating the history of economic ideas and the development of economic policy-making with developments in the real economy. By explaining the deflationary monetary policy of the Bank of Norway and its governor, Nicolai Rygg, as a result of ideological, theoretical, and historical factors, he brought real historical understanding to bear on a problem that had hitherto been analyzed in political and moralistic terms. Sejersted rejected the somewhat anachronistic interpretation of Rygg's monetary policy, which Keilhau had established in the 1930s and which had been accepted by most economists and historians under the influence of the Keynesian revolution. Instead he offered a defence of Rygg by exposing the logic and relative flexibility of the pre-Keynesian policies that were pursued.[20]

Sejersted's interest in economic policy issues was echoed in the writings of several of his younger colleagues. Tore Jørgen Hanisch and Helge W. Nordvik both wrote on economic policy-making in the inter-war period, and together with the writings of Sejersted, this work contributed to a more sophisticated view of the real policy options available. Hanisch extended and revised Sejersted's analysis of the monetary policies of the 1920s, while Nordvik showed that fiscal policies contributed little to economic recovery in the 1930s. Both authors argued that foreign exchange rate policies and monetary policy played a positive role in initiating and stimulating recovery in the 1930s. These views formed part of a broader movement which revised the established picture of the Norwegian inter-war economy and, more generally, the interplay between economic policy, structural change, and economic growth.[21]

19 Sejersted 1972 and 1988; Basberg and Grytten 1994.
20 Sejersted 1973b.
21 Hanisch 1978 and 1979; Hanisch and Lange 1979; Nordvik 1977 and 1979.

The study of the depression and recovery of the 1930s had by
the early 1970s captured the interest of several historians in the
Scandinavian countries, and the topic figured prominently in the
1974 meeting of Nordic historians at Uppsala, Sweden.[22] Graduate students associated with Sejersted's seminar in economic history collaborated on a broad study of the recovery from the depression, concentrating on growth and structural change in the manufacturing sector. The project members rejected the established
view of an export-led recovery, arguing along Schumpeterian lines
that innovation and restructuring in the manufacturing industries
based on the home market were the driving forces in the recovery
process. Through detailed studies of sectors and branches as well
as individual firms, the members of this group presented a coherent and well-documented picture of the process of industrial
change induced by the challenge of economic crisis.[23]

Technological change was a central explanatory variable in the
Sejersted group's approach to the analysis of economic development. Inspired by the writings of economic historians such as
David Landes and Nathan Rosenberg, and ultimately by those of
Joseph Schumpeter, young scholars examined innovation and
technological diffusion in particular industries. As the world economy went into crisis in the 1970s, these structural approaches
enjoyed renewed interest among both economists and historians,
who found that macro-economic Keynesian explanations failed to
account for economic crisis both in the 1970s and in the 1930s.

Norwegian economic history has accordingly had a pronounced tendency to stress the history of technology, reinforced
by an early interest in the role of micro-economic and business
processes in economic development. As we have already seen, the
study of individual business firms had a long tradition. However, it
was only from the end of the 1970s that business history became
an integral part of academic historiography and an important
arena for professional economic historians.

The multi-volume history of the Mathiesen–Eidsvold Værk

22 Nilsson, Hildebrand, and Öhngren 1974.
23 Results of the project are presented in Sejersted 1982a; Hanisch and Lange
1979.

forestry and wood-processing firm constituted an important point of departure for the new role of business history. This unique project, based on records reaching back to the seventeenth century, ran for more than forty years, financed entirely by the family-owned firm.[24] During the 1970s Sejersted published two volumes which essentially covered the nineteenth century. His books demonstrated the value of business history as a way of illuminating central features of the nineteenth-century Norwegian economy, stressing institutional factors and supply-side mechanisms. Sejersted's work in business history was an important catalyst for his subsequent comprehensive reinterpretations of Norwegian economic and social development since 1814. Stressing the specific nature of the business system and social structure after the Napoleonic Wars, Sejersted claims that Norway has followed a *"Sonderweg"* to industrialization, deviating from the general European pattern.[25] The importance of the Mathiesen project is also evident in the fact that all three scholars who participated as main authors became professors of social or economic history, partly because of the academic standard of the project's monographs.

Echoing the new status of a formerly "despised" field, and inspired by international models like the Business History Unit at the London School of Economics, a Centre for Business History was established at the National Archives in 1979. The Centre was organized by Even Lange, who had participated in the work of the Sejersted group from the start and carried the work on Mathiesen–Eidsvold Værk forward into the industrial age. The Centre organized a series of projects linking business and general economic history, and this helped to lay the foundations for the vital development of business history in the late 1980s and early 1990s.[26]

Parallel to the development in Oslo, the 1970s also saw a

---

24 Holmsen 1946 and 1971; Sejersted and Schou 1972; Sejersted 1979; Lange 1985.

25 Sejersted 1993. The project also generated other work addressing central themes in Norwegian economic history; Lange 1977 and 1982. Analysis of the forest-based industries has been carried on by younger scholars; Moen 1991 and 1994.

26 Nerheim 1983; Nordvik 1984; Hanisch and Lange 1985 and 1986; Amdam, Hanisch, and Pharo 1989; Lange 1988 and 1989.

strengthening of the small group of economic historians in Bergen. With the appointment in 1972 of Trygve Solhaug as professor of economic history at the NHH, and the promotion of Thorolf Rafto to a personal chair, the section of economic history at the school consisted of three permanent posts as well as a research fellowship. This became the basis for a small but growing band of graduate students during the 1970s and 1980s which gave rise to several Master's and doctoral dissertations in economic history.

Neither Rafto nor Solhaug were prolific writers, but their research focused on subjects of particular interest to the coastal communities. Although Rafto for many years researched the history of the Norwegian deep-sea fisheries, his manuscript on the Norwegian North Sea fisheries in the period 1880–1920 remained unpublished at his death. His major contribution to Norwegian economic history literature remains his history of the Norwegian telegraph and telephone sector. Solhaug's major contribution is his massive two-volume history of Norwegian fisheries in the nineteenth century, published in 1974.[27]

The economic history of another part of the primary sector became the subject of a special chair when Stein Tveite was appointed professor of agricultural history at the Norwegian Agricultural University in 1970. His duties left him ample time both to supervise doctoral students inside and outside his institution and to act as general adviser and counsellor to the growing band of historians specializing in economic and business history.[28]

An important aspect of the intellectual climate of the 1970s was a growing interest in economic and social history among students at different levels of the rapidly expanding system of higher education. The demand for teaching materials in Norwegian economic history induced several authors to write new texts aimed at students. Indicating the enhanced status of the discipline in general, these first textbooks also mirrored the formation of distinct groups of scholars within the field.

27 Rafto 1955; Solhaug 1974.
28 Tveite's influence is attested to by the *Festschrift* produced on the occasion of his 60th birthday in 1990, which includes contributions from most economic historians holding academic positions at the time; Hovland, Lange, and Rysstad 1990.

In connection with his teaching at the University of Oslo, Sejersted published a general introduction to economic history, historiography, and methodology in 1973.[29] Six years later a group of historians mainly connected to the University of Bergen published the first volume of a general economic history textbook for university students on the 1500–1850 period.[30] A group of four young scholars doing commissioned research in Oslo published in English an account of Norway's economic development from the 1830s for distribution to civil servants and policy-makers abroad. The amended Norwegian version, published in paperback in 1983, became widely used as an introductory survey text for students at universities and elsewhere.[31]

In 1975 Fritz Hodne at the NHH published a preliminary English-language version of an economic history of Norway from 1815 to 1970. A longer and more polished version in Norwegian was published in 1981. As well as applying a "dual economy" model of development, the book synthesized a large body of secondary literature, in particular a number of commissioned business histories. Though uneven, the book was influential, particularly through its ability to stimulate controversy and new research.[32]

These textbooks revised established views on Norwegian economic history. Central issues were the nature and periodization of Norwegian economic development and, in particular, the pattern of industrial growth. In the 1960s and early 1970s, foreign writers on Scandinavian economic development had argued that the backwardness of Norwegian agriculture seriously delayed industrial development and placed the industrial breakthrough in Norway as late as the decade preceding the First World War.[33] Some of the elements of this interpretation were also prominent in Hodne's textbook, including the unimportance of the agricultural sector for economic development and the substantial role of export earnings in economic growth. Export earnings from timber, fishing,

29 Sejersted 1973a (1985).
30 Dyrvik *et al.* 1979.
31 Bergh *et al.* 1981 (1983).
32 Hodne 1975 and 1981 (revised and abridged versions have been published later); Hodne 1983; Hodne and Grytten 1992.
33 Liberman 1965; Jörberg 1971.

and shipping services were seen as the engine of growth in the nineteenth century, while industrial growth came to the fore only after the turn of the century.

Bergh and his colleagues presented a somewhat different view of the development process. While admitting that export surges were of fundamental importance during periods of rapid economic growth (e.g. in the 1850s and prior to World War I), they opposed the previous presentation of Norwegian economic development as a mere reflection of world market forces. In particular, they argued for a more multi-faceted periodization of industrial growth, emphasizing the importance of domestic factors in the course and pattern of industrialization. Much in line with the Schumpeter-inspired interpretation of the 1930s mentioned above, they drew attention to the importance of supply responses to economic crises as an important determinant in the growth process. They thus played down the role of autonomous demand factors also in the nineteenth century. They further argued that the Norwegian industrial revolution had to be understood as a series of separate spurts in the nineteenth century, and that the decisive stage of Norway's transition to industrialism took place before the advent of large-scale capital-intensive industrialization based on hydroelectric energy, from around 1905.[34]

The development of the new discipline in Norway in the 1970s and 1980s to a large extent reflected the surge in activity in the field of economic history internationally. Nevertheless, Norway still lagged behind its Scandinavian neighbours in terms of the status of economic history both inside and outside academia. However, the institutional foundations had been established in the form of new and permanent teaching and research positions, and the stage was set for a burst of activity in the following years. The synthesizing approach to Norwegian economic history represented by the first university textbooks proved particularly stimulating. Much subsequent research has indeed purported to cast light on the fundamental questions raised by the effort at synthesis towards the end of the formative period.

34 Bergh *et al.* 1983:230–5.

The past decade

The past decade has been one of considerable expansion for Norwegian economic history. One sign of this has been institutional growth. However, the number of economic and business historians has increased much more than the number of teaching positions. In reality, the market for economic and business historians has grown considerably, largely thanks to commissioned work on firms and business institutions, but also to large research projects financed through research councils.

Institutional development took place both through expansion at existing departments and through the growth of new centres. At the University of Oslo, Sejersted organized a large research programme which sought to combine the expertise of economic historians and historians of technology in investigating the development of the Norwegian electronics industry after 1945. By the end of the 1980s, this and related projects on science and research policy were incorporated into a new Centre for Technology and Culture. The Centre was partly modelled on the many American projects on society, science, and technology, popular in the 1970s, and signalled a general increase in the public interest in modern technological development. The historians associated with the Centre have made a significant contribution to the growing literature on innovation studies and the history of technology, as well as to business history and general economic history.[35]

A related development took place at the University of Trondheim. A group of historians and social scientists, some of them associated with the history of electronics project mentioned above, established a Centre for Technology and Society. Both the overall approach and the methodologies employed by the Centre's academics owe more to sociology and history of technology than to

35 An early project associated with the Centre was the history of *Det norske Veritas;* Andersen and Collett 1989. A later project was the history of the Norwegian oil industry; Hanisch and Nerheim 1993. The Centre has in particular managed to combine the history of technology, business history, and science policy. Working at the Norwegian Institute for Defence Studies, Olav Wicken became associated with many of the projects and has published several important contributions in these fields; Wicken 1983 and 1994.

economic history. A joint leader of the group was Håkon With Andersen, subsequently appointed professor of history at the University. With Andersen continued the work of establishing the history of technology as a recognized academic discipline in Norway. He forged important links between Norwegian historians of technology and the network of international scholars interested in the field, including many economic historians.[36]

Institutions of higher education outside the university system also responded to the growing interest in economic and business history. In 1988 the Norwegian School of Management, a large independent business school, appointed Even Lange to a new professorship in economic history. The Centre for Business History that he directed also moved there, with a permanent staff of three research fellows. Combining business history and institutional history, both publicly and privately financed, the Centre expanded rapidly. By the early 1990s, some ten researchers worked at the Centre, constituting one of the largest groups of business historians in Europe. The initial research team comprised Rolv Petter Amdam, Finn Erhard Johannesen, and Lars Thue. From this group emanated a series of publications on firms and institutions dealing with themes ranging from managerial education and electricity supply to the chemical industry, glass-making, and pharmaceuticals.[37] Building on this research, the staff has also engaged in teaching, both through independently developed courses in economic and business history, and by introducing topics of economic history into other parts of the school's teaching programme.

More generally, the growth of business history is a striking fea-

---

36 Andersen was a co-organizer of the first international conference of the Society for the History of Technology in Stockholm, 1992. His doctoral work on technical change in Norwegian shipbuilding in the period 1935–70 was linked to a comparative project on British and Swedish shipbuilding, based at the Institute of Economic History at the University of Gothenburg; Andersen 1989 and 1991.

37 Amdam 1991, 1993, and 1994; Amdam and Sogner 1994; Bergh and Lange 1989; Espeli 1992; Johannessen 1989, 1991, and 1992; Thue 1994. Results from several of the projects organized by the Centre are presented in Amdam and Lange 1994.

ture of the past decade. In Norway as elsewhere, business history has become a meeting-place for economists, historians of technology, social historians, and economic historians. The sheer quantity of output suggests that business history has had a large impact on contemporary Norwegian economic history. In the process, business history has itself been widened to include the history not only of companies and firms, but also of industrial sectors and of the interplay between business and government.

As mentioned, central business history projects, such as that on Mathiesen–Eidsvold Værk, have been conducted by historians with a genuine interest in economic history. One of the advantages of a thorough training in general history is the ability to use a wide variety of sources to analyze complex issues of economic policy-making and business decisions. Scholars trained in political history have thus made valuable contributions to the literature. Trond Bergh is one of the prominent authors combining political and economic history, and Edgar Hovland, associate professor at the University of Bergen, is another example of this trend.[38] Recent business histories have also been written by authors approaching the subject-matter from other disciplines. Tore J. Hanisch and Helge W. Nordvik were both trained as economists, while Gunnar Nerheim came into the field by way of the history of ideas and subsequently the history of technology.[39] Nevertheless, the largest influx of new recruits to the field of business history came from graduates in history at the universities. Many of them had originally worked in political and social history, but several were recruited to the field by collaborating with established economic and business historians.

Occasionally an economic historian trained abroad is recruited to the widely defined circle of business historians. An example is Kristine Bruland, whose doctorate in economic history at Oxford was awarded for a thesis on the transfer of textile pro-

38 Bergh has written extensively on economic policy after World War II. His business history contributions include Bergh 1975 and Bergh and Lange 1989. Hovland's studies on agricultural and industrial regulation and policy integrate political and business history in a well-balanced way; Hovland 1979. Cf. Nordvik 1984.
39 Nerheim 1983; Nerheim and Nordvik 1986; Nordvik 1984.

duction methods and machinery from Britain to Norway in the nineteenth century. Her study was inspired by an interest in the history of technology, and she used the sources and some of the methodologies familiar to business historians.

Bruland later expanded her interest in the role of technology transfer by studying the development of the nineteenth-century mechanical engineering industry, and she edited a collection of articles on aspects of technological change and Scandinavian industrialization. She is perhaps the Norwegian economic historian who has most consistently focused on processes of industrial growth before 1914, stressing the importance of British technology in the early phase of the Norwegian industrialization. Appointed to a new chair in economic history at the University of Oslo in 1993, she is one of the few Norwegian economic historians to have made an internationally recognized contribution to one of the perennial and great concerns of economic history: the debate on the Industrial Revolution.[40]

Although the comparatively "new" fields of business history and the history of technology have played an important role in developing Norwegian economic history, some old and established fields have also contributed to the expansion. The study of the formulation and execution of economic policy continues to be an area where economic and political historians frequently collaborate. One such collaboration resulted in a book analyzing the development of the economics profession in Norway and its relationship to economic policy-making, written to commemorate the 100th anniversary of the Norwegian Political Economy Association in 1983. Given the crucial role played by economists in formulating and implementing central elements of the managed mixed economy since 1945, this study underlined the importance of economic history as a way of understanding political, social, and intellectual developments in Norwegian society.[41]

One of the authors, Trond Bergh, extended his analysis, integrating economic thought and political decision-making in several articles on industrial democracy and in his volume of the history

40 Bruland 1989 and 1991.
41 Bergh and Hanisch 1984.

of the labour movement after World War II.[42] His co-author, Tore J. Hanisch, on the other hand, pursued the study of economic policy with an emphasis on monetary and fiscal aspects. Participating in several projects of institutional and business history, he has brought important elements of economic analysis into the predominantly historical tradition of Norwegian economic history. Of particular interest in his later work is his analysis of the role of the oil sector in the Norwegian economy of the 1970s.[43]

Banking and financial history constitutes another expanding field with strong roots in Norwegian economic historiography. Several early works have already been mentioned, many of them written by economists outside mainstream economic history. The first modern economic historian to take an active interest in financial and banking history was Francis Sejersted. Starting with his 1966 Master's thesis on the history of the Bank of Norway in the 1840s, he renewed his interest in central banking in his 1973 book on Nicolai Rygg as governor and architect of the Bank of Norway's "return to gold" policy after World War I.

Some of Sejersted's students have gone on to make their mark as historians of banking and finance. Åsmund Egge worked for many years studying aspects of Norwegian banking in the nineteenth century, culminating in a doctoral thesis on the government-controlled discounting commissions and their role in the nineteenth-century credit market. Egge's work is placed firmly in an empirically oriented historical tradition. Although he was not a student of Sejersted, the same can be said of Øystein Hveding, who investigated the role of government financial support for agriculture through a state bank established for that purpose.[44]

---

42 An early excursion into the post-1945 history of economic policy was Bergh's chapter in Bergh and Pharo 1977. This book also contained a chapter on post-war industrial policy by Tore Grønlie, who developed the theme extensively in his dissertation on state ownership of industry; Grønlie 1989.

43 Hanisch and Nerheim 1993. With a background in political history, Harald Espeli has also written extensively on economic policy issues, focusing on industrial and agricultural issues in the twentieth century. His doctoral dissertation on the mechanization of farming exhibits the characteristic Norwegian interest in the role of technology discussed earlier; Espeli 1990 and 1992.

44 Egge 1983 and 1988; Hveding 1982.

The role of government in banking was a traditional interest of political historians. An alternative point of departure was provided by the business history approach to private banking, a long tradition in Norwegian historiography. From the mid-1970s these two perspectives were brought together in a series of projects initiated by professional historians writing commissioned business histories of banking institutions. In his book on the Norwegian Postal Savings Bank, Trond Bergh placed the bank in a government-institutional setting. He analyzed the bank both as a new competitor for private savings in relation to the established private banks and as a tool of increased government activism.[45] The gap between the old politically oriented approach and the new business history approach was also closed from the other direction. In the early 1980s Sejersted led a team of historians who investigated aspects of commercial and investment banking in a volume celebrating the 125th anniversary of the largest Norwegian commercial bank, Den norske Creditbank. The book also represented a new approach insofar as the authors in individual chapters analyzed a number of areas of interaction between the bank, its clients, and central and local government.[46]

Two further banking histories illustrated a shift in focus from national to local and regional economic development and to the role of financial institutions in furthering economic growth. Combining business history with a structural approach to modernization, the authors of a volume of the role of savings banks in the economic development of south-western Norway documented the changing functions of these institutions in the Norwegian banking system. A similar approach was employed in the volume on Nordlandsbanken, where the authors analyzed the economic development of Northern Norway through the prism of the leading regional commercial bank.[47]

Much recent research in financial history has dealt with the role of banking in the modernization process. Nineteenth-century banking has been taken up by economic historians investigating

45 Bergh 1975.
46 Sejersted 1982b. The book written for the 50th anniversary of the state-owned Norwegian Bank for Industry is another example of this development; Hanisch and Lange 1986.
47 Nordvik, Nerheim, and Brandal 1989; Fygle, Lundestad, and Strand 1993.

aspects of the Norwegian credit market first noted by Sejersted and Egge. Among the characteristics that have been singled out are the strong and sustained role of the state, the early and enduring importance of savings banks, the slow growth of commercial banking, and the relative failure of commercial banks in financing industrial development. Because of the depth and duration of the banking crisis, the financial history of the inter-war period has also attracted substantial interest.[48]

A considerable part of this research has been financed through a comprehensive interdisciplinary programme called Bank Capital and Society. Several economic historians have been involved in structural long-term studies of the financial system. The main purpose of the project has been to obtain a deeper understanding of the role of financial institutions and markets in furthering economic growth under different regulatory regimes. Participation in the recent development of Nordic and European research networks has made financial history one of the fields where Norwegian economic historians publish internationally.[49]

Unlike financial and banking history, maritime economic history has not had much attention from academic economic historians until quite recently. Nonetheless, maritime history has been a growing field within Norwegian economic history and is now quite well-established within several institutions of higher learning. The first economic historian to take a doctorate in maritime economic history (in 1979) was Ole Gjølberg at the NHH. Although the thesis never appeared in print, his main findings were presented in scholarly journals. Gjølberg broke with the traditional historical approach to maritime history by applying economic theory to maritime history in his analysis of technological change, investment, and profitability in Norwegian shipping. This thesis is also worth special note since it was the first time that an economic historian had made use of the massive accumulation of price and wage data collected by Ingvar Wedervang and his associates in the 1930s and early 1940s.[50]

48 Knutsen 1991 and 1994; Lange 1994a; Nordvik 1993.
49 Knutsen 1995; Lange 1994b.
50 See Gjølberg 1979 and Fischer and Nordvik 1987.

The *Yearbook of Norwegian Maritime History*, published by the Bergen Maritime Museum, is the most important outlet for Norwegian maritime economic history. Trained as a political historian, the current director of the museum, Atle Thowsen, has also made a strong personal contribution to the reorientation of maritime history towards economic history in his study of the Bergen shipping industry in the period 1914–39 and his volume on the organization of the Norwegian shipping and trade mission in England during World War II (Nortraship). Thowsen has been joined by several economic historians in the revival of Norwegian maritime history. Starting from an early interest in whaling, Bjørn Basberg, with a doctorate in economic history from NHH in 1985, has written both on whaling and on the history of Norwegian shipping during the Second World War. Together with Thowsen and Lauritz Pettersen, Basberg has written the definitive volumes on the history of the Norwegian merchant fleet during the Second World War. This large and well-financed project also stimulated interest among other historians in the economic history of Norwegian shipping in the twentieth century. It has resulted in several graduate theses, many of them published in the yearbook of the Bergen Maritime Museum.[51] In addition, the history departments of the universities in Bergen and (to a lesser degree) Oslo have consistently produced interesting Master's theses on maritime history, dealing with shipping and shipbuilding as well as fisheries and whaling. All these activities are important in Norwegian economic history, but they have formerly been neglected by professional historians.

The field also enjoys growing international interest. A scholarly partnership between Helge W. Nordvik and the Canadian maritime historian Lewis R. Fischer has resulted in a large number of articles on aspects of Norwegian maritime economic history. Supported by both Canadian and Norwegian funding, they established in 1989 the *International Maritime History Journal*, which has become the leading journal for international maritime economic historians.[52]

51 See the survey in Nordvik 1991.
52 Within the last decade there has been considerable interest in the history of shipbuilding and associated maritime construction activities. Andersen 1989a, 1989b, and 1991; Basberg 1985; Hanisch and Nerheim 1993; Nerheim and Utne 1990. For further details see Nordvik 1991.

While banking and maritime history have recently received much attention, and business history has tended to predominate in Norwegian economic historiography, other fields have been relatively neglected. "New economic history", defined broadly as quantitative economic history and even more narrowly as econometric history, has never gained a strong foothold in Norway. This must no doubt be attributed to the fact that economic historians have by and large been recruited from and trained within history departments. An exception is provided by the Department of Economic History at the NHH, where the doctoral programme provides a thorough knowledge of economics and quantitative methods. Nevertheless, as a recent survey of the field makes clear, there are signs of a growing body of research employing increasingly sophisticated methodologies by both economists and economic historians.[53]

Since the first real chairs in economic history were filled in the early 1970s, Norwegian economic history has made considerable progress. Although it was a late-developer, increasing international contacts bear witness to the fact that Norwegian economic history has developed very much along the same lines as the subject elsewhere in the western industrialized countries. One trend has been an increasing specialization and diversification within the field. In this process the associations between economic history and other expanding subdisciplines have changed. The interface between economic and social historians, long a feature of both international (notably British) and Norwegian economic history, has almost completely vanished.

On the other hand, national peculiarities continue to exert a strong influence on Norwegian economic historiography. As stated, the subject remains very much part of history as opposed to economics. Furthermore, the notable importance of business history spills over into other specialities, such as the history of technology, maritime history, and financial history. Linked to the importance of business history is the substantial role of privately

---

53 Basberg and Grytten 1994. One of the economists who have published extensively internationally in this field is Jan Tore Klovland, whose work is discussed in their article.

financed research as opposed to research financed by universities and research councils. Traditionally, historians have regarded this kind of research with scepticism. For economic history, however, commissioned business histories also have certain positive effects, illustrated in the literature under review. One of these is access to source material often closed to historians in other countries, such as banking and private business records. Another is the opportunity to cover areas commonly neglected by historians limited to official records. In particular, the analysis of the modern business enterprise is necessary to better understand twentieth-century capitalist economies.

The divorce of economics from history has been a characteristic of Norwegian economic historiography since the 1930s. This has tended to reduce the relevance of economic history for policymakers and to impoverish public debate. Current developments seem to offer an opportunity to bridge the gap. Business and institutional history may in fact be the key to closer contacts between economic historians and economists. Modern economic science has recently moved in the direction of institutional analysis and a renewed interest in the economics of the firm. In our view, the future challenge for Norwegian economic history must be to exploit these opportunities by building on the strong general historical tradition and by developing the institutional approach to economic history, while stimulating an eclectic use of economic theory and methodology.

11. Women's History[1]
Ida Blom

The forgotten tradition

In 1970 the Norwegian Historical Association celebrated its centenary. On the occasion Edvard Bull jun. claimed that historians had largely limited themselves to studying themes of interest to the Western European bourgeoisie – "and to that bourgeoisie's men". In the future historical research should begin to also examine "large groups of people who have hitherto been omitted: children, old people and women".[2] A few years later, in 1974, the concept of women's history was taken up for the first time in a broad forum of Norwegian historians. The following year an interdisciplinary conference organized by the Norwegian Humanities Research Council (NHRC, later renamed the NRC) discussed the matter, and in 1977 this was a main theme at the triennial meeting of Nordic historians. Had a new subdiscipline broken through in Norwegian (and Nordic) historical research? It might appear so. But it was soon evident that the subdiscipline was not new, and that one could hardly say that it had broken through in historical circles.

Within Norwegian historical research there was a trace of a tradition for the study by historians of fields which particularly concerned women. This went back as far as the period of the union with Denmark, and can be seen as a result of contemporary European interest in comparative cultural history. With the nineteenth century's rise in interest in the history of the nation–state, the cultural history perspective disappeared, along with interest in women's history. At the end of the nineteenth century, however, a woman active in women's affairs, Ragna Nielsen, posed the question whether women had a history of their own, which historians

1 Translated by Eamonn Noonan.
2 Bull 1970.

neglected to research. Halvdan Koht accepted that this was indeed
the case, but thought that the explanation was the concentration
of research on the country's political history. When historians
were busy with the study of "the actually productive, value-creat-
ing members of society", this would change. "With working people, farmers and town-dwellers, women also become visible in history", claimed Koht in 1904 in reply to Ragna Nielsen's critique.[3]

In the period up to the First World War, however, it was left to
historians not linked to the academic world to treat women's history subjects. Anna Caspari Agerholt and Mimi Sverdrup Lunden
performed pioneering work on political and social women's history.[4] But the gender perspective was ignored in Norwegian
research in the 1950s and 1960s, and also by the few women historians employed at the universities.

Academic women's history

It is thus unsurprising that women's history was regarded as something fundamentally new in the 1970s when graduate students
and younger female researchers took up the subject. The proportion of Master's theses treating themes of women's history soared,
and the NHRC sponsored research projects in the field. Since then
many monographs have appeared, *Historisk tidsskrift* has regularly
printed articles with women's history material, and much has also
been published in English-language journals.[5] Women's history

3 Blom 1983 and 1994a:11–33. Ludwig Holberg and Lauritz Engelstoft, both
  professors at Copenhagen University (at the time the only university in the
  Danish–Norwegian state), wrote works which took up women's history in
  1745 and 1796 respectively. Engelstoft was strongly influenced by the Scot-
  tish academic John Millar, who in 1773 produced a work in which the living
  conditions of women in a series of different cultures had a prominent place.
  See also Harbsmeier 1989 for eighteenth-century German women's history.
4 Agerholt 1973; Sverdrup Lunden 1941 and 1948. Sverdrup Lunden took a
  Master's in history in 1931. Although she did not have academic training,
  Margarethe Bonnevie wrote many works which sought to trace the gender
  perspective in the history of ideas in Europe; Blom 1993e.
5 Hubbard 1993; Fløystad 1990a, 1990b, and 1991. Articles in English
  include Hagemann 1985b; Melby 1991; Sogner 1983, 1984, and 1993;
  Sogner and Sandvik 1989b; Blom 1980a, 1990b, 1991b, 1991c, 1992d,
  and 1993d. One article is translated into Japanese: Blom 1992c.

has become established as a specialist field in its own right, a subdiscipline with its own conferences and with a network of researchers linked to the Nordic and the broader international environment.

Factors both internal and external to the discipline help explain the interest in illuminating women's history. Koht suggested as early as 1904 that the focus on social history, "history from below", meant that new groups stepped into the historians' spotlight. Interest shifted from the governing to the governed, from the country's political history to the social history of everyday life, from public to private, and to family history. A parallel growth in research in historical demography reinforced this tendency, and the same can be said of the interest in studies of the history of mentalities. In short the blossoming of what has since been called "hyphenated history" went in the same direction as research in women's history. A research field with a range of new perspectives was created, complementing traditional political history in differing ways.

Inspiration also came from outside the history discipline. As often before, the historian's own times proved significant for research.[6] There was a clear parallel to developments in the USA and many European countries. At the end of the 1960s, voices critical of the profession and associated with radical political circles took issue with ideas about value-neutral research. This started a discussion in Norwegian historical circles on the concept of objectivity. Inspired by the new women's movement of the early 1970s, parts of this criticism attacked gender neutrality as well as the so-called making invisible of women's history. The women's movement opened many problems for debate, all of which had a history. A need for historical knowledge arose which could not be met from existing presentations. Women had a right to get to know their own, gender-specific history.

From a voyage of discovery to social analysis

Early women's history research had an element of a voyage of discovery.[7] Analyses of women's responsibility for human reproduc-

6 Kjeldstadli 1992; Blom 1975, 1976, and 1983.
7 A comprehensive overview of this research up to 1989 is Fløystad 1990b.

tion, through birth, care for children, and socialization within the household and the family, lay on the dividing line between social history, everyday history, and historical demography. Blom's study of birth control in Christiania from the end of the 1800s to 1930 directed attention towards both reproductive practices and motives for reducing the number of births. It analyses both the practice and the discussion of contraception and abortion. In an extensive research project dealing with the same period, Sogner, Randborg, and Fure revealed and evaluated regional patterns in the decline in fertility. Another work analysed the growing influence of medical science on birthing assistance in town and country through the nineteenth and twentieth centuries, and the shifting of births from home to institutions.[8]

Studies of women's work in the private household and in public, in factories, schools, hospitals, and telecommunications, highlight women's importance for the economy of the family and the society, and their possibilities for providing for themselves outside the family and the household. Avdem and Melby built on their own and others' investigations in this field in their account of the history of domestic work since 1850. Both this work and Fløystad's thorough study of changes in women's work in a Vestland district clearly reveal the great importance of this work at both the family and the societal level. Martinsen's and Melby's works on religious health care workers (*diakonisser*) and secular nurses showed the significance of the female labour force for the building of a modern health service. Contrasts and similarities between related but different caring professions also appeared.[9] This research was hardly marked by a "victim perspective", and it emphasized the active role of women in changes in society.

Hagemann has thrown new light on the significance of gender for industrialization and working life and has further developed central theories about the process of industrialization. In her analysis of how the gender hierarchy was reproduced within both old and new occupations, despite the great changes in production

8 Blom 1990b; Sogner, Randsborg, and Fure 1984; Blom 1988b.
9 Avdem and Melby 1985; Fløystad 1986; Martinsen 1984 and 1989; Melby 1990.

conditions and in the labour market which followed industrialization, she points to the existence of two different types of labour force. One was the young, unskilled, cheap, and relatively poorly organized female labour force, the other was the skilled, expensive, well-organized male labour force; found in every age group. This gender-divided labour market became a central factor in the process of industrialization and was important for both technological and organizational changes.[10]

Within political history the way in which women had participated in, been excluded from, or shown themselves indifferent to, political power was uncovered. A long series of Master's theses treated the growth of female public life. This came about from the end of the nineteenth century through participation in party politics, trade unions, and socially involved women's organizations, as well as through various feminist organizations. For the centenary of the Norwegian Association for the Rights of Women, Aslaug Moksnes wrote the association's history from 1885 to 1913. She analyzed the conflicts behind the establishment of the organization. She showed the complex interaction entailed by an ambivalent perception of the women's question: partly as a struggle for equality with men, and partly as a struggle for the due recognition of the particular qualities of women.[11]

The main focus in women's history research has been on the period from c. 1850 to c. 1940. For the seventeenth and eighteenth centuries, an active research environment has developed, centred on many of Sogner's research projects. A series of theses illuminate criminality and sexuality in a gender perspective. Sandvik has shown that the occupational activity of women was at the end of the 1700s far more extensive and independent than the legal framework apparently allowed. She is now working on an extensive analysis of the relation between the normative stipulations of the law and the variety of actual possibilities open to women up to about 1850. The relatively few works on medieval history illuminate a few main themes, such as women's function in reproduc-

---

10 Hagemann 1994a.
11 See the section "Organisering, kvinnesakskamp" in Fløystad 1990b; Moksnes 1984.

tion and their position in law. The introduction of Christianity has been interpreted as a limitation of the religious activities of women, while the life of the cloister gave new possibilities. In the political area, the growth of the state in the High Middle Ages had been seen as a barrier to women's access to positions of power, but greater emphasis on leadership through intellectual and organizational abilities may have made conditions more suitable for the era's few female leaders.[12]

Like much other Norwegian historical research, research on women's history has been characterized by a strongly empirical approach. A need to establish a profile for women's history as a discipline has, however, been felt. Ida Blom stressed in 1975 the anchoring of the subject in accepted historical methods. She defined women's history as a collective concept for research dealing with women's various activities in the past and analyzing problems of particular relevance to the women of the past.[13] Great emphasis was placed on understanding women's history as an integrated part of other history, and on relating women's historical analysis closely to the society of which they were a part. This approach was in line with what Joan W. Scott later characterized as social historical women's history.[14] This understanding of the concept of women's history entailed a reaction against the view of gender as an innate and unchangeable characteristic. It built on the view that gender was in the main a historical construct. This approach was simultaneously an attempt to find a middle ground between a Marxist-influenced position and a feminist position. The former prioritized class over gender as a category for historical analysis; the latter worked with a clear polarization between the female and the male, and strove for a specifically female research methodology.[15]

12 Fløystad 1990a and 1990b; Øye 1990. Research on the decline of fertility, family history, and the court records project, led by Sølvi Sogner, have all been fruitful starting-points for women's history research. See Eliassen and Sogner 1981 and Sogner 1990. The court records project has to date resulted in ten theses, many with a women's history perspective. See also Sogner and Sandvik 1989a and 1989b.
13 Blom 1975, 1976, and 1977.
14 Scott 1983.
15 Melby 1978; Blom 1978.

It was later suggested that the concept of women's history which had been generally accepted in women's history circles from the mid-1970s had both strengths and weaknesses.[16] The strength was in setting women and gender in focus, while at the same time warning against loose generalization and emphasizing the wish for integration within the discipline. This definition was regarded as broad-ranging, and it enabled professional co-operation between very different groups. Gro Hagemann, however, raised the question whether this starting-point, which in an early phase could be a strength, might not in time entail a weakness. Might it bind women's history too closely to other historical research, and thus allow too little room for innovation?

This self-critical reflection pointed towards lines of development in women's history circles. Research has been conducted at the historical institutes of all the country's universities. University teachers interested in the field have taught and supervised women's history, and there have not been great controversies among Norwegian women's historians. Women's history has, however, remained a special discipline, and the process of integration has not been undisputedly successful. Is this because the earlier definition was a hindrance to innovation, clipping the wings of women's historians?

Striking parallels in the development of women's history in other countries seem to suggest that the Norwegian situation is by no means peculiar.[17] One may, however, suggest that the strong prioritization of the empirical aspect, in women's history as in historical circles generally, has been an obstacle to creative thinking among women's historians. But it may also appear that self-criticism has tended to overlook a range of important theoretical innovations which occurred within women's history research.

The purely empirical approach to women's history research, a "her-story" tradition, had parts of its roots in the debate on objectivity and subjectivity in historical research of the 1960s and early 1970s. Women's historians accepted the researcher's objective starting-point regarding the elaboration of problems to study and

16 Hagemann 1990.
17 Offen, Pierson, and Rendall 1991.

of theories. As was stated at the time, they wanted to analyze history from the woman's perspective. This brought forward an alternative historical reality which, one thought, had implications for the entire history discipline.[18] It soon transpired that the reconstruction of the past which resulted from women's history research was often difficult to combine with the concepts historians had hitherto used. Reflections critical of the concepts led to a recognition that what was apparently gender-neutral often reflected a male-influenced norm. When, for instance, the concept of "work" was blithely limited to the sense of paid work, this had implications for our understanding of economic, social, and political history. It was pointed out that social analyses which neglected the functions occurring within the family and household could not produce a satisfactory understanding of how a society worked. The concept of work had to include not just the work of human care, but also unpaid work in the household and the work of producing new individuals, most of which fell particularly to women. The value of the labour force was linked to gender. Analysis of the process of industrialization and of changes in the labour market which neglected the gender dimension were accordingly incomplete. A series of central concepts – burgher, franchise, farmer, nation, people – gradually became the object of critical analysis which revealed that the (specifically) male had come to stand for the universal.[19]

By emphasizing the gender-determined in what was apparently gender-neutral, women's historians also initiated discussion on the misleading signals which could reside in the dichotomy between concepts such as public and private. They rejected an understanding of society which mainly limited women to the private, and men to the public. They urged comprehensive social analysis as essential for the best possible understanding of how society functioned.[20]

Large parts of the theoretical debate took place within the interdisciplinary world of women's studies. The question how

18 Blom 1979; Hagemann 1982.
19 Blom 1979, 1984, 1985a, and 1985b; Berggreen 1985; Hagemann 1986a, 1986b, and 1989; Blom 1980a, 1993b, and 1994a.
20 Hagemann 1986; Sogner and Sandvik 1989a and 1989b.

empirical findings should be interpreted (i.e., which comprehensive understanding should be applied) gradually won greater attention. Concepts such as "oppression" and "liberation" were soon put in question through an emphasis on the contextual understanding of such core ideas. Empirical studies stressed the uncovering of differences between genders in the same class, and between classes in the life and work of women, in their political activities, and in their ideological roots. The interplay between gender and class was from the beginning an essential theme of Norwegian women's history research.[21]

Theories of patriarchy, strongly influential in international women's history research, were received sceptically. The concept of patriarchy was regarded as unclear, since not only women but also men could be subjected to a patriarchal hierarchy. It was also seen as a simplification of gender relations, underestimating both women's power over men, as well as interaction and co-operation between the sexes.[22] The "victim perspective" became peripheral.

At the same time it was considered important to analyze biologically determined sex in the light of a social understanding of gender, a parallel to the English and American use of the terms "sex" and "gender". The socialization of gender was regarded as a key to the understanding of mediation between the biological and the social. Women's history studies of subjects related to biology – contraception, midwifery, prostitution – included both the social historical and the ideological.[23]

Even if theories of patriarchy were peripheral, studies of the power relationship between the genders were by no means lacking. The systematic unequal distribution of goods and means of power was interpreted as an indication of a subservience relationship. Analysis of conflicts between women and men within the same organization and the same area of work cast light on gender-based asymmetrical power mechanisms.[24] Important themes were analyses of power relations between women (for example, between housewives and

21 Blom 1979; articles in Blom and Hagemann 1977.
22 Hagemann 1985a, 1985b, and 1986b; Blom 1987; Aas 1993a.
23 Fløystad 1979; Blom 1984; Melby 1980. See also the section "Reproduksjon, familie" in Fløystad 1990a.
24 Hagemann 1985a and 1989; Melby 1980; Blom 1988b.

servant girls) and of conflict and co-operation between women
across class or political alignment.[25] Women's historians worked
from an understanding of the research area which put more
emphasis on the putting into question of gender and its historical
construction than on an essentialistic understanding of gender.
Inspired by American women's history research, Hagemann
took up the concept of "gender system" or "gender order" in an
important 1986 article. The concept was embraced as a unified
theoretical framework for a social analysis in which gender was
systematically placed in relation to other central analytical categories. She suggested that gender comprises social divisions of fundamental significance for each society, and that the gender variable is
therefore important for each subsection of the history discipline.
Starting from within her own research, she pointed out the significance of the gender system for research into working life and for
the understanding of economic development. Blom later used the
concept "gender system", with emphasis on the dynamic within
gender relations, as a tool to integrate women's history analyses
into other historical research, especially in political history.[26]
    In recent years the research field has further developed in the
direction of the more recent concept of gender history. This concerns research which tries to investigate "the often silent and hidden operations of gender", to quote Joan W. Scott.[27] In this perspective women's historians have begun to focus on the "gen-
dered" within central areas of the past, such as nation-build-
ing/nationalism, defence policy, public life, and modernity.[28]

25 Fløystad 1990b.
26 Hagemann 1986a; Blom 1992a, 1992b, and 1994a.
27 Scott 1986 and 1988.
28 Hagemann 1994a, 1994b, and 1994c, Hagemann and Krokstad 1994.
    Many new research projects are gathered in the interdisciplinary NRC pro-
    gramme *Kjønnenes møte med det moderne:* Gro Hagemann, *Norskdomsrørsla –
    en maskulin motkultur?;* Kari Melby, *Kjønn og politikk: Frederike Marie Qvam og
    Ole Anton Qvam;* Hilde Sandvik, *Frihet og likhet i nordiske lovbøker i første halv-
    del av 1800-tallet;* Kari Teiste, *Seksualitet og ære i møtet med det moderne: End-
    ringer i forholdet mann–kvinne 1700–1900;* and Hanna Mellemsether,
    Martha Sanna – kvinne i to verdener. In May-Britt Ohman Nielsen's research
    on the Farmers' Party in the inter-war period, the gender perspective is one
    element; Nielsen 1994. See also Blom 1994b and 1994c.

When characteristics like feminine and masculine are separated from a straightforward linking to female and male individuals, the involvement of male politicians in the construction of the welfare state, for example, can be analyzed also as a kind of policy of caring. A state where political power has lain with men can therefore be seen in some contexts to have been characterized by a "feminine" policy. Such analyses reduce the polarization of gender and highlight the ambiguous in the traditional dichotomy between the sexes.[29] The inspiration for this tendency within women's history research lies for the most part in culture-analytical and post-structural theories, with an interdisciplinary aspect in the direction of linguistics, semantics, philosophy, and literature research.

Another tendency within women's history emphasizes the analysis of men and masculinity as gender. Like women's history in general, this tendency is especially influenced by the USA and Great Britain, and takes up historical studies of masculinity as ideology, as mentality, and as praxis. This research tendency may prove to be an interesting further development of women's history, but it is still very weakly represented in Norwegian historical circles.[30]

Legitimacy: Women's history in history research circles

The growth of the discipline of women's history and its further development into gender history has, of course, not occurred in a vacuum. Institutionally the emphasis has been on both an autonomous line, bringing together specialists within the field, and an integration line, where women's history research is aired in broader historical forums. While a professorship in women's history has been established and positions for research assistants and graduates have been created in this field, other historians have also worked to some degree on issues related to women's history. A few compilations and anthologies include contributions both from women's historians and other historians, and *Historisk tidsskrift*

29 Hagemann 1993; Blom 1994c.
30 Moland 1992; Storevik 1993; Blom 1994a:50–3.

has continually published articles and debates on women's history themes. Though a certain measure of institutional autonomy has been upheld, the earlier goal of integration has to some extent been achieved. Women's history has recently been designated both as a study area within the history discipline and as a perspective on the past which may be found in each of the various branches of history.[31]

One can roughly delineate three differing attitudes towards women's history within Norwegian historical circles. A small group of historians have explicitly defined themselves as women's historians and have through their research had main responsibility for the development of the field. As stated, inspiration came initially from both external and internal factors. Though it can generally be said that inspiration from outside the profession produced an especially strong activity in the early stages, there have not been clear divisions between the effects of the two approaches. It is perhaps been significant that both sources of inspiration have been seen as important from the start.

The second group consists of individual historians who have taken the initiative for a debate on women's history as a research field, and who have themselves occasionally taken up women's history topics, either explicitly or as part of larger presentations. The third and largest group has adopted a passive, waiting attitude towards women's history research.

The debate on women's history research has followed three main lines. Firstly, it has been suggested that gender relations are in the main based on biology – that women's particular reproductive functions and men's particular physical strength explain the division of labour and of power.[32] Such a perception of gender will naturally place limits on the explanatory power linked to these analytical categories. This viewpoint is seldom stated explicitly; this does not, of course, imply that it is without its supporters.

Another main line in criticism has been that women's historians have overestimated the importance of gender as an analytic category and have uncritically applied the problems and judgements of their own times to the past. This criticism was particu-

31 Aas 1993b.
32 Benedictow 1985a.

larly formulated by in the early 1980s by Kåre Lunden, who suggested that division between sexes had played a subordinate role in history. He therefore warned against historical analyses which prioritized gender ahead of class and built on theories of the oppression of women. The warning might seem natural, given the clear connection between the contemporary women's movement and professional women's history, but it may nevertheless be seen as based on limited knowledge of the transformations which had occurred among women's historians up to then. Hagemann rejected Lunden's viewpoint and referred especially to the need to further develop existing theories and methods with a view to integrating issues of women's history into other historical research.[33]

Inadequate knowledge of women's history research could to an extent also explain Ottar Dahl's later distancing from women's history as a discipline in its own right, a view he justified, for instance, in a portrayal of women's history as descriptive, as research "fast and loose about women", and as having a tendency to prioritize simple moral–political conclusions.[34] Dahl's criticism was, however, mainly based on theoretical reflections, and it represented the third and most important line in the debate. He suggested that women's history did not have sufficient theoretical context or delineation to be regarded as a separate discipline within the history profession. His main purpose was to plead that women's history should abandon its conceptual anchoring within the category "women" and instead systematically use the category "gender" as its variable. Here he apparently unwittingly touched upon the discussion which was then in progress among women's historians, both in Norway and elsewhere. But his viewpoint was noticeably different, in that he thought gender analyses would mainly be applicable in family history and demography.[35]

Dahl's proposal for a debate became an occasion to present the development of women's history "from compensating history to integrated social history", and to discuss qualifications to be met by historical subdisciplines. It provided the inspiration for a con-

33 Lunden 1980 and 1982; Hagemann 1982.
34 Dahl 1985.
35 Kelly-Godal 1975–6; Genovese 1982; Hewitt 1985; Hagemann 1982 and 1986b; Blom 1983 and 1986; Offen, Pierson, and Rendall 1991.

structive rethinking of the importance of gender for social historical analyses. This in turn became significant for the perception of
women's history research among historical circles.[36]

Without distancing themselves from the concept of women's
history, other historians have suggested that the family's combined
resource base, the working community, and the membership of
family and household have been more important for the
individual's social position than gender.[37] It may, of course, be
appropriate to warn against according gender a universal explanatory power. The main tendency within women's history research
has thus from the outset explicitly examined the significance of
gender in relation to other variables, such as class and marital
status, and in relation to culturally and socially determined variations between rural and urban areas.[38]

The question of extent to which historians can link explanatory
power to the category of gender, and of the areas in which this analytical category is appropriate, has been important for the way in
which the integration of results of women's history research has
proceeded. Large variations have emerged in the integration of the
fruits of women's history research in other historical work. Individual town histories, for example, have distinguished themselves with
a balanced and successful integration, while others have had a
deplorable lack of women's historical material.[39] In a six-volume
work on the history of the labour movement, the attention given to
the women's history aspect has also varied. A recently published
textbook in Norwegian history is marked by a haphazard and thin
treatment of this field. Voluminous syntheses on the national and
international levels have hitherto included women's history
research to a small extent – to such a small extent that one Norwegian publisher, after producing a twenty-two-volume world history,
decided to bring out a specific women's history – in three volumes.[40]

36 Hagemann 1986a; Österberg 1985; Blom 1985b.
37 Bjørgum 1985; Benedictow 1985b.
38 Blom and Hagemann 1977; Gotaas et al. 1980; Blom 1980b; Hagemann
    1992.
39 Balsvik 1989 has been especially mentioned for a good integration.
40 Blom 1992e and 1993.

There are many possible explanations for these variations. The historian's personal priorities about issues to address and choice of material are, of course, important. To neglect women's history research in a presentation rarely calls forth particularly heavy criticism from anyone other than women's historians. Reading lists, teaching, and exams at Norwegian universities do not provide significant stimulation of the study of women's history material.

It must, however, be underlined that the integration of women's and gender history perspectives is no simple matter. It presupposes knowledge of women's and gender history, a critical evaluation of central concepts in social analysis, and a will to examine systematically the importance of gender for continuity and change in the material and cultural structures of society. It also presupposes a will to weigh gender as an analytical category against other categories such as class, religion, age, and marital status, to name the most obvious. But a successful integration can raise our understanding of how a given society functioned, economically, politically, and culturally. A presentation which underlines joint activities and membership in the family and the household, and which proposes that social position was decisive for an individual's living conditions and career, is not necessarily incompatible with an analysis emphasizing an understanding of the individual's gender-specific tasks and position of authority in the family and in society. Sølvi Sogner and Hilde Sandvik have shown that a focus on differences between legally specified rights and day-to-day reality can be an excellent approach to social analysis.[41]

The strongest consensus on gender-specific research has been in the field of social history, particularly in family history and historical demography. In relation to political history, especially on the national level, there has been much disagreement about the explanatory potential of the introduction of gender as an analytical category. This can make the process of integration difficult, as demonstrated in the debate between Per Maurseth and Hagemann on gender blindness in research on the history of the labour movement.[42] Hagemann suggested that gender conflicts within one and

41 Sogner and Sandvik 1989a and 1989b; Bjørgum and Benedictow 1985.
42 Hagemann 1989; Maurseth 1989.

the same class had been underestimated or entirely neglected. Where women's history was included, there was often a tendency to see women as "the others" – as an exception or a problem. For example, historians often held that they were difficult to organize, or that they were competitors in the labour market. Even if such perceptions partly reflected the historical reality, they also occasionally rested on the historian's personal stance, and therefore needed to be put in question and compared with alternative interpretations. Maurseth, however, felt that gender had little explanatory power in an analysis of the growth of the labour movement or in its transformation from opposition to government party. It is noteworthy that he simultaneously raised the question whether the absence of women from the leadership of the labour movement in the inter-war period may have helped make revolutionary ideology stronger. Maurseth thus points implicitly to the other side of the gender variable, the understanding of masculinity, and falls back on a perception of male politicians as more disposed to aggressive radicalism than women.

In medieval history Sverre Bagge has explicitly linked gender and politics. He interprets clan systems and inheritance rules as channels to political power, and points to the connection between the growth of the centralized, bureaucratic royal authority and a trend to a more masculine political power. Blom has stressed that the transfer of political power to public democratic institutions in the nineteenth century may have entailed in the first phase a weakening of women's potential for power, but that the study of private organizations and other informal networks gives a more nuanced picture.[43] Gender in this analytical framework becomes a relevant category when it comes to estimating the importance of structural political changes.

In ancient history there have been analyses which draw the contours of a society divided in two, where either sex had its areas of influence. Christian Meyer accords great importance to biology in gender relations, but sees biological and physiological phenomena as changeable and, precisely because of this, as important in explaining gender relations. Qviller places biology within changes

43 Bagge 1989 and 1992; Blom 1994c.

of a structural kind, where demographic, economic, and political changes are accorded decisive importance for women's history and for the relation between the sexes.[44]

When it comes to understanding the significance of gender for political history, an important potential lies in seeking not just explicit but also implicit and hidden meanings of gender. Only in very recent times have Norwegian historians attempted to apply this perspective to national conflicts such as the dissolution of the union in 1905, to presentations of the rise of nationalism at the end of the nineteenth century, and to the political ideology of the Farmers' Party in the inter-war years.[45]

If women's historians declined to regard gender as a biologically determined category and strongly emphasized the historical and social aspects in the perception of gender, this must be seen against the background of the absence of a history of women entailed by a biologically determined perception of gender. Women's history has nonetheless taken up research in which biologically determined gender and socially constructed gender intersect. Studies of problems closely linked to women's reproductive functions have considered the implications these biologically determined functions had for the position of women, in private and in public, as well as the manner in which the interaction between the biological and the social changed over time. Knowledge of continuity and slow change in this field of history has led to reflections on the burden of conscious and unconscious cultural baggage with roots in physiological differences. Women's historians have thus been open to a way of thinking within historical circles which has great potential.

Gender identity and other identities

There is a certain tension among historians in this area. Some mainly stress class and family as analytical categories, and regard large parts of political and economic history as gender-neutral. Others mainly stress gender as a historical construction, and see gender as a decisive factor both within and across class and family.

44 Meyer 1992; Qviller 1981 and 1985.
45 See, for instance, Hagemann, Melby, Nielsen, and Blom as in note 28; also Blom 1993c.

The latter search for both explicit and implicit effects of gender in apparently gender-neutral historical phenomena.

Can we speak of being right or wrong in the choice of theory, or are there ways to combine these two starting-points?

Firstly, it must be emphasized that ongoing dialogue between historians of differing views is an enrichment of the profession. It presupposes, as Hagemann has stressed, respect for disagreement and a common discussion.[46]

Secondly, I believe that an understanding of identity, including gender identity, as contextual is a good starting-point for the study of human relations, both in the present and in the past. Even if gender identity in certain contexts may have gone across class identity, for instance, membership of a class can have been primary in other connections. In the same way membership of a nation can at times have been more important in modern history than either class or gender, while both class and gender identity in other contexts can have cut across national identity. When identity is perceived as a contextual phenomenon, the historian can work from an assumption that different identities have coexisted, though with varying relevance, in a specific individual or group.[47] Identitites derived from gender, class, or nationality do not necessarily have an inherent and immutable hierarchy of priority. The historian's task is, rather, to uncover whether (and, if so, how) gender identity can influence class identity or national identity and vice versa. The historian's task is also to study when a single identity becomes primary, and to account for shifts between identities. Transitions may be studied as a response to challenges, or as reactions to feelings of marginalization or injustice, and may be expressed in the demand for justice, whether this concerns class identity, national identity, or gender identity. In other words it is precisely the individual's or group's *search for* identity, and the struggle to *define* this identity, which in each case catches the historian's attention. When identity is not regarded as essence, it is simpler to understand alliances and conflicts which cut across differing identities, as, for example, between women and men of the

46 Hagemann 1993.
47 There is an extensive literature on these questions. I have found inspiration especially in Pulkkinnen 1991 and Pascoe 1991. See also Blom 1991a.

same class, or within one gender across different classes. For the historian the challenge is to explain the conditions under which gender identity, class identity, or national identity becomes the most important, when they all move in the same direction, and when conflicts arise between them.

A similar point of view can apply when the question concerns gender as biology or as historical construction. In some situations the purely biological will have particularly strong significance; in others it is precisely the historical variations on a biological theme which are crucial. The historian's task will again be to examine when biology and social context are in harmony, when conflicts occur, and how the very perception of the biological has varied through history.

Such a perspective in historical research would form a good starting-point for dialogue among historians.

An international perspective

If one ultimately allows national identity to be primary, one may ask how Norwegian women's history research stands in relation to women's history of other countries.

International contacts have from the beginning been very important sources of inspiration, and the work to develop the International Federation for Research in Women's History has strengthened international links.[48] The closest contacts have naturally been with other Nordic women's history circles. Women's history issues have been considered at meetings of Nordic historians at intervals since 1978. Regular meetings of Nordic women's historians have taken place since 1983, and the many joint Nordic research projects have resulted in a series of monographs and articles.[49] In medieval

48 Offen, Pierson, and Rendall 1991.
49 The initiative for the first Nordic women's history project, "Women's work in society and family in the nineteenth and twentieth centuries", came from the Nordic historians meeting in 1978. The project rested mainly on Norwegian historians. It resulted in two Danish and three Norwegian monographs. In later joint projects, Norwegian women's historians have participated with researchers from other European countries and from the USA. Sogner and Sandvik 1989; Bock and Thane 1991; Andreassen 1991; Sogner 1993; Wikander 1994.

research Nordic seminars have had a clear interdisciplinary profile which includes archaeology.[50]

Compared with that in Denmark and Sweden, theoretical debate among Norwegian women's historians has been pallid. Resistance in Norwegian historical circles to the adoption of sociological models seems to have inhibited theoretical reflections which also embrace women's historians. In Denmark discussion initially centred particularly on the relation between Marxism and feminism. In recent years culture-analytical theories have been central, both as a supplement and as an alternative to post-structuralism.[51] There has been a lively Swedish debate on different forms of patriarchy theories. In recent years this has come to focus on the pros and cons of the theory of the "genus system". A central dual concept, equality versus difference, which later assumed an important position in international women's history through American historians, was aired in Sweden as early as 1982. There the understanding of the concept of women's history has been discussed in detail.[52] Many of the same themes are also found in Finland, even though it was a relative latecomer in terms of women's history.[53]

It would not, however, be correct to draw altogether clear divisions between the debates on women's history in the Nordic countries. They take place to a great extent across national boundaries. The Swedish theory of a "genus system" has been criticized in Norway for a lack of flexibility, but it has also been seen as an important counterweight to the tendency to relativize and individualize asymmetrical gender relations. The Danish historian Bente Rosenbeck, who has operationalized culture-analytical theories, has met with support in Norwegian circles.[54] In a relatively homogeneous language area, inspiration has crossed borders, and at international conferences Nordic women's historians have presented joint projects.

As far as research methodology is concerned, Norwegian

50 Øye 1990.
51 Rosenbeck 1983, 1990, and 1992; Damsholt 1991; Liljeström 1994.
52 Hirdmann 1988 and 1991; Hagemann 1994a.
53 Korppi-Tommola 1990; Liljeström 1994.
54 Blom 1993a and 1994e; Hagemann 1994d; Rosenbeck 1992. See also Tønnesson 1994a.

women's historians are in some fields closer to the British than the American tradition.[55] It should be particularly mentioned that interest for the class perspective seems to be more explicit in Norwegian and British than in American women's history research. In America, by contrast, the question of women and ethnicity and/or race has been strong, especially in recent years. This theme is barely touched on by Norwegian women's historians.[56] But it must be assumed that there are interesting possibilities in an explicitly comparative coupling of gender-historical analyses within Sami and Norwegian history.

American colleagues have nevertheless had a very influential role in relation to Norwegian women's history. There have been very close contacts, with exchanges of visiting lecturers and researchers, and participation in the same international conferences. In particular the theory of a gender system and the interest in post-structuralist theories and methods have come from the USA. To some extent the same is true for the debate on equality and difference strategies in women's organizational and political ability, and on definitions of the concept of feminism.[57]

But the idea of a separate women's culture, or of women as a homogeneous group, has not been as strong in Norwegian circles as in the USA. To the extent to which there has been talk of a separate women's culture, it has been analyzed in the light of variables such as class, regional and cultural variations, marital status, generational differences, and so on. With this approach to women's history research, post-structuralism's relativization of gender may perhaps appear less foreign in Norwegian than in North American circles, although a certain scepticism can also be noted among Norwegian women's historians when it comes to overemphasizing analyses of language and systems of symbols.[58]

55 Rendall 1991; Blom 1990a and 1994a.
56 Blom 1991 and 1994e.
57 Melby 1991.
58 Report of the NRC conference Konstituering av kjønn fra antikken til moderne tid, Oslo, May 1994. The discussion also arose at the 22nd Norwegian historians meeting in Oslo in August 1994. The debate about priority between the concepts of women's history and gender history is centred on this theme, among others.

The "social historical" perspective in Norwegian women's history and the express wish for integration in a common historical research milieu can be seen against the background of the strong egalitarian tradition in a small and relatively homogeneous society. An influential institution like the NHRC/NRC provided in the initial stage practical and economic support for women's history, as for other research in women's affairs. The strong position achieved by women in recent decades in central political institutions may also have been important for a theoretic development involving greater appreciation of the contextual, as opposed to the essential, in gender identity. Conditions thus seem favourable for continued professional dialogue and, in time, for a successful implementation of the project of integration.

12. Historical Demography
William H. Hubbard[1]

Norway is blessed, in theory, with remarkably rich source materials for the study of population behaviour in past time. The state church began to keep official registers of baptisms (births), burials (deaths), and marriages in the late seventeenth century, and such lists exist for most parishes from the first quarter of the eighteenth century. From 1736 there are also registers of church confirmations, and from 1812 priests were to record the names of individuals moving into or out of parishes. Aggregate vital statistics, organized by diocese on the basis of the parish registers, have been compiled annually since 1735, one of the longest such time-series available in Europe. Statewide counts of adult males were taken in 1664–6 and 1701, and a first census of the entire population was held in 1769. The second statewide census, taken in 1801, was an individual-level, nominative enumeration of the entire resident population; it is considered quite reliable and one of the best early censuses in all of Europe. The next nominative censuses conducted over the entire country came in 1865 and 1875, and then decennially beginning in 1890.[2] Several other individual-level nominative sources also exist over long periods: probate records, conscription rolls, tax registers, and the like.

Nonetheless, the long-standing primacy of the political in Norwegian historiography resulted in the neglect of these sources except for the purposes of genealogical research. Until the 1960s the study of population was the domain of non-historians, primar-

---

1 I wish to thank especially Ståle Dyrvik and Sølvi Sogner for assistance and encouragement in preparing this chapter and for good-natured generosity in tolerating a new Norwegian's adjudication of their field.
2 Backer 1947; Ofstad 1949; for a preliminary list of available parish registers, see Sogner 1965.

ily political economists and social statisticians, and population issues were rarely mentioned in general history books. Three nineteenth-century researchers have had a lasting influence in the field. Torkel H. Aschehoug, jurist and economist, developed methods to compute the country's total population in the seventeenth century from the male counts. Social scientist Eilert Sundt and statistician Anders N. Kiær conducted wide-ranging investigations of then-contemporary demographic behaviour. Sundt's study of mid-nineteenth-century marital behaviour and Kiær's investigations of late-nineteenth-century fertility patterns are still of great value to the modern researcher.[3] In the 1930s the publication of Alva and Gunnar Myrdal's book on the population crisis and its remedies provoked a lively debate on abortion, family support policy, and related issues of social reform. Yet the inter-war debate on population policy in Norway, unlike in Sweden, had no spin-off for historical demographic studies: Norway produced no equivalent of Dorothy Swaine Thomas's pioneering study of the social and economic consequences of population growth.[4]

Beginnings of historical demographic research

International intellectual and institutional developments played a decisive role in awakening the field in Norway, as in many other countries. Demographers, especially in France, began to be interested in the past, and historians, especially those investigating economic growth, began to be interested in population. These interests converged in 1960 at two international academic meetings in Stockholm. At the World Congress of the International Committee of the Historical Sciences, the French demographer Louis Henry demonstrated his methodology of reconstituting families from seventeenth- and eighteenth-century parish registers, which thereby enabled researchers to obtain data on demographic behaviour before the existence of official statistics. At the First International Conference of Economic History, the English economic historian D. E. C. Eversley explained the use of parish registers to investigate

3 Dyrvik 1972.
4 Thomas 1941.

the role of population in English economic growth in the eighteenth century.

Henry's lecture in Stockholm directly inspired Sølvi Sogner, a specialist in the Early Modern Period affiliated with the Norwegian Institute of Local History, to embark upon research in historical demography. A scholarship enabled her to study with Eversley and David Glass in Britain, where she first worked on English parish registers. For some time few other Norwegians took up the subject. At the first International Congress on Historical Demography, held in Liège in 1963, Sogner had to report that little work in historical demography was yet being undertaken in Norway and that no attempt had thus far been made to use parish registers systematically for historical demographic analysis.[5]

Several developments came together in the late 1960s to revise this negative assessment.[6] In 1964 Scandinavian demographers met in Oslo and agreed to establish a Scandinavian Demographic Society, which then became an engine for demographic research, both historical and contemporary. The first Scandinavian Demographic Symposium, organized by the Society, was held in August 1968 and has been followed by others at two- to three-year intervals. In 1969 the Society established a newsletter to communicate ongoing research. The Society also promoted the training of demographers and organized several summer courses to that end. The dominant orientation of the symposia has been towards contemporary demographic issues, but historical demography has been represented regularly. Also during this decade the Norwegian Central Statistical Bureau produced two fundamental studies of long-term population movements, even though it did not establish a separate research division on demography until 1970.[7] Moreover, the gradual shift from high politics to social history awakened attention, especially among Knut Mykland and other specialists in the Danish period (1536–1814) at the University of Bergen, to the study of population as a means to the analysis of social structures.

The take-off of historical demographic research in Norway was

5 Sogner 1965.
6 Moen and Dyrvik 1994.
7 Backer 1961; Backer 1965.

signalled by the appearance in 1969 of Michael Drake's study of population trends between 1735 and 1865.[8] Using the published and unpublished diocesan lists of vital movements in addition to drawing extensively on Sundt's nineteenth-century social studies, Drake identified several features of Norwegian demographic development that became subjects of subsequent research: the pre-industrial demographic regime dominated by periodic demographic crises and regional variations, the break in that regime around 1815 leading to a steady fall in mortality and one of the most rapid rises in population in Europe in the first half of the nineteenth century, and then a second break in the 1860s. According to Drake, Norway's population growth then outran the country's resources, provoking a mass emigration that, relative to the country's size, was second only to Ireland's.

Drake's work was initially given a rough reception by some Norwegian historians, but it brought out the importance of the subject-matter, showed the strengths and weaknesses of the traditional aggregate statistical sources, and provoked other historians to scrutinize them carefully.[9] Henceforth, as Lajos Juhasz remarked in his review of Drake's work, progress in the historical demographic knowledge of Norway would have to come through intensive studies of individual parishes. Juhasz, the director of the Oslo State Archives, had begun to promote this point of view in the mid-1960s in reviews of basic methodological works in historical demography by Henry, Dupâquier, and Wrigley, and began a family reconstitution of the parish of Gjerdrum (Akershus county).[10] Yet despite Juhasz's intervention, the initial centre of activity was in Bergen, where Mykland encouraged students to write degree theses on population growth during the seventeenth and eighteenth centuries.[11] Most of these early parish studies restricted themselves to a positiv-

8 Drake 1969; the original version of the work, completed in 1963, was a doctoral dissertation in economic history at Cambridge University.
9 Herstad 1975; Dyrvik, Mykland, and Oldervoll 1975.
10 Juhasz never finished the project; the raw material is deposited in the National Archive in Oslo.
11 The time-span covered typically began with the man-count of 1665 and ended with the census of 1801. In the mid-1970s Mykland was general editor of a multi-volume history of Norway published by Cappelen in which population was treated seriously for the first time in a general survey.

istic presentation of the data contained in parish registers and censuses, but one of them – the investigation of the fjord parish of Etne
(Hordaland county) submitted by Ståle Dyrvik in 1971 – contained
the first complete application of Henry's methodology of family
reconstitution in Norway.[12] By this time Sogner had also begun a
family reconstitution study of Rendalen parish (Hedmark county)
in eastern Norway as the core of a doctoral dissertation on population growth in Akershus diocese in the late eighteenth century.[13]
Both Dyrvik and Sogner thereafter took up teaching positions at,
respectively, the universities of Bergen and Oslo, where they have
been the country's chief practitioners of historical demography
and the primary sponsors of degree theses in the field, with emphasis on the use of family reconstitution methodology.

The awakening of enthusiasm in the early 1970s for social historical modes of research, especially micro-historical and quantitative approaches, also promoted student interest in historical
demography. Between 1970 and 1990 over 100 theses (out of a
total of 1,500) dealt with topics related to population. Population
movements in fifty parishes have been investigated for either the
eighteenth or nineteenth century; approximately one-half of these
studies used family reconstitution as the core of analysis.[14]

Demographic crises and the decline in mortality

According to the aggregate statistics, the steady decline in mortality that began in late-eighteenth-century Norway became a dramatic drop in 1815. The most compelling reason at first glance

---

12 Dyrvik was trained in historical demography while a scholarship student in
Paris; in Mykland's Cappelen history he wrote the volume covering the
years 1720 to 1784, using the pre-industrial demographic regime as the
central organizing concept; see his informative manual, Dyrvik 1983.

13 Sogner 1979; the dissertation was finished in 1974 and remains the only
doctorate in historical demography completed in Norway.

14 The majority of the parishes covered are located in south-western Norway;
the next largest cluster is in south-eastern Norway. Bibliographic information on Master's theses can be obtained from the Norwegian on-line cata-
logue BIBSYS on Internet.

was the disappearance of mortality crises, but then what lay behind that? Determining the cause and nature of these crises would also explain the overall phenomenon.

Juhasz was first out with a strong endorsement of the classic Malthusian-economic interpretation of Meuvret and Goubert: Norway's demographic crises were subsistence crises reflecting the inherent tendency of pre-transition or traditional populations to exceed food supply.[15] Several researchers, including Drake, supported Juhasz's position,[16] but studies by Dyrvik, Sogner, and their students showed that the crises were considerably more complex. On the one hand, the incidence of crises differed regionally: Bergen diocese experienced its last demographic crisis in 1741; the dioceses of Kristiansand and Trondheim in 1772–3; and the eastern diocese of Akershus in 1809; moreover, coastal communities were often harder hit than inland communities.[17] On the other hand, close examinations of the timing of births, deaths, and marriages – and of the socio-economic status of victims – indicated that hunger was not necessarily always the chief cause of death: disease also played a major role, sometimes the chief role.[18] The reorientation towards an epidemiological interpretation also brought out the growing role of public health policies in containing the spread of contagious diseases and thus in preventing mortality crises.[19]

The contest between nutritional and medical models has continued with regard to mortality in the early nineteenth century. Here, too, parish-level studies have shown that the nutritional benefits of the introduction of potatoes and the medical benefits of mandatory vaccination against smallpox (from 1810) were weaker than generally thought.[20] The causes of the substantial reduction in infant mortality, a major component of the overall decline in mortality, have been little studied.[21] One of the few such

15 Juhasz 1970.
16 Haarstad 1980.
17 Dyrvik, Mykland, and Oldervoll 1976; Sogner 1979.
18 Aaraas 1978; Løvlien 1977; Knudtsen 1986; Karlsen 1982; Engelsen 1983.
19 Sogner 1976.
20 Dyrvik 1988; Solberg 1993.
21 Dyrvik 1974.

studies, an investigation of the town of Moss (Østfold) between 1776 and 1825, found that infant mortality declined first among middle-class families and attributed the reduction to better infant care (breast-feeding) and basic hygiene.[22]

In short, one still does not know quite why Norwegian mortality fell so far so early. For the moment all that can be said with real confidence is that the decline in mortality was an exceedingly complex phenomenon. Dyrvik has proposed that the ultimate cause is a changed epidemiological climate – a new mortality regime – with some diseases losing virulence and human beings becoming more resistant.[23] That this suggestion accords with recent international scholarship on mortality in other countries does not make it easier to prove with tangible evidence.[24]

Fertility and birth-control

Fertility has attracted more attention in Norwegian historical demographical research than mortality. This is perhaps partly due to the inherent predisposition of family reconstitution methodology towards the analysis of fertility; Henry developed it to study the early decline of the birth-rate in France. In addition births are more obviously and persistently related to social structures and social behaviour than are deaths.

The parish studies covering the eighteenth and the early nineteenth century show the now-familiar West European marriage–fertility pattern: relatively late age at marriage for both men and women, high proportion of adults never marrying, and women continuing to bear children into their forties. Fertility was thus high, but it was not uncontrolled. Age at marriage, especially of the woman, was the central mechanism by which a couple's potential fertility was adapted to its economic resources, primarily land. A typical consequence was that farm owners married younger and had more children than cottars, whose average age at

22 Lahn 1986. At the University of Trondheim, Margunn Skjei Knudtsen is currently writing a doctoral dissertation on infant mortality in the Trøndelag region in the eighteenth and nineteenth centuries.
23 Dyrvik 1979.
24 Schofield, Reher, and Bideau 1991; Chesnais 1986.

marriage was several years older and whose families were smaller. So far no synthesis of the individual micro-studies has been undertaken, but it is nonetheless clear that the regional differentiation identified for mortality also applied to fertility.[25]

In contrast to the country's early transition to low mortality, Norway's fertility did not fall substantially until the end of the nineteenth century, but then it dropped by half in one generation. Legal restrictions on access to parish registers and census manuscripts from 1907 have hampered research on this quiet revolution, but two major investigations are noteworthy, in part because they show the relative strengths and weaknesses of the macro- and the micro-approach. Sogner and her former students Hege Brit Randsborg and Eli Fure modelled their study of the decline of fertility from 1890 to 1930 on the Princeton Fertility Study, focusing on multiple regression analysis of demographic and socio-economic data aggregated for the country's 549 towns and townships.[26] The authors considered both materialist and non-materialist variables (see Chapter 14); the variables most strongly correlated with fertility levels were two that expressed the degree of industrialization in the labour force, suggesting that "modernization" was the major promoter of birth-control. Following this, Dyrvik and Marit Karin Alsvik undertook a micro-study of fertility in the western Norwegian city of Stavanger between 1900 and 1935.[27] Although Stavanger was one of Norway's most industrialized cities in terms of occupational structure, fertility declined later there than in Oslo or Bergen. The Dyrvik–Alsvik study used a random sample of 609 families extracted from the manuscript censuses of 1920 and 1930, the census data being supplemented by data on migration and income from population registers and tax records. It thus could focus on individual-level reproductive behaviour and go beyond ecological correlations. The study's central conclusion, however, that "birth-control is ... an essentially *cultural* [sic] phenomenon"[28] associated with a couple's urban background, is

25 Halvorsen and Indseth 1975; Randsborg 1979; Øygarden 1979; Fure 1980; Veland 1981; Gjønnes 1982; Kristoffersen 1983.
26 Sogner, Randsborg, and Fure 1984; Sogner *et al.* 1986.
27 Dyrvik and Alsvik 1987; Dyrvik 1988.
28 Dyrvik 1988, 139; see also Blom 1980.

HISTORICAL DEMOGRAPHY 319

not really a much more precise "cause" than that proffered by Sogner–Randsborg–Fure. Nonetheless, a micro-study reveals the mechanisms and paths of such cultural diffusion much more clearly than an aggregate analysis, and the Stavanger study points out the need for closer examination of fertility decline in cities as well as in rural townships.[29]

Nuptiality, family formation, and household structures

The sharp focus on mortality and fertility in Norwegian historical demography hereto has resulted in the relative neglect of the third major component of vital movements: nuptiality. However, the topic has not been completely ignored. All of the family-reconstitution studies have dutifully computed spousal ages at marriage and showed how completed fertility – and hence regulation of the number of births – depended on the woman's age, a point that Drake (and Sundt) had emphasized earlier.[30] Early on Dyrvik and Sogner each pointed out the central importance of the marriage mechanism and household formation in the emergence of the cottar system and in maintaining agrarian social structures.[31] According to Dyrvik, the relatively high age at marriage, and hence lower fertility, among cottars worked against the proletarianization of rural society. Marriage and age at marriage as mechanisms of birth regulation and social differentiation were not limited to the countryside. Jørgen Eliassen's thesis on Moss in the late eighteenth century shows that they applied to urban society just as strongly: working-class women married markedly later than middle-class women.[32] Aside from these isolated studies, there has been little work directly on marriage as a social institution.[33]

29 The Dyrvik–Alsvik study focuses on individual behaviour as advocated recently in Tilly, Gillis, and Levine 1992.
30 Drake 1969.
31 Dyrvik 1970; Sogner 1976; Dyrvik 1987.
32 Eliassen 1979.
33 But see Kneppen 1976; Haavet 1981; Sogner and Oldervoll 1981; Dyrvik 1981; Olsen 1994.

The same applies to the study of family and household structures. Clearly, Henry's methodology and concerns have dominated over those of Peter Laslett's Cambridge Group. Despite the easy availability of manuscript censuses, with their rich information on household composition and social structure, few researchers have taken up the subject as a central concern.[34] More often, it has been a side issue in projects focusing on the position of women or children and social welfare.[35]

This assessment may change soon. Although Eli Fure's innovative analysis of family formation and life-cycle in the communities of Asker and Bærum (just west of Oslo) in the first half of the nineteenth century still awaits completion,[36] there is new work under way, especially at the University of Bergen, where a group of faculty and students involved in historical computing have begun comparative analyses of household and family structures. Dyrvik has also rekindled an interest in the topic with a study of the remarkable fisher–farmer household economy of Northern Norway.[37] For the moment, though, the informed impressionism of Sogner's short survey of the history of the family in Norway reflects the research situation.[38]

Internal migration and emigration

Migration complicates the task of family reconstitution by removing couples from parish registers before the maximum period of child-bearing has been obtained. Demographic historians following Henry's mode of enquiry thus typically regard it as an interfering factor to be endured rather than explored, and leave its investigation to others.[39]

The great Norwegian emigration in the nineteenth century captured historians' attention relatively early. It was, and still is, a dramatic phenomenon that aroused social consciences and political

34 Higley 1976; Bakkemoen 1984; Aase 1987.
35 Sogner 1980; Wishman 1983; Avdem 1984; Dyrvik 1984.
36 Fure 1983; Fure 1986.
37 Dyrvik 1993.
38 Sogner 1990.
39 Sogner's doctoral dissertation is a major exception; Sogner 1979.

controversy. Between 1865 and 1920 Norway's resident population rose from 1.7 million to 2.6 million. This increase occurred despite the loss through emigration of almost 700,000 inhabitants. During the peak years of emigration, more than one-half of the country's natural population surplus (births minus deaths) was lost. In some years more than 1 percent of the total Norwegian population left: the record was 1.5 percent in 1882. Ingrid Semmingsen's pioneering work in the 1940s established the major findings and interpretations.[40] She related emigration to population pressure and the progressive dissolution of traditional agrarian society in interior and coastal Norway. For several decades families constituted the majority of emigrants, but from the 1890s individuals, especially younger, single men, predominated. North America came to function partially as an extension of the Norwegian labour market, as a substantial percentage of the later emigrants returned to Norway after a few years. Subsequently, local studies as well as econometric and quantitative ecological analyses have largely corroborated the general picture while revealing its complexities.[41]

A number of important issues remain unresolved. The plausibility of a close interconnection between internal migration and emigration is widely accepted, but Semmingsen's suggestion that much emigration occurred as a last stage of migration to ever-larger urban areas was met with scepticism.[42] There are few studies of emigration from urban areas, and the usual sources – censuses and shipping registers – seldom enable the establishment of a migrational chain.[43] Moreover, internal migration and urbanization in general have been little investigated in spite of the fact that most city monographs now contain some demographic information.[44] De-

40 Semmingsen 1941–50; see English-language summary in Semmingsen 1960.
41 Gjerde 1985; Engen 1978; Moe 1971; Svalestuen 1977; Svalestuen 1983; Lowell 1987; Norman and Runblom 1988.
42 Semmingsen 1971.
43 Rinnan 1979; Engelsen 1987.
44 Langholm 1975; Myhre 1977; Gjerdåker 1981; Myhre, 1991. Gunnar Thorvaldsen is currently researching geographic mobility in the county of Troms between 1865 and 1900 using the machine-readable databases generated by the Norwegian Historical Data Centre, of which he is scientific director (see below).

tailed analyses of the socio-demographic recruitment of urban communities are still very few; the most notable ones deal with the Oslo region or Northern Norway.[45] This neglect is especially regrettable given the considerable number of isolate communities that shot up around economic enterprises, especially hydroelectric power stations and mines, towards the turn of the nineteenth century.[46] The seasonal migrations in fisheries and agriculture are another important area needing more research. And the linkages between migrational behaviour and reproductive behaviour – skewing of age structures, marriage markets, diffusion of cultural attitudes, and so on – are still largely unexplored.[47]

Historical demography and historical computing

Because of the enormous amounts of data involved, research in historical demography has increasingly turned to the computer for help and salvation. Norwegian scholars have been actively engaged in historical computing from early on. In the 1960s Stein Rokkan, a social scientist at the University of Bergen, organized a machine-readable database of historical socio-economic data on Norwegian townships, which led to the foundation of the Norwegian Social Science Data Services (NSD) in Bergen in 1971; the following year the Norwegian Centre for Computing in the Humanities was also established there. The first major foray of historians into computing was the registration of the entire 1801 manuscript census undertaken in the early 1970s under the technical

---

45 Myhre 1978; Myhre 1981; Myhre 1990; Drivenes 1985b; Thorvaldsen 1984. Hubbard has begun a study of migration in the town of Haugesund (Rogaland) from 1865 to 1920; the town was founded in 1855.

46 See Gåskjenn and Haugen 1990 on Tyssedal, whose generators supply the power to the smelting works in Odda in Hardanger's south fjord.

47 For an interpretation of migratory behaviour as a part of demographic "culture", see Dyrvik and Alsvik 1987. In separate, unpublished studies, Dyrvik and Tore Thonstad, an economist at the University of Oslo, have estimated that without loss from emigration, Norway's population today would be over 6 million instead of just over 4 million. I am grateful to Ståle Dyrvik for this information.

supervision of Jan Oldervoll at the University of Bergen.[48] The Ullensaker and Christiania social history projects carried out at the University of Oslo during these years also promoted the use of manuscript censuses, parish registers, and quantitative historical analysis (see Chapter 8).

An important spin-off of these activities in both historical demography and social history was the establishment of the Norwegian Historical Data Centre (NHDC) at the University of Tromsø in 1981. Based on the model of Swedish Demographic Data Archives at the University of Umeå, the NHDC has a mandate to prepare machine-readable editions of manuscript censuses and parish registers for use by university researchers and private genealogists.[49] It has focused hitherto on the censuses of 1865, 1875, and 1900, but the National Archive has lately approved controlled access to the censuses of 1910 and 1920. Moreover, the national telephone company, Telenor, has now joined the NHDC in registering the entire 1900 census, using Oldervoll's CensSys program, which is especially designed for the registration and analysis of structured census data.[50] To co-ordinate these projects and the computing activities of the country's extensive community of genealogists, the NHDC has set up a national advisory committee to formulate a set of universal standards for registration.

Conclusion

Space limitations have compelled this survey to be brutally concise.[51] Although the comment that research is lacking appears here frequently, the achievements of demographic historians in Norway have been nonetheless remarkable, given the modest resources available. Much of the archival research has been conducted by students seeking the *cand. philol.* degree, and such Master's theses are often very descriptive with little synthetic, comparative, or theoretical perspective. There is little provision in the Nor-

48 *Population Census 1801 Reprocessed* 1980.
49 See the repertory of machine-readable files in *Historiske persondata i Norge* 1992.
50 Oldervoll 1992.
51 See earlier reviews of the literature in Dyrvik 1972 and Sogner 1986.

wegian university system for long-term, co-ordinated research projects such as those found in neighbouring Sweden. Full-time historians in the area are few, and they have other research interests and obligations as well. As regards the future of the field, advances in historical computing and increased availability of electronic editions of parish registers and censuses should give a fillip to the field by reducing the mechanical tedium of source preparation. A degree course on population and social change in Northern Norway has recently commenced at the University of Tromsø, and the University of Oslo will soon offer full training in demography.

One is still a considerable distance away from being able to write a Norwegian equivalent of the recent, magisterial *Histoire démographique de la France*, but then that comment applies to almost all other European countries.

13. History of Minorities: The Sami and the Kvens

Einar Niemi

Until recent years the history of the minorities has been rather neglected, despite the fact that ethnic minority groups – Gypsies,[1] Jews,[2] Sami, and Kvens – have existed in Norway for centuries. Until the last few decades literature about the minorities was rarely written by historians. Rather, scholars from other disciplines took an interest. This disciplinary trend probably reflects strong scholarly traditions in which historical research for a long time was intimately and strictly related to written source material in public archives. Moreover, cultures and societies regarded as "primitive", exotic, or "foreign" were traditionally not among historians' priorities.

To an extent Norwegian nationalism also helps explain why the minorities did not attract the historians' attention earlier. Modern Norwegian historical research broke through in parallel to the rise of Norwegian nationalism, which was based on the ideas of the nation–state and a homogenous national culture. History and historians were mobilized to nurture these ideas.[3] Thus, historiography at least partly reflects societal and minority political attitudes.[4]

This chapter will focus on the historiography of the two northern minority groups, the *Sami* and the *Kvens*. Until recently the Sami were usually called Lapps, both in Norway and throughout the world, and in Norway sometimes even called Finns, which confused outsiders. Because of ethnopolitical mobilization, ethnic self-awareness, and a changed state minority policy, the minority's own traditional ethnonym has been adopted by the society at

1 Schlüter 1990; *Stortings melding nr 37, 1972–73.*
2 Mendelsohn 1969–86.
3 Sørensen 1994:25–33.
4 Salvesen 1980.

large.[5] "Kven" was originally the Scandinavian name for the Finnish people living in the area around the Gulf of Bothnia, known as early as the Middle Ages. Later the ethnonym was applied to the Finnish farmers who colonized the interior parts of Lapland. From the fifteenth century onwards, they moved from the coastal regions of the Gulf of Bothnia and eventually reached the fiords and coastal areas of Northern Norway. In the nineteenth and twentieth centuries, "Kven" has been used for the contemporary Finnish immigrants in Northern Norway and their descendants.[6] In contrast to the Norwegian Gypsies and Jews, there is quite an extensive literature about these two ethnic groups, and in particular about the Sami; but historical studies as such are few. This is one reason to focus on them. Another reason is that these two minorities have for centuries been objects of state policies, more than other minority groups in Norway.

The hypothesis that the literature mirrors these policies and public attitudes is worth testing. It is also of interest to compare the development of research on the Sami and the Kvens respectively, particularly from the perspectives of policies and attitudes. State minority policy can be divided into distinct chronological periods. Our historiographical outline is organized accordingly.

1700–1850: State-building, "natural" integration, and exotism

Until the early 1700s one could hardly say that Norway (before 1814 the kingdom of Denmark–Norway) had a minority policy in its own right. In the north large parts of the interior areas were a *terra nullius* from the point of view of the states. It was not until 1751 and 1826 respectively that the state borders between Norway and Sweden and Norway and Russia were formally agreed. These territories, inhabited mainly by Sami and partly by Kvens, had for centuries been the focus of rivalries between the states involved. In the early eighteenth century, the Danish–Norwegian

5 Skotvedt 1993:163.
6 Niemi 1992:131–2.

state intensified missionary activities among the Sami, supervised by a special governmental body. The new mission sprang from the pietistic movement of the time. However, it could also be regarded as a governmental state-building measure in the high north, as a part of the "whole state" ideology. With this new missionary impetus, a policy regarding the Sami was introduced.

Even if views on the eventual aims of the policy have differed, its ways and means were mild for most of the period. One barometer is language policy. The missionary and teaching language through most of the period was Sami, even if the language policy was debated. Missionaries were obliged to learn Sami; a special college was established for this purpose in Trondheim, the seat of the northernmost bishopric. Several of the missionaries sent to Sami districts had scholarly interests in addition to their religious engagement. One result was a series of studies on Sami culture, society, language, and traditional religion. An example is the voluminous monograph written by the missionary Knud Leem, who worked in the county of Finnmark in the mid-1700s.[7] Secular civil servants also carried out studies on the Sami and the northern regions in general, in the tradition of the topographical studies of the time. Examples are the pioneering study of the Swedish scholar Johannes Schefferus on Lapland[8] and the monumental, illustrated work of the governor of Finnmark, Hans Lilienskiold, *Speculum Boreale*, dedicated to the king in 1698.[9]

The literature of this period generally treats the northern minorities sympathetically, stressing aspects such as the Sami people's love of freedom and their ability to adapt to natural resources. Towards the end of the period, romantic ideology clearly flavoured descriptions, focusing on pictures of "the noble wild"; yet the positive attitude towards the Sami remained. A well-known representative of this school of early "lappologists" is the clergyman and scholar N. V. Stockfleth, who started his northern studies in the 1820s.

Policy towards the Kvens illustrates some central features of state ideology with regard to the northern minorities.

7 Leem 1767.
8 Schefferus 1673.
9 Lilienskiold 1932–45.

Mercantilist and physiocratic ideas favoured agriculture and farming in the northern areas as elsewhere, both as a means to improve the economy and as a tool of state-building. Hitherto Sami agriculture, i.e. husbandry, had to a large extent been based on seasonal migrations and extensive territorial use. For Norwegians in the northernmost areas, fishing had been by far the most important trade; farming had been limited to small-scale cattle breeding. The Kvens, however, with roots in traditional Nordic agriculture, introduced more intensive cattle breeding and fodder production, and even grain production in the most fertile areas. In the eyes of the authorities, this implied more settlements and greater population density, important national markers in an area where state borders were new or not yet settled. Hence, the authorities welcomed the Kvens.

This positive attitude was reflected in contemporary literature, which described the Kvens as industrious, inventive, and loyal subjects to the Crown. In particular their agriculture was portrayed as an important contribution to the area's economy.[10]

The various Sami ways of resource adaptation, such as reindeer herding in the border regions, were also praised. It was politically important to the authorities that Norwegian reindeer herds were kept here.

During this period, the multicultural and multiethnic dynastic Danish–Norwegian state largely recognized the Sami people's traditional rights as indigenous rights.[11] This also helps explain why minority policy was quite mild and very nearly a non-policy. Although there were local ethnic conflicts between Sami groups and others on questions of rights, the authorities believed that the large, sparsely populated areas would accommodate all groups and that, in the long run, they would integrate in a natural way within the state borders.

10 For example, Sommerfeldt 1799/1800.
11 Tønnesen 1972.

1850–1940: Nation-building, "foreign" minorities, and assimilation policy

To the extent that defined minority policy existed in Northern Norway before the middle of the nineteenth century, it was related to cultural matters, and especially to the question of the fate of the Sami language. Until the middle of the 1800s, a pro-Sami line was followed.

Then, it changed. After a fervid language debate in the 1840s and early 1850s, the Storting voted in favour of a new language and school policy towards both northern minorities. This was defined as a policy of assimilation, with a clearly stated ultimate aim: The languages of the minorities should be replaced by the national language, Norwegian. A special state fund to implement the policy was raised through annual grants and called the Sami fund (*Finnefondet*).[12]

After a transition phase, a strict one-language policy was pronounced in the early 1880s, first and foremost in primary school education, but also in church affairs. In the following decades, minority policy considerations gradually covered economic matters, communications, and military and defence questions. In the inter-war period, the different sectors were co-ordinated under a joint body.[13]

There is no doubt that the state authorities invested much effort and resources in a minority policy with clearly defined nationalistic aims. The official designation of the policy was apt: *Norwegianization*. The second half of the nineteenth century witnessed many examples of this kind of minority policy in different European countries. Rooted in nationalism and in the notion of the nation–state, it was epitomized by the slogan "one state, one language".

However, Norwegian minority policy had some specific features. In terms of regulations and other measures, the policy strictly and consistently discriminated against the minorities over an unusually long period, without the modifications seen else-

12 Eriksen and Niemi 1981:48–9.
13 Ibid.: 188.

where in Europe. Also, security policy considerations formed a very strong element of the policy's real motivations, even if this was not openly admitted.[14] How can this be explained?

As a result of the Napoleonic Wars, Sweden lost the province of Finland to Russia in 1809, and Denmark lost Norway to Sweden in 1814. Finland acquired the status of an autonomous, tsarist grand duchy, while Norway became a country with its own constitution in "personal union" with the kingdom of Sweden. Norway's restricted sovereignty was evidenced by the fact that foreign affairs was a matter for the Swedish government in Stockholm. Even if subsequent research has suggested that there was no real reason to fear Russian expansionism into the northern territories of Scandinavia, anti-Russian suspicions developed in both Norway and Sweden, as in other European countries. There were frequent references to "the Russian Menace". Several factors account for this fear. One general, underlying factor was the November Treaty of 1855, which implied a reorientation of Swedish (and Norwegian) foreign policy. Signed by Sweden, France, and Britain, it was a mutual defence agreement directed against Russia and created a general atmosphere of distrust and watchfulness regarding Russia.[15]

Another factor which heightened tension in the north was the increased settlement of Finns in Northern Norway. Western authorities regarded these people as Russian subjects and as a potential fifth column in border areas in the event of conflict with Russia; the Finns in the Swedish Torne River valley were so regarded, too.[16] The voluminous influx of Finns – who became Kvens in Northern Norway – peaked in the 1860s and turned into a national problem at a time when ideas of nation-building had widespread support. The fact that half of the population of Finnmark were Sami as late as 1850 added to national insecurities. Although the Norwegian population was now increasing rapidly, the ethnic situation caused nightmares for the central authorities.

Intentions *vis-à-vis* the two ethnic minorities were undoubtedly different at the outset. Attitudes towards traditional Sami rights

---

14 Ibid.: *passim.*
15 Nielsen 1991, 1992, and 1994:94–6.
16 Eriksen and Niemi 1981:36–8.

had changed; state acceptance of indigenous exclusive rights had been replaced by the juridical principle of "equal rights to everybody belonging to the same settlement", and by the doctrine of "the state's registered ground" in Finnmark.[17] Thus, in the nineteenth century, the Sami lost their former juridical status. Positive attitudes towards the Sami as an indigenous people still existed, in particular among scholars and clergymen. However, the Sami and the Kvens clearly became objects of the same vigorous policy of Norwegianization, even if the source material documents that the authorities were more occupied with the "Kven question" than with the Sami in their consideration of practical measures. If a counterfactual hypothesis may be admitted, it seems reasonable to suggest that, without the Kvens, assimilation policy regarding the Sami would not have been so strict.[18]

Nation-building and security considerations thus provide the main explanation for minority policy in the north, defined as "exposed border areas" on the fringes of western civilization. Part of the legitimacy of the nation-building policy was as a kind of European mission on the threshold of Asia. The newly developed ideas of social Darwinism were also frequently appealed to. Ethnic minorities were ranked below Norwegians in all cultural, social, and economic aspects. Only through "enlightenment" could they possibly survive, and this meant integration into Norwegian culture and society on the premises of the host society. These attitudes are somewhat parallel to Kipling's "the White Man's Burden". An element of racism added to the legitimation of the policy.

Literature about the ethnic minority groups and the northern areas published in this period can be subdivided into several groups.

Some of the literature has roots in the scholarly missionary tradition of the eighteenth century, developed into the aforementioned "lappologist school". A characteristic feature was that the lappologists were learned men who had mastered several disciplines, though linguistics and ethnography were their core disciplines.

In the first half of this period, few Norwegian scholars took an interest in the Sami, and even fewer in the Kvens. One who did was

17 Tønnesen 1972; Sandvik 1980; Minde 1991.
18 Eriksen and Niemi 1981:331–3.

the aforementioned N. V. Stockfleth, who produced the greater part of his linguistic and cultural historical writings in the 1840s. Because of his fervent engagement in the public debate on language policy, several of his publications are rather polemical. Stockfleth wrote on both the Sami and the Kvens.[19]

The most outstanding nineteenth-century Norwegian lappologist was Stockfleth's pupil J. A. Friis, whose forty-year career began with field work in Finnmark in the early 1850s. Friis covered a wide range of fields. In addition to ethnographic, historical, and linguistic studies[20], he wrote on folklore, notably on Sami tales and local traditions.[21] He also wrote fiction about the Sami.[22] Although he concentrated mostly on the Sami, Friis studied the Kvens as well, especially in what is regarded as his most important book, *En Sommer i Finmarken, russisk Lapland og Nordkarlen* (A Summer in Finnmark, Russian Lapland and North Karelia, 1871). Like his teacher Stockfleth, Friis regarded both ethnic groups positively, on the basis of a pluralistic societal philosophy, though it should be admitted that there are paternalistic elements in his writings.

In 1874 Friis became the first professor of Sami and Finnish language at the University of Kristiania (Oslo). Hitherto the university, founded in 1811, had had no tradition in studies of the northern peoples. Friis turned to other Nordic academic institutions to find colleagues and relevant material, as had Stockfleth. He turned in particular to Finnish researchers, who had already established a school within Finno-Ugric studies in the northern areas.

One of the very few historians who in this period contributed with writings on Sami and Kven history and culture was Ludvig Kristensen Daae, from 1866 professor of history at the University of Kristiania and also well known as a politician, journalist, and editor. In 1867 he accompanied his relative J. A. Friis on an extensive expedition to the northern regions of Norway, Russia, and Finland. Concerning the first part of the journey, he published a series of articles in the Kristiania newspaper *Aftenbladet* (1870). The rest

---

19 Stockfleth 1848.
20 Friis 1856a, 1856b, and 1885–7.
21 Friis 1871a and 1871b.
22 Friis 1881 and 1884.

of the expedition, together with general descriptions and analyses of different topics, was related in a remarkable book.[23]

Eilert Sundt, regarded as Norway's first sociologist, was another scholar with pluralistic ideas about the cultures in the north, mixed with a touch of well-meaning paternalism. He described the Sami especially with great understanding and sympathy, and also opposed the strict assimilation policy, notably in a public debate in 1863.[24]

In the second half of the period, from about 1880 or 1890, the attitude of the scholars changed. New ideological elements now coloured their research. Evolutionary ideas, social Darwinism, and even racism made their impact on leading scholars, together with a more outspoken nationalism. This does not mean that attitudes towards the minorities in general changed for the worse, but rather that basic conceptions of culture, ethnicity, and nation resulted in theories that minority cultures were in decay and had seen their heyday, whereas the larger national cultures were progressing.

This is clearly evident in the writings of the leading lappologist in Norway after Friis, Just Qvigstad (1853–1957). Qvigstad's scientific career lasted about seventy years, from the early 1880s to 1950.[25] Qvigstad held several important political and administrative positions nationally, including that of minister of education and church affairs, besides being rector of Tromsø Teachers' College. Like his predecessors, Qvigstad collaborated closely with foreign scholars of Finno-Ugric topics. In addition to Finnish and Baltic colleagues, he collaborated in particular with the Uppsala University scholar K. B. Wiklund. Qvigstad covered an even wider range of topics and fields than Friis, including toponymical studies. The notable characteristics of his writings are that 1) methodologically they are largely based on positivist–empirical ideals and 2) they involved a measure of compilation. According to Qvigstad, the most important task was to collect material while there still was time.[26] Qvigstad's writings reveal a tension, symptomatic of the period, between nationalism and nation-building on the one hand and a desire for objective documentation on the other. This is

23 Daae 1870.
24 Eriksen and Niemi 1981:325.
25 Hansen 1992.
26 Hansen 1992:62.

seen, for example, in his theoretical approach, which is dominated by diffusionism: Sami cultural features are frequently explained as "borrowings" from Scandinavians.[27] Yet Qvigstad's contributions to Sami studies are great, though based on what we are today inclined to see as old-fashioned methods and theories, which show Qvigstad to be a "child of his time". His documentary achievements are particularly outstanding.

In the inter-war period, Qvigstad was the only Norwegian scholar to take an interest in the Kvens.[28] At the same time, Finnish scholars eagerly studied the Kvens[29] as part of a larger research programme in which all Finnish "forgotten tribes" outside Finland proper were to be studied as part of a diaspora. In the wake of Finland's declaration of full independence in 1917, a new "greater Finland" nationalistic movement developed, and this helps explain this new field of scholarly interest.[30]

While lappologists as a group did not develop extreme attitudes towards minorities, racists certainly did. Racism as a science also took an interest in the northern ethnic groups. "Race hygiene" developed into a Norwegian and Swedish scientific school. The most influential and most widely known work with relevance for the Sami and the Kvens was the Finnmark volume (1906) of the standard multi-volume work *Norges Land og Folk* (Norway's Land and People), written by the cultural geographer Amund Helland of the University of Kristiania. Helland was also a central figure among radical Norwegian scholars of the time. On the basis of criteria such as physical anthropological features and mental character, Helland ranked the northern groups into a strict hierarchic scheme, with Norwegians on top, followed by Kvens and diverse Sami groups; the Eastern Sami (the Skolt Sami) had the lowest ranking and were dismissed as a people totally "lacking vitality and with no future".[31] There is no doubt that Helland's description contributed vastly to individual feelings of inferiority, often resulting in denial of identity and loss of integrity.

27 Hansen 1992:60–1; Mathiesen 1994.
28 Qvigstad 1921.
29 Especially Paulaharju 1928; 1935.
30 Nygård 1978.
31 Eriksen and Niemi 1981:325–7.

In the inter-war period, Norwegian nation-building and nationalistic behaviour intensified in the Arctic Ocean regions; this behaviour was later dubbed "Arctic imperialism" by Norwegian historians. Several leading national scholars published studies asserting Norway's "historical rights" in these regions.[32] Oscar Albert Johnsen's *magnum opus* on the political history of Finnmark[33] is an example of intimate co-operation between state authorities and highly qualified scholars. The study was commissioned and financed by the Ministry of Foreign Affairs in connection with ideas for regulations concerning the north-eastern border area including parts of Norway, Finland, and the Soviet Union.[34] This body of literature had hardly any relation to the lappologist tradition, though it drew on the lappologists' great empirical knowledge. It was simply a part of the general academic life of the period.

The inter-war period saw a culmination of unofficial tensions between Norway and Finland in the north. Despite the October Revolution and fear of communist contagion across the northern border, "the Finnish Menace" now preoccupied Norwegian state authorities. However, because the authorities confined "the Finnish question" to the more or less clandestine world of politicians and diplomats, these tensions were rarely considered explicitly by "serious" scholars or by official state spokesmen; this was left to travel writers and sensation-seeking journalists. An example is the Oslo journalist Arthur Ratche's book *Finsk fare for Finnmark* (Finnish threats against Finnmark, 1936), which precisely described the authorities' actual fears and their minority policy motives, but which was spurned by the authorities as speculation by an imaginative journalist.

Despite the tide of nationalism, social Darwinism, and racism throughout the period, sympathies for the Sami as an indigenous people survived among both political and diplomatic decision-makers. The early Sami ethnopolitical movement, starting at the turn of the century,[35] gained support from certain clerical circles and, above all, the reorganized and modernized Sami mission, as

32 For example, Johnsen 1923 and Brøgger 1931.
33 Johnsen 1923.
34 Eriksen and Niemi 1981:169.
35 Jernsletten 1986.

well as from a smaller number of scholars. There was thus some opposition to the Norwegianization policy. This was strongly manifested in a collection of articles published by the Sami mission pastor Jens Otterbech, strikingly titled *Kulturværdier hos Norges finner* (Cultural values among the Norwegian Sami, 1920).

For the Kvens, however, there were very few advocates. With the exception of a few intellectuals, the official attitude towards the Kvens was that they had come to Norway voluntarily and ought to adapt to the host society as soon as possible and in all possible ways. Off the record, the security policy dimension was still of the utmost importance for the state authorities.

1945–1970: The welfare state, awakening pluralism, and modern social sciences

The ideas of the modern welfare state formed the basis for reconstruction after the Second World War, during which the northern areas in particular had suffered heavy damages. Until the middle of the 1950s, the minority question did not receive much attention. Most resources were spent on material reconstruction and on new enterprises to implement the social and economic ideas of the welfare state.

Yet some new elements signalled a possible change in attitudes towards the Sami, partly inspired by international trends. This is seen, for example, in new views about school reforms as early as 1948. Renewed Sami organizational work on both national and international (Nordic) levels helped arouse new interest. So did the foundation of so-called Sami Societies (Samisk Selskap), initiated by Norwegian and Sami scholars and other intellectuals in Oslo. It could be argued that these societies belonged to the paternalistic tradition. However, they were important in spreading knowledge both to the Norwegian general public and to the Sami themselves, particularly through their periodical *Sami aellin* (Sami life).

In the mid-1950s, the Labour government decided to examine "the Sami question" through a committee consisting of scholars, state officials, and prominent Sami: the Sami committee (Samekomiteen). Its report was published in 1959 and suggested a wide range of actions to improve cultural, social, and economic conditions and to make fundamental changes in state policy towards the Sami. State authorities and politicians received the report positively. However, at local and regional political levels in the north, it was fervidly debated and (with a few local exceptions) rejected. The main explanation for this probably lies in ethnic prejudices and a lack of ethnic self-confidence, the results of generations of assimilation policy.[36] The outcome was that a clearly reformed Sami policy did not emerge, although the assimilation policy had already been abandoned, at least formally. However, a long series of *ad hoc* measures were introduced and implemented throughout the 1960s, especially in relation to schools and cultural matters.

In this period scholarly interest in the Sami revived. Remnants of the lappologist tradition were still seen, as in the works of Konrad Nielsen, who spanned the pre-war and post-war periods, e.g. in his *Lapp Dictionary* (four volumes, 1932–62). Despite the fact that the lappologist school was now superseded by specialized disciplines which introduced new methods and theories,[37] the break with the past was not always sharp. An example of this is the work of the Tromsø scholar Ørnulv Vorren, the leader of the Sami-ethnographical department at Tromsø Museum from 1949 and professor in Sami ethnography at the University of Tromsø from 1971. His numerous studies are rooted in the ethnographic tradition established by figures such as Ole Solberg of the Ethnographic Museum in Oslo and the Helsinki scholar V. Tanner in the pre-war period (Vorren had been a student under Solberg). Vorren's ecological and geographical perspectives, along with his thorough field documentation, renewed Sami studies.[38] The cultural geographic approach attracted several scholars in Sweden and Finland as well.[39] Typically, Vorren for many years collaborated closely with a Swedish colleague, Ernst Manker.[40] Another Norwegian to build a bridge between the pre-war and post-war research traditions was the ethnographer J. Falkenberg. Falkenberg contributed funda-

36 Eidheim 1971:17–20; Minde 1980:99–111.
37 Minde 1992:6–22.
38 Especially Vorren 1944, 1951, 1962, and 1986; Vorren and Eriksen 1993.
39 For example, Tegengren 1952; Hultblad 1968.
40 An example of collaboration in writing is Vorren and Manker 1956.

mental studies of the coastal Sami in Finnmark in the 1930s[41] and, after the war, focused especially on the Sami of Røros in southern Norway.[42] Within the discipline of ethnology, Knut Kolsrud of Norsk Folkemuseum and the University of Oslo (professor from 1961) became a prominent scholar both generally and on Sami studies, with special focus on coastal Sami, though, with regard to material and methodology, he did not represent extensive innovation.[43]

Linguistic studies also saw both a continuity and a new development. In Norway Knut Bergsland, professor in Finno-Ugric languages at the University of Oslo from 1947, was the leading figure. In the 1960s he was joined by Thor Frette, senior lecturer at the same university. One of the priorities was toponymical studies, to which both scholars contributed vastly. New insight about the minorities was produced also by pedagogical studies and school history; here Helge Dahl at the University of Oslo was the key figure.[44]

The introduction of modern social sciences to Sami studies was, however, this period's most striking historiographical feature. Disciplines like sociology and social anthropology became established in Norway as a part of the international trend, especially under American influence. In methodology, theory, and techniques, these disciplines represented a radical break with the past, particularly in their synchronic approach and generalizing aim. Sociology's specific contribution was the analysis of mass data based both on sample studies and on censuses covering Sami habitation areas.

The pioneers of this new "school" were non-Scandinavian scholars, who saw the Sami culture as an interesting object for case studies. It had traditional and "exotic" features, resisting forceful modernization processes in the surrounding societies. Sami culture was in a way rediscovered as a fascinating "relic" culture. Early international representatives were scholars such as the anthropologists I. Whitaker[45] and R. Pehrson,[46] who both studied

41 Falkenberg 1941.
42 Falkenberg 1982–3.
43 Kolsrud 1947, 1955, and 1961.
44 Dahl 1957.
45 Whitaker 1955.
46 Pehrson 1957.

the Finnish–Swedish–Norwegian border regions, with special emphasis on reindeer herding. Within Norwegian territories, Robert Paine's studies of a local coastal Sami society in western Finnmark have become classics.[47]

Among Norwegian social scientists, Harald Eidheim of the University of Oslo came to prominence with his study of the Sami in Polmak, a village in the Tana River valley in Finnmark.[48] Through his endogenous perspective, Eidheim was the first scholar to give a thorough description of the post-war experiences of the Sami. This was followed by his fundamental study *Aspects of the Lappish Minority Situation* (1971), which became very influential in the 1970s and 1980s. The Bergen student Siri Lavik (later Dikkanen) was another early representative of this new school, with her study of another Tana local society, Sirma.[49]

At the University of Oslo, Vilhelm Aubert, regarded as the most prominent modern Norwegian sociologist, introduced Sami studies in sociology. From the early 1960s he incorporated the Sami in his ambitious research project on isolated fringe societies.[50] The project found, among other things, that Sami did not partake in the modernization processes to the same degree as Norwegians did. They tended to stay in their relatively isolated societies, with over-population as one result.[51]

Of the two northern ethnic groups, the Sami had dominated scholarly attention so far. The only important exception is Helge Dahl's study of the education system and school policy in Finnmark, which deals fully with the Kven dimensions as well as the Sami.[52] Apart from that and some minor popular works, there was silence about the Kvens, even though they continued as an ethnic group. Several thousand people in Northern Norway still used the Finnish language daily. However, a strict assimilation policy was no longer pursued. The main reason for this was probably that the Kvens were not the object of serious security considerations after

47 Paine 1957–65.
48 Eidheim 1958.
49 Dikkanen 1965.
50 Aubert 1968, 1969, and 1970.
51 Minde 1992:14–9.
52 Dahl 1957.

the Second World War.[53] The non-policy situation had a parallel in the lack of scholarly interest.

1970–1990: Ethnopolitical drama, pluralism, and new paradigms

This period of about twenty years can be subdivided into distinctive phases regarding ethnopolitical and minority political development. The 1970s saw a strongly increasing trend towards Sami ethnopolitical mobilization and organization. Simultaneously, indigenous peoples organized internationally in the WCIP (World Council of Indigenous Peoples) with considerable Sami participation from the start. The question of rights to land and water resources now became a central issue, spurred by the international development of indigenous rights under the UN system.

The years around 1980 saw a dramatic culmination of claims and of conflicts in connection with the state hydroelectric power project in Alta in Finnmark (the Alta-Kautokeino River). Sami rights came to the foreground. During demonstrations against the project and open confrontations at the site, the project turned a spotlight on Sami rights and in particular on territorial rights related to reindeer herding.[54] It also came to symbolize state attitudes towards the Sami.[55]

The project went ahead, but in the aftermath of the conflicts, the government in 1980 set up two committees mandated to investigate the Sami minority situation and to propose suggestions both for a new policy and for specific new measures. One committee was to handle juridical matters and traditional territorial rights (Samerettsutvalget, the Sami rights committee), and the other, cultural and school affairs (Samekulturutvalget, the Sami cultural committee). The latter delivered three reports and concluded its work in 1987. The former has to date also produced three reports, but its final conclusions have not yet been delivered.

---

53 Eriksen and Niemi 1981:373; Niemi and Salvesen 1987:81–4.
54 Bjørklund and Brantenberg 1981; Brantenberg 1985.
55 Paine 1982, 1984, 1985, and 1991; Eidheim 1985.

There is no doubt that the Sami policy climate has shifted considerably since 1980. This is partly a consequence of these two committees' suggestions, partly because of ethnopolitical pressures, and partly because of international developments in attitudes towards indigenous peoples. Official Norwegian Sami policy has definitely changed to a policy of pluralism. The Norwegian constitution now states that the Sami are to be regarded as a people in their own right and that the state has a responsibility to secure the conditions for their protection and development. The Storting has accordingly passed a law which secures the Sami language in teaching and in public use. The most important initiative was probably the establishment of the Sami parliament (Sametinget) in 1989.[56]

The period as a whole has seen the establishment of other Sami institutions such as Sami museums, the Nordic Sami Institute, and the Sami College, all situated in traditional Sami habitation areas and all largely supported by state funds.

There has been a growing self-awareness and a breakthrough of organizational mobilization also among the Kvens in this period. However, the state authorities' attitude towards the Kvens has not changed profoundly, though limited possibilities for language teaching in schools have been provided.[57] In recent years there has been intensified debate on "the Kven question", in which state authorities have played a rather defensive role. They have, for instance, defined the Kvens as "immigrants", placing them in the same category as today's immigrants to Norway.

Research during these two decades reflects the pattern in public interest for the minorities. Research on the Kvens has not been absent, though Sami studies have been dominant by far. With a few exceptions, Kven topics tend to be neglected by social scientists, while linguists, socio-linguists, ethnologists, and historians have taken a greater interest in the Kvens. Another general trend is that Sami and Kven topics have for the first time been integrated generally into all kinds of studies, including general works on national history and local and regional historical studies. This is in stark

56 Brantenberg 1991.
57 Bratrein and Niemi 1994:207–8; Drivenes and Jernsletten 1994:274–7.

contrast to the neglect of former days and to earlier brief and biased descriptions.[58] A third feature is that the volume of research has increased and more disciplines have been involved, with history as a newcomer.

The University of Tromsø (founded in 1968, offering instruction in the social sciences and the humanistic disciplines from the early 1970s) has been of particular importance, together with the Nordic Sami Institute (1973) and other universities and colleges in the northern parts of the Nordic countries. All these northern institutions have felt a special obligation to study their regions' respective societies, cultures, and histories, including the respective ethnic groups. The recruitment of Sami and Kvens to teaching and research has been of the greatest importance. The period has also seen a flood of diverse publications about the Sami, aimed at the general public; an ever increasing market for such publications has developed.

Within the limited scope of this chapter, it is not possible to do more than sketch the historiographical developments in this period.

First, the social scientific tradition established in the preceding period continued after 1970. This continuity is also seen in the fact that many of Aubert's students have become leading figures and prolific writers. Several of the pioneering scholars, such as Eidheim and Vorren, are still active. A figure such as Gutorm Gjessing, who began his academic career in the 1930s as an archaeologist, represented both continuity and renewal. His radical thoughts and his reflections on Sami culture and the minority situation were undoubtedly influenced by the social sciences.[59] Within the disciplines of pedagogy and educational history, impulses from sociology and anthropology are clearly seen, e.g. in studies by A. Hoëm[60] and A. Høgmo.[61] Incidentally, it was a sociologist, P. Otnes, who wrote the first modern general Sami survey history based on a holistic societal theory, *Den samiske nasjon* (The Sami nation).[62]

58 Niemi 1987:69–70; Niemi 1989:201–3; Niemi and Winge 1993:15, 38.
59 Gjessing 1973.
60 Hoëm 1976.
61 Høgmo 1986 and 1989.
62 Otnes 1970.

Social anthropological studies have continued to focus on the Sami minority situation, analysed from diverse points of view.[63] A topic which has attracted considerable attention is the northern fundamentalist Lutheran religious movement *Laestadianism*, studied as a Sami (and Kven) tool for cultural and ethnic survival.[64] Anthropologists working with the northern ethnic groups also have been more oriented towards history, perhaps more so in choice of source material and topics than in methods and theory.[65]

Also, archaeology has contributed to Sami studies, in particular with a high number of doctoral and Master's theses. An outstanding figure is Knut Odner of the University of Oslo, both archaeologist and anthropologist, with studies aiming at a holistic and historical understanding of cultural development.[66]

This leads us to a second feature of the period, namely the theoretical and methodological debate on ethnic studies. This issue was linked to the general and international debate on studies of indigenous peoples. The basic questions were, first, who had the right to do such research ("who owns history?") and, second, what theoretical, methodological, and ethical implications did such research raise?[67] Later the focus shifted to the relations between the social sciences and history. The core question was now whether these two disciplines stood for "the same history".[68] Important theoretical contributions were also made in relation to the Kven projects.[69]

On the one hand, the debate undoubtedly helped to clarify disciplinary positions and identities, and to increase ethical, theoretical, and methodological consciousness. On the other hand, it also helped pave the way for inter- and multidisciplinary approaches. Historical studies of northern local societies and ethnic groups have clearly been influenced by the social sciences' interest in theories and models, prominent examples being Henry Minde's local

63 Thuen 1980, 1983, and 1985.
64 Bjørklund 1978 and 1985.
65 Mathiesen 1974; Bjørklund 1985; Thuen 1987.
66 For example, Odner 1992.
67 Keskitalo 1976; Mathiesen 1976.
68 Drivenes 1985; Bjørklund 1986; Hansen 1986.
69 Kalhama 1982; Olsen 1983 and 1994; Saressalo 1983, 1985, and 1986.

study *Stein og brød* (Stone and bread, 1983) and L. I. Hansen's doctoral thesis *Handel i nord. Samiske samfunnsendringer ca. 1550–ca. 1700* (Trade in the north. Sami societal transformations, *c. 1550–c. 1700*, 1990).

The specific contributions of historians, a third feature of the period, have come especially within three fields. First, historians have studied the demographic and economic history of the minorities, including migrations, covering both older and newer history.[70] A specific achievement is the considerable number of Master's theses, some of which also deal with the Kvens. Second, ethnopolitical and minority political studies have developed as a special field for historians.[71] Third, historians have contributed vastly to local and regional studies in which studies of the ethnic groups have been integrated. It is tempting to name this last feature "the new northern local history school". The list of such studies is already long.

A fourth feature of ethnic research in the period is linked to Sami rights, mirroring public debate and political considerations. Sverre Tønnesen's doctoral thesis *Retten til jorden i Finnmark* (Ground rights in Finnmark, 1972) received great attention, notably because it documented that the state authorities had formerly respected traditional Sami rights. It served as a trailblazer for many projects and minor studies, as did diverse court cases on conflicts between Sami land use – especially for reindeer herding – and the larger society's interests. Studies on historical rights have often provoked public debates on questions of current interest, as in the historical question of the southern border of Sami settlement and of land use in early modern times.[72] The work of the Sami rights committee of 1980 has also resulted in publications on historical

---

70 Examples are Niemi 1977; Nielssen 1986; Hansen 1990a and 1990b; Andresen 1991. A large number of articles by different authors have been published, for example, in the multidisciplinary periodical *Acta Borealia* ("a Nordic Journal of Circumpolar Societies", Novus, Oslo).
71 Minde 1980 and 1985; Eriksen and Niemi 1981; Jernsletten 1986; Andresen 1989; Eriksen 1991; Drivenes 1992; Niemi 1992; Sandvik 1993.
72 Bergsland 1970, 1974, and 1977; Sandnes 1973 and 1974; Haarstad 1981 and 1992.

rights, including contributions written by historians.[73] In Sweden and Finland research on Sami rights also attracts many scholars. Not surprisingly, jurists have been centrally involved in such studies. However, historians have increasingly been engaged, as have anthropologists. A current debate concerns theories and methods related to Sami rights analysed endogenously or exogenously. The latest contributions by historians seem to demonstrate that they are probably more capable than jurists of studying Sami rights "from within".[74]

Conclusion

In the historiography of the northern minorities, we have identified various features.

First, the hypothesis that the studies mirror societal attitudes has to a large extent been confirmed, with regard both to attention as such and to sympathy versus antipathy towards ethnic minorities.

Second, the Sami have, on the whole, received far more scholarly attention than the Kvens. An obvious reason is the Sami status as an indigenous people with roots in Norway back to prehistoric times. Their position as an indigenous people raised sympathy among scholars even during the period of strict assimilation policy, with its widespread discrimination and ideological harassment. Furthermore, the traditional picture of the Sami as representatives of an ancient culture has attracted scholars and other writers. With few exceptions scholars did not take any serious interest in the Kven history and culture until the late post-war period. The 1970s saw a breakthrough in Kven studies, though these were still far behind Sami studies in extent and in general interest. The minority and ethnic political climate then changed in a positive way, especially regarding the Sami.

Third, it was not until the 1970s that *history* and its subdisciplines really took up Sami and Kven studies, with specific contribu-

---

73 NOU 1984:18; NOU 1985:14; NOU 1993:34; NOU 1994:21. Among the contributors are the historians G. Sandvik, S. Pedersen, E. R. Hanssen, and E. Niemi.
74 See also Hansen 1986; Pedersen 1986.

tions on topics like demographic and economic history, minority policy and ethnopolitical history, and local and regional studies. Historians have also contributed considerably in recent years to studies on Sami rights. In the post-war era until *c.* 1970, the modern social sciences were in the forefront in ethnic studies, though there were examples of continuity from the lappologist tradition dating back to the eighteenth century, with linguistics, folklore, and ethnography as core disciplines.

Fourth, the 1970s and 1980s saw paradigmatic changes in scholarly activities related to the minorities as well as in minority politics. Ethical, theoretical, and methodological debates contributed positively to the scientific level of studies, as well as to disciplinary identity and inter- and multidisciplinary approaches. A prerequisite for the new scholarly development was infrastructural change and, specifically, the establishment of new northern universities and colleges, including Sami institutions. These, in turn, contributed vastly to the recruitment of Sami scholars.

To sum up, historians came late to the historiography of the northern ethnic minorities. However, their relatively brief involvement in Sami and Kven studies seems to bode well for the future.

14. History of Mentalities – History of Culture
Sølvi Sogner

The parting of the ways

A famous debate between Norwegian men of letters took place at the beginning of the twentieth century. It concerned the Christianization of Norway in the Early Middle Ages. The Marxist historian Edvard Bull sen., the leading figure in the dominant materialistic school of history in Norway, claimed that no real change of faith had actually taken place: characteristic qualities of the spiritual make-up of the people, such as self-assertion and a strong sense of kin, were too closely linked with the old heathen beliefs and were incompatible with Christian tenets.[1] According to literary historian Fredrik Paasche, however, Norwegians were no less believing Christians than other Europeans.[2]

It is unlikely that this conundrum will ever be solved conclusively. But the debate may be seen as an important cross-roads and a parting of the ways of materialistically oriented historians – the establishment at the time – and others. Not until a generation later did serious, career-minded historians, strongly influenced by, above all, the Annales school, take a similar interest in the spiritual past of their forebears. This delay seems to a certain extent to be true of medieval history as well, although there always remained a certain consensus as to the possible existence of a medieval mind, different from ours (see Chapter 4). As for early modern times and later, it was different. Even renaissance and reformation times were given short shrift in terms of spirituality, and were interpreted overwhelmingly in materialistic terms. *Homo economicus* as an ahistoric being was omnipresent, busily maximizing his (or her)

1 Bull 1912.
2 Paasche 1915.

profits and causing little trouble as regards the motivation behind his acts. Cultural history was seen as "history with politics and economics left out", the concern of other disciplines rather than of History proper. It was left to ethnologists and art historians, separate from general history.[3] Two series of cultural histories have been published, however, with the collaboration of professional historians. The first came around 1940, and the second around 1980; significantly, they were independent publications, outside mainstream history.[4] At present, the winds of change are upon us. A general history of Norway currently in progress has explicitly incorporated a cultural approach.

Theories of race discredited the idea of mental diversity

Several trends evident in the first half of the nineteenth century contributed towards the clear choice of approach, noticeable between the wars. Among the most influential was the growing mistrust of the race theories which had been in vogue from around the turn of the last century. These theories ascribed specific mental qualities to physical appearance, such as skull shape or colour of hair and eyes. The physical anthropological approach was prominent in the most up-to-date community studies published between the wars. The mental characteristics of people with different physical "racial" traits were discussed in full, accompanied by photographs. Even the official multi-volume topographical–statistical description of Norway published in these years presented flamboyant descriptions of the physical and mental make-up of the population.[5] If taken with a grain of salt, this documentation makes humorous and even interesting reading still today. The parts about the Sami population, however, are blatantly offensive and humiliating.

Needless to say, these publications are today "forgotten". The

3 Visted 1908, re-edited 1951–2 by Stigum; Schnitler 1911.
4 Bugge and Steen 1938–42; Semmingsen *et al.* 1979–81.
5 Helland 1899–1918.

example of the Norwegian Institute for Comparative Research in Human Culture is symptomatic. Founded in 1922, and publisher of Franz Boas's *Primitive Art* (1927) and Marc Bloch's *Les caractères originaux de l'histoire rurale française* (1931), among others, the Institute in later years found it opportune to change its old and well-known logo, which depicted the different "races" of the world.

No one can deny, however, that people look different. A popular children's ditty of recent years claims that some children are brown and others yellow, but that is only on the outside; inside we are all alike. But are we? Or were we? What did our ancestors think, what did they feel, what made them tick? Were they like us, or different? The Nobel laureate for literature 1928, Sigrid Undset, has often been quoted for claiming that "the human heart does not change at all, ever". But is that so? In her magnificent historical novels, one can certainly feel akin to the protagonists, as if time did not matter. But do we not fall prey to her masterly hand? Should we not use our proper tools and find out for ourselves?

History of mentalities *avant la lettre*

A courageous, pioneering figure appeared on this difficult stage in 1957. Gabriel Øidne attacked head-on the difficult question of the traditional regional antagonism between the eastern and western parts of Norway.[6] He was trying to solve the problem of divergent voting patterns between the two regions. Why did these regions traditionally and typically react so differently in political matters? Stein Rokkan, professor of political science and internationally known pioneer of electoral analyses, took a great interest in Øidne's article, which has for years been included in the curriculum in the social sciences.[7]

Øidne's article is both suggestive and knowledgeable, and his reasoning is strikingly similar to the way we usually think about the different regions of the country: the phlegmatic earthiness of the interior east as opposed to the introvert sensibility of the coastal west. Political voting patterns differed between the regions.

6 Øidne 1957.
7 Rokkan 1967.

In the west heady support was given to religion, teetotalism, and the revival of the Norwegian language as spoken in the countryside – a combination of attitudes often characterized by the term "counter-culture" – whereas in the east such matters did not raise the political temperature noticably.

Earlier attempts at explaining regional differences in political attitudes had been based on theories about the influence of the landscape, the climate, or – as we have already mentioned – the shape of skulls: people in the east lived on broad, open, fertile lands and were open-minded and liberal, whereas the more narrow-minded people of the west lived in steep valleys and along narrow fjords. Too much rain made the westerners spend much time indoors, and inclined them towards religious pondering. Also, their short skulls, as compared with the long skulls of the easterners, brought on deplorable qualities. The definition of a short skull, by the way, is one whose breadth exceeds 80 percent of its length.

Those were the days when history was struggling within the framework of a positivistic approach and the ardent desire to transform itself into a "human science". Although Øidne was no more able than his predecessors to explain people's voting behaviour, he managed to present hard evidence and to measure quantitatively people's attitudes towards prohibition (votes cast) and their generosity regarding overseas missionary activity (donations given). He correlated these variables with the traditional regions, and thus evoked historical cultural continuity. This was still a difficult field to cultivate, however, and further development had to await new impulses.

Introduction of the mentalities concept

In 1978 an abridged version of Jacques Le Goff and Pierre Nora's *Faire de l'histoire* (three volumes, 1974) was translated into Swedish, making it accessible to all Scandinavians. Norwegian historians – more anglophone than francophone – made acquaintance with the idea of history of mentalities as the "collective unconscious". "The mentality of any one historical individual, however important, is precisely what that individual shares with other men of his time", according to Le Goff, or to paraphrase the words of

Philippe Ariès, it is that which a mundane Frenchman and Henri IV have in common. The historian of mentalities, unlike the economic and social historian, "seeks not the real but the ways in which people considered and transposed reality".[8]

Agrarian historians and local historians took a special interest.[9] They sensed the close relationship, having discussed the question for years, in the so-called debate of the shedding of the serpent's skin. That debate centred on the difficult question of the market-mindedness of Norwegian farmers: had Norwegian farmers always acted in the interest of profit, or was this a modern attitude or mentality adopted during the nineteenth century, along with commercial farming and a general shedding of traditional attitudes and mentalities?

Indeed, some asked, was a history of mentalities really something new? Had we not been discussing mentalities for years, though without putting a name to it or making a fuss? It was very sensibly conceded, however, that mainstream Norwegian historians at least had not made history of mentalities their main concern in general; when they did touch on that kind of issue, they were not very explicit about it. "[A] systematic study of attitudes, ideas etc. of the people at large" was now called for to remedy the situation.[10]

History of mentalities was discussed at a Nordic seminar in 1985.[11] Reactions were mixed, and the Norwegian attitude was overwhelmingly negative. History of mentalities was partly felt as a threat, and

a denial of history. The historian of mentalities is looking for elementary and general fundamental structures, and therefore has to look upon historical events as disturbing elements. History must be "dehistorized" in order to realize its purpose.[12]

In spite of initial scepticism, however, interest remained lively. And when young Norwegian historians organized themselves in an

8 Chartier 1988:43.
9 Salvesen 1980; Sandnes 1981.
10 Sandnes 1981.
11 Kvium and Wåhlin 1987.
12 Hagen 1987.

autonomous organization and arranged their first national conference later in the same year, history of mentalities was their main
theme.[13]

Introducing the theme, the African scholar and contemporary
historian Jarle Simensen expressed the opinion that it was not a
fundamentally new approach: historians had always had to try and
understand the fundamental thinking behind their sources in order
to interpret them. One should not, however, embrace uncritically
all the implications of the new concept of history of mentalities:

> It ought to be dismissed as an idea that in historical reality there exist
> comprehensive, integrated systems of conscious and unconscious ideas,
> norms and ways of thinking that are shared by all members of a collec-
> tive. In the analysis of historical reality, more nuanced definitions are
> called for, which *inter alia* account for the dynamics of spiritual develop-
> ment interacting with social life.

But mentality could be "a good word with which to think"; Norwegian historiography ought to actively include the cultural dimension and set it firmly on the research agenda. All historical topics,
in fact, have "mentality" as one of their dimensions. This is true
even of contemporary political history:

> The wish to uncover the unconscious fundamental concepts and atti-
> tudes that are taken for granted in contemporary society is an impor-
> tant part of such a programme. One way of doing it is to conduct an in-
> depth study of "what is different" in the distant past and in distant cul-
> tures. This is nothing new in the discipline of history. It is in harmony
> with the very essence of the humanities and the hermeneutic method:
> through a dialogue with what is different, in order to see what is histor-
> ically given in our own positions and in that way to ease the pressure of
> tradition.[14]

History of mentalities now seemed to have gained admittance. But
was this really so? In his revised overview of Norwegian historiography from 1990 (originally published in 1959), Ottar Dahl, a
leading Norwegian historiographer and arbiter of the correct his-

13 Reiersen and Slettan 1986.
14 Simensen 1986.

torical approach, never mentions history of mentalities.[15] In a national seminar in June 1994, however, when discussing the future of history as a discipline, Dahl pronounced that history of mentalities is needed in order to deepen our historical understanding. What produced this change in attitude? What had happened in the meantime?

A probable explanation is that in 1990 there was as yet too little active interest or substantive historical writing on the history of mentalities to warrant the theme a place in the national overview. There have been several attempts at supplementing political, economic, social, and demographic research with "mental" dimensions. No single piece of research has surfaced, however, which identifies itself explicitly as history of mentality. References to people's attitudes, norms, ways of thinking, concepts of the world, etc. are legion, but rarely is there any explicit mention of mentality or mentalities. Furthermore, in 1990 it was not yet possible to say what the future trend would be. Since then, however, historians' general attitudes have been steadily more open towards this new perspective. Several historians have written articles which actively seek to arouse a wider interest in new perspectives. They acknowledge inspiration from social anthropology, ethnology, and folklore studies, of both domestic and foreign varieties.[16]

Hesitant attempts at writing history of mentalities/culture

Few, if any, historians have set about demonstrating how research of this kind can actually be carried out. Those who have made partial attempts along these lines have rarely spelled out their intention to do exactly that; they have also been very modest, and rightly so, in their conclusions. It may indeed be said that no piece of research exists which can be termed a whole-hearted attempt at writing history of mentalities. Research work generally shows an

---

15 Dahl 1990.
16 O. Fure 1984; Kjeldstadli 1989 and 1992; E. Fure 1990; Jenssen 1990; Nedkvitne 1991; Slettan 1992; Kaldal 1994; Andersen 1994; Slettan 1994.

interest in the implications of mentalities, but the main undertaking usually deals with something more traditional which can be brought safely to a conclusion.

The new approach has been more visible in some fields of historical research than in others. Already in the 1970s interest grew in "history from below", i.e. that of the little people: the old, the young, women, minorities. Historians immersed themselves in oral history, labour history, the history of underprivileged groups and minorities, women's history, demographic history, and extra-European history. These new interests confronted historians with the urgent problem of interpreting historical evidence produced by actors whose mental make-up was likely to be alien to the researcher and therefore not readily accessible. Hermeneutics has hence become a much-favoured methodology. Historians have sought to uncover the attitudes of anonymous, often illiterate historical actors, who have not articulated the motivations for their deeds and exploits. The mute actors of the past have indeed held a tremendous attraction for historians of recent years.

Within the field of labour history, Edvard Bull jun. pioneered history "from the bottom up" and the use of oral history, conducting interviews with elderly working men and women. In his major work on the rise of the labour movement, he was able to make use of his vast first-hand insight into these matters.[17] However, as Bull sought primarily to explain how class-consciousness emerged, his undertaking was in itself a contradiction in terms in relation to the uncovering of the collective *un*conscious.

Practitioners of historical demography immediately took an active interest in the concept of mentalities. The very idea of unconscious attitudes held in common by king and pauper appealed to people conducting research on anonymous masses, because conscious and explicit reasoning behind demographic practices were not to be found. One had only the acts themselves on which to make judgements and infer attitudes. This approach resembled that of the distinguished nineteenth-century demographer–sociologist Eilert Sundt. A pioneer in his field, Sundt nurtured the ambition of explaining regional and local variations of illegitimacy in nine-

17 Bull 1985.

teenth-century Norway. Modern historical demographers, striving to emulate Sundt, similarly tried to explain the startling regional discrepancies in these figures.[18] The search continues.

A multiple regression analysis of the national decline in fertility in Norway from 1890 to 1930, conducted along the lines of Ansley J. Coale's famous Princeton project, explicitly searched for cultural as opposed to economic explanations.[19] Was it possible to link fertility patterns to cultural attitudes and differing mentalities?

The analysis was carried out at the community level. Adequate cultural variables at the community level for the whole country during the period of the fertility decline were much harder to come by than economic variables, such as proportion of the population working in the different economic sectors. A number of indicators of underlying cultural factors were retained in the analysis. These were variables associated with *stability/mobility* (proportion of the population born and still living in the community at the time of the census); *"counter-culture"* (votes given in 1926 to uphold the prohibition introduced in 1919, in spite of economic setbacks caused by a decline in fish exports to retaliating wine-producing countries); *religiousness* (number of privately erected religious assembly houses, votes given to the Socialist Party after 1900; votes given to the Moderate Left, a Christian–democratic party, in 1891; and *women's status* (women's suffrage achieved in 1913).

These cultural variables did have an influence. However, the analysis showed the pre-eminence of economic variables. The conclusion drawn was that, on a national scale, the country was culturally so homogenous that economic factors had more explicatory power than cultural ones in relation to the problem of declining fertility.

Cultural factors have been highlighted, however, in a more recent analysis of the fertility decline in the city of Stavanger. Ståle Dyrvik was able to demonstrate that

> People born in Stavanger or in another Norwegian city were more likely to limit family size than people born in the countryside.... It has been possible to distinguish a key factor, neither economical nor social. If a

18 Sogner 1978; Sogner and Oldervoll 1981.
19 Sogner *et al.* 1984.

label is to be applied, it must be *cultural*.... When one has shouldered the sacrifice of renouncing good solid variables for the sake of something so woolly and vague as culture, this new perspective lends meaning and coherence to other findings as well.... The key factor is the geographical subdivisions. These constitute more or less complete societies of differing kinds and sizes, but they have some kind of culture in common as the constitutive nucleus.[20]

The idea of a common culture was a driving force when a Nordic research project launched in the 1980s had the explicit objective of studying changing attitudes and the spread of new ideologies in the nineteenth century within the Nordic seafaring region between Norway, Denmark, and Sweden. It focused on the cultural history of the coasts, and was called the Kattegat–Skagerrak project. To date a series of publications have appeared, focusing on sea-traffic, fisheries, religious movements, migration, and holiday visitors.[21] A final (Danish) publication concludes that the region – in spite of the initial assumptions – is not marked by unity or by a common, maritime culture.[22] This fact, as well as the wide spectrum of themes covered, may have contributed to a certain fragmentation in the character of the project results. The project also suffered from the premature death of one of its main initiators, Hans Try. Try was an ardent protagonist of this line of research, and wrote a much-respected national history with the programmatic title *Two cultures – one state*.[23]

The question of the possible existence of a specific coastal culture in Norway, different from the culture of the interior of the country, was further considered at a 1992 conference: do people who live on the coast have a mentality particular to them, or a particular way of life? Experienced researchers from the immensely long Norwegian coast stressed cultural diversity rather than unity, in spite of obvious common features such as the dynamic, ever-changing adaptive character of coastal culture, responsive to impulses from outside.[24]

20 Dyrvik and Alsvik 1987.
21 *Meddelelser* 1982–91.
22 Holm 1991.
23 Try 1979.
24 *Heimen* 4/1992.

The historical records which are most promising in the effort to uncover the mentalities of our anonymous ancestors in the Early Modern Period are judicial documents, from civil as well as criminal cases. At present the social and cultural history of crime and civil litigation is a very lively field of research. It is a real growth sector, and several practitioners explicitly state that their underlying interest in this new approach lies in discovering and understanding the motivations behind the actions that the legal documents bear witness to, as opposed to the criminal pattern as such.[25] To the historian of mentalities – or culture – the interesting part is what lies behind the acts which are labelled as criminal. Whatever this may have been, it was important enough for contemporaries to bring prosecutions, whether it was the authorities or ordinary civil prosecutors who took action. The point of contention may often be difficult to understand if not completely impenetrable to the modern researcher. Pursuing research in this field may give insight into the ways of thinking of our ancestors.

One of the most interesting findings is the importance of honour in early modern times. Libel suits are quite common. Cases are brought before the court through private litigation, by men and women alike. People are adamant about defending their honour and refuting dishonourable accusations of all kinds. Honour lost amounts to loss of social status, and perhaps even of the right to fully recognized membership of the local community. Honour thus appears to be a key variable for our understanding of this society. The question then arises how honour is lost. This may happen in much the same way for either gender, through irrefutable accusations of sorcery, violence, slander, theft, etc. But there are also differences. For young women, it is of extreme importance to refute accusations of sexual frivolity, and their future marriage possibilities may depend on a public defence in court.[26] Publicity is extremely important, and the proceedings of the court serve as the means by which people are reintegrated in the local society after some moral lapse. The outcome of the proceedings is in many dif-

25 Næss 1982; Sandvik (1985) 1992; Natvik 1989; Sandnes 1990; Sandmo 1992; Løyland 1992; Telste 1993.
26 Telste 1993.

ferent ways highly influenced by locals – as jurors or as witnesses – and in-depth analyses of court cases may therefore disclose popular attitudes of the period.[27]

Norwegian researchers also participate in an ongoing comparative Nordic project on social control and the handling of conflicts in pre-industrial society.[28] The civilization perspective is central to the analysis. Among the problems raised is the question whether there is such a thing as a common Nordic culture.

History of mentalities or history of culture?

Today it can be safely claimed that there is a genuine and widespread interest among Norwegian historians in this new approach. This new interest has a variety of names, of which history of mentalities is just one. Others are historical anthropology, history of everyday life, cultural history, and socio-cultural history. As the saying goes, a beloved child has many names.

A change of name seems warranted. Norwegian researchers generally seem to prefer the word "culture" as opposed to "mentality". The term is almost equally slippery, but it has a great tradition and sound fund-raising properties: there is a Ministry of Culture, there are museums of culture, and research programmes for culture have been launched. Whereas a university institute for economic history has never been established, we have recently been endowed with a Centre for Technology and Culture. The Historical Institute at the University of Oslo has been subsumed temporarily into the School for Cultural and Social Studies. Culture is increasingly becoming the preferred term, as opposed to mentality or mentalities.

"Culture" harmonizes better with historians' predilection for the conscious rather than the unconscious. In the words of one of the practitioners,

> "History of culture" focuses more clearly on the individual than the already ageing history of mentalities, on conscious thinking and on the

27 Sandmo 1992.
28 Österberg 1991; Tønnesson 1994b.

use that the individual makes of the culture that he or she is born into....
History becomes not a study of "the mental tools" of a period but of the
hands that held the tools and of what they were used for.[29]

Culture "regarded as the whole way of life of a people"[30] has
immense research possibilities, and it is fast becoming the new jar-
gon. We have seen only the beginnings so far. The grand ambition
must be – in the words of Roger Chartier – to consider

> how all relations, including those that we call economic or social rela-
> tions, are organised according to differing forms of logic that put into
> play and into operation the schemata of perception and appreciation of
> a variety of social objects and consequently, the representations that
> comprise what one can call "culture", be it common to the whole of
> society or particular to a limited group.[31]

29 Sandmo 1994.
30 Jenks 1993.
31 Chartier 1988.

15. International History

Tor Egil Førland

International history – defined as history focused on international relations and the conduct of foreign policy –did not exist as a separate discipline in Norway before World War II.[1] Norway's forced inclusion in the war in 1940 and its accession to the North Atlantic Treaty in 1949 not only served as reminders of the need to study international history, but also provided two major events to study. Today, international history is firmly established – albeit not at the centre of Norwegian historiography, but rather near the borderland between history and political science.

This chapter comprises two main parts. The first outlines major themes, concentrating on that still-dominant part of Norwegian international historiography which examines Norway's relations with other countries. In addition to the German attack and the signing of the North Atlantic Treaty, three themes are discussed: security policy over the long term; alliance policy; and attitudes towards European integration. This section concludes with a brief review of a growing body of studies that are not mainly preoccupied with Norway itself. The second part seeks to identify dominant characteristics of Norwegian international history. The discipline, although thematically spanning the whole world, nevertheless exhibits a coherence and unity of method to such an extent that theoretical debate – indeed, any kind of debate – is missing. Moreover, by ignoring social developments, international history remains an appendix to Norwegian historiography.

---

1 The youthful and wide-ranging Halvdan Koht had, however, published a few studies on international relations. Koht 1906 and 1908.

Main themes

The German attack

In the 1950s Magne Skodvin and Nils Ørvik, pioneers among Norwegian international historians, devoted their energies to the question why Norway was caught so completely off-guard by the German attack on 9 April 1940. The studies they published are still standard works. Skodvin focused on the policies of the great powers and on perceptions within the Norwegian government in 1939–40.[2] He showed how the British and French authorities vacillated between their desire to engage the Germans in a favourable location – i.e. Norway – and their fear that landing troops there would end up instead as a dangerous diversion. The Germans, once Hitler had given the go-ahead signal, had none of the allied dithering – nor did they share British apprehensions about offending the Norwegian authorities, who were fixated on preserving neutrality. As to the question of Norwegian unpreparedness – and the accusation that the government ought to have read the signs better in the early days of April – Skodvin pleaded for empathy with Foreign Minister (and proto-international historian)[3] Halvdan Koht. Admittedly, Koht failed to discern among the welter of conflicting messages and rumours the indications that a large-scale German invasion force was on its way. But so did the British, on the basis of better intelligence. And when the invasion became reality, Koht and the government stood firm. Refusing to bow to German ultimatums, they immediately prepared to continue the fight from abroad.

Ørvik first wrote books on neutrality problems in modern warfare and on Norway's role in the economic warfare of the "phoney war" of 1939–40.[4] He then, in 1960–1, published a magisterial two-volume study of Norwegian security policy from 1920 to 1939.[5] Here he provided the background to the decisions that led to Norway's unpreparedness in 1940: the Labour Party's well-

2 Skodvin 1953, 1975, and 1977.
3 See note 1.
4 Ørvik 1953a and 1953b.
5 Ørvik 1960 and 1961. His ninety-page conclusion is reprinted as Ørvik 1962.

grounded scepticism of the armed forces in general and the military establishment in particular; the general belief that neutrality and Norway's remote location would keep the country out of war; the fear that armed fighting against a great power would lead to increased destruction without preventing defeat; and the confidence that British sea power would deter and, if necessary, repel German designs on Norway.

The North Atlantic Treaty

In the early 1970s Skodvin and his students started mining government and Labour Party archives for evidence regarding Norway's signing of the North Atlantic Treaty. Their excavations produced a spate of publications and an incipient debate rare to Norwegian international history. They also created a greatly increased understanding of why Norway bade farewell its policy of so-called bridge-building – the attempt to maintain good relations with all great powers in the vain hope that the wartime allies would not become antagonists – and chose the Atlantic option instead of a neutral defence union with Sweden and Denmark.

In 1971 Skodvin published a study, based on Foreign Ministry archives, of the government's decision to opt for the Atlantic alliance when the emerging Cold War made bridge-building impossible.[6] For the Norwegian authorities, the lessons of 1940 were (a) that Norway needed guarantees of military assistance from friendly great powers – i.e. Britain and/or the United States – and (b) that in order to be effective, such assistance had to be prepared in peacetime. When the Swedish government insisted that a Scandinavian defence union would have no formal ties to the West, Foreign Minister Halvard Lange (another historian) and the government decided Norway ought to join the Atlantic alliance.

Skodvin's study was less comprehensive in relation to either decision-making within the governing Labour Party or the policies of the great powers. These fields were cultivated by two students of his, Knut Einar Eriksen and Geir Lundestad. On the basis of party archives, Eriksen showed how both Lange and Prime Minister

6 Skodvin 1971.

Einar Gerhardsen had wavered before they concluded that it was impossible to reconcile the Swedish policy of neutrality with the Norwegian *sine qua non* of formal guarantees of western aid.[7] When the leaders had taken their decision, they secured consent from the party, putting their weight behind the effort to convince hesitant party members, though without bending the rules of party democracy, as opponents had claimed.

Using declassified State Department documents, Lundestad demonstrated that the Truman administration in 1948 had an open mind towards associating Scandinavian countries with the incipient Atlantic alliance by arrangements other than formal membership.[8] He argued that Lange could have made fuller use of US flexibility had he wanted to. Eriksen, in response, insisted that the opening provided by Lange's American interlocutors was too small to accommodate guarantees of the kind sought by the Norwegian government.[9] When British government archives were opened, Eriksen and Skodvin wrote an article supporting their earlier views with fresh evidence.[10] Today, only nuances separate the participants in this discussion.[11]

Long-term stability?

It was Olav Riste who took it upon himself to transcend the preoccupation with specific turning-points and offer a long-term view of Norwegian security policy.[12] He was particularly well-suited to the task, having written major monographs on Norway's role in both world wars.[13] Other writers had seen Norwegian foreign policy in the 1940s making sharp turns and even coming full circle:[14] the government-in-exile promoting its notion of an Atlantic alliance

7 Eriksen 1972.
8 Lundestad 1977a, 1977b, and 1980.
9 Eriksen 1977a and 1977b.
10 Eriksen and Skodvin 1981. See also Skodvin 1990.
11 For recent overviews in English, see Riste 1991 and Pharo 1994:210–6.
12 While they were anticipated in a 1973 book review (Riste 1973b), Riste presented his views more comprehensively in Riste 1984, 1985a, and 1985b.
13 Riste 1965, 1973a, and 1979.
14 Udgaard 1973.

in 1941–2;[15] soft-pedalling and seeking shelter in bridge-building when it realized the Soviet Union was not too happy about the Atlantic idea; and eventually turning west again with the acceptance of Marshall Aid[16] and the signing of the North Atlantic Treaty. Riste pointed to the stability in the underlying basis for Norwegian security, namely the guarantee from a western protecting power. In Riste's long-term strategic perspective, it was less significant whether this guarantee was implicit or laid down formally in a treaty; whether Norway juridically was neutral or allied; and whether the protecting power was Britain or the United States. "Norway's accession to the North Atlantic Treaty was more shadow than substance, and far from being a real turning-point", the search for which, in Riste's opinion, is likely to prove futile, since a country's pursuit of security must be seen as a gradual process.[17]

The observation that Norwegian security had rested on British sea power was not novel: it had been a major point in Ørvik's analysis of the inter-war years.[18] By stretching the time frame, however, Riste used this British "implicit guarantee"[19] to turn Norway's accession to the North Atlantic Treaty on its head: it became a symbol of stability rather than change. It is an indication of its strength – and probably of the coherence of the Norwegian international history community as well – that Riste's stability thesis has remained virtually unchallenged.[20]

Norwegian alliance policy

Among students of Norwegian alliance policy, Rolf Tamnes is dominant. In the 1980s he produced a small mountain of studies

---

15 For a short English-language treatment of Norway's so-called Atlantic policy, see Riste 1982.
16 Pharo 1976.
17 Riste 1985a, quotation from p. 147.
18 See Ørvik 1962:37, where he shows that German authorities also were fully aware of this fact. Riste's student Roald Berg (1985) has shown how Norway's leading statesmen put their trust in Britain in the years from the dissolution of the union with Sweden to the integrity treaty provided by the great powers in 1907.
19 An expression adopted from John Sanness (1978).
20 The exception is Førland 1988. For Riste's reply see Riste 1989.

on Norwegian alliance policy and US northern flank policy, culminating in his coining of the twin concept "integration and screening" to describe Norway's policy towards NATO and the United States.[21] Aware that the policy of most European NATO countries included elements of both strategies, Tamnes argued that Norwegian policy has been distinguished by its sustaining "both components so vigorously, and simultaneously".[22] On the one hand, Norway worked very hard to commit Britain and the United States to its defence when NATO set up an integrated command structure after the outbreak of the Korean War, and Norwegian authorities never tired of ensuring that NATO's war plans and resource allocations made provision for a credible defence of the northern flank. On the other hand, until France left NATO's military structure, no country had more restrictions on allied military presence than Norway, with its publicly declared policy of accepting no foreign bases or nuclear weapons on its territory in peacetime. Hence Norwegian alliance policy became one of combining loyalty and strong general support of NATO's military integration with special arrangements providing an escape for Norway from arrangements that might provoke the Soviet Union (as well as domestic left-wing critics).[23]

The critical spot in Tamnes's Janus face of integration and screening is whether Norway really was more in favour of general NATO integration than other alliance members were, or whether its support for integration was reserved for undertakings beneficial to Norway. In the latter case, Norwegian alliance policy may fit better the model provided by Ørvik's observation that when Norway entered the League of Nations in 1920, as well as when in 1937–8 it considered publicly to renege on the League's sanction provisions, Oslo sought "maximum benefits with minimum contributions" by means of some kind of semi-membership.[24] It is tempting to see Norway's post-war reservations against allied bases and

21 On Norwegian alliance policy, Tamnes 1982, 1983, 1985a, 1986a, 1987a, and 1989; on US northern flank policy, Tamnes 1985b, 1986b, and 1991.
22 Tamnes 1987:93.
23 For speculation that part of Norway's motivation for its loyalty is its need of special treatment, see Førland 1990:512 and 1994:175, 181–2.
24 Ørvik 1962:31.

nuclear weapons on its territory in the same light, suggesting that the half-way house is Norway's preferred residence[25] – although the NATO shelter, of course, has a much more solid foundation than the League had. The contrast between the strength of Norway's NATO integration and the earlier tacit trust in the British navy illustrates the limitations of this view. It should also serve as a reminder that the underlying stability of the implicit western great power guarantee should not eclipse completely changes in weapons technology, commitments, and patron powers.

European integration

Long-term syntheses on Norwegian attitudes towards European integration are still wanting, although much knowledge on which such attempts could be based has been produced by Norwegian integration historians. Chief among them is Helge Pharo, who has published several articles on Norway and the Marshall Plan and on Norwegian attitudes towards European integration in the 1950s.[26] In his Marshall Plan studies, two themes stand out. The first is Norway's volte-face from initial reluctance towards Marshall Aid to becoming an avid contender a few months later. In summer 1947, fear of compromising the bridge-building policy combined with an insufficient apprehension of the gravity of Norway's dollar gap to produce an initial lack of interest in the US offer. The turnabout is explained by the government's realization that East–West relations had deteriorated to the point that bridge-building had become impossible; foreign policy considerations therefore prompted a fallback to the reserve position, namely alignment with the West. Pharo's second theme links Marshall Aid and the Labour government's plans for the modernization of the Norwegian economy. The relationship is complex. The government hoped to use aid to invest in national industrial champions that needed protection from international competi-

25 The preference for the half-way house may, of course, apply equally to Norwegian attitudes towards European economic co-operation: see below.
26 English-language articles presenting various (and sometimes overlapping) aspects of the issues are Pharo 1976a, 1984, 1986a, and 1993; Pharo 1989 is more detailed on domestic politics regarding Europe.

tion; this often conflicted with the US insistence that recipients liberalize intra–West European trade and invest in industries in which they had a comparative advantage. At the same time, Washington's liberalization policy could be compatible with a perception in government circles that such liberalization might promote a desired restructuring and modernization of Norwegian industry – a policy that met with considerable opposition both in the party and in the parliament.

The integration history research of Pharo and others[27] has shown that, well into the 1960s, Norwegian policy-makers, including the Foreign Ministry establishment, were generally fearful of European integration efforts – to the limited extent that they paid attention to such activities. Their anxiety had several sources. Partly it was grounded in the general Norwegian preoccupation with sovereignty, achieved only in 1905. Partly it rested in the belief that Norwegian industry and agriculture needed tariff walls to survive – a factor which also explains why the many attempts to create a Scandinavian customs union faltered.[28] And partly it stemmed from an (inflated) impression of the extent to which a deflationary *laissez-faire* ideology dominated Continental economies to the detriment of full employment, in contrast to the policy pursued by Scandinavian and British Labour governments.[29] The anxiety did not lead Oslo into obstructionism: such activities were considered unnecessary given the prevailing view through most of the 1950s that the integration efforts of "the six" were doomed to fail. Probably animated by heavy doses of wishful thinking, Norwegian foreign policy authorities put their faith in a North Atlantic free trade area which would be dominated by the United States and Britain, Norway's favourite patron state, and which Sweden would also be able to join.

---

27 Røhne 1987 and 1989. In this area, too, Ørvik was somewhat of a pioneer, but his publications in the early 1970s (1972 and 1975), pondering Norwegian Euro-scepticism, lacked the empirical base needed to provide new historical insight.

28 Sogner 1993.

29 It is tempting to suggest that because of Norway's particular party system, Norwegian social democrats were unable to comprehend Continental social Christian democracy.

The Norwegian pipe-dream of a trans-Atlantic free trade area is where European integration meets with security studies: Norway's preferred option for both security and economic co-operation was a combination of the Atlantic and Scandinavian concepts. In either area, however, was this a realistic option a fact that provided for painful decisions which did much damage to the cohesion of the governing Labour Party in 1949 as well as in 1972 and 1994.

No preoccupation with Norway

It is perhaps a sign of the Norwegian international history community's having come of age that several of its younger members have published studies in which Norway is altogether absent or accorded no more place than its international significance requires. Historians of the new generation are not the first to show little interest in Norway, however. They had a role model in Geir Lundestad, the Norwegian international historian who enjoys the highest acclaim abroad. Through books based on research in US government archives on early American Cold War policy towards the East European satellites (characterized by Lundestad as a "non-policy") and towards Scandinavia,[30] and probably as much through promoting the term "Empire by Invitation" to characterize the US Cold War hegemony in Western Europe,[31] Lundestad has earned a place among the most widely read and cited Cold War historians – a feat matched by few non-Americans.

Although Lundestad has certainly set an example of what Norwegian international historians can achieve, scholars from the new generation have seldom found their objects of study in the trail blazed by Lundestad. Instead they have spread out in all directions in a most post-modern way. The early 1990s saw major monographs on international history written from a non-Norwegian perspective by scholars graduating in the previous decade. Stein Tønnesson, in *The Vietnamese Revolution of 1945*, argues that Franklin D. Roosevelt's South-east Asian machinations in World

30 Lundestad 1978 and 1980.
31 For the evolution of Lundestad's thinking on this point, see Lundestad 1984, 1986, and 1990.

War II induced the Japanese to topple the French colonial administration for fear of an Allied invasion of Indo-China, thus eventually paving the way for Ho Chi Minh to take over and fill the power
vacuum created when Japan capitulated.[32] Tor Egil Førland, in his
study of the creation and prime of CoCom, the Cold War export
control organization, shows how West European countries reluc-
tantly accepted the US call for strategic export controls on ship-
ments to the Soviet bloc; he contends that the Europeans,
although they agreed to expand controls in the wake of the Korean
War, had considerable success in keeping their most cherished
(and often most strategic) export items off the embargo list.[33] Odd
Arne Westad, in his book on how the embryonic Cold War in the
Far East contributed to the outbreak of full-scale civil war in China
from 1946, concludes that rivalry between the United States and
the Soviet Union meant Jiang Jieshi was no longer able to monopo-
lize great power-backing; realizing that he would be unable to control China and contain Mao's Communists by political means
unless he had such dual backing, Jiang, with considerable US
assistance, tried to achieve his aim through civil war.[34] Olav
Njølstad, in his study of Jimmy Carter's Soviet policy in the first
two years of Carter's presidency, sees more of a cold warrior in the
new president than most previous scholars: he argues that Carter
had basically the same goals and attitudes towards the Soviet
Union as his predecessors; that differences related to means rather
than aims; and that when he departed from their path, it was in
being more ambitious and assertive.[35]

Main traits

Only one school

A shift in emphasis, from substance to methods, is needed to distinguish traits characteristic of all or most parts of the Norwegian
international history community. One reason for such a shift is
that Norwegian international historians do not as a rule till each

32 Tønnesson 1991.
33 Førland 1991b.
34 Westad 1993.
35 Njølstad 1994.

other's fields: scholars hardly ever study the same issue or offer competing syntheses.[36]

The main reason why Norwegian international historians exhibit such peacefulness and respect for each other's territory is perhaps that all are products of the same school, and therefore employ basically the same methods. Hence the conclusions presented by one are respected and accepted by the others. The basic methodological element is a heavy reliance on archival evidence, often gathered in several countries and always carefully sifted. In selecting, interpreting, and presenting the evidence, scholars are guided – more or less consciously – by what has recently been termed a "liberal intergovernmentalist" approach. This seeks to merge the "realist" school of international relations analysis, which sees the states system as basically anarchic and which studies inter-state relations with little regard for internal policy-making, with schools that pay more attention to the role played by domestic politics and interest groups in determining the policy of each state.[37] The outcome is a body of multi-archival, multi-level, and multi-actor studies based on overwhelming empirical evidence and little or no theory. (Theoretical debate is non-existent.)[38] A side effect is to make cross-field cultivation harder. Cross-fertilization by theoretical erudition acquired in one's own area must be expected to produce low yields. Even if one possesses the language requirements to enter someone else's field, the mountains of evidence and the slight chances of reward in the form of conclusions significantly different from what others have offered – since everybody approaches the evidence in basically the same way – are inhibiting. To attempt tillage of a field belonging to

36 Exceptions are (a) the so-called Lundestad–Eriksen debate (with additional contributions from Pharo [1976b] and Skodvin) on Halvard Lange's role in the process leading up to Norway's signing of the North Atlantic Treaty in 1949; and (b) the interest taken by several scholars in the security of Svalbard. For an introduction to this issue, which is excluded here for lack of space, see Pharo 1994:204–6. Although Riste, Eriksen, Lundestad, Tamnes, and others have been occupied with Svalbard security, debate is peculiarly absent: individual scholars have studied different aspects without disagreeing among themselves.

37 Moravcsik 1993.

38 But for Njølstad 1990.

someone else on a less thorough basis is only for the foolhardy or the extremely sure-footed, since the more experienced cultivator will not hesitate to point out a rival's mistakes.[39]

Had there been several competing international history milieux in Norway, the methodological unity might have been broken down. In reality only two institutions – the Department of History at the University of Oslo and the Institute for Defence Studies[40] – have provided what could be called a permanent home for international history,[41] and the overlap between the two has been too close to allow serious competition. The majority of the Institute's historians teach at the University, and several University historians have taken up residence at the Institute for shorter or longer periods. The close relationship is typified in the six-year project to produce a commissioned, multi-author, six-volume account of Norway's foreign relations. This is located at the Institute of Defence Studies and guided by an advisory group chaired by the Institute's director, Riste; it currently employs not only Riste's deputy, Tamnes, but also Pharo, professor of international history at the University. Much of the methodological cohesion among the younger generation of international historians can be attributed to Pharo, mentor to most of them, including Tønnesson, Førland, Westad, and Njølstad. One step up the generation ladder, we find Skodvin, who taught not only Pharo but also Eriksen and Lundestad, and who was responsible for establishing the international history community at the University of Oslo in the 1960s.

Skodvin was assisted by John Sanness and Jakob Sverdrup, both of whom had had their interest in international relations nour-

39 For an example see Rolf Hobson's (1993) rebuke of Øystein Sørensen's (1991) attempt to use the failure of the Schlieffen Plan as a basis for counterfactual speculation.
40 This institution, home to Ørvik in the 1950s and Riste and Tamnes today, is an independent centre attached to the National Defence College. It has changed its name and structure several times. From 1980 to 1988 it was the Research Centre for Defence Studies; before that it was the War History Department of the Armed Forces.
41 The University of Tromsø in the 1970s recruited Lundestad and Eriksen and looked set to establish itself as a third stronghold of international history, but in the 1980s both gravitated to Oslo and became affiliated with the Department of History there.

ished by Arne Ording, history professor at the University, policy advisor to Foreign Ministers Trygve Lie and Halvard Lange, and editor of the foreign policy journal *Internasjonal Politikk* from 1947 to 1959. Sanness and Sverdrup were also part of the Labour Party's foreign policy establishment, and worked as foreign policy editors of the government mouthpiece *Arbeiderbladet* at different times from the 1940s to the 1960s. The dividing line between policy-makers and international history professors was permeable. What Tamnes has called the "Kissinger syndrome" among US international relations scholars, namely an appetite for government positions that often cause the discipline to "gravitate towards established society and established modes of thinking",[42] might perhaps apply to parts of the Norwegian international history community in the first post-war decades. (Ørvik, too, worked with Lange in the 1960s.) The second and third generations of international historians have so far kept more distance from the government and the Labour Party; this perhaps symbolizes an increasing professionalization of international historians, as well as of politicians and political advisors.[43]

Close connections between the social democratic foreign policy establishment and international historians, the Foreign Ministry's practice of allowing Skodvin and his students privileged access to its archives, and Skodvin's ability to emphasize with the decision-makers he was studying, combined to produce the embryo of an alternative international history circle around professor Jens Arup Seip at the Department of History in Oslo. Seip and his students approached the foreign policy decision-making process, and the government and Labour Party in general, more suspiciously than did Skodvin and his circle. The Seipians never came close to establishing a real alternative, however. Their prime interest was Norwegian decision-making, rather than international relations or

---

42 Tamnes 1993:491 (my translation).
43 It is perhaps also symbolic of a shifting balance of power between international historians and international relations scholars that the last Norwegian academic to become foreign minister was Johan Jørgen Holst, international relations scholar and former director of the Norwegian Institute of Foreign Affairs – a position he inherited from Sanness, who had held it in the 1960s and 1970s.

Norway's role in the international community;[44] in order to comprehend Norwegian foreign policy-making on a broader basis, they would have had to take much greater account of the international environment than they cared to.[45] At the same time, the second and third generations of "mainstream" international historians published detailed studies of foreign policy-making exhibiting no lack of scepticism towards the Foreign Ministry and Labour Party's foreign policy establishment.[46] In the 1980s the Ministry's declassification regime was made more liberal. With the mystique of closed archives removed, the Seip school of international history, short on determination and squeezed for room by Skodvin's students, was doomed to cot-death. Despite generous life-support by historiographers,[47] it ought to be buried by Pharo student Hilde Henriksen Waage's in-depth study of Labour and Foreign Ministry attitudes towards the creation of the state of Israel.[48] By disclosing how Foreign Ministry officials tried to circumvent the express wish of Foreign Minister Lange and other Labour leaders, Waage not only exploded the illusion of unity between Labour Party and state, but also created a minor row between Foreign Ministry officials, who insisted that the manuscript had to be changed before publication, and historians of the Skodvin school, who refused to alter anything of substance.[49]

Having turned back – or rather absorbed – the Seipian challenge, graduates from the Skodvin school have been tilling their fields without serious encounters with historians from other subdisciplines, including Seip's own speciality, political history. International historians have constituted a separate community, spe-

44 See Benum 1969.
45 It is indicative that Seip, in his 1963 essay describing the Labour Party establishment's iron grip on the Norwegian state, ignores foreign policy-making and the international environment (Seip 1963).
46 For example, Eriksen 1972; Lundestad 1977a.
47 Tamnes 1986c; Eriksen and Pharo 1994. Tamnes even suggests there exists a third school, the "Hernes school", although he is unable to find any international historians to fit into this category.
48 Waage 1989.
49 Waage had been allowed privileged access to Foreign Ministry documents. The Ministry, basing its claim on its right to check the manuscript before publication, eventually backed down.

cializing in their discipline and taking only a limited interest in exchanges with their more nationally oriented colleagues.[50] This lack of interchange and interest has been fully reciprocated by non-international Norwegian historians. It is perhaps part of the explanation for the concluding observation of this chapter, namely the isolation of international historians from trends shaping the rest of Norwegian historical culture.

International history as an appendix

One can discern two major categories in Norwegian international history: foreign policy decision-making and international relations. (Most studies include both themes but concentrate on one or the other.) On decision-making, the policy-making role of bureaucrats has received particular attention;[51] regarding international relations, Norway's pursuit of security has dominated. This dual emphasis, on decision-making and international relations, sets international historians apart from most of their history colleagues and has made international history an appendix to the main body of Norwegian historiography in two ways.

First, to the limited degree that they make any explicit use of theory at all, Norwegian international historians draw on theories and models from political science (including international relations).[52] One might argue that international historians are thus in

50 There are nuances to this picture. For example, both Pharo and Tønnesson have published monographs on Norwegian sports history (!).
51 Waage 1989 and Førland 1991a and 1991b focus explicitly on bureaucratic foreign policy-making and illuminate the decision-making power of officials. Also belonging to this category are some of Pharo's development aid studies (1986b and 1987b in particular), which lack of space has squeezed from this treatment, and two Svalbard studies: Eriksen 1989 and Holtsmark 1993. The latter is remarkable for showing how Soviet Foreign Ministry officials in 1944–6 pressed for an aggressive Svalbard policy.
52 Of the scholars mentioned in the immediately preceding note, only Førland (esp. 1991b:307–9) employs or relates his findings to decision-making theory, i.e. so-called bureaucratic politics and presidential decision-making. Among Norwegian international relations historians, Tamnes and Lundestad in recent works have exhibited theoretical inclinations, Tamnes (1991a:17–31) with regard to geopolitics and Lundestad (1990 and 1994) with regard to empires: the term and their fall.

fact students of past decision-making and international relations, and have nothing in common with fellow (political) historians but their methods – critical scrutiny of archival evidence.

Second, Norwegian international historians have stood apart from the basic trend of Norwegian historiography (including political history) of the last decades, recently described as "distinguished by the fundamental importance accorded to social factors."[53] Norwegian historians are overwhelmingly concerned with various aspects of socio-economic change. Modernization in general, and industrialization and democratization in particular, figure prominently in almost any recent work on Norwegian nineteenth- and twentieth-century history. Historical studies concerning the post-war period accord similar significance to the development of corporate capitalism, the power of social democracy, and the welfare state. These concepts are conspicuously absent from Norwegian international historiography, which focuses on agents rather than structures, on power relations rather than ideology,[54] and almost all of which is written not only as if the developments caught by the term "modernization" have no relevance – partly explicable by the focus on the period after 1905 – but also as if the evolution of corporate capitalism, social democracy, and the welfare state can be just as easily ignored.[55]

Statist analysis without a social dimension may be the approach best suited to those themes which Norwegian international historians have studied. Modernization and the development of post-war western societies might not have much explanatory power for foreign policy-making and international relations. On the other hand, the achievements of the so-called corporatist school in US international history, which has successfully incorporated socio-economic developments in its interpretation of twentieth-century American foreign policy, indicate that the effort might be worth while.[56] It is, of course, "no small thing to combine mat-

53 Sejersted 1994:241.
54 Except parts of Tvedt 1990, in which development aid is seen in a long-term international relations perspective, namely as cultural imperialism.
55 Pharo 1989 may be counted as an exception.
56 Erdmann 1993:171–3 gives a sympathetic introduction to corporatist historiography, as well as basic references.

ters of social structure, historical change and international relations in a single analysis."[57] Indeed, to integrate these different parts into one body – which incidentally would mean integrating Norwegian international history into the culture of Norwegian historiography – is likely to prove much like Norway's pursuit of security: a long-term quest where success is never certain but where the alternative, certain failure through not trying, is even less satisfactory.

57 Scholte 1994:22.

List of Contributors

Sverre Bagge	University of Bergen
Ida Blom	University of Bergen
Tor Egil Førland	University of Oslo
William H. Hubbard	University of Bergen and Concordia University, Montreal
Knut Kjeldstadli	University of Bergen
Even Lange	Norwegian School of Management, Oslo
Sivert Langholm	University of Oslo
Kåre Lunden	University of Oslo
Jan Eivind Myhre	University of Trondheim and University of Tromsø
Einar Niemi	University of Tromsø
Trond Nordby	University of Oslo
Helge W. Nordvik	Norwegian School of Economics and Business Administration, Bergen
Øystein Rian	University of Oslo
Francis Sejersted	University of Oslo
Sølvi Sogner	University of Oslo
Harald Winge	Institute of Local History, National Archive, Oslo

Addresses may be obtained through Scandinavian University Press, Oslo.

Résumés des articles

traduits par Finn Fuglestad, avec la collaboration de Viviane Fuglestad-Aumeunier

1. *Kåre Lunden, Histoire et société*

L'article donne d'abord un aperçu de la géographie, de la société et de l'histoire de la Norvège. Le trait saillant de son histoire est la perte de l'indépendence au 14e siècle. En effet entre 1319 et 1905 le pays se trouva dans un état de subordination (de jure ou de facto selon les époques) à l'égard de ses voisins. Ce trait a fortement marqué la production historique. On peut dire que les questions concernant la souveraineté de la Norvège constituent l'un des thèmes principaux de l'historiographie norvégienne, et ce depuis le moyen âge.

Les plus anciens récits historiques, les sagas des rois de Norvège, qui datent du 13e siècle, reflètent et expliquent la croissance du royaume norvégien. La maigre littérature historique de l'époque de l'union avec le Danemark, au moins jusqu'au 18e siècle, est basée principalement sur les sagas du Moyen Âge, et avait comme fonction essentielle de maintenir la conscience de l'existence de la Norvège en tant qu'unité distincte avec sa propre identité.

Quant aux historiens du 18e et du 19e siècles, ils cherchèrent avant tout à démontrer que le peuple norvégien était l'un des plus "anciens" de l'Europe avec un passé prestigieux. Ce point de vue fut même explicitement formulé pendant les années 1830 dans un manifeste de "L'école historique norvégienne".

Après l'indépandance en 1905, le rapport entre l'évolution sociale et la manière d'écrire l'histoire se transforma progressivement. Cette tendance fut encore plus marquée après la deuxième guerre mondiale et peut être liée, entre autres, à l'augmentation spectaculaire du nombre d'historiens et à la différenciation thématique qui s'en suivit. Presque tous les aspects de l'évolution historique de la société et de la culture norvégiennes furent progressivement inté-

grés au domaine de l'histoire. Mais du coup le lien traditionnellement fort entre l'histoire, la politique et le social se distendit considérablement et la spécificité professionnelle des historiens devint
plus confuse.
L'histoire locale occupe une position centrale au sein de la littérature historique norvégienne. Cela est à rapprocher du fait que la
périphérie ne s'est jamais laissée véritablement dominer par le centre dans ce pays très étendu et peu peuplé. On peut dire à ce propos
qu'il existe une forte tradition de méfiance à l'égard des "centres",
qu'ils soient nationaux ou plus récemment européens.

2. Knut Kjeldstadli, L'histoire en tant que science
Une approche possible de l'historiographie moderne norvégienne,
qui remonte aux années 1830, est de focaliser sur les cinq génération d'historiens qui se sont succédées depuis. Chaque génération
peut être attachée à l'un des principaux courants de pensée qui ont
marqué l'évolution intellectuelle de l'Occident. La première génération, dite "l'école norvégienne" et dont les figures emblématiques
étaient Peter Andreas Munch et Rudolf Keyser, avait de fortes affi-
nités avec l'école historique allemande. Quant à Ernst Sars, qui do-
mina le milieu historique à partir des années 1870, il était très in-
fluencé par ce qu'il est convenu d'appeler "l'évolutionnisme idéa-
liste". A partir des années 1910 la relève fut assurée par des historiens marxisants, tels Halvdan Koht et Edvard Bull. Les historiens
les plus en vue de la génération de la fin des années trente aux années soixante, Sverre Steen, Jens Arup Seip et Andreas Holmsen,
étaient, eux, empreints d'une sorte de mélange de matéralisme dit
de bon sens et de fonctionnalisme. Quant à la génération montante
des années soixante-dix et quatre-vingt, son intention semble avoir
été de privilégier la théorie critique.
   Cette évolution n'est certes pas propre au milieu historique norvégien. Notons cependant au niveau des particularités:
1) Un fort penchant pour "l'histoire des sociétés", c'est-à-dire pour
   une histoire "ethnographisante"; ceci à cause de l'absence pendant des siècles d'un état norvégien, le "peuple" représentant
   en quelque sorte la continuité.
2) que le matérialisme dit de bon sens hérité de l'époque marxi-

sante s'est maintenu grâce à l'hégémonie des courants socialistes et sociaux-libéraux parmi les historiens.

3) que le climat intellectuel a oscillé entre l'approche analytique et synthétique. L'approche synthétique semble être surtout prisée pendant les périodes de crise. Quant à l'"évolutionnisme" d'Ernst Sars, il fut le compagnon intellectuel de la lutte politique en faveur d'un régime parlementaire (lutte menée à bien en 1884). La montée du marxisme correspondait, elle, à la crise sociale du capitalisme. Et l'orientation contemporaine vers une approche plus synthétisante peut être interprétée comme un reflet de la crise morale et culturelle qui caractérise actuellement la société norvégienne.

4) on note, nonobstant les changements au niveau de l'orientation théorique, une certaine continuité, en ce sens qu'aucune des générations successives n'a totalement rejeté l'héritage des précédentes. La raison majeure semble en être le fort accent mis depuis toujours sur l'histoire nationale. Jusqu'à présent l'état-nation est en effet considéré comme le cadre référentiel naturel des historiens norvégiens.

L'article décrit l'évolution conceptuelle de l'histoire en tant que science et cherche à l'expliquer par deux approches, l'une interne qui prend comme point de départ l'évolution intellectuelle, et l'autre externe, à travers la société en général; et finalement en analysant les mécanismes d'investigation à l'intérieur de la recherche historique et de l'enseignement universitaire de l'histoire

3. Sivert Langholm, L'infrastructure de l'histoire
Une chaire d'histoire fut l'une des premières à être établies dans la nouvelle Université de Christiania (Oslo), fondée en 1813. Après une longue période de croissance continue mais modeste jusque après la deuxième guerre mondiale, le nombre d'étudiants et de postes connut un essor considérable à partir de 1960. Aujourd'hui l'histoire est enseignée dans les quatre universités norvégiennes de Oslo, Bergen, Trondheim et Tromsø, ainsi que dans plusieurs collèges régionaux. Le nombre total d'étudiants en histoire était en 1992 aux alentours de 2000. Un important chaînon dans la structure formative universitaire est le "hovedfag" (à mi-chemin entre

la Maîtrise et le 3e cycle dans le système français) avec sa dissertation. Le "hovedfag" fonctionne en pratique comme la première étape majeure dans l'initiation à la recherche. Entre 1989 et 1992 environ 45 candidats en moyenne annuelle obtinrent leur diplôme de "hovedfag" et le nombre va croissant. Le secteur universitaire norvégien comptait en 1993 soixante-six professeurs et maîtres de conférence d'histoire. A cela s'ajoute un grand nombre d'assistants et d'attachés de recherche. La discipline historique est en général organisée en départements autonomes, l'exception étant l'Université de Tromsø ou la discipline fait partie du Département pluridisciplinaire des Sciences Sociales. L'histoire économique n'est nulle part constituée comme une discipline ou une entité administrative à part. Beaucoup d'historiens sont engagés dans de la recherche dite sur commande, notamment au niveau de l'histoire locale, une discipline traditionnellement très importante en Norvège.

Le Conseil National de la Recherche Scientifique a joué un rôle considérable pour le développement de la recherche historique en Norvège. Parmi les autres institutions centrales il convient naturellement de mentionner surtout les Archives Nationales (Riksarkivet), établies en 1817. La plus importante association d'historiens est la Société historique norvégienne, qui date de 1869, et qui fut réorganisée comme une société professionnelle en 1990. Elle publie notamment la Revue Norvégienne d'Histoire (Historisk Tidsskrift). D'autres revues sont "Heimen" (littéralement "Le foyer") publiée par la Société d'histoire locale, et les deux revues pan-scandinaves, à savoir le Scandinavian Journal of History et le Scandinavian Economic History Review.

4. Sverre Bagge, Le moyen âge
Depuis le début du XIXe siècle, la recherche historique norvégienne sur le moyen âge s'est attachée, d'une part, à souligner l'importance de cette période, âge de la grandeur norvégienne, d'autre part à rédiger une série de grandes synthèses qui précèdent l'historiographie norvégienne concernant le moyen âge semble être caractérisée par deux faits: d'abord l'importance nationale de la période en tant que l'âge de la grandeur de la Norvège; et ensuite une

série de grandes narratives ou synthèses qui furent l'oeuvre principalement d'historiens dits de gauche. Ces historiens cherchèrent à
leur manière à expliquer l'émergence, puis le déclin de la nation, et
à relier le passé au présent. Les plus importants furent Ernst Sars,
qui écrivit à la fin du siècle dernier, Halvdan Koht et Edvard Bull,
deux historiens marxisants de la première moitié de ce siècle. Par
contre, durant la période antérieure à Sars, puis – et surtout –
après 1945, les historiens ont porté leur attention sur des problèmes plus spécifiques et ont été davantage préoccupés par les problèmes posés par les sources. On note cependant depuis quelques
années un regain d'intérêt pour une approche plus synthétisante.
Cette approche semble être inspirée par les sciences sociales et par
l'histoire des mentalités en France et semble donc peu liée à des
considérations d'ordre politique et national.

5. Øystein Rian, La période d'union avec le Danemark
La periode d'union avec le Danemark (1380–1814) fut peu étudiée
par la première génération d'historiens après 1814. Ces historiens
portèrent par ailleurs un regard assez negatif sur cette période
pendant laquelle les norvégiens n'avaient eu, selon eux, guère de
prise sur leur propre destin. Les choses changèrent à partir des années 1860 avec l'éclosion d'une nouvelle génération d'historiens.
On peut classer ces "nouveaux" historiens en deux écoles, une
école dite conservatrice, et une autre dite national-démocrate. Les
historiens de l'école dite conservatrice s'intéressèrent surtout aux
causes de la perte de souveraineté et faisaient valoir que les conditions économiques et démographiques expliquèrent pourquoi la
Norvège se trouva pendant si longtemps dans une position de subordination à l'égard du Danemark. Ils soulignèrent cependant les
signes de renouveau à partir du 16e siècle. Ceux de l'école dite national-démocrate, qui s'érigèrent souvent en juges du passé, con-
damnèrent sévèrement la perte de souveraineté. Mais ils faisaient
valoir que la paysannerie norvégienne était pendant cette période
parmi les mieux loties en Europe du fait de la faiblesse de l'aristo-
cratie locale.

L'école dite matérialiste qui émergea au début de ce siècle con-
tribua à mettre l'accent sur l'histoire économique de cette époque.

C'est ainsi qu'on assista à partir des années 1920 à une efflore-
cence d'études d'histoire agraire. Parmi les thèmes étudiés on note
surtout la répartition et l'oscillation du nombre des exploitations
agricoles, ainsi que les problèmes liés au droit foncier. L'éventail
des thèmes de la recherche s'élargissait considérablement à partir
des années 1970 et des problèmes liés aux rapports de force entre
les différentes catégories de la population furent systématiquement
étudiés à partir de ce moment là.

Quelques grands débats ont marqué l'historiographie durant les
derniers cent ans: le niveau de la pression fiscale, le rôle et la position des paysans, le conflit entre les tendances autoritaires et con-
stitutionnelles, l'évolution démographique, les relations entre les
différentes couches sociales, et l'influence de l'économie de marché
sur l'économie de subsistance de la paysannerie.

6. *Francis Sejersted, Approches de l'histoire moderne norvégienne*
L'article prend comme point de départ la revolte contre l'histori-
cisme et les synthèses totalisantes qui marquèrent les années
1950. L'article montre que cette revolte n'eut en réalité pas d'effets
notables. L'auteur en veut pour preuve le fait que chacun des trois
historiens les plus en vue de l'époque (Steen, Seip et Bull fils) elabora
une synthèse de l'évolution historique de la Norvège dont le but
était d'expliquer l'émergence de l'état social-démocrate. Ces synthèses sont analysées dans l'article à l'aide des concepts de Hayden
White, à savoir respectivement la comédie, la satire et la tragédie.
Un quatrième genre, la romance, est representée par un trait parti-
culier de l'historiographie norvégienne, la mise sur chantier à peu
près tous les vingt ans d'une histoire norvégienne multi-volumes.

La recherche historique norvégienne a longtemps mis l'accent
sur le rôle et l'importance des facteurs d'ordre social. On note cependant, à partir des années 1980, un nouvel intérêt pour le rôle
des institutions. Il s'agirait d'une révolte contre la révolte des années cinquante.

7. *Trond Nordby, Construire l'état et la nation*
L'état norvégien fut consolidé en tant qu'unité politique et administrative au 19e siècle. Ceci dans le cadre de l'union personnelle

avec la Suède (1814–1905). Au moment où la Norvège obtint son indépendance (en 1905) l'emprise de l'état sur la société s'était déjà considérablement renforcée par rapport à 1814. Le fait qu'une écrasante majorité opta pour la dissolution de l'union lors du referendum de 1905 démontre par ailleurs les progrès accomplis au niveau de l'identification nationale.

Pendant la période où la Norvège devint véritablement un pays industrialisé, c'est-à-dire les dernières décennies avant la première guerre mondiale, on assista à une radicalisation et donc à une marginalisation de la classe ouvrière. Cette radicalisation toucha également le parti travailliste. Mais après avoir adhéré pendant quelque temps à l'internationale communiste, les travaillistes adoptèrent une position plus réformiste à partir de 1923. En 1935 le parti accepta la responsabilité du gouvernement d'une société capitaliste en crise. L'arrivée au pouvoir du parti travailliste confirma l'intégration de la classe ouvrière au sein de la communauté nationale.

On notera, par rapport aux thèmes principaux de l'article, que les historiens les plus influents de la deuxième moitié du 19e siècle cherchèrent à renforcer la conscience nationale de la société. Leurs analyses étaient de ce fait fortement appuyées sur une argumentation nationaliste. Les historiens cherchèrent en même temps à élaborer des synthèses susceptibles de capter le jeu conjugué des évolutions sociétale, culturelle et politico-institutionnelle. Ce paradigme orienté vers la synthèse fut le trait marquant de la recherche norvégienne jusqu'à la deuxième guerre mondiale.

L'après-guerre constitua cependant une rupture, caractérisée par un scepticisme profond à l'égard des synthèses, ainsi que par une plus grande rigueur au niveau empirique. On s'intéressa davantage à des questions de motivation, notamment en ce qui concerne les élites politiques. Mais il est à remarquer qu'on ne tenta point d'insérer des idéologies comme le nationalisme dans un contexte social et économique. Nous sommes redevables à cette génération d'historiens de travaux qui ont contribué à approfondir notre compréhension des institutions politiques et des partis politiques.

Depuis les années 70 on assiste de nouveau à une réorientation vers une manière plus synthétisante d'écrire l'histoire. L'un des points de départs a été la forte et continue tradition de recherche en histoire sociale. Mais ce changement de paradigme doit également être mis en rapport avec l'émergence du neo-marxisme qui a connu une percée au sein de l'intelligentsia norvégienne après 1968. Par rapport aux thèmes principaux de cet article, le thème de l'évolution et du développement de l'état a été pendant longtemps celui qui a suscité le plus d'intérêt parmi les historiens. On note cependant un regain d'intérêt pour les problèmes liés à ce qu'il est convenu d'appeller la construction de la nation. L'auteur de l'article, ayant beaucoup travaillé sur ces problèmes, termine, en décrivant d'une manière détaillée – et en prenant comme point de départ les travaux politico-sociologiques de Stein Rokkan – précisément le processus de la construction de la nation norvégienne.

8. Jan Eivind Myhre, L'histoire sociale
L'évolution de l'histoire sociale en Norvège peut être divisée en deux phases bien distinctes, avant et après 1970. Ce n'est en effet qu'après 1970 qu'on peut parler d'historiens spécialisés dans l'histoire sociale. Avant les années soixante-dix l'histoire sociale faisait en quelque sorte partie intégrante de l'histoire générale. Ou plus exactement, l'histoire générale était dans une large mesure l'histoire de la société norvégienne et non par exemple celle de la politique norvégienne (on notera au passage que très peu d'historiens s'intéressèrent à l'histoire extra-norvégienne). Ceci s'explique notamment par le fait que la Norvège fut pendant longtemps dominée par ses voisins. C'était donc au niveau de la société, et non au niveau de la politique ou du gouvernement qu'on retrouvait la spécificité et la continuité nationales.

L'essor d'une histoire sociale distincte de l'histoire générale à partir du début des années soixante-dix peut être liée à la radicalisation du milieu historique, ainsi qu'à l'augmentation considérable du nombre d'étudiants. Une histoire vue autrement, une histoire des "sans-grades", ceux qui avaient été négligés jusque là, devint à la mode. Les historiens se mirent à souligner la contribution des masses, et faisaient valoir que l'histoire sociale devait être basée sur des théories et des méthodes empruntées aux sciences sociales.
Un trait marquant de l'histoire sociale norvégienne est l'appro-

che micro-historique de Sivert Langholm et ses adeptes, et la variante anthropologique ou culturelle de Bull et ses acolytes. Bien que l'histoire sociale doive sa position actuelle en grande partie à l'histoire locale professionnelle, on peut dire qu'elle a réussi à garder une perspective globalisante. En effet, les spécialistes de l'histoire sociale ont toujours cherché à placer les sujets sur lesquels ils travaillent, et quels qu'ils soient, dans un contexte plus vaste, tels l'industrialisation, l'urbanisation et la transformation du monde rural après les années 1850.

9. Harald Winge, L'histoire locale

L'article présente un survol de l'histoire dite locale: ses origines, son évolution et sa position actuelle en tant que mouvement populaire et en tant que l'une des branches de la recherche historique. Les principaux genres littéraires consacrés à l'histoire locale norvégienne sont présentés. Un genre important est constitué par ce qui est appelé en norvégien "bygdebøker" (littéralement "livres cantonaux"), un terme intraduisible strictement parlant, mais qui qualifie les monographies consacrées à l'histoire d'une communauté locale, que ce soit une exploitation agricole et la famille qui s'y attache, ou une municipalité, rurale ou urbaine. Aujourd'hui la majorité de ces monographies est écrite par des historiens professionnels. Mais comme il s'agit d'ouvrages destinés à un public local, le genre en question pose des problèmes particuliers aux historiens. Comment en effet satisfaire les exigences du public auquel il est destiné tout en maintenant un niveau scientifique acceptable? L'article propose différentes manières d'y parvenir.

10. Even Lange et Helge W. Nordvik, L'histoire économique

En Norvège l'histoire économique fut reconnue comme un sujet d'étude à part entière il y a seulement une génération. L'article retrace les origines de cette branche depuis le siècle dernier, au moment où une tradition puissante de statistique déscriptive émergea.

Au vingtième siècle les historiens universitaires ont dominé l'histoire économique au détriment des économistes. Les conséquences ont été d'abord que cette branche s'est développée en tant

que sous-discipline de l'histoire, aussi bien sur le plan institution-
nel que sur le plan thématique (quoiqu'on trouvât pendant longtemps parmi ceux qui pratiquèrent l'histoire économique bon
nombre d'écrivains formés par les sciences sociales ou venant du
journalisme). Parmi les autres conséquences on notera la place importante occupée par le "business history" (histoire des affaires
et/ou des entreprises); le lien assez lâche entre l'histoire économique et l'histoire sociale; et le rôle assez marginal jusqu'à récemment de la théorie économique et des méthodes quantitatives.

La branche est maintenant solidement établie comme une matière à part entière dans les universités norvégiennes, ainsi que
dans les Ecoles des Hautes Etudes Commerciales, surtout à Oslo et
à Bergen. Les spécialistes de l'histoire économique se sont surtout
intéressés à l'histoire des technologies et au "business history" particulièrement dans l'industrie. En plus la modernisation des activi-
tés liées à la pêche, à l'exploitation des forêts et à l'agriculture, ainsi
que le rôle important joué par la marine marchande dans le développement de l'économie nationale ont suscité l'intérêt des chercheurs. Le soutien d'entreprises aussi bien privées que publiques,
notamment en commanditant des monographies, ont puissament
contribué à élargir le rôle de l'histoire économique au sein de l'historiographie norvégienne.

11. Ida Blom, L'histoire des femmes
Après avoir rappelé les maigres traditions de la recherche en matière d'histoire des femmes, qui remontent en ce qui concerne la
Norvège au 18e siècle, l'article retrace le développement de cette
nouvelle approche en histoire depuis les années 1970. L'histoire
des femmes est perçue en partie comme la conséquence du besoin
d'une identité historique féminine, un besoin lié à la montée du
mouvement féministe. L'article présente un résumé de la recherche effectuée dans ce domaine en Norvège, ainsi que des discussions qui ont eu lieu entre les historiens concernant les problèmes
de définition et de méthodologie. Une évaluation critique des concepts clés ainsi qu'une approche sceptique à l'égard des théories de
patriarcat ont caractérisé cette recherche.

Des analyses des relations entre sexe et "gender",[1] entre biologie et culture en somme, ont ouvert la voie vers une discussion des theories concernant les systèmes de "gender". Ceci, ainsi que l'influence de l'analyse culturelle et des théories post-structuralistes ont abouti à élargir le domaine de l'histoire des femmes, devenue en fait "gender history".

La discussion concernant la pertinence de "gender" et des rapports entre les sexes pour la compréhension du passé est âpre en Norvège comme ailleurs. Les opinions exprimées reflètent en grande partie le niveau d'intégration de l'histoire des femmes, ce niveau étant particulièrement bas en histoire politique. On note cependant un intérêt croissant pour les concepts et les modes d'analyse mis au point par cette nouvelle branche de l'histoire.

Les spécialistes norvégiens ont noué des contacts étroits au niveau international et ont contribué à l'élaboration du consensus qui s'est petit à petit dégagé concernant la méthodologie en matière de recherche du "gender history". On notera enfin que la longue tradition égalitaire qui caractérise la société norvégienne explique peut-être pourquoi en Norvège une compréhension contextuelle plutôt que essentialiste de "gender" prévaut.

1 un mot anglais intraduisible, mais qui se refère aux constructions sociales et surtout culturelles concernant les deux sexes.

12. William H. Hubbard, La démographie historique

A part quelques cas isolés, la recherche historique sur la population de la Norvège ne commença qu'à la fin des années 60. Dans la décennie suivante la discipline fut développé par des universitaires qui s'inspirèrent des méthodes mises au point par l'école française d'histoire démographique. La technique de reconstruction familiale élaborée par Louis Henry fut surtout à l'honneur.

Trois thèmes ont surtout retenu l'attention des chercheurs: les crises démographiques et le début du déclin de la mortalité au 18e siècle (c'est-à-dire le début de la transition démographique); le déclin de la fécondité vers la fin du 19e siècle; et l'émigration. En revanche des thèmes comme la nuptialité, l'évolution de la structure familiale et le flux migratoire interne ont été quelque peu negligés. Le cadre géographique habituel de la majeure partie des études est la paroisse. Compte tenu des grandes disparités qu'on enregistre même entre des localités relativement proches, on peut dire que nous sommes encore loin d'avoir une vue d'ensemble suffisamment précise de l'évolution du "comportement" démographique des norvégiens. On note par ailleurs, depuis quelques années, un certain essoufllement de la recherche. Mais il est permis de penser que le développement de l'informatique contribuera à la relancer.

13. Einar Niemi, L'histoire des minorités: les lappons et les kvènes
Le thème de l'article est la recherche historique concernant les lappons et les kvènes, les deux minorités ethniques du nord de la Norvège. L'hypothèse est que intérêt du monde scientifique pour ces deux minorités a oscillé en fonction de l'attention (elle-même très variable) que la communauté norvégienne leur a portée.

Ce n'est qu`à partir du début du 18e siècle qu'on peut parler d'une politique clairement définie à l'égard des minorités du nord; c'est-à-dire à partir de l'installation des premiers missionnaires norvégiens parmi les lappons. Cette politique, dont la littérature scientifique de l'époque se fait l'écho, peut être qualifiée de "bienveillante", surtout sur le plan linguistique.

On constate cependant un changement très net d'attitude des autorités norvégiennes à l'égard des minorités à partir du milieu du 19e siècle. La nouvelle politique peut être caractérisée comme étant une politique stricte d'assimilation. Elle fut maintenue jusqu'à la deuxième guerre mondiale et elle peut s'expliquer par des considérations militaro-stratégiques liées à la sécurité du Royame. Ceci n'empêcha cependant pas les lappons de continuer à jouir d'une certaine sympathie en tant que population indigène. Bon nombre de leurs droits héréditaires furent maintenus. La littérature (surtout ethnographique et linguistique) de l'époque concernant les lappons est étendue. Il s'agit en fait de l'âge d'or de la "lapponologie". Il n'en demeure pas moins que des attitudes paternalistes et social-darwinistes, voire racistes, commencèrent petit à petit à se manifester.

Après 1945 la politique à l'égard des lappons fut progressivement modifiée, et se transforma en une politique dite pluraliste. Mais les kvènes continuèrent à être negligés, aussi bien par les au-

torités que par les chercheurs. La recherche lappone de son côté
connut un remarquable essor, et un renouveau prononcé, le tout
en grande partie grâce à l'évolution politique. Après 1970 environ
les kvènes furent également "découverts" par les chercheurs, un
phénomène qui est probablement lié à la montée générale de l'intérêt pour les cultures des minorités et des questions d'ethnicité. Surtout des disciplines comme l'histoire, la linguistique (y compris la
linguistique sociologique) et l'ethnologie se sont montrées actives.
Par contre, les nouvelles sciences sociales ont continué à privilégier les études lappones.

On peut dire somme toute que les historiens n'ont rejoint la recherche sur les minorités que très tardivement. Leur contribution
a surtout été axée sur les domaines de l'histoire démographique et
économique, ainsi que de l'histoire de l'ethnopolitique et de la politique à l'égard des minorités, puis sur celui de l'histoire locale et regionale. On note depuis peu un certain intérêt pour l'histoire du
droit.

14. Sølvi Sogner, L'histoire des mentalités – l'histoire culturelle
Les historiens norvégiens, quand ils cherchent à dégager les motivations et les causes qui expliquent le processus historique, ont traditionnellement tendance à privilégier les facteurs d'ordre économique au détriment de ceux d'orde culturel. La conception matérialiste de l'histoire prédomine en effet dans l'école historique norvégienne aussi. Cette dominance fut en quelque sorte renforcée par
l'attrait exercé, au début de ce siècle, par des théories raciales qui
établirent un lien entre les caractéristiques physiologiques et mentales des peuples. Ces théories furent certes rapidement discredi-
tées, mais elles dissuadèrent un peu plus les historiens de chercher
des explications au niveau des mentalités et des attitudes.

C'est seulement depuis quelques années, sous l'influence de l'é-
cole des Annales, qu'on assiste à un regain d'intérêt pour les mentalités en tant que variable explicative. Mais il ne s'agit nullement
d'une percée véritable pour ce genre d'approche.

La "nouvelle histoire culturelle" a été dans un certain sens
mieux accueillie, puisqu'elle met l'accent sur le conscient et non le
subconscient. Les sources et les méthodes des historiens sont en ef-

fet mieux à même de percer la manière dont les acteurs historiques tentèrent consciemment de manipuler leur époque, que de cerner leurs structures mentales au niveau du subconscient. Il y a aujourd'hui une tendance de plus en plus marquée parmi les historiens – même parmi ceux qui s'occupent d'histoire économique – de prendre en considération la dimension culturelle au sens large.

15. Tor Egil Førland, Histoire internationale
Les relations extérieures de la Norvège constituent toujours la partie dominante de l'histoire internationale telle qu'elle est conçue en Norvège. Dans la première partie de l'article sont discutés cinq thèmes: l'attaque allemande du 9 avril 1940; la signature du traité de l'Atlantique-nord en 1949; la politique de défense et de sécurité dans la longue durée; la politique d'alliances; et l'attitude à l'égard de l'intégration européenne. Cette première partie contient également un rappel du nombre croissant d'études d'histoire internationale faites en Norvège mais qui ne concernent pas ce pays.

Dans la deuxième partie de l'article l'auteur cherche à dégager les traits dominants de l'histoire internationale en Norvège. Le point de vue de l'auteur est que cette discipline, qui embrasse le monde entier sur le plan thématique, est caractérisée par une cohérence et une unité de méthode très fortes. Les historiens norvégiens spécialisés en matière d'histoire internationale sont en effet empiristes à l'extrême; ils ne sont pas particulièrement préoccupés par des problèmes de méthode ou d'ordre théorique. On constate par ailleurs qu'ils respectent leurs "chasses gardées" respectives et qu'ils ne contestent que rarement les interprétations de leurs collègues. L'explication de ce phénomène réside peut-être dans le fait qu'il n'existe en réalité qu'une seule école d'histoire internationale, celle dite de Skodvin.

La conclusion de l'article est que les spécialistes de l'histoire internationale, en concentrant leur attention sur la manière dont la politique étrangère est élaborée et sur les relations internationales, tout en ignorant l'évolution sociale, ont fait de leur discipline un élément quelque peu marginal de l'historiographie norvégienne.

List of References

Agerholt, Caspari Anna. 1973 (1st ed. 1937). *Den norske kvinnebevegelses historie.* Oslo.

Ahlmann, Hans W. 1962. *Norge. Natur og næringsliv.* Oslo.

Alsvik, Ola. 1993. *Fagfelt og folkerørsle. Norsk lokalhistorie i det 20. århundre.* Oslo.

Amdam, Rolv Petter. 1991. Industrial espionage and the transfer of technology to the early Norwegian glass industry. In Bruland 1991.

Amdam, Rolv Petter. 1993. *For egen regning: BI og den økonomisk–administrative utdanningen 1943–1993.* Oslo.

Amdam, Rolv Petter. 1994. Foreign influence on the education of Norwegian Business Managers before World War II. *Business History* 36:79–94.

Amdam, Rolv Petter, Tore Jørgen Hanisch, and Ingvild Pharo. 1989. *Vel blåst! Christiania Glasmagasin og norsk glassindustri 1739–1989.* Oslo.

Amdam, Rolv Petter, and Even Lange (eds.). 1994. *Crossing the Borders. Studies in Norwegian Business History.* Oslo.

Amdam, Rolv Petter, and Knut Sogner. 1994. *Rik på kontraster. Nyegaard & Co – en norsk farmasøytisk industribedrift 1874–1985.* Oslo.

Amundsen, Leiv. 1961a. *Universitetet i Oslo 1911–1961,* Vol. I. Oslo.

Amundsen, Leiv. 1961b. *Det historisk-filosofiske fakultet. Universitetet i Oslo 1911–1961,* Vol. II:63–88. Oslo.

Andersen, Håkon With. 1989a. *Fra det britiske til det amerikanske produksjonsideal. Forandringer av tekinologi og arbeid ved Aker mek. Verksted og i norsk skipsbyggingsindustri 1935–1970.* Trondheim.

Andersen, Håkon With. 1989b. Norsk skipsbyggingsindustri gjennom 100 år. In Lange 1989.

Andersen, Håkon With. 1991. Laggards as Leaders: Some Reflections on Technological Diffusion in Norwegian Shipping 1870–1940. In Bruland 1991.

Andersen, Håkon With. 1994. Mennesker, meninger og medlemmer – En skisse av nye muligheter for en kulturhistorie. In H. W. Andersen *et al.* (eds.), *Clios tro tjener. Festskrift til Per Fuglum:*13–44. Trondheim.

Andersen, Håkon With, and John P. Collett. 1989. *Anchor and Balance: Det Norske Veritas 1864–1989.* Oslo.

Andersen, Per Sveaas. 1960. *Rudolf Keyser. Embetsmenn og historiker.* Oslo.

Andersen, Per Sveaas. 1977. *Samlingen av Norge og kristningen av landet 800–1130.* Oslo.

Anderson, Benedict. 1983. *Imagined Communities.* London.

Andreasen, Tayo (ed.). 1991. *Moving On. New Perspectives on the Women's Movement.* Acta Jutlandica LXVII:1. Humanities Series 66. Århus.

Andresen, Astri. 1989. *Sii'daen som forsvant. Østsamene i Pasvik etter den norsk–russiske grensetrekning i 1926.* Kirkenes.

Andresen, Astri. 1991. *Omstillingstid. Nomadisk reindrift i Torne lappmark og Troms 1840–1920.* Unpublished doctoral dissertation. University of Tromsø.

Annual Report, University of Oslo. See *Aarsberetning, Det Kongelige Frederiks Universitets / Årsberetning. Universitetet i Oslo.*

Aschehoug, Torkel H. 1866. *Statsforfatningen i Norge og Danmark indtil 1814.* Christiania.

Aubert, Vilhelm. 1968. Den samiske minoriteten i lagdelingsstrukturen. In N. R. Ramsøy (ed.), *Det norske samfunn.* Oslo.

Aubert, Vilhelm, 1969. Ein nasjonal eller ein sosial minoritet? In L. R. Homme (ed.), *Nordisk nykolonialisme.* Oslo.

Aubert, Vilhelm, *et al.* 1970. *Isolation and Integration. A Community Study in Northern Norway.* Oslo.

Aukrust, Odd. 1990. *Økonomisk forskning og debatt. Utvalgte artikler av Odd Aukrust.* Sosiale og økonomiske studier 75. Oslo.

Avdem, Anna Jorunn. 1984. *... gjort ka gjerast skulle. Om arbeid og levekår for kvinner på Lesja ca. 1910–1930.* Oslo.

Avdem, Anna Jorunn, and Kari Melby. 1985. *Oppe først og sist i seng. Husarbeid i Norge fra 1850 til i dag.* Oslo.

Backer, Julie E. 1947–8. Population Statistics and Population Registration in Norway. *Population Studies* 1:212–26 and 2:318–38.

Backer, Julie E. 1961. *Dødeligheten og dens årsaker i Norge 1856–1955.* Samfunnsøkonomiske studier 10. Oslo.

Backer, Julie E. 1965. *Ekteskap, fødsler og vandringer i Norge 1856–1960.* Samfunnsøkonomiske studier 13. Oslo.

Bagge, Sverre. 1987. *The Political Thought of the King's Mirror.* Odense.

Bagge, Sverre. 1989. Kvinner i politikken i middelalderen. *Onsdagskvelder i Bryggens Museum IV:*5–30. Bergen.

Bagge, Sverre. 1991. *Society and Politics in Snorri Sturluson's Heimskringla.* Berkeley, Calif.

Bagge, Sverre. 1992. Ekteskap og politikk. In Blom 1992e:353–9.

Bagge, Sverre. 1994. *Samfunnsvitenskapenes historie ved Universitetet i Bergen 1957–1994.* Unpublished manuscript. Bergen.

Bagge, Sverre. 1995. *From Gang Leader to the Lord's Anointed.* Odense.

Bagge, Sverre, and Knut Mykland. 1987. *Norge i dansketiden 1380–1814.* Oslo.

Bakkmoen, Per Kr. 1984. *Hushold i ei overgangstid. En sosialhistorisk undersøkelse av et arbeiderstrøk i Bergen 1900–1912.* Unpublished Master's thesis. University of Bergen.

Balsvik, Randi. 1989. *Vardø – grensepost og fiskevær.* 2 vols. Vardø.

Basberg, Bjørn. 1985. Technological Transformation of the Norwegian Whaling Industry in the Interwar Period. *Scandinavian Economic History Review* 33:83–107.

Basberg, Bjørn, and Ola H. Grytten. 1994. Økonometrisk historie. Iakttagelser om fagfeltets utvikling i Norge. *Historisk tidsskrift* 73:430–49.

Beckman, Svante. 1990. *Utväcklingens Hjälter.* Stockholm.

Benedictow, Ole Jørgen. 1977. *Fra rike til provins* (K. Mykland [ed.], *Norges historie,* Vol. 5). Oslo.

Benedictow, Ole Jørgen. 1985a. See Bjørgum and Benedictow 1985.

Benedictow, Ole Jørgen. 1985b. Reproduksjon og undertrykkelse. In Vogt 1985, Vol. 1:121–5.

Benedictow, Ole Jørgen. 1992. *Plague in the Late Medieval Nordic Countries: Epidemiological Studies*. Oslo.

Benum, Edgeir. 1969. *Maktsentra og Opposisjon*. Spaniasaken i Norge 1946 og 1947. Oslo.

Benum, Edgeir. 1979. *Sentraladministrasjonens historie*, Vol. 2, 1845–1884. Oslo.

Berg, Roald. 1985. "Det land vi venter hjælp af". England som Norges beskytter 1905–1908. *Forsvarsstudier* IV/1985:111–68. Oslo.

Berggreen, Brit. 1985. Fra kvinnebonde til bondekvinne. In Vogt 1985, Vol. 2:107–14.

Bergh, Trond. 1975. *Fra Fædrelandssag til storbank*. Norges Postsparebank 1950–1975. Oslo.

Bergh, Trond. 1987. *Storhetstid (1945–1965)* (E. Bull *et al.* [eds.], Arbeiderbevegelsens historie, Vol. 5). Oslo.

Bergh, Trond, and Tore J. Hanisch. 1984. *Vitenskap og politikk*. Linjer i norsk sosialøkonomi gjennom 150 år. Oslo.

Bergh, Trond, Tore J. Hanisch, Even Lange, and Helge Ø. Pharo. 1981. *Growth and Development. The Norwegian Experience 1830–1980*. Norwegian Foreign Policy Studies, No. 37. Oslo. (Norwegian edition 1983. *Norge fra u-land til i-land*. Oslo.)

Bergh, Trond, and Even Lange. 1989. *Foredlet virke. Historien om Borregaard 1889–1989*. Oslo.

Bergh, Trond, and Helge Ø. Pharo (eds.). 1977. *Vekst og velstand. Norsk politisk historie 1945–1965*. Oslo.

Bergh, Trond, and Helge Ø. Pharo (eds.). 1989. *Historiker og veileder. Festskrift til Jakob Sverdrup*. Oslo.

Bergsgård, Arne. 1932. *Ole Gabriel Ueland og bondepolitikken*, Vol. 1. Oslo.

Bergsgård, Arne. 1946. *Nasjonaliteten i europeisk historie*. Oslo.

Bergsgård, Arne. 1958. *Frå 17. mai til 9. april*. Oslo.

Bergsland, Knut. 1970. Om middelalderens finnmarker. *Historisk tidsskrift* 49:365–409.

Bergsland, Knut. 1974. Synsvinkler i samisk historie. *Historisk tidsskrift* 53:1–36.

Bergsland, Knut (ed.). 1977. *Samenes og sameområdenes rettslige stilling historisk belyst*. Oslo.

Berntsen, Harald. 1969. Objektivitet og historie. *Syn og Segn* 75(8).

Beyer, Harald. 1979. *A History of Norwegian Literature*. New York.

Birkeland, Michael. 1919. *Historiske skrifter*, Vol. I. Kristiania.

Bjerke, Juul. 1966. *Langtidslinjer i norsk økonomi 1865–1960*. Samfunnsøkonomiske studier 16. Oslo.

Bjørgum, Jorunn, and Ole Jørgen Benedictow. 1985. Kvinneliv i norsk middelalder. In Vogt 1985, Vol. 1:114–21.

Bjørklund, Ivar. 1978. *Kvæn – same – norsk*. En sosial–antropologisk analyse av "De tre stammers møte". University of Tromsø.

Bjørklund, Ivar. 1985. *Fjordfolket i Kvænangen*. Fra samisk samfunn til norsk utkant 1550–1980. Bergen–Oslo–Tromsø–Stavanger.

Bjørklund, Ivar. 1986. Om samfunnsvitenskap, historie og livet i Kvænangen. *Historisk tidsskrift* 65:39–43.

Bjørklund, Ivar, and Terje Brantenberg. 1981. *Samisk reindrift – norske inngrep*. Bergen–Oslo–Tromsø.

Bjørkvik, Halvard. 1983. Helge Salvesen: Fire forskningsfaser i studiet av bosetning og bruksmåter i det gamle bondesamfunnet. Opposisjonsinnlegg ved doktordisputas 27.11.1982. *Historisk tidsskrift* 1983:320–39.

Bjørkvik, Halvard, and Andreas Holmsen. 1972. *Kven åtte jorda i den gamle leilendingstida? Fordelinga av jordeigedomen i 1661.* Trondheim.

Bjørnson, Øyvind. 1987. *Den nye arbeidsdagen. Bedriftsledelse og arbeidere ved Stordø kisgruber 1911–1940.* Bergen.

Blom, Grethe Authén. 1967a. *Kongemakt og privilegier i Norge inntil 1387.* Oslo.

Blom, Grethe Authén. 1967b. *Norge i union på 1300-tallet.* 2 vols. Trondheim.

Blom, Grethe Authén (ed.). 1977. *Urbaniseringsprosessen i Norden.* 3 vols. Oslo.

Blom, Ida. 1975. Oversikt over igangværende kvinneforskning: Historiske fag. *Kvinneaspekter i humanistisk forskning. En konferanserapport*:114–41. NAVF, Oslo.

Blom, Ida. 1976. Women's History – No Longer a Neglected Field of Study? *Research in Norway* 1976:4–10. Oslo.

Blom, Ida. 1978. Kvinnehistorie – hva og hvordan? *Kjerringråd. Kvinnepolitisk tidsskrift* 4:51–5.

Blom, Ida. 1979. Kvinneforskning – en metodisk–teoretisk revolusjon? *Kvinneforskning i de humanistiske fag. Konferanserapport NOS-H*:34–43. Oslo.

Blom, Ida. 1980a. The Struggle for Women's Suffrage in Norway, 1885–1913. *Scandinavian Journal of History* 5:1–22.

Blom, Ida. 1980b. *Barnebegrensning – synd eller sunn fornuft?* Bergen.

Blom, Ida. 1983. Kvinder og samfundsforandring. Politiske/ideologiske aspekter ved oppkomsten av kvindehistorie/forskning. *Usynlige historie. Studier i historisk metode nr. 17*:107–18. Oslo.

Blom, Ida. 1984. Barneoppdragelse. In Hodne and Sogner 1984:37–50. Oslo.

Blom, Ida. 1985a. Nødvendig arbeid – skiftende definisjoner og praktiske konsekvenser. *Historisk tidsskrift* 64:117–41.

Blom, Ida. 1985b. Kvinnehistorie – ledd i historieforskningen og ledd i kvinneforskningen. *Historisk tidsskrift* 64:414–24.

Blom, Ida. 1986. Mentalitetshistorie og kvinnehistorie. In Fredriksen and Rømer 1986:14–26.

Blom, Ida. 1987. Patriarkatsteorier i kvinnehistorisk forskning. *Nytt om kvinneforskning* 2:7–14.

Blom, Ida. 1988b. *Den haarde Dyst. Fødsler og fødselshjelp gjennom 150 år.* Oslo.

Blom, Ida. 1990a. En annen historie? Kvinnehistorie i et internasjonalt perspektiv. *Historisk tidsskrift* 69:416–34.

Blom, Ida. 1990b. "Hun er den Raadende over Husets økonomiske Anliggender"? Changes in Women's Work and Family Responsibilities in Norway since the 1860's. In P. Hudson and W. R. Lee (eds.), *Women's Work and the Family Economy in Historical Perspective*:157–82. Manchester.

Blom, Ida. 1991a. Global Women's History: Organising Principles and Cross-Cultural Understandings. In Offen, Pierson, and Rendall 1991:135–50.

Blom, Ida. 1991b. The History of Widowhood: A Bibliographical Overview. *Journal of Family History* 16:191–210.

Blom, Ida. 1991c. Voluntary Motherhood 1900–1930: Theories and Politics of a Norwegian Feminist in an International Perspective. In Bock and Thane (eds.) 1991:21–39.

Blom, Ida. 1992a. Kjønnssystem som et element i syntesedannelse. In Marthinsen and Winge 1992:85–92.

Blom, Ida. 1992b. Refleksjoner over *Grunntrekk i norsk historie*. *Historisk tidsskrift* 71:315–29.
Blom, Ida. 1992c. "On the Shelf"? – Single Women in Modern European History. *Rekishi Hyoron*, March 1992 (in Japanese).
Blom, Ida. 1992d. Widowhood: From the Poor Law Society to the Welfare Society. The Case of Norway, 1875–1964. *Journal of Women's History* 4:53–81.
Blom, Ida (ed.). 1992e–93. *Cappelens kvinnehistorie*. 3 vols. Oslo.
Blom, Ida. 1993a. Språk, mentalitet og virkelighetsforståelse. *Historisk tidsskrift* (Denmark) 93:155–68.
Blom, Ida. 1993b. Refleksjoner over Grunntrekk i norsk historie. *Historisk tidsskrift* 72:315–29.
Blom, Ida. 1993c. En nasjon – to kjønn. *Historisk tidsskrift* 72:420–39.
Blom, Ida. 1993d. "Margarete Bonnevie – skisse av et liv". In *Portretter fra norsk historie*:161–84. Oslo.
Blom, Ida. 1993e. Equality and the Threat of War in Scandinavia, 1884–1905. In T. G. Fraser and K. Jeffery (eds.), *Men, Women and War. Historical Studies* XVIII:100–18. Dublin.
Blom, Ida. 1994a. *Det er forskjell på folk – nå som før. Om kjønn og andre former for sosial differensiering*. Oslo.
Blom, Ida. 1994b. Demokrati, forsvarspolitikk og nasjonalisme. In *Konferanserapport fra det 18. nordiske historikermøte*. Oslo. In press.
Blom, Ida. 1994c. Refleksjoner over kjønn og stat. In A.-H. Nagel (ed.), *Kjønn og velferdsstat*. Oslo.
Blom, Ida, and Gro Hagemann (eds.). 1977 (2nd ed. 1980). *Kvinner selv ... Sju bidrag til norsk kvinnehistorie*. Oslo.
Bock, Gisela, and Pat Thane (eds.). 1991. *Maternity and Gender Policies. Women and the Rise of the European Welfare States, 1880s–1950s*. London.
Brantenberg, Terje. 1985. The Alta–Kautokeino Conflict, Saami Reindeer Herding and Ethnopolitics. In J. Brøsted et al. (eds.), *Native Power. The Quest for Autonomy and Nationhood of Indigenous Peoples*. Bergen–Oslo–Stavanger–Tromsø.
Brantenberg, Terje. 1991. Constructing Indigenous Self-government in a Nation–State: Samediggi – The Sami Parliament in Norway. In P. Jull and S. Robarts (eds.), *The Challenge of Northern Regions*. Darwin.
Bratrein, Håvard Dahl. 1972. Fisker, kremmer og proprietær i Nordland. *Heimen* 15:641–8.
Bratrein, Håvard Dahl, and Einar Niemi. 1994. Inn i riket. Politisk og økonomisk integrasjon gjennom tusen år. In E.-A. Drivenes, M. A. Hauan, and H. A. Wold (eds.), *Nordnorsk kulturhistorie*, Vol. I. Oslo.
Brox, Ottar. 1984. *Nord-Norge: Fra allmenning til koloni*. Oslo.
Bruland, Kristine. 1989. *British Technology and European Industrialisation. The Norwegian textile industry in the mid-nineteenth century*. Cambridge.
Bruland, Kristine (ed.). 1991. *Technology Transfer and Scandinavian Industrialisation*. Oxford.
Bruland, Kristine. 1992. *Levekår under det industrielle gjennombrudd*. Working paper 52, TMV-sentret. Oslo.
Brøgger, A. W. 1931. *Nord-Norges bosetningshistorie*. Oslo.
Bugge, Alexander. 1911. Historie. *Det Kongelige Fredriks Universitet 1811–1911* II:211–89. Kristiania.
Bugge, Anders, and Sverre Steen (eds.). 1938–41. *Norsk kulturhistorie*. 5 vols. Oslo.

Bull, Edvard. 1912. *Folk og kirke i middelalderen; studier til Norges historie.* Oslo.
Bull, Edvard. 1920. Norsk historisk forskning 1869–1919. In *Norsk historisk videnskap i femti år. 1869–1919*:52–129. Kristiania.
Bull, Edvard. 1922–36. *Kristianias historie.* 3 vols. Oslo.
Bull, Edvard. 1933. Professor Karl Lamprecht. In J. Schreiner (ed.), *Historie og politikk.* Oslo.
Bull, Edvard. 1958. *Arbeidermiljø under det industrielle gjennombrudd.* Oslo.
Bull, Edvard. 1966. Håndverkssvenner og arbeiderklasse i Kristiania. Sosialhistoriske problemer. *Historisk tidsskrift* 1966:89–113.
Bull, Edvard. 1969. *Sozialgeschichte der Norwegischen Demokratie.* Stuttgart.
Bull, Edvard. 1970. Historisk vitenskap foran 1970-årene. *Historisk tidsskrift* 49:245–59.
Bull, Edvard. 1972 (originally published 1958). *Arbeidermiljø under det industrielle gjennombrudd.* Oslo.
Bull, Edvard. 1975. Fra bøndenes og husmennenes samfunn til den organiserte kapitalisme. In O. Dahl et al. (eds.), *Makt og motiv. Et festskrift til Jens Arup Seip*:225–40, 265–6. Oslo.
Bull, Edvard. 1976 (1922). Arbeiderbevægelsens stilling i de tre nordiske land 1914–1920. *Tidsskrift for arbeiderbevegelsens historie* 1/1976:3–28. First time in Norwegian as a pamphlet, Oslo 1922; in German: Die Entwicklung der Arbeiterbewegung in den drei skandinavischen Ländern 1914–1920. *Archiv für die Geschichte des Sozialismus und der Arbeiterbewegung* 10 (1922): 329–61.
Bull, Edvard. 1979. *Norge i den rike verden. Tiden etter 1945* (K. Mykland [ed.], *Norges historie*, Vol. 14). Oslo.
Bull, Edvard. 1981. *Retten til en fortid. Sosialhistoriske artikler.* Oslo.
Bull, Edvard. 1985. *Arbeiderklassen blir til (1850–1900)* (E. Bull et al. [eds.], *Arbeiderbevegelsens historie i Norge*, Vol. 1). Oslo.
Bull, Francis. 1958. *Norges litteratur. Fra reformasjonen til 1814.* Oslo.
Butterfield, Herbert. 1931. *The Whig Interpretation of History.* London.
Castberg, Frede. 1961. Statsforbindelsen mellom Danmark og Norge. *Juridiske stridsspørsmål i Norges politiske historie*:5–19. Oslo.
Castberg, Frede. 1964. *Norges statsforfatning*, Vol. 1. Oslo.
Chadwick, Owen. 1978. *Catholicism and History. The Opening of the Vatican Archives.* London.
Chartier, Roger. 1988. *Cultural History.* Cambridge.
Chesnais, Jean Claude. 1986. *La Transition démographique.* Paris.
Clausen, H. P. 1963. *Hvad er Historie?* Copenhagen.
Coldevin, Axel. 1938. *Næringsliv og priser i Nordland 1700–1880.* Det hanseatiske museums skrifter XI. Bergen.
Collingwood, Robin G. 1946, 1961. *The Idea of History.* Oxford.
Comité International des Sciences Historiques. *Bulletin d'Information.* 1926ff. Paris.
Dahl, Hans Fredrik. 1980. Seip, Jens Arup. *Pax leksikon.* Oslo.
Dahl, Helge. 1957. *Språkpolitikk og skolestell i Finnmark 1814 til 1905.* Oslo.
Dahl, Helge. 1959. *Norsk lærerutdanning fra 1814 til idag.* Oslo.
Dahl, Ottar. 1955. Noen teoretiske problemer i sosialhistorien. *Historisk tidsskrift* 34:185–203.
Dahl, Ottar. 1956. *Om årsaksproblemer i historisk forskning. Forsøk på en vitenskapsteoretisk analyse.* Oslo.

Dahl, Ottar. 1967. *Grunntrekk i historieforskningens metodelære*. Oslo.
Dahl, Ottar. 1970. Innledning. In *Hundre års historisk forskning*. Oslo.
Dahl, Ottar. 1974. *Historisk materialisme. Historieoppfatningen hos Edvard Bull og Halvdan Koht*. Oslo.
Dahl, Ottar. 1975. Politikk, makt og motiv. Synspunkter på Jens Arup Seips historiske forfatterskap. In O. Dahl *et al.* (eds.), *Makt og motiv. Et festskrift til Jens Arup Seip*:3–11. Oslo.
Dahl, Ottar. 1978. Historisk institutt 25 år, 1953–1978. *Universitetet i Oslo. Årsberetning 1978*:51-6. Oslo.
Dahl, Ottar. 1984. *Problemer i historiens teori*. Oslo.
Dahl, Ottar. 1985. "Kvinnehistorie". Kategorihistorie eller samfunnshistorie? *Historisk tidsskrift* 64:262–74.
Dahl, Ottar. 1986. *Problemer i historiens teori*. Oslo.
Dahl, Ottar. 1987. Aktuelle Tendenzen und Hauptgebiete in norwegischer Geschictswissenschaft. In *Bericht über das 1. deutsch–norwegische Historikertreffen in Bergen, Mai 1986. Historiographie. Protoindustrialisierung. Arbeiterbewegung. Faschismus*:22–32. Oslo.
Dahl, Ottar. 1990. *Norsk historieforskning i det 19. og 20. århundre*. 4th ed. (1st ed. 1959.) Oslo.
Dahl, Ottar. 1991. Teoristrid i norsk historievitenskap. *Nytt norsk tidsskrift* 8(3).
Dahl, Ottar. 1992a. Hva er syntese? In Marthinsen and Winge 1992:93–6.
Dahl, Ottar. 1992b. *Jens Arup Seip. Minnetale i Det Norske Videnskaps-Akademi*. Oslo.
Damsholt, Nanna. 1991. The State of Women's History in Denmark. In Offen, Pierson, and Rendall 1991:231–8.
Danielsen, Rolf. 1958. *Det nye bysamfunn 1880–1914 (Trondheim bys historie,* Vol. 4). Trondheim.
Danielsen, Rolf. 1961–2. Samlingspartiet og unionen. *Historisk tidsskrift* 41.
Danielsen, Rolf. 1964. *Det norske storting gjennom 150 år,* Vol. 2, *Tidsrommet 1870–1908*. Oslo.
Danielsen, Rolf. 1984. *Borgerlig oppdemmingspolitikk (Høyres historie,* Vol. 2). Oslo.
Dent, John. 1957. *Norway*. London.
Derry, T. K. 1957. *A Short History of Norway*. London.
Derry, T. K. 1973. *A History of Modern Norway, 1814–1972*. Oxford.
Det Kongelige Fredriks Universitet 1811–1911. Festskrift I-II. 1911. Kristiania.
Det nordiske forskningsprojektet Centralmakt och lokalsamhälle – beslutsprocess på 1700-talet. Publ. I–VI. Oslo 1982–5; Lund 1994.
Dikkanen, Siri Lavik. 1965. Sirma: Residence and Work Organization in a Lappish-speaking Community. *Samiske samlinger* 8. Oslo.
Drake, Michael. 1969. *Population and Society in Norway 1735–1865*. Cambridge.
Drake, Michael. 1972. Fertility controls in pre-industrial Norway. In D. V. Glass and R. Revelle (eds.), *Population and Social Change*:185–98. London.
Drake, Michael. 1979. Norway. In W. R. Lee (ed.), *European Demography and Economic Growth*:284–318. London.
Drivenes, Einar-Arne. 1985a. Do Social Scientists and Historians Write the Same Minority Histories? *Acta Borealia* 34 (Norwegian version in *Historisk tidsskrift* 64(1985)).
Drivenes, Einar-Arne. 1985b. *Fiskarbonde og gruveslusk*. Oslo.

Drivenes, Einar-Arne. 1992. Religion, Church and Ethnic Minorities of Norway up to 1940. In D. Kerr (ed.), *Religion, State and Ethnic Groups. Governments and Non-dominant Ethnic Groups in Europe, 1850–1940*, Vol. II. New York–Dartmouth.

Drivenes, Einar-Arne, and Regnor Jernsletten. 1994. Det gjenstridige Nord-Norge. Religiøs, politisk og etnisk mobilisering 1850–1990. In E.-A. Drivenes, M. A. Hauan, and H. A. Wold (eds.), *Nordnorsk kulturhistorie*, Vol. I. Oslo.

Dyrvik, Ståle. 1970. Om giftarmål og sosiale normer. Ei studie av Etne 1715–1801. *Tidsskrift for samfunnsforskning* 11:285–300.

Dyrvik, Ståle. 1972. Historical Demography in Norway 1660–1801. A Short Survey. *Scandinavian Economic History Review* 20:27–44.

Dyrvik, Ståle. 1974. Infant Mortality about 1800. *Scandinavian Population Studies* 3:125–34.

Dyrvik, Ståle. 1978. *Den lange fredstiden 1720–1784*. (K. Mykland [ed.], *Norges Historie*, Vol. 8). Oslo.

Dyrvik, Ståle. 1979. The Decline of Mortality ca. 1740–1850. *Scandinavian Population Studies* 5:98–103.

Dyrvik, Ståle. 1981a. Gagne-pain ou sentiments? Traits du remariage en Norvège au XIXe siècle. In J. Dupâquier *et al.* (eds.), *Marriage and Remarriage in Populations of the Past*:297–306. London.

Dyrvik, Ståle. 1981b. Lokalsamfunnet i historieforskninga. *Søkelys på lokalhistoria*:7–19. Oslo.

Dyrvik, Ståle. 1983. *Historisk demografi. Ei innføring i metodane*. Oslo.

Dyrvik, Ståle. 1984. Hushaldsutviklinga i Norge 1800–1920. In *Familien i forandring i 18- og 1900-tallet & mødeberetning*, Rapporter til den XIX nordiske historikerkongres Odense 1984, Vol. III. Odense.

Dyrvik, Ståle. 1987. The Norwegian Rural Proletariat 1650–1900. In *Bericht über das 1. deutsch–norwegische Historikertreffen in Bergen, Mai 1986. Historiographie. Protoindustrialisierung. Arbeiterbewegung. Faschischmus*:45–61. Bergen.

Dyrvik, Ståle. 1988a. Économie ou culture? L'introduction de la prévention des naissances dans la ville de Stavanger, Norvège, 1900–1935. *Annales de Démographie Historique* 1988:127–39.

Dyrvik, Ståle. 1988b. The Effects of Smallpox Vaccination on Mortality. A Norwegian Case Study 1770–1840. In A. Brandström and L.-G. Tedebrand (eds.), *Society, Health and Population during the Demographic Transition*: 495–512. Stockholm.

Dyrvik, Ståle. 1993. Farmers at Sea: A Study of Fishermen in North Norway, 1801–1920. *Journal of Family History* 18:341–56.

Dyrvik, Ståle *et al.* 1979. *Norsk økonomisk historie 1500–1970*, Vol. 1, *1500–1850*. Bergen.

Dyrvik, Ståle, and Marit Karin Alsvik. 1987. *Gjennombrotet for fødselsregulering i Stavanger 1900–1935*. Bergen.

Dyrvik, Ståle, Knut Mykland, and Jan Oldervoll. 1976. *The Demographic Crises in Norway in the 17th and 18th Centuries*. Bergen.

Døssland, Atle. 1990. *Med lengt mot havet. Fylkeshistorie for Møre og Romsdal*, Vol. 1, *1671–1835*. Oslo.

Daae, Ludvig K. 1870. *Skisser fra Lapland, Karelstranden og Finland*. Kristiania.

Daae, Ludvig K. 1871. *Det gamle Christiania 1624–1814*. (Revised edition by Roar Tank 1924.) Christiania.

400 MAKING A HISTORICAL CULTURE

Edding, Elisabeth. 1983. *"Brytningstider" – Sverre Steens syn på historisk utvikling*. Unpublished Master's thesis. University of Oslo.

Educational Statistics. Universities and Colleges. Central Bureau of Statistics of Norway. Oslo/Kongsvinger.

Egge, Åsmund. 1974. Empirisme eller marxisme? *Historisk tidsskrift* 53: 332–52.

Egge, Åsmund. 1983 Transformation of bank structures in the industrial period: The case of Norway. *Journal of European Economic History* 12: 271–294.

Egge, Åsmund. 1988. *Statens Diskonteringskommisjoner. Finansdepartementet som statsbank i det 19. århundre*. Unpublished doctoral dissertation. University of Oslo.

Eidheim, Harald. 1958. Erhverv og kulturkontakt i Polmak. *Samiske samlinger* 4. Oslo.

Eidheim, Harald. 1971. *Aspects of the Lappish Minority Situation*. Oslo–Bergen–Tromsø.

Eidheim, Harald. 1985. Indigenous Peoples and the State: The Saami Case in Norway. In J. Brøsted *et al.* (eds.), *Native Power*. Bergen–Oslo–Stavanger–Tromsø.

Einarsen, Einar. 1904. *Gode og daarlige tider*. Christiania.

Eliassen, Finn Einar. 1972. *Det gamle embetsverk og det nye. Norske embetsmenns kamp mot Generalforstamtet 1739–46*. Unpublished Master's thesis. University of Oslo.

Eliassen, Jørgen. 1979. *"Gud give dem et mindre sandseligt Sindelag". Trekk ved giftermålsinngåelser med særlig vekt på begynnelsen av det seksuelle samlivet for arbeidsfolk i Moss 1776–1814*. Unpublished Master's thesis. University of Oslo.

Eliassen, Jørgen, and Sølvi Sogner (eds.). 1981. *Bot eller Bryllup – Ugifte mødre og gravide bruder i det gamle samfunnet*. Oslo.

Elster, Jon. 1971. *Nytt perspektiv på økonomisk historie*. Oslo.

Elster, Jon. 1978. *Logic and Society*. Chichester.

Elster, Jon. 1979. *Forklaring og dialektikk*. Oslo.

Engelsen, Kirsten M. 1987. *Utvandringen fra Bergen til Amerika 1874–1890*. Unpublished Master's thesis. University of Bergen.

Engelsen, Rolf. 1983. Mortalitetsdebatten og sosiale skilnader i mortalitet. *Historisk tidsskrift* 62:161–202.

Engen, Arnfinn (ed.). 1978. *Utvandringa – det store oppbrotet*. Oslo.

Erdmann, Andrew P. N. 1993. Mining for the Corporatist Synthesis: Gold in American Foreign Economic Policy, 1931–1936. *Diplomatic History* 17:171–200.

Eriksen, Knut Einar. 1972. *DNA og NATO*. Oslo.

Eriksen, Knut Einar. 1977a. Norden, NATO og den "utro tjener" Halvard Lange. *Internasjonal Politikk* 2/1977:261–302.

Eriksen, Knut Einar. 1977b. Sluttreplikk. *Internasjonal Politikk* 4/1977:747–52.

Eriksen, Knut Einar. 1989. Svalbardspørsmålet fra krig til kald krig. In Bergh and Pharo 1989:112–62.

Eriksen, Knut Einar. 1991. Norwegian and Swedish Educational Policies *vis-à-vis* Non-dominant Ethnic Groups. In J. Tomiac (ed.), *Schooling, Educational Policy and Ethnic Identity. Comparative Studies on Governments and Non-dominant Ethnic Groups in Europe, 1850–1940*, Vol. I. New York–Dartmouth.

Eriksen, Knut Einar, and Einar Niemi. 1981. *Den finske fare. Sikkerhetsproblemer og minoritetspolitikk i nord 1860–1940*. Oslo–Bergen–Tromsø.
Eriksen, Knut Einar, and Helge Ø. Pharo. 1994. Norsk sikkerhetspolitikk som etterkrigshistorisk forskningsfelt. *Etterkrigshistorisk Register* 21. Bergen.
Eriksen, Knut Einar, and Magne Skodvin. 1981. Storbritannia, NATO og et skandinavisk forsvarsforbund. *Internasjonal Politikk* 3/1981:437–502.
Erslev, Kristian. 1911 (1961). *Historisk Teknik. Den historiske Undersøgelse fremstillet i sine Grundlinier*. Copenhagen.
Espeli, Harald. 1990. *Fra hest til hestekrefter*. Unpublished doctoral dissertation. Norwegian College of Agriculture, Ås.
Espeli, Harald. 1992. *Industripolitikk på avveie. Motkonjunkturpolitikken og Norges Industriforbunds rolle 1975–1980*. Oslo.
Fagerbakk, Terje. 1989. *Om å gå bakover. Andreas Holmsen i norsk lokalhistorisk forskning*. Unpublished Master's thesis. University of Tromsø.
Falkenberg, Johs. 1941. Bosetningen ved Indre Laksefjord i Finnmark. *Nordnorske samlinger* 2. Oslo.
Falkenberg, Johs. 1982–3. Samiske bruksområder og stedsnavn i Rørostraktene. *Åarjel-Saemieh/Samer i sør* I. Snåsa.
Finberg, H. P. R. 1954. *The Local Historian and His Themes*. Leicester.
Finberg, H. P. R., and V. H. T. Skipp 1973. *Local History. Objective and Pursuit*. 2nd ed. Newton Abbot.
Fischer, Lewis R., and Helge W. Nordvik. 1987. From Namsos to Halden: Myths and Realities in the History of Norwegian Seamen's Wages 1850–1914. *Scandinavian Economic History Review* 35:41–64.
Fladby, Rolf. 1963. *Fra lensmannstjener til Kongelig Majestets Foged*. Oslo.
Fladby, Rolf. 1965. Local History in Norway. *The Amateur Historian* 6(8):262–6.
Fladby, Rolf. 1970. Bygdehistorien og den lokalhistoriske forskning 1920–1970. In *Lokalhistorie i forskning og kulturarbeid gjennom 200 år. Landslaget for bygde- og byhistorie 50 år 6. juli 1970*:55–74. Oslo.
Fladby, Rolf. 1986. *Samfunn i vekst – under fremmed styre 1536–1660*. Oslo.
Fladby, Rolf, and Harald Winge. 1981. *Søkelys på lokalhistorien*. Oslo.
Fløystad, Ingeborg. 1979. Vi lærte tidlig å arbeide! Barnearbeid i Norge i de siste 200 år. In *Å være barn i gamle dager. Forskningsnytt* 4:20–31.
Fløystad, Ingeborg. 1986. *Kvinnekår i endring. Kvinner sitt arbeid i Arna, Hordaland 1870–1930*. Bergen.
Fløystad, Ingeborg. 1990a. Kvinnehistorie i Norge 1970–1990. *Historisk tidsskrift* 69:403–15.
Fløystad, Ingeborg. 1990b. Kvinnehistorie i Norge. En bibliografi. *Historisk tidsskrift* 69:598–621.
Fløystad, Ingeborg. 1991. Women's History in Norway: A Short Survey. In Offen, Pierson, and Rendall 1991:221–30.
Fossen, Anders Bjarne. 1979. *Borgerskapets by 1536–1800 (Bergen bys historie, Vol. 2)*. Bergen.
Fredriksen, Inge, and Hilde Rømer (eds.). 1986. *Kvinder, mentalitet og arbejde. Kvindehistorisk forskning i Norden. Rapport fra det 2. nordiske kvinnehistorikermøte 1985*. Århus.
Friis, J. A. 1856a. *Lappisk Grammatikk*. Kristiania.
Friis, J. A. 1856b. *Lappiske Sprogprøver*. Kristiania.
Friis, J. A. 1871a. *En Sommer i Finmarken, russisk Lapland og Nordkarelen*. Kristiania.

402 MAKING A HISTORICAL CULTURE

Friis, J. A. 1871b. *Lappisk Mytologi, eventyr og folkesagn.* Kristiania.

Friis, J. A. 1881. *Lajla.* Kristiania.

Friis, J. A. 1884. *Klosteret i Petchenga.* Kristiania.

Friis, J. A. 1885–7. *Ordbog over det Lappiske Sprog med latinsk og norsk Forklaring.* Kristiania.

Fulsås, Narve. 1989–90. National–historical synthesis as a function of narrative "emplotment" in J. E. Sars' "Udsigt". In *Bericht über das 4. deutsch–norwegische Historikertreffen in Berlin, Mai 1989.* Die Hanse und Nord-Europa: Handel-Politik-Kultur. *Synthesekonzepte in der Geschichtsschreibung*:122-38. Oslo.

Fulsås, Narve. 1993. *Universitetet i Tromsø 25 år.* Tromsø.

Fulsås, Narve. 1994. *Ernst Sars, positivismen og 1800-talets historievitskap.* Unpublished manuscript. Tromsø.

Fure, Eli. 1980. *Den ekteskapelige fruktbarhet i Kolbu på Toten ca. 1870–1910. En studie av fruktbarhetsfallets innledningsfase.* Unpublished Master's thesis. University of Oslo.

Fure, Eli. 1983. Are Children Poor Men's Riches? *Scandinavian Economic History Review* 31:161–77.

Fure, Eli. 1986. Gamle i flergenerasjonsfamilier – en seiglivet myte? *Historisk tidsskrift* 65:16–35.

Fure, Eli. 1990. Oppkalling og familiementalitet. *Historisk tidsskrift* 69:146–62.

Fure, Odd-Bjørn. 1976. Synspunkter og historieteoretiske tendenser i forskningen om den norske arbeiderklasse og -bevegelse i den radikale fase 1918–1933. *Tidsskrift for arbeiderbevegelsens historie* 1/1976.

Fure, Odd-Bjørn. 1983. Problemer, metode og teori i historieforskningen, Historie- og vitenskapsoppfatning i Jens Arup Seips teoretiske produksjon. *Historisk tidsskrift* 62:373–401.

Fure, Odd-Bjørn. 1984a. Jens Arup Seips *Utsikt over Norges historie* 1–2. *Historisk tidsskrift* 63:117–56.

Fure, Odd-Bjørn. 1984b. Hverdagshistorie i tysk historieforskning. Problemer – perspektiver – potensiale. *Historisk tidsskrift* 63:349-83.

Fure, Odd-Bjørn. 1993. Kritisk empirisme. Historie og vitenskapsteori i Ottar Dahls *Grunntrekk i historieforskningens metodelære. Historisk tidsskrift* 72:37–66.

Furre, Berge. 1991. *Vårt hundreår 1905–1990.* Oslo.

Fygle, Svein, Svein Lundestad, and Inge Strand. 1993. *Banken, folket og bygda. Nordlandsbanken og Nordlands næringsliv gjennom 100 år 1893–1993.* Bodø.

Førland, Tor Egil. 1988. 1949 som "vendepunkt": Er NATO-medlemskapet bare kulisse? *Internasjonal Politikk* 6/1988:69–85.

Førland, Tor Egil. 1990. An Act of Economic Warfare? The Dispute over NATO's Embargo Resolution, 1950–1951. *International History Review* 12:490–513.

Førland, Tor Egil. 1991a. "Selling Firearms to the Indians": Eisenhower's Export Control Policy, 1953–54. *Diplomatic History* 15:221–44.

Førland, Tor Egil. 1991b. *Cold Economic Warfare: The Creation and Prime of Co-Com, 1948–1954.* Unpublished doctoral dissertation. University of Oslo.

Førland, Tor Egil. 1993. *Europeisk fellesskap?* Oslo.

Førland, Tor Egil. 1994. Foreign Policy Profiles of the Scandinavian Countries: Making Use of CoCom. *Scandinavian Journal of History* 19:165–84.

Galensen, Walter. 1986. *A Welfare State Strikes Oil: The Norwegian Experience.* Lanham, Mass.

Gellner, Ernest. 1983. *Nations and Nationalism*. Oxford.
Genovese, Fox Elisabeth. 1982. Placing Women's History in History. *New Left Review* 133.
Geyl, Pieter. 1955. *Debates with Historians*. New York.
Gissel, Svend et al. 1981. *Desertion and Land Colonization in the Nordic Countries c. 1300–1600*. Stockholm.
Gjerde, Jon. 1985. From Peasants to Farmers. *The Migration from Balestrand, Norway, to the Upper Middle West*. Cambridge.
Gjerdåker, Brynjulv. 1974. *Geografisk og sosial mobilitet i Ullensaker på 1800-tallet. Ein kohort-analyse*. Unpublished Master's thesis. University of Oslo.
Gjerdåker, Brynjulv (ed.). 1981. *På flyttefot. Innanlands vandring på 1800-talet*. Oslo.
Gjessing, Gutorm. 1973. *Norge i Sameland*. Oslo.
Gjessing, Helge. 1920. Arkeologien. *Norsk historisk videnskap i femti år 1869–1919*:161–205. Kristiania.
Gjølberg, Ole. 1979. *Økonomi, teknologi og historie. Analyser av skipsfart og økonomi 1866–1913*. Unpublished doctoral dissertation. Norwegian School of Economics and Business Administration, Bergen.
Gjønnes, Siri. 1982. *Fruktbarhetsfallet i Elverum. En studie av den ekteskapelige fruktbarhet i perioden 1875–1930*. Unpublished Master's thesis. University of Oslo.
Gotaas, Anne-Marie et al. 1980. *Det kriminelle kjønn*. Oslo.
Greve, Tim. 1964. *Det norske storting gjennom 150 år*, Vol. 3. *Tidsrommet 1908–1964*. Oslo.
Grønlie, Tore. 1989. *Statsdrift. Staten som industrieier i Norge 1945–1963*. Oslo.
Gåskjenn, Albert, and Håkon Haugen. 1990. *Tyssedal 1900–1935*. Unpublished Master's thesis. University of Bergen.
Hagemann, Gro. 1982. Hva er kvinnehistorie? In *Litt frukt fra kunnskapens tre. Fagkritikk og kvinnekritikk*:89–100. Oppland Distriktshøgskole Informasjonsserien nr. 30.
Hagemann, Gro. 1985a. Om kjønnsskiller og kvinneundertrykking i historien. *Materialisten* 1–2/1985:73–82.
Hagemann, Gro. 1985b. Feminism and Sexual Division of Labour. Female Labour in the Norwegian Telegraph Service around the Turn of the Century. *Scandinavian Journal of History* 10:143–54.
Hagemann, Gro. 1986b. Kapitalisme, lønnsarbeid og kjønnsarbeidsdeling. In Fredriksen and Rømer 1986:50–63.
Hagemann, Gro. 1986c. Kvinnehistorie – faglig blindspor eller fruktbar disiplin? *Historisk tidsskrift* 65:343–60.
Hagemann, Gro. 1989. De osynliga kvinnorna. Historien om den manlige arbetarklassen, og Könsstrukturerna ignoreras. Svar till Per Maurseth. *Arbetarhistoria, Meddelande från Arbetarrörelsens Arkiv och Bibliotek* 13(51):15–23, 33–4.
Hagemann, Gro. 1990. Om å gjøre det enkle komplisert og det usynlige synlig – noen dilemmaer i kvinnehistorien, *Kvinnohistoria i teoretiskt perspektiv*. Uppsala.
Hagemann, Gro. 1992. *Skolefolk. Lærernes historie i Norge*. Oslo.
Hagemann, Gro. 1993. Om å utfordre fornuften – kvinneforskningen som kritisk mot offentlighet. In Langholm et al. 1994:101–24.
Hagemann, Gro. 1994a. *Kjønn og industrialisering*. Oslo.

Hagemann, Gro. 1994b. Det kvinnelige element lutret og styrket. Kvinnesak og kvinnelighet i forrige århundres Kristiania. In Hagemann and Krogstad 1994.

Hagemann, Gro. 1994c. Bohemer, kvinnesakskvinner og hanskemoral. Fra en strid om normene for offentlig debatt. In Hagemann and Krogstad 1994.

Hagemann, Gro. 1994d. Postmodernismen en användbar men opålitlig bundsförvant. Kvinnovetenskaplig tidskrift 15:19–34.

Hagemann, Gro, and Anne Krogstad (eds.). 1994. Høydeskrekk. Artikler om kvinner og offentlighet. Oslo.

Hagen, Rune. 1987. Mentalitetshistorie: Hva og hvorfor? In Kvium and Wåhlin 1987.

Halvorsen, Bjørg, and Kari Indseth. 1975. Befolkningsutviklingen i Ullensaker 1733–1845. Unpublished Master's thesis. University of Oslo.

Hanisch, Tore J. 1978. The Economic Crisis in Norway in the 1930s: A Tentative Analysis of its Causes. Scandinavian Economic History Review 26:145–55.

Hanisch, Tore J. 1979. Virkninger av paripolitikken. Historisk tidsskrift 58:239–68.

Hanisch, Tore J., and Even Lange. 1979. Krise og vekst. Norsk økonomi i 1930-årene. Tidsskrift for Arbeiderbevegelsens Historie 2/1979:51–67.

Hanisch, Tore J., and Even Lange. 1985. Vitenskap for industrien. NTH – en høyskole i utvikling gjennom 75 år. Oslo.

Hanisch, Tore J., and Even Lange. 1986. Veien til velstand.Industriens utvikling i Norge gjennom 50 år. Oslo.

Hanisch, Tore J., and Gunnar Nerheim. 1993. Norsk oljehistorie, Vol. I. Oslo.

Hansen, Lars Ivar. 1986a. Modeller uten metodologi? Perspektiver på rekonstruksjon av samisk fortid. Unpublished paper. University of Tromsø.

Hansen, Lars Ivar. 1986b. Samiske rettigheter til jord på 1600-tallet. "Finnejorder" i Sør-Troms. Tromsø Museums skrifter XX. Tromsø.

Hansen, Lars Ivar. 1990a. Samisk fangstsamfunn og norsk høvdingeøkonomi. Oslo.

Hansen, Lars Ivar. 1990b. Handel i nord. Samiske samfunnsendringer ca. 1550–ca. 1700. Unpublished doctoral dissertation. University of Tromsø.

Hansen, Lars Ivar. 1992. Just K. Qvigstad's Contribution to the Study of Sami Culture. Acta Borealia 41.

Harbsmeier, Michael. 1989. World Histories before Domestication. The Writing of Universal Histories, Histories of Mankind and World Histories in Late Eighteenth Century Germany. Culture and History:93–131. Copenhagen.

Haugen, Einar. 1966. Language Conflict and Language Planning: The Case of Modern Norwegian. Cambridge, Mass.

Heimen 1/1977. Articles on "Det store hamskiftet" by Jørn Sandnes, Hans Try, Tore Pryser, and Kjell Haarstad.

Heimen 2/1989:67–114.

Heimen 3–4/1992. Thematic issues devoted to cultural history.

Helland, A. 1906. Finmarkens Amt. Norges Land og Folk. Kristiania.

Helland, Amund Theodor. 1898–1921. Norges land og folk. 20 vols. Kristiania.

Helle, Knut. 1961. Tendenser i nyere norsk høymiddelalderforskning. Historisk tidsskrift 40:337–70.

Helle, Knut. 1964–74. Norge blir en stat 1130–1319. Oslo.

Helle, Knut. 1972. Konge og gode menn i norsk riksstyring ca. 1150–1319. Bergen.

Helle, Knut. 1981. Norway in the High Middle Ages: Recent Views on the Structure of Society. Scandinavian Journal of History 6:161–89.

Helle, Knut. 1994. Samfunnshistoriske synteser. In Langholm *et al.* 1994.
Helvig, Magne *et al.* 1974. *Norway: Land, People, Industries.* Oslo.
Hernes, Gudmund. 1966. Tsarens strømper. Om historie og sosiologi. *Kontrast* 2/1966.
Hernes, Gudmund. 1977. Modellenes maskerade. *Historisk tidsskrift* 56:80–90.
Herstad, John. 1975. Bispelistene som kilde til eldre norsk befolkningsstatistikk. *Heimen* 16:609–28, 689–704.
Hertzberg, Ebbe. 1882. Norges Industri. En historisk og statistisk oversigt. *Polyteknisk tidsskrift* 4/29:94–112
Hewitt, Nancy. 1985. Beyond the Search for Sisterhood: American Women's History in the 1980s. *Social History* 10(3).
HIFO-nytt/HiFo-nytt. 1983–. Oslo–Trondheim–Tromsø.
Higgs, John. 1960–2. Lokalhistorisk forskning i England og Wales. *Fortid og Nutid* 21:113–20. Copenhagen.
Higley, Lisbeth. 1976. *Husholdningsstruktur i Ullensaker i 1801 og 1865.* Unpublished Master's thesis. University of Oslo.
Hirdman, Yvonne. 1988. Genussystemet – reflexioner kring kvinnors sociale underordning. *Kvinnovetenskapligt tidskrift* 9(3):49–63.
Hirdman, Yvonne. 1991. The State of Women's History in Sweden. In Offen, Pierson, and Rendall 1991:239–58.
Historisk statistikk 1978. Norges offisielle statistikk XII 291. Oslo.
Historisk tidsskrift 1991. Special issue: *Tingbøker som historisk kilde* 70(2): 149–351.
Historiske persondata i Norge 1992. Registreringssentral for historiske data. Tromsø.
Hobsbawm, Eric J. 1990. *Nations and nationalism since 1780.* Cambridge.
Hobson, Rolf. 1993. Stormaktenes krigsplanlegging før 1914. *Historisk tidsskrift* 72:440–71.
Hodne, Bjarne, and Sølvi Sogner (eds.). 1984. *Barn av sin tid. Fra norske barns historie.* Oslo.
Hodne, Fritz. 1975. *An Economic History of Norway, 1815–1970.* Trondheim.
Hodne, Fritz. 1981. *Norsk økonomisk historie 1815–1980.* Oslo.
Hodne, Fritz. 1983. *The Norwegian Economy, 1920–1980.* London.
Hodne, Fritz, and Ola H. Grytten. 1993. *Norsk økonomi 1900–1990.* Oslo.
Hoëm, Anton. 1976a. *Makt og kunnskap.* Oslo.
Hoëm, Anton. 1976b. *Yrkesfelle, sambygdning, same eller norsk.* Oslo.
Hohle, Per. 1956. *Mountain World of Norway.* Oslo.
Holberg, Ludvig. 1732–5. *Dannemarks riges historie.* 3 vols. Copenhagen.
Holm, Edvard. 1891–1912. *Danmark–Norges historie fra den store nordiske krigs afslutning til rigernes adskillelse (1720–1814).* 7 vols. Copenhagen.
Holm, Poul. 1991. *Kystfolk. Kontakter og sammenhænge over Kattegat og Skagerrak ca. 1550–1914.* Esbjerg.
Holmsen, Andreas. 1933. Kulturskiftet i Noreg kring midten av 19. hundradaaret. *Syn og Segn* 39. Also in *Gard, bygd, rike,* 1966. Oslo.
Holmsen, Andreas. 1936–41. *Eidsvoll bygds historie,* Vol. I:1, *Bygdehistorien til omkring 1700.* Oslo.
Holmsen, Andreas. 1939. *Norges historie. Fra de eldste tider til 1660.* (Also several later editions.) Oslo.
Holmsen, Andreas. 1940. Nye metoder innen en særskilt gren av norsk historieforskning. *Historisk tidsskrift* 32:27–45.

Holmsen, Andreas. 1941–50. *Eidsvoll bygds historie*, Vol. II:1, *Gardene på østsiden av Vorma*. Oslo.

Holmsen, Andreas. 1946. *Fra Linderud til Eidsvold Værk*, Vol. I, *Grunnleggelsen av Linderudgodset*. Oslo.

Holmsen, Andreas. 1966. Menneske, mønster og masse i historien. *Historisk tidsskrift* 45:330–9.

Holmsen Andreas. 1971. *Fra Linderud til Eidsvold Værk*, Vol. II–1, *Familiebedriften i Kristiania–patrisiatets tid: 1742–1792*. Oslo.

Holmsen, Andreas. 1982. *Før bonden ble forretningsmann*. Oslo.

Holtedahl, Olaf. 1960. *Geology of Norway*. Oslo.

Holtsmark, Sven G. 1993. A Soviet Grab for the High North? USSR, Svalbard, and Northern Norway 1920–1953. *Forsvarsstudier* 7/1993.

Hosar, Hans P. 1981. *Herre og bønder ved Jens Bjelkes adelsgods kring midten av 1600-talet. Ein studie i føydal utbytting i Norge*. Unpublished Master's thesis. University of Oslo.

Hoskins, W. G. 1972. *Local History in England*. 2nd ed. London.

Hovland, Edgar. 1979. Smør og margarin blir ett fett. *Historisk tidsskrift* 58:305–24.

Hovland, Edgar, Even Lange, and Sigurd Rysstad (eds.). 1990. *Det som svarte seg best. Studier i økonomisk historie og politikk*. Oslo.

Hroch, Miroslav. 1985. *Social Preconditions of National Revival in Europe. A Comparative Analysis of the Social Composition of Patriotic Groups among Smaller European Nations*. Cambridge.

Hubbard, William H. 1992. History Theses in Norway 1945–1990. A Note on Numbers and Subject-Matter. *Historisk tidsskrift* 71:3–10.

Hultblad, Filip. 1968. *Övergången från nomadism till agrar bosättning i Jokkmokk socken*. Lund.

Hveding, Øistein. 1982. *Landbrukets gjeldskrise i mellomkrigstiden. Statens lånekasse for jordbrukere*. Oslo.

Hvor er kildene? Institusjoner til hjelp for lokalhistorikere. Småskrifter fra Norsk lokalhistorisk institutt. 4th ed. 1994. Oslo.

Høgmo, Asle. 1986. Det tredje alternativ. *Tidsskrift for samfunnsforskning* 27: 395–416.

Høgmo, Asle. 1989. *Norske idealer og samisk virkelighet. Om skoleutvikling i det samiske området*. Oslo.

Haarstad, Kjell. 1976a. *Bondenæringen i støpeskjeen. Strukturendringer i jordbruket i Selbu 1850–1900*. Oslo.

Haarstad, Kjell. 1976b. Perspektiver på hamskiftet. *Historisk tidsskrift* 55: 113–24.

Haarstad, Kjell. 1980. Sult, sykdom, død. *Historisk tidsskrift* 59:4–25.

Haarstad, Kjell. 1981. *Samiske vandringer i Sør-Norge*. Trondheim.

Haarstad, Kjell. 1992. *Sørsamisk historie: ekspansjon og konflikter i Rørostraktene*. Trondheim.

Haavet, Inger Elisabeth. 1982. *Avvik eller uhell? Ugifte foreldre omkring 1800 – en sosialanalyse*. Unpublished Master's thesis. University of Bergen.

Iggers, Georg C. 1984. *New Directions in European Historiography*. 2nd ed. Hanover, NH.

Imsen, Steinar. 1987. Den tronfølgerettslige situasjonen i Norge ved utgangen av middelalderen. *Historisk tidsskrift* 66:169–79.

Imsen, Steinar. 1990. *Norsk bondekommunalisme fra Magnus Lagabøte til Kristian Kvart*, Vol. 1. Trondheim.

Ingstad, Anne Stine. 1985. *The Norse Discovery of America*. Oslo.

Iversen, Tore. 1994. *Trelldommen. Norsk slaveri i middelalderen*. Unpublished doctoral dissertation. University of Bergen.

Jahn, Gunnar, Alf Eriksen, and Preben Munthe. 1966. *Norges Bank gjennom 150 år*. Oslo.

Jenks, Chris. 1993. *Culture*. London.

Jensen, Arne, Preben Munthe, Francis Sejersted, and Arnljot Strømme Svendsen (eds.). 1972. *Studier i sparing og sparebankvesen i Norge 1822–1972*. Oslo.

Jensen, Olav Harald, and Arnljot Strømme Svendsen. 1986. *Norges Handelshøyskole femti år*. Bergen.

Jenssen, Dag. 1990. *Mentalité: en vitenskapsteoretisk studie i mentalitetshistoriske tekster av Ariès, Mandrou og Vovelle*. Bergen.

Jernsletten, Regnor. 1986. *Samebevegelsen i Norge. Idé og strategi 1900–1940*. University of Tromsø.

Johannessen, Finn E. 1989. *Challenge and Change. The History of Protan 1939–1989*. Lillehammer.

Johannessen, Finn E. 1991. *Lær og skinn i tykt og tynt. Den norske garveri–industris historie*. Oslo.

Johannessen, Finn E. 1992. *I støtet. Oslo Energi 1892–1992*. Oslo.

Johannessen, Knut. 1992. Riksarkivets bygninger 1817–1992. *Arkivmagasinet. Informasjon fra Riksarkivaren* 2/92:26–31.

Johnsen, Oscar Albert. 1920. Den nyere lokalhistoriske forskning. In *Norsk historisk videnskap i femti år 1869–1919*. Kristiania.

Johnsen, Oscar Albert. 1923. *Finnmarkens politiske historie*. Kristiania.

Johnsen, Oscar Albert. 1939. *Norwegische Wirtschaftsgeschichte*. Jena.

Juhasz, Lajos. 1971. Demografiske kriser. *Heimen* 15:397–417; also appeared in French: Les Crises démographiques en Norvège (XVIIe–XVIIIe siècles). *Annales de Démographie Historique 1972*.

Jörberg, Lennart. 1973. The Nordic Countries 1850–1914. In Carlo M. Cipolla (ed.), *The Fontana Economic History of Europe* 4(2):375–485. London.

Jørgensen, Hans-Jørgen. 1969. *Det norske tollvesens historie. Fra middelalderen til 1814*. Oslo.

Kaldal, Ingar. 1994. Historie som forteljing. In M.-B. Ohman Nielsen (ed.), *Form og forskerens forståelse*. Oslo.

Kaldal, Ingar. 1994a. *Alltagsgeschichte og mikrohistorie*. Trondheim.

Kaldal, Ingar. 1994b. *Arbeid og miljø ved Follafoss Tresliperi og Ranheim Papirfabrikk 1920–1970*. Trondheim.

Kalhama, Maija-Liisa (ed.). 1982. *Suomalaiset jäämeren rannoilla/Finnene ved Nordishavets strender*. Turku.

Karlsen, Trond. 1982. *Dødelighetskrisene i Trøndelag på 1770- og 1780-tallet*. Unpublished Master's thesis. University of Trondheim.

Keilhau, Wilhelm. 1927. *Norge og verdenskrigen*. Oslo

Keilhau, Wilhelm. 1935–8. *Det norske folks liv og historie gjennem tidene*, Vols. X–XI. Oslo.

Kelly-Godal, Joan. 1975–6. The Social Relations of the Sexes: Methodological Implications of Women's History. *Signs* 1(1).

Keskitalo, Alf Isak. 1976. Research as an Inter-ethnic Relation. *Acta Borealia* 25.
Kirkhusmo, Anders. 1983. *Akademi og seminar. Norges lærerhøgskole 1922–1982.* Trondheim.
Kjeldstadli, Knut. 1978. Standssamfunnets oppløsning. *Kontrast 77* 7/1978: 50–61.
Kjeldstadli, Knut. 1980. Hvorfor historie? *Spor* 6.
Kjeldstadli, Knut. 1989a. Historisk Antropologi. *Historisk tidsskrift* 68:50–65.
Kjeldstadli, Knut. 1989b. *Jerntid. Fabrikksystem og arbeidere ved Christiania Spigerverk og Kværner Brug fra om lag 1890 til 1940.* Oslo.
Kjeldstadli, Knut. 1990. *Den delte byen. 1900–1948 (Oslo bys historie,* Vol. 4). Oslo.
Kjeldstadli, Knut. 1991. Struktur, norm, interesse – om historikernes behov for en handlingsteori. *Historisk tidsskrift* 70:50–61.
Kjeldstadli, Knut. 1992a. Synteser og språk. In Marthinsen and Winge 1992:72–82.
Kjeldstadli, Knut. 1992b. *Fortida er ikke hva den en gang var. En innføring i historiefaget.* Oslo.
Kjeldstadli, Knut. 1992c. Hverdagslivet – et godt emne å studere? *Dugnad* 18.
Kjeldstadli, Knut. 1993a. En ny historie? *Historie* 3(2).
Kjeldstadli, Knut. 1993b. Verken relativisme eller absolutisme, men et relasjonelt standpunkt. *Historisk tidsskrift* 72:517–21.
Kjeldstadli, Knut. 1994. *Et splittet samfunn 1905–35 (Aschehougs Norges historie,* Vol. 10). Oslo.
Kjærheim, Steinar. 1958. Norwegian Timber Exports in 18th Century. A Comparison of Port Books and Private Accounts. *Scandinavian Economic History Review* 5:188–201.
Kneppen, Alf Steinar. 1976. *Giftermål og sosiale ulikheter i Ullensaker fra 1730-åra til 1840-åra.* Unpublished Master's thesis. University of Oslo.
Knudtsen, Margunn Skjei. 1986. *Befolkningsutviklinga i Stod prestegjeld ca. 1665–1801.* Unpublished Master's thesis. University of Trondheim.
Knutsen, Sverre. 1991. From Expansion to Panic and Crash. The Norwegian Banking System and its Customers 1913–1924. *Scandinavian Economic History Review* 39:41–71.
Knutsen, Sverre. 1994. Norwegian banks and the legacy of the interwar years. In A. Teichova, T. Gourvish, and A. Pogany (eds.) *Universal Banking in the Twentieth Century.* Aldershot.
Knutsen, Sverre. 1995. Phases in the development of the Norwegian banking system 1910–1980. In Youssef Cassis, Gerald Feldman, and Ulf Olsson (eds.) *The Evolution of Financial Institutions and Markets in Twentieth–Century Europe.* Leicester.
Koht, Halvdan. 1906. *Fredstanken i Noregs-sogo.* Kristiania.
Koht, Halvdan. 1908. *Die Stellung Norwegens und Schwedens im deutsch-dänischen Konflikt, zumal während der Jahre 1863 und 1864.* Kristiania.
Koht, Halvdan. 1910. Bonde mot borgar i nynorsk historie. Revised edition (1970) in *Hundre års historisk forskning. Utvalgte artikler fra Historisk Tidsskrift.* Oslo.
Koht, Halvdan. 1920. Historieskrivning og folkevokster. In *Norsk historisk videnskap i femti år 1869–1919:*1–18. Kristiania.
Koht, Halvdan. 1921. Sagaenes opfatning av vår gamle historie. In *Innhogg og utsyn.* Kristiania.

Koht, Halvdan. 1951. *Historikar i lære*. Oslo.
Koht, Halvdan. 1953. *På leit etter liner i historia*. Oslo.
Koht, Halvdan. 1955. *Historisk innleiing til 1905. Syn og Segn* 61.
Koht, Halvdan. 1965. *Minnearv og historie*. Oslo.
Koht, Halvdan. 1975 (1926). *Norsk bondereising*. Oslo.
Koht, Halvdan. 1977 (1908). Henrik Wergeland og den norske folkearven. *Norsk vilje:*75–97. Oslo.
Koht, Halvdan. 1977 (1917). J. E. Sars. *Norsk vilje:*24–39. Oslo.
Koht, Halvdan. 1977 (1920). Nasjonalkjensla i Noreg. *Norsk vilje:*1–12. Oslo.
Koht, Halvdan. 1977 (1921). Vitskap og nasjonalt liv. *Norsk vilje:*40–53. Oslo.
Koht, Halvdan, J. S. Worm-Müller, and Sverre Steen. 1935. *Trin i norsk historieforskning*. Universitetets radioforedrag. Oslo.
Kolsrud, Knut. 1947. Finnefolket i Ofoten. En studie i Ofotens demografi og sjøfinnenes etnografi i eldre tid. *Nordnorske samlinger* 8. Oslo.
Kolsrud, Knut. 1955. Sjøfinnene i Rognsund. *Studia septentrionalia* 6. Oslo.
Kolsrud, Knut. 1961. Sommersete. *Samiske samlinger* 4. Oslo.
Kongsrud, Helge. 1984. *Den kongelige arveretten til Norge 1536–1661*. Oslo.
Kongsrud, Helge. 1987. Den kongelige arveretten til Norge –både politisk pretensjon og almen rettsoppfatning? *Historisk tidsskrift* 1987:533–47.
Korppi-Tommola, Aura. 1990. Kvinnohistoria i kris? In *Kvinnohistoria i teoretisk perspektiv:*52–61.
Kraft, Jens. 1820–35. *Topographisk–statistisk Beskrivelse over Kongeriget Norge*. Christiania.
Krag, Claus. 1991. *Ynglingatal og ynglingasaga: en studie i historiske kilder*. Oslo.
Kringsjå. Informasjon fra Norsk lokalhistorisk institutt. Oslo.
Kristoffersen, Dag. 1983. "*To bønder på en bergmann*". *Befolkningsutvikling i Sandsvær 1750–1801*. Unpublished Master's thesis. University of Oslo.
Krogseth, Otto. 1983. *Den tyske historismen. En idéhistorisk undersøkelse av den tyske historismens utviklingshistorie*. Unpublished doctoral dissertation. University of Oslo.
Krokann, Inge. 1976 (1942). *Det store hamskiftet i bondesamfunnet*. Etterord av Tore Pryser. Oslo.
Kuhnle, Stein. 1983. *Velferdsstatens utvikling. Norge i komparativt perspektiv*. Oslo.
Kvinnohistoria i teoretiskt perspektiv. Konferanserapport från det tredje nordiska kvinnohistorikermøtet 1989. Uppsala Papers in Economic History 1990, Working Paper No. 8. Uppsala.
Kvium, Christian, and Birgitte Wåhlin (eds.). 1987. *Mentalitetsforandringer. Oplæg fra den 19. Nordiske fagkonference i historisk metodelære, Ljusterø, 31. maj–3. juni 1985*. Århus.
Kyvik, Svein, and Jens-Are Enoksen. 1992. *Universitetspersonalets tidsbruk. NAVFs utredningsinstitutt. Rapport 10/92*. Oslo.
Kaartvedt, Alf. 1956. *Kampen mot parlamentarisme 1880–1884. Den konservative politikken under vetostriden*. Oslo.
Kaartvedt, Alf. 1964. *Det norske storting gjennom 150 år*, Vol. 1, *Fra Riksforsamlingen til 1869*. Oslo.
Kaartvedt, Alf. 1980a. The Economic Basis of Norwegian Nationalism in the Nineteenth Century. In R. Mitchison (ed.), *The Roots of Nationalism: Studies in Northern Europe*. Edinburgh.
Kaartvedt, Alf. 1980b. Samlingspolitikk og unionslojalitet. Francis Hagerups dilemma 1902–1905. *Historisk tidsskrift* 59:140–63.

Lafferty, William M. 1981. *Participation and Democracy in Norway*. Oslo.

Lahn, Janneke. 1986. *Livsvilkår og levesjanser i Moss, 1776–1825*. Unpublished Master's thesis. University of Oslo.

Lange, Even. 1977. The Concession Laws of 1906–09 and Norwegian Industrial Development. *Scandinavian Journal of History* 2:311–30.

Lange, Even. 1982. Konjunkturer og teknologisk tilpasning. En case–study fra norsk treforedlingsindustri. In F. Sejersted (ed.), *Vekst gjennom krise. Studier i norsk teknologihistorie*. Oslo.

Lange, Even. 1985. *Fra Linderud til Eidsvold Værk*, Vol. IV, *Treforedlingens epoke: 1895–1975*. Oslo 1985.

Lange, Even. 1988. Business History som innfallsvinkel til økonomisk historie. *Historisk tidsskrift* 67:283–95.

Lange, Even (ed.). 1989. *Teknologi i virksomhet. Verkstedindustrien i Norge etter 1840*. Oslo.

Lange, Even. 1994a. The Norwegian banking system before and after the interwar crises. In A. Teichova, T. Gourvish, and A. Pogany (eds.), *Universal Banking in the Twentieth Century*. Aldershot.

Lange, Even. 1994b. Financial institutions and markets in twentieth–century Scandinavia. In Gerald D. Feldman, Ulf Olsson, Michael Bordo, and Youssef Cassis (eds.), *The evolution of modern financial institutions in the twentieth century*. Proceedings B12, 11th International Economic History Congress, Milan.

Langholm, Sivert. 1967. *Historisk rekonstruksjon og begrunnelse. En innføring i historiestudiet*. Oslo.

Langholm, Sivert. 1970a. Periferi og sentrum i historieforskningen. *Historisk tidsskrift* 49:260–70.

Langholm, Sivert. 1970b. De nordiske fagkonferanser om historisk metodelære i 1960-årene. *Historisk tidsskrift* (Sweden) 1/1970:68–79.

Langholm, Sivert 1972. The Historian, the Sociologist – and the Third Man. *Historisk tidsskrift* (Sweden) 4/1972:474–89.

Langholm, Sivert. 1974. Historie på individnivå. Omkring Ullensaker-undersøkelsen – et mikrohistorisk eksperiment. *Historisk tidsskrift* 53: 243–72.

Langholm, Sivert. 1975. Short-distance Migration, Circles and Flows: Movement to and from Ullensaker According to the Population Census Lists of 1865. *Scandinavian Economic History Review* 23:36–62.

Langholm, Sivert. 1976a. The Christiania Project – Historians Investigate the Making of Urban Society. *Research in Norway* 1976:49–57.

Langholm, Sivert. 1976b. On the Scope of Micro-history. *Scandinavian Journal of History* 1:1–24.

Langholm, Sivert. 1982. *The Role of Local History in Historical Research*. Unpublished paper.

Langholm, Sivert. 1984. *Elitenes valg. Sosial avstand og politisk oppslutning blant Christianiavelgerne i 1868*. Oslo.

Langholm, Sivert. 1994. Den norske historiske forening 125 år. *HiFo-nytt* 3/1994:41–3.

Langholm, Sivert et al. (eds.). 1994. *Den kritiske analyse. Festskrift til Ottar Dahl på 70-årsdagen den 5. januar 1994*. Oslo.

Laursen, Laurs. 1920. *Danmark–Norges traktater 1523–1750 med dertil hørende aktstykker*. V:215–43, 297–313, 345–75. Copenhagen.

Leem, Knud. 1767. *Beskrivelse over Finmarkens Lapper.* Copenhagen.
Leuillot, Paul. 1968. Forsvar for lokalhistorien. *Heimen* 14:273–84. Oslo.
  Translation by G. Sandvik of P. Leuillot, Apologie pour l'histoire locale. *Annales* 1967:154ff.
Lieberman, Sima. 1970. *The Industrialization of Norway 1800–1920.* Oslo.
Lilienskiold, H. 1932–45. Speculum Boreale. *Nordnorske samlinger* 4, 7. Oslo.
Liljeström, Marianne. 1994. Kvinnohistorisk forskning i Norden: Om historiografi och problemorientering. *Rapport fra det 18. nordiske historikermøte,* Oslo, August 1994:5–15.
Liljeström, Marianne, Pirjo Markkola, and Sari Mäenpää (eds.). 1994. *Kvinnohistoriens nya utmaningar: Från sexualitet till världshistoria.* Konferensrapport från det IV Nordiska Kvinnohistorikermötet 1993, Tampereen Yliopisto, Historiatieteen laitoksen julkaisuja 17. Tampere.
Lindbekk, Kari 1978. *Lofoten og Vesterålens historie 1500–1700.* Stokmarknes.
Lorange, Erik, and Jan Eivind Myhre. 1991. Urban Planning in Norway. In T. Hall (ed.), *Planning and Urban Growth in the Nordic Countries:*116–66. Oslo.
Lorentzen, Bernt. 1952. *Omkring et kjøpmannsskap. Kløverhuset.* Bergen.
Lorentzen, Bernt. 1954. *Dale Fabrikker 1879–1954.* Bergen.
Lowell, Briant Lindsay. 1987. *Scandinavian Exodus. Demography and Social Development of 19th-century Rural Communities.* Boulder, Colo.
Lunden, Kåre. 1965. Mellomalder. *Heggen og Frøland* I:149–311. Askim.
Lunden, Kåre. 1972. *Økonomi og samfunn.* Oslo.
Lunden, Kåre. 1974. Some Causes of Change in a Peasant Economy. *Scandinavian Economic History Review* 22:117–35.
Lunden, Kåre. 1977. *Norge under Sverreætten* (K. Mykland [ed.], *Norges historie,* Vol. 3). Oslo.
Lunden, Kåre. 1978. *Korn og kaup.* Oslo.
Lunden, Kåre. 1979. Gardar, bruk og menneske i høgmellomalderen. *Historisk tidsskrift* 58:111–58.
Lunden, Kåre. 1980a. Kjettarar, prestar og sagakvinner. Om historie og historieproduksjon. Oslo.
Lunden, Kåre. 1980b. Lokalsoga – i kvé eller på viddene? *Heimen* 18:313–17.
Lunden, Kåre. 1980c. Norsk økonomi under dansk styre. *Historisk tidsskrift* 59:88–108.
Lunden, Kåre. 1981. Øydegardsprosjektet – metodar og resultat. Svar til Jørn Sandnes. *Historisk tidsskrift* 60:26–49.
Lunden, Kåre. 1982. Nora jager det "vidunderlige" – Kva er kvinnehistorie? In *Litt frukt fra kunnskapens tre. Fagkritikk og kvinnekritikk:*68–88. Oppland Distriktshøgskole Informasjonsserien nr. 30.
Lunden, Kåre. 1985a. *Dialog med fortida.* Oslo.
Lunden, Kåre. 1985b. Val for historia. Motsetnader hos Jens Arup Seip som metodolog og venstrepolitisk legtimator. In Lunden 1985a:220–68. Oslo.
Lunden, Kåre. 1986. Norsk tronfylgjerett i seinmellomalderen og lovgjevingssuvereniteten. *Historisk tidsskrift* 65:393–419.
Lunden, Kåre. 1991a. *Biletet av fortida. Innhogg i historisk fagteori.* Oslo.
Lunden, Kåre. 1991b. Offentleg bruk av historie i Noreg. In Lunden 1991a:242–8. Oslo.
Lunden, Kåre. 1992. *Norsk grålyning. Norsk nasjonalisme 1770–1814 på allmenn bakgrunn.* Oslo.
Lunden, Kåre. 1993. *Nasjon eller union? Refleksjonar og røynsler.* Oslo.

Lunden, Kåre. 1994a. Min klassiker. E. H. Carr. *HiFo-nytt* 3/1994:13–21.
Lunden, Kåre. 1994b. Was there a Norwegian National Identity in the Middle Ages? *Scandinavian Journal of History* 19.
Lundestad, Geir. 1972. Anmeldelse av Magne Skodvins *Norden og NATO. Historisk Tidsskrift* 52:221–4.
Lundestad, Geir. 1977a. USA, skandinavisk forsvarsforbund og Halvard Lange: en revurdering. *Internasjonal Politikk* 1/1977:139–73.
Lundestad, Geir. 1977b. Sluttreplikk. *Internasjonal Politikk* 3/1977:561–6.
Lundestad, Geir. 1978. *The American Non-policy towards Eastern Europe 1943–1947: Universalism in an Area Not of Essential Interest to the United States.* Oslo.
Lundestad, Geir. 1980. *America, Scandinavia, and the Cold War 1945–1949.* Oslo.
Lundestad, Geir. 1984. Empire by Invitation? The United States and Western Europe, 1945–1952. *The Society for Historians of American Foreign Relations Newsletter* 15(3):1–21.
Lundestad, Geir. 1986. Empire by Invitation? The United States and Western Europe, 1945–1952. *Journal of Peace Research* 23:263–77.
Lundestad, Geir. 1990. *The American Empire.* Oxford.
Lundestad, Geir. 1994. The Fall of Empires: Peace, Stability, and Legitimacy. In G. Lundestad (ed.), *The Fall of Great Powers: Peace, Stability, and Legitimacy*:383–402. Oslo.
Lægereid, Per, and Johan P. Olsen. 1978. *Byråkrati og beslutninger.* Oslo.
Løberg, Lars. 1987. *Bidrag til lokal historie. Bibliografi over hovedfags- og magistergradsavhandlinger med lokal- og regionalhistorisk ramme.* Oslo.
Løvlien, Astrid. 1977. *Dødelighetskrisa på 1740-tallet.* Unpublished Master's thesis. University of Bergen.
Løyland, Margit. 1992. *Slagsmål, leiermål og bøtlagde egder 1600–1700.* Oslo.
Løyland, Margit. 1993. Bygdebokdekninga i Noreg. Resultat frå NLI-prosjektet 1992. *Heimen* 30:276–85.
Låg, Jul *et al.* 1959. *Norges Landbrukshøgskole 1859–1959.* Oslo.
Mannsåker, Dagfinn. 1954. *Det norske presteskapet i det 19. hundreåret. Sosialhistoriske studiar.* Oslo.
March, James G., and Johan P. Olsen. 1989. *Rediscovering Institutions.* New York.
Marthinsen, Liv (ed.). 1990. *Tingboka som kilde.* Oslo.
Marthinsen, Liv. 1993. *Kringsjå. Informasjon fra Norsk lokalhistorisk institutt.* No. 21. Oslo.
Marthinsen, Liv, and Harald Winge (eds.). 1992. *Syntese i historieskrivingen – innspill fra et seminar.* Oslo.
Martinsen, Kari. 1984. *Freidige og uforsagte diakonisser. Et omsorgsyrke vokser fram 1860–1905.* Oslo.
Martinsen, Kari. 1989. *Omsorg, sykepleie og medisin. Historisk–filosofiske essays.* Oslo.
Marxism och historieforskning 1973. *Studier i historisk metode nr. 8.* Oslo.
Mathiesen, Per. 1974. *Grunnfjord–Dypfjord. En analyse av tilpassingsprosesser i to nord-norske lokalsamfunn.* University of Tromsø.
Mathiesen, Per. 1976. Har samfunnsfagene noen bruksverdi? *Acta Borealia* 25.
Mathiesen, S. R. 1994. Etnisitet, nasjonalisme og modernitet. Norsk sameforskning i "lappologiens" periode. *Dugnad* 20.
Matricul, Det Kongelige Fredriks Universitets. Kristiania.
Maurseth, Per. 1979. *Sentraladministrasjonens historie,* Vol. 1, *1814–1844.* Oslo.

Maurseth, Per. 1984. Mellom Seip og Bull. Tilbakeblikk på en jubileumsdebatt. In P. Fuglum and J. Simensen (eds.), *Historie nedenfra. Festskrift til Edvard Bull på 70-årsdagen*:138–49. Oslo.

Maurseth, Per. 1987a. *Gjennom kriser til makt (1920–1935)* (E. Bull et al. [eds.], Arbeiderbevegelsens historie, Vol. 3). Oslo.

Maurseth, Per. 1987b. The Norwegian Bourgeoisie and the "Beamtenstaat" of the 19th Century. Class and State: A Historiographical and Theoretical Discussion. In *Bericht über das 2. deutsch-norwegische Historikertreffen in Bonn, Mai 1987. Bürgertum und Bürokratie im 19. Jahrhundert. Technologie. Innovation. Technologietransfer*:3–13. Oslo.

Maurseth, Per. 1989. Kön och historia. Åtta teser och en slutvinjett, and En skev polemik. Kommentar til Gro Hagemann. *Arbetarhistoria, Meddelande från Arbetarrörelsens Arkiv och Bibliotek*, Vol. 13, no. 51:24–9, 30–2.

Meddelelser fra Kattegat–Skagerrak-prosjektet. Nos. 1–17. 1982–91.

Melby, Kari. 1978. Kvinnehistorie – hva og hvordan? *Kjerringråd. Kvinnepolitisk tidsskrift* 3/1978:27–32.

Melby, Kari. 1980. Prostitusjon og kontroll. In Gotaas et al. 1980.

Melby, Kari. 1990. *Kall og kamp. Norsk Sykepleierforbunds historie.* Oslo.

Melby, Kari. 1991. Women's Ideology: Difference, Equality or a New Femininity. Women Teachers and Nurses in Norway 1912–1940. In T. Andreasen et al. (eds.), *Moving On. New Perspectives on the Women's Movement.* Acta Jutlandica LXVII:1, Humanities Series 66:138–54.

Mendelsohn, Oskar. 1969–86. *Jødenes historie i Norge gjennom 300 år.* 2 vols. Oslo.

Meyer, Jørgen Christian. 1992. Urtiden. In Blom 1992e: 13–139.

Midbøe, Hans. 1960. *Det Kongelige Norske Videnskabers Selskabs historie I.* Trondheim.

Minde, Henry. 1980. Samebevegelsen, Det norske Arbeiderparti og samiske rettigheter. In T. Thuen (ed.), *Samene – urbefolkning og minoritet.* Tromsø, Oslo, Bergen.

Minde, Henry. 1983. *Stein og brød.* Alta.

Minde, Henry. 1985. The Sami Movement, the Norwegian Labour Party and Sami Rights. In *L'image de l'autre. Étrangers – Minoritaires – Marginaux.* Stuttgart.

Minde, Henry. 1991. Ei politisk handling i normal tyding av ordet? Sameforskningen i et hundreår. *Historisk tidsskrift* 70:539–65.

Minde, Henry. 1992. *Samenes historie som etterkrigshistorisk forskningsfelt.* LOS-senter Notat 9228. Bergen.

Minde, Kjell Bjørn. 1987. Levestandarden i Norge 1750–1914. In G. Karlsson (ed.), *Levestandarden i Norden 1750–1914*:46–66. Reykjavik.

Minde, Kjell Bjørn, and Jan Ramstad. 1986. The Development of Real Wages in Norway 1730–1910. *Scandinavian Economic History Review* 34:90–121.

Moe, Moltke, and Johan Ernst Sars. 1914. Norsk folkekarakter. In *Norge 1813–1914*, Vol. II:1–8. Kristiania.

Moe, Thorvald. 1977. *Demographic Development and Economic Growth in Norway, 1740–1940.* New York.

Moen, Bjørg, and Ståle Dryvik. 1994. *Demografi som etterkrigshistorisk forskningsfelt.* LOS-senter Notat 9356. Bergen.

Moen, Eli. 1991. Norway's entry into the age of paper: The development of the pulp and paper industry in the Drammen district. In Bruland 1991.

Moen, Eli. 1994. Technological change and the decline of the traditional pulp

and paper industry in Norway. *Scandinavian Economic History Review* 42.
Moksnes, Aslaug. 1984. *Likestilling eller særstilling? Norsk Kvinnesaksforening 1884–1913*. Oslo.
Moland, Tallak. 1992. *Fotball og maskulinitet*. Unpublished seminar paper in History. University of Bergen.
Moravcsik, Andrew. 1993. Preferences and Power in the European Community: A Liberal Intergovernmentalist Approach. *Journal of Common Market Studies* 31:473–524.
Morgenstierne, Bredo. 1911. Universitetet fra 1813 til 1911. *Det Kongelige Frederiks Universitet 1811–1911* I:1–401. Kristiania.
Munby, Lionel M. 1969. Lokalhistorie i England. *Heimen* 14:487–97.
Munch, Peter Andreas. 1852–63. *Det norske Folks Historie*, Vols. 1–4; 2nd part, Vols. 1–2. Christiania.
Munch, Peter Andreas. 1853. *Om den saakaldte nyere historiske Skole i Norge*. Christiania.
Munthe, Wilhelm. 1920. Den Norske Historiske Forening 1869–1919. In *Norsk historisk videnskap i femti år 1869–1919*:322–52. Kristiania.
Myhre, Elin. 1990. *Generasjonsskifte eller transaksjon? Om handlingsmønstre og normer når jord skiftet eier i Ullensaker på 1800-tallet*. Unpublished Master's thesis. University of Oslo.
Myhre, Jan Eivind. 1977. Urbaniseringen i Norge i industrialiseringens første fase ca. 1850–1914. In G. A. Blom (ed.), *Urbaniseringsprosessen i Norden. Det XVII nordiske historikermøte i Trondheim 1977*, Vol. 3:13–94. Oslo.
Myhre, Jan Eivind. 1978a. The Christiania Study. *Industrial Buildings and Dwellings* 2/1978:25–33.
Myhre, Jan Eivind. 1978b. *Sagene – en arbeiderforstad befolkes 1801–1875*. Oslo.
Myhre, Jan Eivind. 1981. Vest for byen – bærumsbefolkningen 1800–1920. In R. Fladby and H. Winge (eds.). *By og bygd – stad og omland*:61–87. Oslo.
Myhre, Jan Eivind. 1983. Urbaniseringen i Norge etter første verdenskrig. *Historica IV, Föredrag vid det XVIII Nordiska historikermøtet Jyväskylä 1981, Studia Historica Jyväskylänsia* 27:157–70. Jyväskylä.
Myhre, Jan Eivind. 1986. Research into Norwegian Living Conditions in the Period 1750–1914. *Scandinavian Economic History Review* 34:159–66.
Myhre, Jan Eivind. 1987. Tilnærminger til byhistorien. På leting etter de urbane variabler. *Historisk tidsskrift* 66:180–95.
Myhre, Jan Eivind. 1990. *Hovedstaden Christiania 1814–1900 (Oslo bys historie*, Vol. 3). Oslo.
Myhre, Jan Eivind. 1991. The Urbanization of Norway 1850–1980. In T. Hall (ed.), *Planning the Nordic Countries*:122–9. London.
Myhre, Jan Eivind. 1993. The Nordic Countries. In R. Rodger (ed.), *European Urban History: Prospect and Retrospect*:170–90. Leicester.
Myhre, Jan Eivind. 1994a. Den norske historiske kultur. Om sammenheng og fragmentering i norsk historieforskning. *Historisk tidsskrift* 73:320–37.
Myhre, Jan Eivind. 1994b. Verdien av lokalhistorie. *Heimen* 31:227–35.
Myhre, Jan Eivind, and Jan Sigurd Østberg (eds.). 1979. *Mennesker i Kristiania. Sosialhistorisk søkelys på 1800-tallet*. Oslo.
Mykland, Knut. 1955a. *Fra Søgaden til Strandgaten 1807–1880 (Trondheim bys historie*, Vol. 3). Trondheim.
Mykland, Knut. 1955b. *Grandeur et décadence. En studie i Ernst Sars' historiske grunnsyn*. Oslo.

Mykland, Knut (ed.). 1967. *Om 1814*. Oslo.
Mykland, Knut (ed.). 1976–80. *Norges historie*. 15 vols. Oslo.
Mykland, Knut. 1978. *Kampen om Norge. 1784–1814* (K. Mykland [ed.], *Norges historie*, Vol. 9). Oslo.
Myklebost, Hallstein *et al.* 1963. *Norge*. 4 vols. Oslo.
Nagel, Anne-Hilde (ed.). 1994. *Kjønn og velferdsstat*. Oslo.
Natvik, Oddvar. 1989. *Brotsatferd i Sogn og Sunnfjord på 1600-talet. Brotsstrukturar i dei to bygdelaga ut frå sakefallslistene*. Unpublished Master's thesis. University of Oslo.
Nedkvitne, Arnved. 1983. *Utenrikshandelen fra det vestafjelske Norge*. Unpublished doctoral dissertation. University of Bergen.
Nedkvitne, Arnved. 1988. *"Mens Bønderne seilte og Jægterne for". Nordnorsk og vestnorsk kystøkonomi 1500–1730*. Oslo.
Nedkvitne, Arnved. 1991. Mentalitetshistorie – en historiografisk blindgate? *Historisk tidsskrift* 70:62–71.
Nedkvitne, Arnved, and Per Norseng. 1991. *Byen under Eikaberg (Oslo bys historie*, Vol. 1). Oslo.
Nerbøvik, Jostein. 1976. *Norsk historie 1870–1905*. Oslo.
Nerheim, Gunnar. 1983. *Growth Through Welding. Perspectives on the history of a Norwegian Welding Firm. Norgas A/S 1908–1983*. Oslo.
Nerheim, Gunnar, and Helge W. Nordvik. 1986. *Ikke Bare Maskiner: Historien om IBM i Norge 1935–1985*. Oslo.
Nerheim, Gunnar, and Bjørn S. Utne. 1990. *Under samme stjerne: Rederiet Peder Smedvig 1915–1990*. Stavanger.
Nielsen, J. P. 1991. Ønsket tsaren seg en isfri havn i nord? *Historisk tidsskrift* 70:604-21.
Nielsen, J. P. 1992. "Den norske trussel". Et lite kjent aspekt ved de russisk–norske forbindelser 1826–1917. In E. Niemi (ed.), *Pomor. Nord-Norge og Nord-Russland gjennom tusen år*. Oslo.
Nielsen, J. P. 1994. The Barents Region in Historical Perspective. In O. S. Stokke and O. Tunander (eds.), *The Barents Region. Cooperation in Arctic Europe*. Oslo–London–New Delhi.
Nielsen, Konrad. 1932–62. *Lappisk (samisk) ordbok/Lapp Dictionary*. 5 vols. Oslo.
Nielsen, Mai-Brith Ohman. 1994a. *"The Gospel of the Soil". Gender in Constitution of a Political Ideology. The Creation of Norwegian Agrarian Nationalism 1914–1940*. Paper presented to the ESTHER-seminar "New Issues, Fields and Approaches in Women's and Gender History", October 1994. University of Bielefeld.
Nielsen, May-Brith Ohman. 1994b. Framtid for den faglige frimodigheten? *HiFo-nytt* 3/1994:28–37.
Nielsen, Yngvar. 1911. Indledning. *Det Kongelige Fredriks Universitet 1811–1911* I:iii–lx. Kristiania.
Nielssen, Alf Ragnar. 1986. Economic Adaption among the Coast Sami Population in Finnmark *c.* 1700. *Acta Borealia* 35.
Niemi, Einar. 1977. *Oppbrudd og tilpasning. Den finske flyttingen til Vadsø 1845–1885*. Vadsø.
Niemi, Einar. 1987. Nord-norsk lokalhistorie – kulturaktivitet, vitenskap og politisk redskap. *Heimen* 24:58–72.
Niemi, Einar. 1989. Norsk lokalhistorie på 1970- og 80-tallet – paradigmeskifte eller kontinuitet? *Heimen* 26:195–204.

Niemi, Einar. 1991. Har lokalhistorien behov for teori? In L. Marthinsen and H. Winge (eds.), *Bygdesamfunnet – en sammensatt helhet*:7–22. Oslo.

Niemi, Einar. 1992. The Kvens in Vadsoe, Northern Norway, 1850–1940. In M. Engman (ed.), *Ethnic Identity in Urban Europe. Comparative Studies on Governments and Non-dominant Ethnic Groups in Europe, 1850–1940*, Vol. VIII. New York–Dartmouth.

Niemi, Einar, and Helge Salvesen. 1987. Samene og kvenene/finnene i minoritetspolitisk perspektiv. In G. Karlsson (ed.), *Nationale og etniske minoriteter i Norden*. Reykjavik.

Niemi, Einar, and Hallvard Tjelmeland (eds.). 1992. *Nyere byhistorie i Norden*. Tromsø.

Niemi, Einar, and Harald Winge. 1993. *Lokalhistorie som etterkrigshistorisk forskningsfelt*. LOS-senter Notat 9311. Bergen.

Nilsson, Sven A., Karl–Gustaf Hildebrand, Bo Öhngren (eds.). 1974. *Kriser och krispolitik i Norden under mellankrigstiden*. Nordiska historikermøtet i Uppsala 1974. Møtesrapport. Uppsala.

Njølstad, Olav. 1990. Learning from History? Case Studies and the Limits to Theory-building. In N. P. Gleditsch and O. Njølstad (eds.), *Arms Races: Technological and Political Dynamics*:220–46. London.

Njølstad, Olav. 1994. *Peacekeeper* and *Troublemaker: Jimmy Carter and the Soviet Union, 1977–1978*. Unpublished doctoral dissertation. University of Oslo.

Nordby, Trond. 1983. *Venstre og samlingspolitikken 1906–08. En studie i partioppløsning og gjenreisning*. Oslo.

Nordby, Trond. 1989. "Roll-call Analysis" within Historical Theory – with Examples from Norwegian Party History. *Scandinavian Journal of History* 14:39–56.

Nordby, Trond. 1991. *Det moderne gjennombruddet i bondesamfunnet. Norge 1870–1920*. Oslo.

Nordvik, Helge W. 1977. Krisepolitikken og den teoretiske nyorienteringen av den økonomiske politikken i Norge i 1930–årene. *Historisk tidsskrift* 56:286–315.

Nordvik, Helge W. 1979. Finanspolitikkens og den offentlige sektors rolle i norsk økonomi i mellomkrigstiden. *Historisk tidsskrift* 58:223–37.

Nordvik, Helge W. (ed.). 1984. *Rent mel i posen. Bjølsen Valsemølle A/S og mølleindustriens utvikling 1884–1984*. Stavanger.

Nordvik, Helge W. 1991. Norwegian Maritime Historical Research during the Past Twenty Years: A Critical Survey. *Sjøfartshistorisk Årbok 1990*:241–79. Bergen.

Nordvik, Helge W. 1993. The Banking System, Industrialization and Economic Growth in Norway 1850–1914. *Scandinavian Economic History Review* 41: 51–72.

Nordvik, Helge W. 1994. Nicolai Rygg – vitenskapsmann og sentralbanksjef. In *Portretter fra norsk historie*. Oslo.

Nordvik, Helge W., Gunnar Nerheim, and Trygve Brandal. 1989. *Penger spart, penger tjent. Sparebankene og den økonomiske utvikling på Sør–Vestlandet 1839–1989*. Stavanger.

Norges allmennvitenskapelige forskningsråd 1973. *Rapport om status og perspektiver i historisk forskning i Norge i 1973*. Part 2. Oslo.

Norges forskningsråd. Prosjektkatalog 1993. Humaniora. Oslo.

Norman, Hans, and Harald Runblom. 1988. *Transatlantic Connections. Nordic Migration to the New World after 1800*. Oslo.
Norsk biografisk leksikon, I–XIX. 1923–83. Oslo.
Norsk historisk videnskap i femti år 1869–1919. Published by Den norske historiske forening to mark its 50th anniversary, 21 December 1919:277–306. Kristiania.
Norsk lokalhistorisk litteratur 1946–1970. Published by the University Library of Oslo 1976–81.
Norsk lokalhistorisk litteratur 1971–1990. Published by the University Library of Oslo 1993–4.
Norske historikeres organisasjonsforhold. *Historisk tidsskrift* 68:113–21.
NOU 1984:18. *Om samenes rettsstilling*. Oslo.
NOU 1985:14. *Samisk kultur og utdanning*. Oslo.
NOU 1991:24. *Organisering for helhet og mangfold i norsk forskning. Norges offentlige utredninger*. Oslo.
NOU 1993:24. *Lov og rett i Norges-nett. Lov om universiteter og høgskoler. Norges offentlige utredninger*. Oslo.
NOU 1993:34. *Rett til og forvaltning av land og vann i Finnmark. Bakgrunnsmateriale for Samerettsutvalget*. Oslo.
NOU 1994:21. *Bruk av land og vann i Finnmark i historisk perspektiv. Bakgrunnsmateriale for Samerettsutvalget*. Oslo.
Novick, Peter. 1988. *That Noble Dream. The "Objectivity Question" and the American Historical Profession*. Cambridge.
Nygård, Toivo. 1978. *Suur-Suomi vai lähiheimolaisten auttaminen*. Keuruu.
Næss, Hans Eyvind. 1982. *Trolldomsprosessene i Norge på 1500–1600-tallet. En retts- og sosialhistorisk undersøkelse*. Oslo.
Odén, Birgitta. 1975. *Lauritz Weibull och forskarsamhället* (Bibliotheca historica Lundensis, 39). Lund.
Odner, Knut. 1992. *The Varanger Saami. Habitation and Economy AD 1200–1900*. Oslo.
Offen, Karen, Ruth Roach Pierson, and Jane Rendall (eds.). 1991. *Writing Women's History: International Perspectives*. London–Bloomington, Ind.
Ofstad, Kåre. 1949. Population Statistics and Population Registration in Norway. Part 3, Population Censuses. *Population Studies* 3:66–75.
Oldervoll, Jan. 1992. *Eden or Babylon? On Future Software for Highly Structured Historical Sources*. St. Katharein, FRG.
Olsen, Berit E. 1994. *Giftermålsmønsteret i Sauda på 1800-tallet*. Unpublished Master's thesis. University of Bergen.
Olsen, Kr. Anker. 1953. *Kværner Brug gjennom 100 år*. Oslo.
Olsen, Kr. Anker. 1955. *Norsk Hydro gjennom 50 år*. Oslo.
Olsen, Kr. Anker. 1961. *Wilh. Wilhelmsen i hundre år*. Oslo.
Olsen, Venke. 1983. Finsk etnisitet mellom norsk storsamfunn og samisk minoritet belyst ut fra begrepet etnonym. In J. Sandnes *et al.* (eds.), *Folk og ressurser i nord*. Trondheim.
Olsen, Venke. 1994. International Minority Rights and the Finnish Situation in North Norway. *Migration/Siirtolaisuus*. Turku.
Olstad, Finn. 1978. *Medlemmene i Christiania Arbeidersamfund 1864–1896*. Unpublished Master's thesis. University of Oslo.
Olstad, Finn. 1980. Standssamfunn, klassesamfunn og historisk forskning. *Historisk tidsskrift* 59:406–13.

Olstad, Finn. 1991. *Arbeiderklassens vekst og fall. Hovedlinjer i 100 års norsk historie*. Oslo.

Otnes, Per. 1970. *Den samiske nasjon*. Oslo.

Otterbech, Jens (ed.). 1920. *Kulturværdier hos Norges Finner*. Kristiania.

Paine, Robert. 1957–65. *Coast Lapp Society*, I–II. Tromsø 1957/Tromsø–Oslo–Bergen 1965.

Paine, Robert. 1982. *Dam a River, Damn a People? Saami (Lapp) Livelihood and the Alta/Kautokeino Hydro-electric Project and the Norwegian Parliament*. Copenhagen.

Paine, Robert. 1984. Norwegians and Saami: Nation–State and Fourth World. In G. L. Gould (ed.), *Minorities and Mother Country Imagery*. St. John's, Newfoundland.

Paine, Robert. 1985. Ethnodrama and the "Fourth World": The Saami Action Group in Norway, 1979–81. In N. Dyck (ed.), *Indigenous Peoples and the Nation–State: "Fourth World" politics in Canada, Australia and Norway*. St. John's, Newfoundland.

Paine, Robert. 1991. The Claim of Aboriginality: Saami in Norway. In R. Grønhaug *et al.* (eds.), *The Ecology of Choice and Symbol. Essays in Honour of Fredrik Barth*. Bergen.

Pascoe, Peggy. 1991. Introduction: The Challenge of Writing Cross-cultural Women's History, and Race, Gender and Intercultural Relations: The Case of Interracial Marriages. *Frontiers* 12:1–18.

Paulaharju, S. 1928. *Ruijan Suomalaisia*. Helsinki.

Paulaharju, S. 1935. *Ruijan äärimmäisillä saarilla*. Porvoo.

Pedersen, Steinar. 1986. *Laksen, allmuen og staten. Fiskerett og forvaltning i Tanavassdraget for 1888*. Diedut 2. Kautokeino.

Pehrson, Robert. 1957. *The Bilateral Network of Social Relations in Könkämä Lapp District*. Bloomington, Ind.

Petersen, Erling. 1957. *Den norske Creditbank 1907–1957*. Oslo.

Petersen, Kaare. 1982. *Bankkriser og valutauro. Forretningsbankenes historie i mellomkrigstiden*. Oslo.

Pharo, Helge Ø. 1976. Bridgebuilding and Reconstruction: Norway Faces the Marshall Plan. *Scandinavian Journal of History* 2:125–53.

Pharo, Helge Ø. 1984. Domestic and International Implications of Norwegian Reconstruction. *European University Institute Working Papers* 81/1984. Florence.

Pharo, Helge Ø. 1986a. The Third Force, Atlanticism and Norwegian Attitudes towards European Integration. *European University Working Papers* 255/1986. Florence.

Pharo, Helge Ø. 1986b. *Hjelp til selvhjelp. Det indisk–norske fiskeriprosjektets historie 1952–72*. 2 vols. Oslo.

Pharo, Helge Ø. 1987. Conflict and Cooperation in the Indo-Norwegian Fisheries Project 1952–1972. In Clive Dewey (ed.), *The State and the Market: Studies in the Economic and Social History of the Third World*:319–51. New Dehli.

Pharo, Helge Ø. 1989. Gjenreisning og utenrikspolitikk. In T. Bergh and H. Ø. Pharo (eds.), *Historiker og veileder. Festskrift til Jakob Sverdrup*:163–202. Oslo.

Pharo, Helge Ø. 1993. The Norwegian Labour Party. In R. T. Griffiths (ed.), *Socialist Parties and the Question of Europe in the 1950s*:201–20. Leiden.

Pharo, Helge Ø. 1994. Scandinavia. In D. Reynolds (ed.), *The Origins of the Cold War in Europe*:194–223. New Haven, Conn.

Popper, Karl. 1957. *The Poverty of Historicism*. Norwegian edition 1971: *Samfunnsvitenskap og profeti*. Oslo.

Popperwell, Ronald G. 1972. *Norway*. London.

Population Census 1801 Reprocessed. 1980. Central Bureau of Statistics, NOS B134. Oslo.

Pryser, Tore. 1977a. *Klassebevegelse eller folkebevegelse? En sosialhistorisk undersøkelse av thranittene i Ullensaker*. Oslo.

Pryser, Tore (ed.). 1977b. *Thranerørsla i norske bygder*. Oslo.

Pryser, Tore. 1985. *Norsk historie 1800–1870. Frå standssamfunn til klassesamfunn*. Oslo.

Pryser, Tore. 1988. *Klassen og nasjonen (1935–1946)* (E. Bull et al. [eds.], Arbeiderbevegelsens historie, Vol. 4). Oslo.

Pryser, Tore. 1989. Noen konsekvenser av fagpolitikken i 1980-åra. *Historisk tidsskrift* 68:463–78.

Pulkkinen, Tuija. 1993. *Citizens, Nations and Women: The Transition from Ancient Regime to Modernity and Beyond*. Paper presented to a symposium of The International Federation for Research in Women's History: "Rethinking Women and Gender Relations in the Modern State", April 1993. University of Bielefeld.

Paasche, Fredrik. 1915. *Kristendom og kvad; en studie i norrøn middelalder*. Oslo.

Qvigstad, Just. 1921. *Den kvænske indvandring til Nord-Norge*. Tromsø.

Qviller, Bjørn. 1981a. Fra polygyni til misogyni: Metodeutvikling og kvinnehistorie belyst ved studiet av kvinneadferd i arkaiske samfunn. *Usynlig historie. Studier i historisk metode nr. 17*:132–56. Oslo.

Qviller, Bjørn. 1981b. The Dynamics of the Homeric Society. *Symbolae Osloensis* LVI.

Qviller, Bjørn. 1985. Kvinneliv i Roma. In Vogt 1985, Vol. 1:43–8.

Rafto, Thorolf. 1955. *Telegrafverkets historie 1855–1955*. Bergen.

Ramstad, Jan. 1982. *Kvinnelønn og pengeøkonomi. En studie av kvinners lønn i tekstilindustrien i Kristiania ca. 1850–1910*. Unpublished Master's thesis. Norwegian School of Economics and Business Administration, Bergen.

Ramsøy, Natalie Rogoff (ed.). 1974. *Norwegian Society*. Oslo.

Randsborg, Hege Britt. 1979. *Befolkningsutviklingen i Bø i Telemark 1727–1815*. Unpublished Master's thesis. University of Oslo.

Reiersen, Elsa, and Dagfinn Slettan (eds.). 1986. *Mentalitetshistorie. Muligheter og problemer*. Trondheim.

Reinton, Lars. 1938. *Folk og fortid i Hol*, I. Oslo.

Reinton, Lars. 1955–61. *Sæterbruket i Noreg*. 2 vols. Oslo.

Reinton, Lars. 1970. Den lokalhistoriske rørsla og den moderne bygdehistorie 1900–1920. In *Lokalhistorie i forskning og kulturarbeid gjennom 200 år. Landslaget for bygde- og byhistorie 50 år 6. juli 1972*:33–54. Oslo.

Reksten, Erling. 1985. *Krongods og kongsmenn. Jordsalg og sosial endring på Vestlandet 1650–1700*. 2 vols. Oslo.

Rendall, Jane. 1991. Uneven Developments: Women's History, Feminist History and Gender History in Great Britain. In Offen, Pierson, and Rendall 1991:45–58.

Renvall, Pentti. 1965. *Den moderna historieforskningens principer*. Stockholm.

RHD-Årsrapport 1993. Registreringssentral for historiske data. Universitetet i Tromsø. Tromsø.

Rian, Øystein. 1975. *Jens Juels stattholderskap. En studie i stattholderembetets kompetanse og funksjoner.* Oslo.

Rian, Øystein. 1980. *Vestfolds historie. Grevskapstiden 1671–1821.* Tønsberg.

Rian, Øystein. 1984. Skogpolitikk i Norge 1724–1740. In K. Bäck et al. (eds.), *Skog och brännvin. Studier i näringspolitiskt beslutsfattande i Norden på 1700-talet*:129–78. Oslo.

Rian, Øystein. 1985. State and Society in Seventeenth-century Norway. *Scandinavian Journal of History* 10:337–63.

Rian, Øystein. 1990. Giftermål og familie som elitedannende faktorer i 1600-tallets Bratsberg. *Historisk tidsskrift* 69:471–83.

Rian, Øystein. 1992. Den frie og stolte norske bonden. Myter og realiteter. In H. Winge (ed.), *Lokalsamfunn og øvrighet i Norden ca. 1550–1750*:117–59. Oslo.

Ringdal, Nils Johan. 1981. *Statsoppfatningen hos Jens Arup Seip.* Bergen–Oslo–Tromsø.

Ringdal, Nils Johan (ed.). 1983. *Frontlinjer i historiefaget – moderne historieskrivning i internasjonalt perspektiv.* Oslo–Bergen–Stavanger–Tromsø.

Rinnan, Peter. 1979. *Utvandringen fra Kristiania 1880–1907. En studie i urban utvandring.* Unpublished Master's thesis. University of Oslo.

Riste, Olav. 1965. *The Neutral Ally. Norway's Relations with Belligerent Powers in the First World War.* Oslo.

Riste, Olav. 1973a. *London-regjeringa. Norge i krigsalliansen 1940–1945,* Vol. I, *1940–1942: Prøvetid.* Oslo.

Riste, Olav. 1973b. Alliansepolitikk og brubygging. *Historisk tidsskrift* 52: 261–7.

Riste, Olav. 1979. *London-regjeringa. Norge i krigsalliansen 1940–1945,* Vol. II, *1942–1945: Vegen heim.* Oslo.

Riste, Olav. 1982. The Genesis of North Atlantic Defence Cooperation: Norway's "Atlantic Policy" 1940–1945. *Forsvarsstudier 1981*:10–19. Oslo.

Riste, Olav. 1984. Frå integritetstraktat til atompolitikk: det stormaktsgaranterte Norge 1905–1983. *Forsvarsstudier* III/1983–4:13–44. Oslo.

Riste, Olav. 1985a. Was 1949 a Turning Point? Norway and the Western Powers 1947–50. In O. Riste (ed.), *Western Security. The Formative Years*:128–49. Oslo.

Riste, Olav. 1985b. The Historical Determinants of Norwegian Foreign Policy. In J. J. Holst (ed.), *Norwegian Foreign Policy in the 1980s*:12–25. Oslo.

Riste, Olav. 1987. *Norge i krig,* Vol. 1, *Overfall.* Oslo.

Riste, Olav. 1989. Merkeår i norsk utanrikspolitikk: Vendepunkt eller ledd i ein gradvis prosess? *Internasjonal Politikk* 1–2/1988:187–91.

Riste, Olav. 1991. Nordic Union or Western Alliance? In E. Di Nolfo (ed.), *The Atlantic Pact Forty Years Later: A Reappraisal*:127–42. Berlin.

Rokkan, Stein. 1967. Geography, Religion, and Social Class: Crosscutting Cleavages in Norwegian Politics. In S. M. Lipset and S. Rokkan (eds.), *Party Systems and Voter Alignments: Cross-National Perspectives*:367–444. New York.

Rokkan, Stein. 1970. Nation-building, Citizenship and Political Mobilization: Approaches and Models. In S. Rokkan, *Citizens, Elections and Parties. Approaches to the Comparative Study of the Processes of Development.* Oslo.

Rokkan, Stein. 1975. Sentrum og periferi, økonomi og kultur: Modeller og data i kliometrisk sosiologi. In *Periferi og sentrum i historien. Studier i historisk metode nr. 10.* Oslo.

Rosenbeck, Bente. 1983. Teoriutvikling og kvinnehistorie. *Usynlig historie. Studier i historisk metode nr. 17*:119–31. Oslo.

Rosenbeck, Bente. 1990. Kvindehistorisk forskning i Norgen. Hvor står vi, hvor går vi? *Kvinnohistoria i teoretiskt perspektiv. Konferensrapport från det tredje nordiske kvinnohistorikermötet april 1989*. Uppsala Papers in Economic History, Working Paper No. 8:37–51. Department of Economic History. Uppsala.

Rosenbeck, Bente. 1992. *Kroppens politik. Om køn, kultur og videnskab*. Copenhagen.

Rygg, Nicolai. 1918-54. *Norges Banks historie*. 2 vols. Kristiania-Oslo.

Røhne, Nils A. 1987. Norge – en lunken europeer. Norsk Europa-politikk fram til 1950. *Forsvarsstudier* VI/1987:144–80.

Røhne, Nils A. 1989. De første skritt inn i Europa. Norsk Europa-politikk fra 1950. *Forsvarsstudier* V/1989.

Salvesen, Helge. 1979. *Jord i Jemtland. Bosetningshistoriske og økonomiske studier i grenseland ca. 1200–1650*. Östersund.

Salvesen, Helge. 1980a. "Annales-skolen" i Frankrike og oversettelsespolitikk i Skandinavia. *Heimen* 18:330–4.

Salvesen, Helge. 1980b. Tendenser i den historiske sameforskning – med særlig vekt på politikk og forskning. *Scandia* 46:21–52.

Salvesen, Helge. 1982. The Strength of Tradition: A Historiographical Analysis of Research into Norwegian Agrarian History during the Later Middle Ages and the Early Modern Period. *Scandinavian Journal of History* 7:75–133.

Sandal, Per. 1983. *Lokalhistorie*. Oslo.

Sandmo, Erling. 1992. *Tingets tenkemåter. Kriminalitet og rettssaker i Rendalen 1763–97*. Oslo.

Sandmo, Erling. 1993. Er relativismen absolutt? En kommentar til Knut Kjeldstadlis *Fortida er ikke hva den en gang var. Historisk tidsskrift* 72:512–16.

Sandmo, Erling. 1994. Æren og ærekrenkelsen. Domstolene i samspill med lokalsamfunnet. In K. Tønnesson (ed.), *Rapport II. Normer og sosial kontroll i Norden ca. 1550–1850*:330–4. Oslo.

Sandnes, Jørn. 1970. Lokalhistorisk litteratur til omkring 1900. In *Lokalhistorie i forskning og kulturarbeid gjennom 200 år. Landslaget for bygde- og byhistorie 50 år 6. juli 1972*:13–32. Oslo.

Sandnes, Jørn. 1973. Om samenes utbredelse mot sør i eldre tid. *Historisk tidsskrift* 52:113–37.

Sandnes, Jørn. 1974. Sørsamenes eldre historie igjen. Replikk til Knut Bergslund. *Historisk tidsskrift* 54:415–21.

Sandnes, Jørn. 1975. Rikshistorie og lokalhistorie – sentrum og periferi i historieforskningen. *Periferi og sentrum i historien. Studier i historisk metode nr. 10*:159–67. Oslo.

Sandnes, Jørn. 1979. Ødegårdsprosjektet og tallet på gårdsbruk i Norge i høymiddelalderen. *Historisk tidsskrift* 58:397–410.

Sandnes, Jørn. 1981. Totalhistorie og mentalitetshistorie. *Heimen* 18:561–70.

Sandnes, Jørn. 1983. *Handbok i lokalhistorie. Faget og metodene*. Oslo.

Sandnes, Jørn. 1990. *Kniven, ølet og æren. Kriminalitet og samfunn i Norge på 1500- og 1600-tallet*. Oslo.

Sandnes, Jørn, and Helge Salvesen. 1978. *Ødegårdstid i Norge. Det nordiske ødegårdsprosjekts norske undersøkelser*. Oslo.

Sandvik, Gudmund. 1975. *Det gamle veldet. Norske finansar 1760–79*. Oslo.

Sandvik, Gudmund. 1980. Ei forelda lære: Statens umatrikulerte grunn i Finn-
mark. In T. Thuen (ed.), *Samene – urbefolkning og minoritet*. Bergen–Oslo–
Tromsø.
Sandvik, Gudmund. 1987. *300 års jubileet for Christian Vs norske lov på Køben-
havns Universitet 29. april 1987*. Oslo.
Sandvik, Gudmund. 1993. The Non-existent Sami Language Rights in Norway.
In S. Vilfan (ed.), *Ethnic Groups and Language Rights. Comparative Studies on
Governments and Non-dominant Ethnic Groups in Europe, 1850–1940*. New
York–Dartmouth.
Sandvik, Hilde. (1985) 1992. *"Umyndige" kvinner i handel og håndverk. Kvinner i
bynæringer i Christiania i siste halvdel av 1700-tallet*. Oslo.
Sanness, John. 1978. Norsk alliansefri politikk? *Atlanterhavskomiteens skriftserie*
44. Oslo.
Saressalo, Lassi. 1983. Om etniska stereotypier. In J. Sandnes *et al.* (eds.), *Folk og
ressurser i nord*. Trondheim.
Saressalo, Lassi. 1985. Measuring Change in Culture. *Nord nytt* 8.
Saressalo, Lassi. 1986. From Oicotype (Ecotype) to the Study of Ethnotypes.
Acta Borealia 35.
Sars, Ernst. 1873–91. *Udsigt over den norske Historie*. 4 vols. Christiania. Revised
edition: *Samlede værker*, I–II. Kristiania–Copenhagen 1911–12.
Sars, Ernst. 1906. Unionsoppløsningen og Skandinavismen. *Samtiden* 17.
Schefferus, J. 1673. *Lapponia*. Frankfurt am Main.
Schier, Kurt. 1970. *Sagaliteratur*. Stuttgart.
Schiøtz, Aina. 1977. *Prostitusjonen i Kristiania ca. 1870–1890*. Unpublished
Master's thesis. University of Oslo.
Schiøtz, Aina. 1980. Prostitusjon og prostituerte i 1880-årenes Kristiania. In
Gotaas *et al.* 1980.
Schlüter, Ragnhild. 1990. *De reisende: en glemt minoritet*. Levanger.
Schnitler, Carl Wille. 1911. *Slegten fra 1814*. Oslo.
Schofield, Roger, David Reher, and Alain Bideau (eds.). 1991. *The Decline of Mor-
tality in Europe*. Oxford.
Scholte, Jan Aart. 1994. New Border Crossings: Christopher Thorne and Inter-
national History. *The Society for Historians of American Foreign Relations
Newsletter* 25:1–28.
Schreiner, Johan. 1934. *Nederland og Norge 1625–1650. Trelastutførsel og han-
delspolitikk*. Published by Det norske videnskapsakademi i Oslo 1933, II,
nr. 2.
Schreiner, Johan. 1944. *Akers Sparebank gjennom hundre år*. Oslo.
Schreiner, Johan. 1963. *Norsk skipsfart under krig og høykonjunktur 1914–1920*.
Oslo.
Schrumpf, Ellen. 1978. *Tjenestepikespørsmålet i Kristiania. Tjenestepikenes kår og
organisering ca. 1880–1900*. Unpublished Master's thesis. University of Oslo.
Schurer, Kevin. 1991. The Future for Local History: Boom or Recession? *The
Local Historian* 21:99–108.
Schweigaard, Anton Martin. 1840. *Norges Statistik*. Christiania.
Scott, Joan Wallach. 1983. Survey Articles – Women in History: The Modern
Period. *Past and Present* 101:141–57.
Scott, Joan Wallach. 1986. Gender: A Useful Category of Historical Analysis.
American Historical Review 91(4).

Scott, Joan Wallach. 1988. *Gender and the Politics of History*. New York.

Seip, Anne-Lise. 1981. *Om velferdsstatens framvekst*. Oslo.

Seip, Anne-Lise. 1984a. *Sosialhjelpstaten blir til. Norsk sosialpolitikk 1740–1920*. Oslo.

Seip, Anne-Lise. 1984b. Motive Forces behind the New Social Policy after 1870. Norway on the European Scene. *Scandinavian Journal of History* 9:329–41.

Seip, Anne-Lise. 1975. *Vitenskap og virkelighet. Sosiale, økonomiske og politiske teorier hos T. H. Aschehoug 1845 til 1882*. Oslo.

Seip, Anne-Lise. 1986a. Eilert Sundt. A Founding Father of the Social Sciences in Norway. *Scandinavian Journal of History* 11:220–42.

Seip, Anne-Lise. 1986b. Velferdsstaten Norge. In L. Alldén *et al.* (eds.), *Det norske samfunn*:197–232. Oslo.

Seip, Anne-Lise. 1994. *Veier til velferdsstaten. Norsk sosialpolitikk 1920–75*. Oslo.

Seip, Jens Arup. 1934. *Lagmann og lagting i senmiddelalderen og det 16de århundre*. Published by Det norske videnskapsakademi i Oslo, II, nr. 2.

Seip, Jens Arup. 1940. Problemer og metode i norsk middelalderforskning. *Historisk tidsskrift* 32:49–131. Reprinted in Seip, Jens Arup, 1983a.

Seip, Jens Arup. 1945. *Et regime foran undergangen*. Oslo.

Seip, Jens Arup. 1958. Årsaksproblemer. Innlegg ved doktordisputas: Ottar Dahl, Om årsaksproblemer i historisk forskning. Forsøk på en vitenskapsteoretisk analyse (1957). *Historisk tidsskrift* 38. Reprinted in Seip, Jens Arup, 1983a.

Seip, Jens Arup. 1959. "Det norske system" i den økonomiske liberalismens klassiske tid (1850–1870). *Historisk tidsskrift* 39:1–58.

Seip, Jens Arup. 1963. Fra embedsmannsstat til ettpartistat. In *Fra embedsmannsstat til ettpartistat og andre essays*. Oslo.

Seip, Jens Arup. 1968. *Tanke og handling i norsk historie*. Oslo.

Seip, Jens Arup. 1970. Historieforskningen i fremtiden. *Historisk tidsskrift* 49: 271–85.

Seip, Jens Arup. 1973. Friheten i gave. In *Fra embedsmannsstat til ettpartistat og andre essays*:43–50. Oslo.

Seip, Jens Arup. 1974–81. *Utsikt over Norges historie I–II*. Oslo.

Seip, Jens Arup. 1975. Modellenes tyranni. In *Periferi og sentrum i historien. Studier i historisk metode nr. 10*. Oslo.

Seip, Jens Arup. 1980. *Dyd og nødvendighet. Høyres historie gjennom hundre år 1880–1980*. Oslo.

Seip, Jens Arup. 1983a. *Problemer og metode i historieforskningen. Artikler, innlegg, foredrag 1940–1977*. Oslo.

Seip, Jens Arup. 1983b. Forspilte muligheter som historisk forklaringsfaktor. In Seip, Jens Arup. 1983a:148–58. Oslo.

Seip, Jens Arup. 1994. Flerpartistaten i perspektiv. *Nytt Norsk Tidsskrift* 3–4/1994:203–20.

Sejersted, Francis. 1972. Apologi for den gammeldagse økonomiske historie. *Historisk Tidskrift* (Sweden) 92:461–73.

Sejersted, Francis. 1973a (2nd ed. 1985). *Historisk introduksjon til økonomien*. Oslo.

Sejersted, Francis. 1973b. *Ideal Teori og Virkelighet. Nicolai Rygg og pengepolitikken i 1920–årene*. Oslo.

Sejersted, Francis. 1978. Rettsstaten og den selvdestruerende makt – noen refleksjoner over det 19. århundres embetsmannsstat. In R. Slagstad (ed.), *Om staten*. Oslo. Reprinted in Sejersted 1984a.

Sejersted, Francis. 1979. *Fra Linderud til Eidsvold Værk*, Vol. III, *Den gamle bedrift og den nye tid: 1842–1895*. Oslo.

Sejersted, Francis (ed.). 1982a. *Vekst gjennom krise. Studier i norsk teknologihistorie*. Oslo.

Sejersted, Francis (ed.). 1982b. *En storbank i blandingsøkonomien: Den norske Creditbank 1957–1982*. Oslo.

Sejersted, Francis. 1984a. *Demokrati og rettsstat. Politisk–historiske essays*. Oslo.

Sejersted, Francis. 1984b. Arven fra 1905. In Sejersted 1984a.

Sejersted, Francis. 1988. The Development of Economic History in Norway. *Scandinavian Economic History Review* 36:42–50.

Sejersted, Francis. 1989. Norsk historisk forskning ved inngangen til 1990-årene. Et oppgjør med den metodologiske individualisme. *Historisk tidsskrift* 68(4). Oslo. Reprinted in Sejerstad 1993a:305–28.

Sejersted, Francis. 1993a. *Demokratisk kapitalisme*. Oslo.

Sejersted, Francis. 1993b. Politikk og kultur. Om den politiske histories fall og vekst. In Sejersted 1993a.

Sejersted, Francis. 1994. Den truede idyll. Om de vekslende perspektiver i studiet av moderne norsk historie. In Langholm *et al.* 1994:229–49.

Sejersted, Francis, and August Schou 1972. *Fra Linderud til Eidsvold Værk*, Vol. II–2, *Hurdalsbruket 1792–1842*. Oslo

Selbygg, Arne. 1986. *Norway Today. An Introduction to Modern Norwegian Society*. Oslo.

Semmingsen, Ingrid. 1938. Utvandringen til Amerika 1866–73. *Historisk tidsskrift* 31:237–79.

Semmingsen, Ingrid. 1941–50. *Veien mot vest. Utvandringen fra Norge 1825–1915*. 2 vols. Oslo.

Semmingsen, Ingrid. 1954. The Dissolution of Estate Society in Norway. *Scandinavian Economic History Review* 2:166–203.

Semmingsen, Ingrid. 1960. Norwegian Emigration in the Nineteenth Century. *Scandinavian Economic History Review* 8:237–79.

Semmingsen, Ingrid. 1971. Family Emigration from Bergen 1874–92. *Americana Norvegica* 3:38–63. Oslo.

Semmingsen, Ingrid. 1972. Emigration from Scandinavia. *Scandinavian Economic History Review* 20:45–60.

Semmingsen, Ingrid. 1978a. Nordic Research into Emigration. *Scandinavian Journal of History* 3:197–229.

Semmingsen, Ingrid. 1978b. *Norway to America: A History of the Migration*. Minneapolis. (Norwegian original 1975: *Drøm og dåd. Utvandringen til Amerika*. Oslo.)

Semmingsen, Ingrid, Nina Karin Monsen, Stephan Tschudi-Madsen, and Yngvar Ustvedt (eds.). 1979–81. *Norges kulturhistorie*. 8 vols. Oslo.

Sigurdsson, Jón Vidar. 1993. *Goder og maktforhold på Island i fristatstiden*. Unpublished doctoral dissertation. University of Bergen.

Simensen, Jarle. 1986. Mentalitetshistorie – er det mulig? In Reiersen and Slettan 1986.

Simensen, Jarle, and Sten Helland. 1984. The Nordic Historians' Conferences on Historical Method 1965–1983. *Scandinavian Journal of History* 9:239–53.

Skobba, Ingvar. 1994. *Edvard Bull d.e. og jakten på den egentlige historien.* Unpublished Master's thesis. University of Oslo.

Skodvin, Magne. 1953. Norge i stormaktspolitikken opp til 9. april. *Historisk tidsskrift* 36.

Skodvin, Magne. 1971. *Norden eller NATO?* Oslo.

Skodvin, Magne. 1975. *Samtid og historie. Utvalde artiklar og avhandlingar.* Oslo.

Skodvin, Magne. 1977. Norwegian Neutrality and the Question of Credibility. *Scandinavian Journal of History* 2:123–45.

Skodvin, Magne. 1990. Nordic or North Atlantic Alliance? The Postwar Scandinavian Security Debate. *Forsvarsstudier* 3/1990.

Skodvin, Ole-Jacob. 1989. *Den store utfordringen! Rekruttering til de humanistiske vitenskapene fram mot år 2010. NAVFs utredingsinstitutt, Notat* 5/89. Oslo.

Skoie, Hans. 1992. Det regionale systemet – noen prinsipielle spørsmål i et historisk perspektiv. In N. Roll-Hansen (ed.), *Forskning i de regionale høyskolene – noen prinsipielle spørsmål. NAVFs utredningsinstitutt. Rapport* 12/92:33–47. Oslo.

Skotvedt, T. 1993. Sami: The Indigenous Peoples of Norway. In A. C. Kiel (ed.), *Continuity and Change. Aspects of Contemporary Norway.* Oslo.

Skånland, Hermod. 1967. *Det norske kredittmarked siden 1900.* Samfunnsøkonomiske studier 19. Oslo.

Slagstad, Rune. 1987. *Rett og politikk. Et liberalt tema med variasjoner.* Oslo.

Slagstad, Rune. 1992. Frederik Stangs ideologiske lederskap. *Nytt norsk tidsskrift* 2/1992:136–54.

Slettan, Dagfinn. 1978. *Dreng og taus i Verdal. Eksperiment med en kollektiv sjølbiografi.* Oslo.

Slettan, Dagfinn. 1989 (ed.). *Bondesamfunn i oppløsning? Trønderske bondesamfunn 1930–1980.* Lesjå.

Slettan, Dagfinn. 1992. Editorials in *Heimen* 29(3–4), introducing articles by Arnved Nedkvitne, Harald Winge, Atle Døssland, Anna Tranberg, Brynjulv Gjerdåker, Håvard Dahl Bratrein, and Kjell J. Bråstad.

Slettan, Dagfinn. 1994. *Minner og kulturhistorie. Teoretiske perspektiver.* Trondheim.

Smith, Anthony D. 1971. *Theories of Nationalism.* London.

Sogner, Ingrid. 1993. The European Idea: The Scandinavian Answer: Norwegian Attitudes towards a Closer Scandinavian Economic Cooperation 1947–1959. *Scandinavian Journal of History* 18:307–27.

Sogner, Sølvi. 1965. Historical Demography in Norway To-day. Sources, Literature and the Present Situation. In Les congrès et colloques de l'Université de Liège, Vol. 33, *Problèmes de mortalité. Méthodes, sources et bibliographie en démographie historique:*199–216. Liège.

Sogner, Sølvi. 1976a. A Demographic Crisis Averted? *Scandinavian Economic History Review* 24:114–28.

Sogner, Sølvi. 1976b. Freeholder and Cottar. *Scandinavian Journal of History* 1:181–99.

Sogner, Sølvi. 1978. Illegitimacy in the Old Rural Society. Some Reflections on the Problem Arising from Two Family-reconstitution Studies. In S. Åkerman et al. (eds.), *Chance and Change. Social and Economic Studies in Historical Demography in the Baltic Area.* Odense.

Sogner, Sølvi. 1979. *Folkevekst og flytting. En historisk demografisk studie i 1700-årenes Øst-Norge.* Oslo.

Sogner, Sølvi. 1984. "... a prudent wife is from the Lord." The Married Peasant

Woman of the Eighteenth Century in a Demographic Perspective. *Scandinavian Journal of History* 9:113–33.

Sogner, Sølvi. 1986. Bilan de la recherche en démographie historique dans les pays scandinaves 1976–1985. *Annales de Démographie Historique 1986*: 275–310.

Sogner, Sølvi. 1990. *Far sjøl i stua og familien hans. Trekk fra norsk familiehistorie før og nå.* Oslo.

Sogner, Sølvi. 1993. Historical Features of Women's Position in Society. In N. Federici, K. O. Mason, and S. Sogner (eds.), *Women's Position and Demographic Change*:245–58. Oxford.

Sogner, Sølvi, and Jan Oldervoll. 1981. Illegitimate Fertility and the Marriage Market in Norway, 1800–1850. In J. Dupâquier *et al.* (eds.), *Marriage and Remarriage in Populations of the Past*:495–510. London.

Sogner, Sølvi, Hege Brit Randsborg, and Eli Fure. 1984. *Fra stua full til tobarnskull. Om nedgangen i barnetall i norske familier i de siste 200 år, med særlig vekt på perioden 1890–1930.* Oslo.

Sogner, Sølvi, Hege Brit Randsborg, Eli Fure, and Lars Walløe. 1986. Le déclin de la fécondité en Norvège (1890–1930). *Annales de Démographie Historique 1986*:361–78.

Sogner, Sølvi, and Hilde Sandvik. 1989a. Ulik i lov og lære; lik i virke og verd? Kvinner i norsk økonomi i by og på land ca 1500–1800. *Historisk tidsskrift* 68:434–46.

Sogner, Sølvi, and Hilde Sandvik. 1989b. Minors in Law, Partners in Work, Equals in Worth? Women in the Norwegian Economy in the 16th to 18th Century. In Simonetta Cavaciocchi (ed.), *La Donna nell-economia Secc. XIII–XVIII.* Istituto Internazionale di Storia Economica "F. Datini", Prato Serie II – Atti delle "Settimane dei Studi" e altri Covegni 21.

Solberg, Aud Ross. 1993. *Mortalitet, offentlige helsetiltak og økonomisk utvikling i Sogndal fra ca. 1820 til 1880.* Unpublished Master's thesis. University of Bergen.

Solhaug, Trygve. 1974. *De norske fiskeriers historie 1815–1880.* 2 vols. Bergen.

Sommerfeldt, H. O. 1799/1800. Kort Beskrivelse over Finmarken. In *Topographisk Journal.* Christiania.

Sprauten, Knut. 1992. *Byen ved festningen. Fra 1536 til 1814 (Oslo bys historie,* Vol. 2). Oslo.

Statistisk Årbok for Norge. Annual. Oslo.

Steen, Sverre. 1923. *Kristiania postvæsens historie 1647–1921.* Kristiania

Steen, Sverre. 1930–3. Review of Arne Bergsgård, *Ole Gabriel Ueland og bondepolitikken. Historisk tidsskrift* 29.

Steen, Sverre. 1930–5. *Det norske folks liv og historie gjennem tidene,* Vols. IV, *1500–1640* (1935); V, *1640–1720* (1930); VI, *1720–1770* (1932); and VII, *1770–1814* (1933). Oslo.

Steen, Sverre. 1935. Siste slektledds historiegransking. In Koht *et al.* 1935:41–56.

Steen, Sverre. 1948a. De frivillige organisasjoner og det norske demokrati. *Historisk tidsskrift* 34:581–600.

Steen, Sverre. 1948b. *Kristiansands historie,* Vol. I, *Fredens århundre 1814–1914.* Oslo.

Steen, Sverre. 1951. *1814 (Det frie Norge,* Vol. 1). Oslo.

Steen, Sverre. 1951–62. *Det frie Norge.* 5 vols. Oslo.

Steen, Sverre. 1957. *Det gamle samfunn (Det frie Norge*, Vol. 4). Oslo.
Steen, Sverre. 1958 (1938). Brytningstider. *Tusen års norsk historie*. Oslo.
Steen, Sverre. 1967. *Langsomt ble landet vårt eget*. Oslo.
Steen, Sverre. 1973. *Drømmen om frihet*. Oslo.
Steen, Sverre. 1976. *På egen hånd*. Oslo.
Steen, Sverre. 1977. *Frihet og liv er ett*. Oslo.
Steinnes, Asgaut. 1928–31. *Gamal skatteskipnad*. 2 vols. Oslo.
Stockfleth, N. V. 1848a. *Bidrag til Kundskab om Qvænerne i Kongeriget Norge*. Christiania.
Stockfleth, N. V. 1848b. *Bidrag til Kundskab om Finnerne i Kongeriget Norge*. Christiania.
Stoltz, Gerhard. 1955. *Økonomisk utsyn 1900–1950*. Samfunnsøkonomiske studier 3. Oslo.
Stonehill, Arthur. 1965. *Foreign Ownership in Norwegian Enterprises*. Samfunnsøkonomiske studier 14. Oslo.
Storevik, Rune. 1993. Menn, maskulinitet og mannnshistorie. *Historie* 3(2): 61–76.
Stortings melding nr 37, 1972–73.
Strømberg, Erling. 1977. *Telegrafistene 1855–1890. En gruppe offentlige funksjonærer vokser fram*. Unpublished Master's thesis. University of Oslo.
Strømme Svendsen, Arnljot. 1961. *Elektrostål og industri–innovasjon*. Bergen.
Strømme Svendsen, Arnljot. 1973. *Union 1873–1973. En norsk treforedlingsbedrifts liv og eksistenskamp*. Oslo.
Studieplan for alle Fakulteter. 1897. Kristiania.
Studieplan for Sproglig–Historisk Embedeksamen. 1907. Kristiania.
Sundt, Eilert. 1967 (1855). *Om giftermaal i Norge*. Oslo–Gjøvik. In English translation (1980): *On Marriage in Norway*. Cambridge.
Sundt, Eilert. 1976 (1856). *Om sædelighetstilstanden i Norge*. Oslo–Gjøvik.
Supphellen, Steinar. 1978. Supplikken som institusjon i norsk historie. Framvokster og bruk særleg først på 1700-talet. *Historisk tidsskrift* 57:152–86.
Svalestuen, Andres A. 1972. *Tinns emigrasjonshistorie*. Oslo.
Svalestuen, Andres A. 1977. Five Local Studies of Nordic Emigration and Migration. *American Studies in Scandinavia* 9:17–63.
Svalestuen, Andres A. 1983. Emigration from the Community of Tinn, 1837–1907: Demographic, Economic, and Social Background. *Norwegian-American Studies* 29:43–88.
Svalestuen, Andres A. 1992. Noen hovedlinjer i Riksarkivets historie 1817–1992. Administrasjon og organisasjon. *Arkivmagasinet. Informasjon fra Riksarkivaren* 2/92:13–25.
Sverdrup Lunden, Mimi. 1941. *De frigjorte hender. Et bidrag til forståelse av kvinners arbeid i Norge etter 1814*. Oslo.
Sverdrup Lunden, Mimi. 1948. *Den lange arbeidsdagen*. Oslo.
Sømme, Axel (ed.). 1959. *Jordbrukets geografi i Norge*. Oslo.
Sørensen, Øystein (ed.). 1994. *Nordic Paths to National Identity in the Nineteenth Century*. Oslo.
Sørensen, Øystein. 1991. Det germanske Europa fra Bismarck til Kohl. Hvorfor Tyskland burde ha vunnet første verdenskrig. *Nytt Norsk Tidsskrift* 3/1991:245–64.
Tamnes, Rolf. 1982. Den norske holdningen til atomfrie soner i Sentral-Europa 1957–1965. *Forsvarsstudier 1981*:82–122. Oslo.

Tamnes, Rolf. 1983. Den norske holdningen til en nordisk atomvåpenfri sone 1958–1983. *Forsvarsstudier 1982*:11–86. Oslo.

Tamnes, Rolf. 1985a. Norway's Struggle for the Northern Flank. In O. Riste (ed.), *Western Security: The Formative Years*:215–43. Oslo.

Tamnes, Rolf. 1985b. Nordområdene i amerikansk strategi etter andre verdenskrig. *Internasjonal Politikk* 2/1985:7–56.

Tamnes, Rolf. 1986a. Kamp mot russerne på tysk jord? Tysklandsbrigaden og den kalde krigen 1947–1953. *Forsvarsstudier* V/1986:82–172.

Tamnes, Rolf. 1986b. Fra SAC til MAB. Nordområdene i amerikansk strategi 1945–1986. *FHFS-notat* 1/1986.

Tamnes, Rolf. 1986c. Ettpartistat, småstat og særinteresser. Tre skoler i norsk sikkerhetspolitikk. *Nytt Norsk Tidsskrift* 3/1986:42–64.

Tamnes, Rolf. 1987. Integration and Screening. The Two Faces of Norwegian Alliance Policy, 1945–1986. *Forsvarsstudier* VI/1987:59–100. Oslo.

Tamnes, Rolf. 1989. Handlefrihet og lojalitet. Norge og atompolitikken i 1950-årene. In Bergh and Pharo 1989:203–36.

Tamnes, Rolf. 1991. *The United States and the Cold War in the High North*. Oslo.

Tamnes, Rolf. 1993. Forskningen omkring den kalde krigen – status og fremtid. *Historisk tidsskrift* 72:487–503.

Tegengren, Helmer. 1952. *En utdød lappkultur i Kemi Lappmark*. Åbo.

Telste, Kari. 1993. *Mellom liv og lov. Kontroll av seksualitet i Ringerike og Hallingdal 1652–1710*. Oslo.

Terjesen, Einar A. 1982. Sozialgeschichtliche Forschung in Norwegen. *Internationale Tagung der Historiker der Arbeiterbewegung. 16. Linzer Konferenz 1980. ITH-Tagungsberichte* 15:459–77. Vienna.

Thomas, Dorothy Swaine. 1941. *Social and Economic Aspects of Swedish Population Movements, 1750–1933*. New York.

Thorvaldsen, Gunnar. 1984. Befolkningsutvikling i Tromsø 1866–1900. *Heimen* 21:95–106.

Thowsen, Atle. 1981. Historikernes syn på Norges statsrettslige stilling 1536–1814. Norges-artikkelen av 1536. In S. Imsen (ed.), *Studier i norsk historie 1537–ca.1800. Lydriket 1537–1660. Norske historikere i utvalg*, VII:56–70.

Thue, Fredrik W. 1992. *Empirisme og demokrati. Arne Næss og fremveksten av et norsk institutt for samfunnsforskning, 1939–1950*. Unpublished Master's thesis. University of Bergen.

Thue, Fredrik W. 1994. *Bergens universitetshistorie. De humanistiske fagene 1825–1994*. Unpublished manuscript. Bergen.

Thue, Lars. 1977. *Framveksten av et industriborgerskap i Kristiania 1840–1875*. Unpublished Master's thesis. University of Oslo.

Thue, Lars. 1994. *Statens Kraft 1890–1947. Kraftutbygging og samfunnsutvikling*. Oslo.

Thuen, Trond (ed.). 1980. *Samene – urbefolkning og minoritet*. Bergen–Oslo–Tromsø.

Thuen, Trond. 1983. Meaning and Transaction in Saami Ethnopolitics. In R. Grønhaug (ed.), *Transaction and Signification*. Bergen–Oslo–Tromsø.

Thuen, Trond. 1985. Acculturation and ethnic survival? Some problems in the study of so-called "Norwegianized" Sami communities. *Acta Borealia* 34.

Thuen, Trond. 1987. One Community – One People? Ethnicity and Demography in a North-Norwegian Community 1865–1930. *Acta Borealia* 36.

Tilly, Louise, James Gillis, and David Levine. 1992. *The European Experience of Declining Fertility: A Quiet Revolution, 1750–1970*. London.

Tingbokprosjektet 1992–94. *Publikasjoner fra Tingbokprosjektet, I–IX*. Department of History, University of Oslo.

Torstendahl, Rolf. 1964. *Källkritik och vetenskapssyn i svensk historisk forskning 1820–1920*. Uppsala.

Torstendahl, Rolf. 1966. *Historia som vetenskap*. Stockholm.

Tranberg, Anna. 1993. *Korn og klasseskille. Ringsakboka, III*. Ringsaker.

Try, Hans. 1969. *Gardsskipnad og bondenæring. Sørlandsk jordbruk på 1800-tallet*. Oslo.

Try, Hans. 1977. Sosial holdningsendringar i norske bygdesamfunn på 1800-tallet. In E. Hovland (ed.), *Folket, bygda og historia*:39–52. Oslo.

Try, Hans. 1979. *To kulturer en stat 1851–1884* (K. Mykland [ed.], *Norges historie*, Vol. 11). Oslo.

Tvedt, Terje. 1990. *Bilder av de andre. Om utviklingslandene i bistandsepoken*. Oslo.

Tveite, Stein. 1959. *Jord og Gjerning. Trekk av norsk landbruk i 150 år*. Oslo.

Tveite, Stein. 1962. *Engelsk–norsk trelasthandel 1640–1710*. Oslo.

Tvethe, Braun. 1848. *Norges Statistik*. Christiania.

Tønnesen, Sverre. 1972. *Retten til jorden i Finnmark*. Bergen–Oslo–Tromsø.

Tønnessen, J. N. 1967–70. *Den moderne hvalfangsts historie*. Vols. II–IV. Sandefjord.

Tønnesson, Kåre D. (ed.). 1994a. *Fra kvinnehistorie til kjønnshistorie? Det 22. nordiske historikermøte 1994. Rapport III*. Oslo.

Tønnesson, Kåre D. (ed.). 1994b. *Normer og sosial kontroll i Norden ca. 1550–1850*. Oslo.

Tønnesson, Kåre D. 1979. *Sentraladministrasjonens historie*, Vol. 4, *1914–1940*. Oslo.

Tønnesson, Stein. 1991. *The Vietnamese Revolution of 1945: Roosevelt, Ho Chi Minh and de Gaulle in a World at War*. London.

Udgaard, Nils Morten. 1973. *Great Power Politics and Norwegian Foreign Policy. A Study of Norway's Foreign Relations November 1940–February 1948*. Oslo.

Valen, Henry, and Daniel Katz. 1964. *Political Parties in Norway*. Oslo.

Veland, Gunnar. 1981. *Demografiske og sosiale forhold i ei befolkning i nedgang: Granvin 1875–1920*. Unpublished Master's thesis. University of Bergen.

Villstrand, Nils Erik. 1992. Lokalhistoria som den är och kunde vara. *Heimen* 29:76–83.

Visted, Kristofer. 1908. *Vor gamle bondekultur*. Oslo. Revised by Hilmar Stigum 1951–2, published as Visted and Stigum, *Vår gamle bondekultur*.

Vogt, Kari (ed.). 1985. *Kvinnenes kulturhistorie*. 2 vols. Oslo.

Vorren, Ørnulf. 1944. Dyregraver og reingjerder i Varanger. *Nordnorske samlinger* 6. Oslo.

Vorren, Ørnulf. 1951. *Reindrift og nomadisme i Varangertraktene*. Tromsø.

Vorren, Ørnulf. 1962. *Finnmarkssamenes nomadisme*. 2 vols. Oslo.

Vorren, Ørnulf. 1986. *Reindrift og nomadisme i Helgeland*. 2 vols. Oslo.

Vorren, Ørnulf, and Hans Kristian Eriksen. 1993. *Samiske offerplasser i Varanger*. Stonglandseidet.

Vorren, Ørnulf, and Ernst Manker. 1956. *Samekulturen*. 1st ed. Oslo.

Wasberg, Gunnar Christie, and A. Strømme Svensen. 1969. *Industriens historie i Norge*. Oslo.

Weibull, Lauritz. 1948. Kritiska undersøkningar in Nordens historia omkring år

1000. In *Nordisk historia. Forskningar och undersøkningar*, Vol. 1:245–360. Stockholm.

Weidling, Tor. 1988. *Adelig godsøkonomi og sagbruksinteresser i Østfold på 1600-tallet*. Unpublished Master's thesis. University of Oslo.

Westad, Odd Arne. 1993. *Cold War and Revolution: Soviet–American Rivalry and the Origins of the Chinese Civil War, 1944–1946*. New York.

Whitaker, Ian. 1955. Social Relations in a Nomadic Lappish Community. *Samiske samlinger 2*. Oslo.

White, Hayden. 1973. *Metahistory. The Historical Imagination in the Nineteenth-century Europe*. Baltimore.

Wicken, Olav. 1983. Industrial Change in Norway during the Second World War. *Scandinavian Journal of History* 8:119–50.

Wicken, Olav (ed.). 1994. *Elektronikkentreprenørene. Studier av norsk elektronikk-forskning og -industri etter 1945*. Oslo.

Wikander, Ulla. 1994. *Comparative Perspectives on Protective Labor Legislation for Women*. Urbana, Ill.

Winge, Harald. 1992. Hvordan skal vi skrive lokalhistorie? *Heimen* 29:83–92.

Winsnes, A. H. 1924. *Det Norske Selskab 1772–1812*. Kristiania.

Wishman, Merete. 1983. *"Han vil ha meg sånn hjemmekvinne". Middelklassehus-mødre i Trondheim 1900–1940. En studie av den borgerlige familie*. Unpublished Master's thesis. University of Trondheim.

Worm-Müller, Jacob S. 1920. Synet på Norges historie. In *Norsk historisk viden-skab i femti år 1869–1919*:19–51. Kristiania.

Worm-Müller, Jacob S. 1922. *Kristiania og krisen efter Napoleonskrigene*. Kristiania.

Worm-Müller, Jacob S. (ed). 1923–51. *Den norske sjøfart fra de ældste tider til vore dage*. 3 vols. Kristiania/Oslo.

Worm-Müller, Jacob S. 1935. Ernst Sars. In Koht *et al*. 1935:21–339.

Worm-Müller, Jacob S. 1954. *Ideer og mennesker*. Oslo.

Waage, Hilde Henriksen. 1989. *Da staten Israel ble til. Et stridsspørsmål i norsk politikk 1945–49*. Oslo.

Ødegaarden, Olav. 1989. *Et historiefaglig portrett. Perspektiv på Ottar Dahls metodelære*. Unpublished Master's thesis. University of Oslo.

Øhren, Andreas J. 1977. *Arbeiderne ved Kværner Brug 1869–1885. En sosialhis-torisk undersøkelse*. Unpublished Master's thesis. University of Oslo.

Øidne, Gabriel. 1957. Litt om motsetninga mellom Austlandet og Vestlandet. *Syn og Segn* 63(3):97–114.

Ørvik, Nils. 1953a (2nd ed. 1971). *The Decline of Neutrality*. Oslo.

Ørvik, Nils. 1953b. *Norge i brennpunktet*. Oslo.

Ørvik, Nils. 1960. *Sikkerhetspolitikken 1920–1939*, Vol. I, *Solidaritet eller nøytra-litet*. Oslo.

Ørvik, Nils. 1961. *Sikkerhetspolitikken 1920–1939*, Vol. II, *Vern eller vakt*. Oslo.

Ørvik, Nils. 1962. *Norsk sikkerhetspolitikk 1920–1939*. Oslo.

Ørvik, Nils (ed.). 1972. *Fears and Expectations. Norwegian Attitudes toward Euro-pean Integration*. Oslo.

Ørvik, Nils (ed.). 1975. *Norway's No to Europe*. Pittsburgh.

Österberg, Eva. 1975. Rikshistoria och lokalhistoria. En fråga om centrum och periferi, centralt och perifert i historieforskningen? *Periferi og sentrum i his-torien. Studier i historisk metode nr. 10*:168–89. Oslo.

Österberg, Eva. 1985. Några krumelurer till Ottar Dahls inlägg om kvinnohis-toria. *Historisk tidsskrift* 64:425–8.

Österberg, Eva. 1991. Social Arena or Theatre of Power? The Courts, Crime and the Early Modern State. In H. Pihlajamäki (ed.), *Theatres of Power. Social Control and Criminality in Historical Perspective*. Jyväskylä.

Østerud, Øyvind. 1975. Nytt perspektiv på det store hamskiftet. *Historisk tidsskrift* 54:120–9.

Østerud, Øyvind. 1978a. *Agrarian Structure and Peasant Politics in Scandinavia. A Comparative Study of Rural Response to Economic Change*. Oslo.

Østerud, Øyvind. 1978b. *Utviklingsteori og historisk endring. En kritisk fremstilling av utviklingsteoretiske posisjoner innen samfunnsforskningen*. Oslo.

Østerud, Øyvind. 1984. *Nasjonenes selvbstemmelsesrett. Søkelys på en politisk doktrine*. Oslo.

Østerud, Øyvind. 1994. *Hva er nasjonalisme?* Oslo.

Øye, Ingvild. 1990. Middelalderkvinner i tverrfaglig belysning. *Historisk tidsskrift* 69:435–54.

Øygaarden, Sven Gabrielsen. 1979. *Avaldsnes 1758–1801*. Unpublished Master's thesis. University of Bergen.

Aardal, Bernt. 1994. Hva er en politisk skillelinje? En begrepsmessig grenseoppgang. *Tidsskrift for samfunnsforskning* 35:218–49.

Aarsberetning, Det Kongelige Frederiks Universitets / Årsberetning. Universitetet i Oslo. Kristiania/Oslo, 1904/05ff.

Aarsæter, Nils, Ragnar Nilsen, and Jan Einar Reiersen (eds.). 1982. *Folkemakt og regional utvikling*. Oslo.

Aaraas, Tronn. 1972. *Befolkningskrisa i Norge 1770–74. Sult eller sykdom?* Unpublished Master's thesis. University of Bergen.

Aas, Kristin Natvig. 1993a. Patriarkatsteoriernas maktförståelse bör nyanseras. *Kvinnovetenskaplig tidskrift* 14(2):27–44.

Aas, Kristin Natvig. 1993b. Kvinne- og kjønnshistorie. Hva er det, og hva kan det tilføye historiefaget? *Historie* 3(2):76–81.

Aase, Hildur Gerd. 1987. *Sjømannsfamilier i Haugesund i mellomkrigstida*. Unpublished Master's thesis. University of Bergen.

Index of Names

Viking expeditions in the 9th and 10th centuries.
The political situation c. 900

ICELAND
Holar
Borg
Tingvellir
Skálholt
c. 870

NORWEGIAN SEA

Bjarkøy
Borg
Lofoten

*LAPPS
(SAMER)*

Tjøtta

KVENS

Faeroe I.
c. 850

Mære
Øreting • Lade

FINNS

**Shetland
(Hjaltland)**
Before 800

NORWEGIANS

Åker
SWEDES

Hebrides
c. 800
Orkney I.
**Caithness
(Katanes)**
Iona
SCOTLAND

Borre
Oseberg • Tune
Hafrsfjord ★
Skiringssal
(Kaupang)

Uppsala
Sigtuna
Birka
Helgö

Åland
(Alland)
c. 800
(VIRLAND)
ESTONIANS

BALTIC

Daugava

IRELAND
Limerick
(Lymrek)
840
Waterford
(Vedrafjord)

Lindisfarne   793
840
Man (Mon) *850*
Dublin
(Dyflinn)
York (Jorvik)

NORTH SEA

DANES
Viborg

GOTHS

Lund

Gotland
Öland (Evland)   *BALTS*
(KURLAND)

**WALES
(BRETLAND)**
840

**DANE
LAW**

Ribe
Haithabu (Hedeby)
845 Hollingsted
Hamburg

Bornholm (Borgundarholm)

Wolin
(Jumne, Jomsborg)

London
(Lundun)

865

FRISIA

WENDS

(SAXONY)

Oder

Wista

Njemen

**(FLÆMING-
LAND)**
Dorestad

BRITTANY

**NOR-
MANDY** *845*
Rouen (Ruda)
Paris
Nantes
Orléans
856 Tours

*Seine
(Signa)*
Loire

**LOTHAR-
INGIA**
Trier
Mainz *832*
Köln

Elben

Praha
CZECHS
BOHEMIA
Krakow

POLES

Pripjat

EAST FRANCONIA

Regensburg

WEST FRANCONIA

Vienna

Danube

HUNGARY
MAGYARS

Dnestr

Bordeaux

844
844
Roncevaux
NAVARRA
Pamplona Narbonne

BURGUNDY

(PÉTALAND)

Inn

LOMBARDY

Venice

CROATIA

ROMANIANS

Arles
860 Marseille

Barcelona
860
Tortosa

859

Ebro

Corsica

Pisa
ITALIA

Rome
(Romaborg)

Sardinia

Napoli

ADRIATIC SEA

BULGARIA

**BYZANTINE
EMPIRE**

Athens

(GRIKLAND)

→ Mainly Danish
→ Mainly Norwegian   } Viking thrusts in the 9th
→ Mainly Swedish   and 10th centuries

Dates along the routes indicate time of thrust
Areas with mainly Danish ▨ Norwegian ▨ and Swedish ▨ settlement
— Eastern limit of ravagings in the Franconian empires
- - - The main trade routes of the Vikings
Names in parentheses are those used by the Vikings

From *Cappelens historiske atlas.* © J. W. Cappelens Forlag AS, Oslo 1994.